DEFENSE, SECURITY AND STRATEGY SERIES

STRATEGIZING RESILIENCE AND REDUCING VULNERABILITY

DEFENSE, SECURITY AND STRATEGY SERIES

Military Satellites: Issues, Goals and Challenges
Abel Chirila (Editor)
2009. ISBN: 978-1-60741-238-0

Evaluating Military Compensation
Jaime G. Duenas (Editor)
2009. ISBN: 978-1-60741-476-6

The Army's Future Combat System Program
Christian N. Feliciano (Editor)
2009. ISBN 978-1-60741-262-5

Strategizing Resilience and Reducing Vulnerability
Peter R. J. Trim and Jack Caravelli (Editor)
2009. ISBN 978-1-60741-693-7

DEFENSE, SECURITY AND STRATEGY SERIES

STRATEGIZING RESILIENCE AND REDUCING VULNERABILITY

PETER R. J. TRIM
AND
JACK CARAVELLI
EDITORS

Nova Science Publishers, Inc.
New York

Copyright © 2009 by Nova Science Publishers, Inc.

All rights reserved. No part of this book may be reproduced, stored in a retrieval system or transmitted in any form or by any means: electronic, electrostatic, magnetic, tape, mechanical photocopying, recording or otherwise without the written permission of the Publisher.

For permission to use material from this book please contact us:
Telephone 631-231-7269; Fax 631-231-8175
Web Site: http://www.novapublishers.com

NOTICE TO THE READER

The Publisher has taken reasonable care in the preparation of this book, but makes no expressed or implied warranty of any kind and assumes no responsibility for any errors or omissions. No liability is assumed for incidental or consequential damages in connection with or arising out of information contained in this book. The Publisher shall not be liable for any special, consequential, or exemplary damages resulting, in whole or in part, from the readers' use of, or reliance upon, this material. Any parts of this book based on government reports are so indicated and copyright is claimed for those parts to the extent applicable to compilations of such works.

Independent verification should be sought for any data, advice or recommendations contained in this book. In addition, no responsibility is assumed by the publisher for any injury and/or damage to persons or property arising from any methods, products, instructions, ideas or otherwise contained in this publication.

This publication is designed to provide accurate and authoritative information with regard to the subject matter covered herein. It is sold with the clear understanding that the Publisher is not engaged in rendering legal or any other professional services. If legal or any other expert assistance is required, the services of a competent person should be sought. FROM A DECLARATION OF PARTICIPANTS JOINTLY ADOPTED BY A COMMITTEE OF THE AMERICAN BAR ASSOCIATION AND A COMMITTEE OF PUBLISHERS.

LIBRARY OF CONGRESS CATALOGING-IN-PUBLICATION DATA
Strategizing resilience and reducing vulnerability / Peter R.J. Trim , Jack Caravelli.
 p. cm.
 Includes index.
 ISBN 978-1-60741-693-7 (hardcover)
 1. Emergency management--Congresses. 2. Security, International--Congresses. 3. National security--Congresses. I. Trim, Peter R. J. II. Caravelli, Jack, 1952-
 HV551.2.S76 2009
 355'.0335--dc22
                                                                                                2009015630

Published by Nova Science Publishers, Inc. ✦ *New York*

CONTENTS

Preface		vii
Chapter 1	New Policy Directions in Confronting Terrorism: Challenges for the Obama Administration *Jack Caravelli*	1
Chapter 2	Examining the Linkages between National Security Frameworks and Security Sector Reform (SSR): The Need For 'Value-Based' Strategic Planning *Ann M. Fitz-Gerald*	15
Chapter 3	Dealing with Disaster – Paradox and Perception *Robert Hall*	29
Chapter 4	The Growing Competition for Water: An Emerging Global Flashpoint *Marc Glasser*	39
Chapter 5	A Strategic View of Security *Nick Edwards, Peter R.J. Trim and Jack Caravelli*	65
Chapter 6	Open Source Software, Information Entrepreneurs and Issues of National Security *Peter R.J. Trim and Yang-Im Lee*	75
Chapter 7	Collaborative Security: Pointers for Government Representatives and Corporate Security Personnel *Peter R.J. Trim*	91
Chapter 8	Isomorphic Learning in Business Continuity: A Review of How the "Lessons Identified" Were Shared after the 7th July, 2005 Terrorist Incidents *Kevin Brear*	103
Chapter 9	A Journey Towards Resilience: Lessons from the British Experience *Andrea C. Simmons*	131

Chapter 10	Towards the Hardened Organization *Maitland Hyslop*	**149**
Chapter 11	Establishing A Security Culture: Pointers For Senior Management *Nigel A. Jones and Peter R.J. Trim*	**165**
Chapter 12	Strategic Transformational Management in the Context of Inter-Organizational and Intra-Organizational Partnership Development *Yang-Im Lee*	**181**
Chapter 13	Some Suggestions for Making Emergency Response Exercises More Consistent and More Successful *David Upton*	**197**
Chapter 14	Placing Disaster Management Policies and Practices within a Stakeholder Security Architecture *Peter R.J. Trim*	**213**
Chapter 15	A Conceptual Environmental and Infrastructural Risk Assessment Model to Facilitate Security Management At Major Sporting Events *Peter R.J. Trim and Jack Caravelli*	**229**
About the Contributors		**245**
Index		**249**

PREFACE

This book stems in the main from papers presented at the Third CAMIS Security Management Conference entitled: *Strategizing Resilience and Reducing Vulnerability*, which was held at Birkbeck College, University of London, from 5th to 7th September, 2007. As the reader will note, the papers span a wide area of study and encompass subject areas such as national security, corporate security, various aspects of intelligence work, and disaster/emergency management and planning. One of the advantages of the material presented is that the varied range of papers provide different perspectives and are representative of a range of disciplines, approaches and styles. This can be considered a strength in the sense that the issues covered are complex and intellectually challenging, and will no doubt provide senior managers, security and intelligence experts, law enforcement personnel, disaster and emergency management practitioners, as well as policy makers and their advisors, and academics and university students, with a rich body of knowledge from which to gain insights and embark on theory building.

Jack Caravelli has, in Chapter 1, provided a glimpse into the strategic decision- making process at the highest political level, and suggests that although there have not been any successful terrorist attacks on US soil since 2001, some experts are of the view that "there remains a widely held perception that the US remains inadequately prepared to respond to, mitigate the effects of and recover from a future terrorist attack". In his discussion, the author notes that the Obama administration will be required to address a number of security challenges, and this will mean that the issue of devising an effective counterterrorism strategy will be given prominence.

In Chapter 2, Ann M Fitz-Gerald, has provided a number of insights into the linkages between national security frameworks and security sector reform, and has entered into discussion and made reference to why policy makers need to engage in 'value-based' strategic planning. Indeed, policy advisors appear to be paying increased attention to what have become known as "Whole of Government (WGA)" approaches to security and development, and as a consequence policy makers are focusing increased attention on security issues, overseas assistance programmes and the development of strategic national security frameworks. It has been acknowledged that "Whole of Government (WGA)" approaches have brought significant benefits to processes supporting policy development and this has resulted in shared knowledge and experience that supports analysis, planning and programmatic formulation. There is also an emerging trend towards improved macro-strategic planning in support of second order security and development programmes, and this can be placed in the context of a strategic multilateral approach to security and development planning. Building a strong foundation upon which national security planning processes can be based is important and can be assisted through the articulation and codification of national interests and core values, which should provide the central pillar for a national security strategy process.

Robert Hall makes clear in Chapter 3, that the perception of risk is changing and that it is necessary to overcome what amounts to a collective fear of risk through the development of trust based relationships. He also states that: "Realizing the upside of risk can confer confidence, strength and resilience to a business". As regards policy formulation and implementation, it is suggested that a structural change needs to be accompanied by a change in policy, and this demands firm leadership.

In Chapter 4, Marc Glasser highlights the fact that the demand for water worldwide is increasing and as a result there are likely to be increased tensions due to the pressure from economic growth, which in turn will have ramifications for food production and the sustainability of a population. Water supply cannot therefore, be considered from a domestic perspective only and the crucial point to note is that failure to effectively manage water and limit pumping to a sustainable level, may well have disastrous security related consequences. Marc makes reference to the issue of water mismanagement, and suggests that it is necessary to place this in context vis-à-vis the spread of infectious diseases, food insecurity and forced migration.

Nick Edwards, Peter R.J. Trim and Jack Caravelli provide a strategic view of security in Chapter 5, and state that identifying areas of vulnerability are no longer to be viewed as just the priority of government. Indeed, the authors explain that managers need to think in terms of physical security and the technical aspects of security, and this means implementing various international Business Continuity standards. They also make reference to the concept of risk management and refer to Sarbanes Oxley, Basel II and the Information Security Forum for example.

Several issues relating to open source software, the emergence of information entrepreneurs and a range of national security issues are addressed by Peter R.J. Trim and Yang-Im Lee in Chapter 6. The development of networked communities is given attention and so too are the activities of computer hacker groups. The problems facing law enforcement officers, intelligence and security officers, and corporate intelligence officers are referred to. A central argument throughout the paper is that greater co-operation is needed between staff from both the public and private sectors vis-à-vis counterintelligence, and reference is made to an effective intelligence and security monitoring system.

In Chapter 7, Peter R.J. Trim writes about the concept of collaborative security and provides a number of pointers for government representatives and corporate security personnel. Reference is made to the possible alliances between international criminal organizations and international terrorist groups, and how government representatives and corporate security experts need to work together in order to counteract the threats posed. Peter also suggests that policy makers need to think in terms of "integrating homeland security objectives in their country with homeland security objectives in other countries" so that a collectivist approach to security emerges.

Kevin Brear pays attention to a number of security issues in Chapter 8, and makes a case for senior managers to utilize what is known as Isomorphic Learning. The author is of the view that business continuity practitioners can learn lessons from the events in London of the

7th of July, 2005. Indeed, Kevin pays attention to the methods of research and some of the barriers encountered, and reports on some of the successes and positive outcomes. He states: "Some of the lessons identified during the research process are reported in the chapter and it is shown that much of the available information was held in silos (stovepipes) and not shared with the wider industry". The implications of this are discussed and solutions offered.

Andrea C. Simmons, has in Chapter 9, examined the journey from 'disaster recovery', through 'business continuity' to 'corporate resilience', and has outlined the various operational concepts that senior managers need to be aware of. Specific reference has been made to IT security and information assurance, and the link between business continuity, information security and incident management has been made public. Various aspects of crisis management and corporate resilience have been covered, and the people element has been placed in context. Furthermore, the topic of risk management has been addressed and a connection made with management theory. Reflection is entered into and policy recommendations offered.

In Chapter 10, Maitland Hyslop focuses attention on what is known as the hardened organization, and suggests that senior managers need to think in terms of making the organization resilient. However, he goes beyond this and states that: "A hardened organization requires certain characteristics not found in resilient organizations. Some of these may be surprising e.g. the type of staff required". It is important, therefore, to note that technology is important but that technology is not the complete answer. Issues of governance, business strategy, management, marketing, and human resources are all important and need to be in balance. It is essential therefore, that senior managers understand what risk management involves and that they embrace it fully.

Nigel A. Jones and Peter R.J. Trim explain in Chapter 11 how senior managers can establish a security culture within their organization and they also indicate that senior managers will in the years ahead be required to pay more attention to the human and behavioural aspects of security. By anticipating future threats and putting in place necessary management systems, the organization will become more resilient and better able to withstand future shocks. Networked partnerships are covered and so too are important issues such as the organization's value system.

In Chapter 12, Yang-Im Lee, writes about "Strategic transformational management in the context of inter-organizational and intra-organizational partnership development", and covers in detail the concept of organizational learning. An argument is put forward which suggests that top management need to encourage staff to develop their knowledge and skill base through time, and this is underpinned by the fact that senior managers need to ensure that the organization adapts to a changing international environment. Hence senior managers need to manage changes in organizational culture and ensure that the process of institutionalizing organizational learning is effective. In order to be effective, "senior managers need to make a distinction between transformational leadership and transactional leadership, and take notice of the fact that a dual leadership style can be deployed in a culturally sensitive organizational environment". Attention is also given to how senior managers can implement a leadership style that puts into place relevant management controls and workable partnerships with external organizations.

In Chapter 13, David Upton makes a case for emergency response exercises/crisis management simulations to be used as they represent "essential tools for testing and validating response plans and building organizational resilience". David outlines the criteria for successful exercises, and it is not surprising to note that these include consistency of design, adequate documentation and the ability to create a learning environment. As regards the latter, it is important to understand that those involved in emergency response exercises can learn from their experience and develop their skill and knowledge base in a way that is beneficial to their career development. Reference is also made to a software framework for exercise design and assessment, and various examples are presented throughout the paper, which bring into focus the constraints and challenges associated with organizing and administering large simulation exercises.

Peter R.J. Trim provides in Chapter 14, guidance as to how to produce a security architecture that embraces disaster and emergency management policies and practices. Attention is given to stakeholder considerations, and intra-government and inter-government working arrangements. Aspects of international disaster relief management operations are covered and advice is provided as to how a more pro-active approach can be adopted for dealing with disaster and emergency situations vis-à-vis the international community.

In Chapter 15, Peter R.J. Trim and Jack Caravelli pay specific attention to security issues relating to major sporting events. They argue that law enforcement officers, and security and intelligence officers, are becoming increasingly concerned that activists, criminals and terrorists, may be able to disrupt major sporting events for their own purposes. In order to counteract a potential disruption, it is advocated that a range of experts, drawn from both the public and private sectors, work together in the form of a collectivist security partnership and produce workable strategic security management policies. A conceptual environmental and infrastructural risk assessment model is outlined which can be used by security experts as a framework to identify possible threats and to neutralize them in due course. Hence, by putting in place robust counterterrorist measures, it should be possible for the authorities to ensure that a major sporting event is a cultural, social and economic success.

Peter R.J. Trim, London, UK

Jack Caravelli, Washington, D.C., USA

In: Strategizing Resilience and Reducing Vulnerability
Editors: Peter R.J. Trim and Jack Caravelli

ISBN 978-1-60741-693-7
© 2009 Nova Science Publishers, Inc.

Chapter 1

NEW POLICY DIRECTIONS IN CONFRONTING TERRORISM: CHALLENGES FOR THE OBAMA ADMINISTRATION

Jack Caravelli

ABSTRACT

The terrorist attacks of September 11, 2001 against the United States have resulted in a tectonic shift in US national security policies and priorities. The Bush administration implemented an aggressive set of foreign policy responses abroad, centered on the use of force in Iraq and Afghanistan. Concurrently, it has pursued a series of domestic policies, including unprecedented degrees of surveillance and warrantless searches described as essential to preempting terrorist activities on the US homeland. To date, there have been no successful terrorist attacks on US soil since 2001. Nonetheless, there remains a widely held perception that the US remains inadequately prepared to respond to, mitigate the effects of and recover from a future terrorist attack. Developing and enhancing these elements of resilience are likely to emerge as one of the Obama administration's most pressing security challenges. It also will be left with the "legacy" of the Bush administration's counterterrorism strategy, elements of which almost certainly require modification given evolving circumstances in the Middle East and elsewhere.

INTRODUCTION

In ways it could never have imagined upon taking office in early 2001, the Bush administration's legacy will be defined not only by a protracted confrontation with Islamic fundamentalism but also the controversial nature of the United States government's strategy against it. After the attacks against New York City and Washington, DC on September 11, 2001, the administration had little, if any, guiding precedent in US history to draw upon in shaping its domestic or foreign counterterrorism strategy. Terrorism, in its broadest context, has a long and complex history, dating to ancient times when the Zealots violently confronted

Roman rule and the Assassins, an extremist Shia Muslim sect, operated in the Middle East during medieval times [1].

Within US history, however, there had never been anything comparable to the small group of foreign nationals poorly equipped and trained by Western military standards but imbued with messianic fervor and an eagerness for martyrdom. This ragged group inflicted vast physical destruction and psychological trauma on a nation that had emerged after the 1991 breakup of its former rival the Soviet Union as a global political colossus and sole military superpower.

The September 11, 2001 attacks ushered in a new and asymmetric type of warfare against the United States. In so doing America's seemingly unlimited material, technological and psychological advantages, including its capacity to deter attacks against its homeland, were largely neutralized. For all the resources and sophistication of its intelligence, law enforcement and armed forces, the US government failed to uncover or prevent the September 11 attacks [2]. That failure—and fear of a second successful attack against the United States-- has been the catalyst for vast changes in America's worldview, national security policy and its approach to homeland security, a phrase that was not even in the political lexicon when George Bush entered office but is now inherited by Barack Obama.

As this chapter was being drafted initially in the first part of 2008, it was unclear who would be elected to the US presidency in November. What is clear is that George Bush has left a now well understood set of counterterrorism priorities, perspectives and practices that will serve as the de facto starting point for the Obama administration. The Bush administration's counterterrorism strategy, known to some as the Bush Doctrine, evolved since 2001 and at the end of the president's second term incorporated the following key elements:

- Reorganization of major elements of the US government's national security infrastructure with the creation of a Department of Homeland Security and revision of the US intelligence community as reflected in the creation of a Director of National Intelligence.
- Aggressive expansion of domestic and on occasion warrantless domestic surveillance operations, justified as necessary for the timely interdiction of possible terrorist actions.
- The central policy role for the use of force in retaliation for the attacks on the United States as seen in the war in Afghanistan and an avowed embrace of preventive military strategies against prospective terrorist enemies reflected in the war in Iraq.
- A counterterrorism strategy featuring political rhetoric describing the threat to the United States in Manichean terms whereby any given nation is viewed through the prism of being either "with us or against us."
- Prevention of terrorist acquisition of various types of weapons of mass destruction [3].

As noted, most elements of the administration's counterterrorism strategy were not derived from historical "lessons learned" and the accumulated precedents of hard experience. At the same time, some elements represented a significant departure from established US national security principles and practices in the eyes of many observers. The nation's most prominent newspaper, The New York Times, has been an unrelenting critic in its editorial pages of what it has described as the administration's unjustified and flagrant abuse of human rights and civil liberties in the pursuit of suspected terrorists. Moreover, for a democratic nation to undertake in Iraq what essentially was a preventive war stood on its head over two hundred years of foreign policy practice in which America at times was slow to resort to war, even in the face of aggression. Bush administration spokesmen acknowledged an aggressive and ground breaking set of policies in these areas and stridently embraced their choices, asserting that new threats require new approaches. In some fundamental respects the strategy has had successes. The first duty of government is to protect its citizens and, as noted, there has been no successful terrorist attack on US soil since September 11, 2001. Whether that positive development was the artifact of good fortune, skill or some combination of both could be debated but the Bush administration continued to view the possibility of terrorist attacks, at home and abroad, as a permanent part of the political and security landscape throughout its term in office.

There was ample reason for that assessment. A handful of planned attacks in various parts of the United States, including Los Angeles, California, John F. Kennedy Airport in New York and the military base at Fort Dix, New Jersey, had been detected and interdicted [4]. Great Britain, America's most important ally in confronting terrorism, has confronted even more severe events. London was victimized by attacks on its transport system on July 7, 2005 and other more recent planned attacks such as the summer 2007 car bombings outside London night clubs had been disrupted or, in the case of the attack against the airport in Glasgow, Scotland, were largely unsuccessful [5]. Underscoring the continuing nature of the threat was the assessment of Jonathan Evans, the director of MI-5, the British security service, that his organization was tracking as many as 4,000 suspected terrorists living in the United Kingdom [6]. These events, along with continuing military operations in Iraq and Afghanistan, were proof positive in George Bush's eyes that confronting Islamic fundamentalism had to remain the administration's overriding security concern.

From its first days in office the Obama administration will inherit the vexing and myriad problems of finding a path forward in Iraq and Afghanistan, dealing with the fragile and volatile political situation in Pakistan, and developing an overarching strategy for confronting Islamic fundamentalism in other regions. How a new administration perceives and conceptualizes these challenges will translate into policy and resource decisions. While President Obama, almost certainly would take significantly differing approaches to the development of a new set of counterterrorism policies, this chapter does not offer a prophecy of those likely choices. There also may be more continuity than some might have predicted immediately after the November 2008 election with Obama's decision to retain Robert Gates as Secretary of Defense. Rather, this chapter attempts to present a taxonomy of those issues that in early 2009 appear as the most pressing in developing a new counterterrorism strategy. The approach herein takes as its starting point and focuses on those criticisms, from both political parties, of the Bush administration's strategies and resource priorities. Government is about choosing and the Bush administration chose a path that emphasized some elements of a comprehensive counterterrorism strategy at the expense of others. Moreover, even those well developed elements of the administration's strategy will need to be reviewed and possibly modified in light of changing circumstances. It is within those critiques, especially existing policy gaps, that key elements of the new administration's counterterrorism strategy are likely to emerge.

DEFINING VICTORY AND A LONG-TERM STRATEGY TO ACHIEVE IT

It is impossible to develop any reasonable counterterrorism strategy—or at least one with any prospect of success or political support at home or abroad-- without an end goal in mind. This seemingly obvious dictum was not always reflected in the Bush administration's actions. For example, clear articulation of what "winning the war on terror" means in practice often has been sorely lacking. (Because terrorism is only a tactic whether that phrase even accurately captures the reality of the threat to the West is debated in some policy and academic circles.) Does it mean the complete absence of attacks against Western interests? If so, that goal seems hopelessly unrealistic given the diverse and widespread organizations operating under the rubric of Islamic fundamentalism. What the mass media describe as al Qaeda today is as much if not more a widespread and often loosely organized movement rather than a well-defined organization. But if the US goal is something short of the complete capitulation of the Islamic fundamentalists then where is the line drawn?

Answers to that question will not be formulated in a vacuum. Policy makers will have to assess that question in light of a broader reassessment of US national security strategy. Albeit a central and critical element of US foreign policy, the strategy for winning the war on terror must be shaped against the backdrop of other US policy objectives with their own claims on US resources and attention. Nation states, their policy objectives and challenges to US interests still matter as vividly demonstrated by Russia's summer 2008 invasion of Georgia. The Obama administration will confront evolving myriad issues that will place their own demands on official Washington's time and resources, ranging from an increasingly confrontational Russia to China's emergence as a global power, to the security and stability of global energy supplies to name a few. In addition to these known policy challenges, the biggest surprise for any administration, as George Bush would attest, would be if there were no policy surprises.

Given the forgoing, the new administration might find itself choosing between a strategy of actively trying to shatter the al Qaeda movement as a threat or pursuing the alternative approach of containing it [7]. Such distinctions are far more than policy semantics. A strategy of annihilation, whether pursued unilaterally or multilaterally, implies al Qaeda and associated terrorist elements continue to pose the overriding threat to US interests at home and abroad. Those perceptions derive from what is believed here to be the correct understanding of al Qaeda's aims; namely, forcing the United States from the Middle East and establishing Islamic governments in the region. A heavy reliance on military force, overtly or covertly, also is implied by the annihilation strategy along with equally heavy reliance on timely and accurate intelligence. The strategy of "killing (or capturing) the bad guys" might resonate positively with an American public that historically has viewed its foreign wars in moral terms as well as black and white tones. Implementation of this strategy, however, would be anything but clear cut. For example, the United States likely would continue to seek the assistance of like-minded nations in tracking and bringing to bear their far more limited but often unique law enforcement and intelligence resources on terrorists. As appealing as such an approach would appear, nations have their own agendas and perceptions of threats that can be expected to lead from time to time to their own set of frictions with the United States government.

The Bush administration learned these lessons painfully. One of Washington's most pressing problems in Afghanistan, for example, remains securing the commitment of some NATO countries to increase the number of troops to those areas where the fighting is most severe as opposed to deploying forces to regions far from hostilities. America's priorities, even among those that might share the Obama administration's broad assessment of the nature of the threat, almost certainly will not be uncritically embraced by the new administration's putative allies. Obama supports the shifting of American military forces from Iraq to Afghanistan but there is a limit to how far those redeployments can be sustained. Moral suasion from Washington is likely to be put to the test in the new administration's early stages and in that arena it will be handicapped by widespread perception of its predecessor as ignoring the advice and concerns of its friends. In addition, history shows that those friends from time to time will be inclined to exact other concessions from Washington in exchange for supporting American policy goals [8].

Containment represents the clearest alternative to the counterterrorism strategy based on shattering al Qaeda through the aggressive use of force. Long the central element of US strategy against communism throughout the Cold War, containment also represented the de facto preferred US counterterrorism strategy in the late twentieth century as President Bill Clinton defined US counterterrorism policies largely through the prism of reliance on law enforcement while selectively targeting individual terrorists from the Abu Nidal Organization, the Lebanese Hezbollah and Greece's November 17 Organization [9]. A policy of containment allows for perhaps substantial reduction in resources spent on counterterrorist activities overseas but, if conditions demand, also can provide for an aggressive posture against terrorist planning or activities on the US homeland. Containment also would define "victory" largely along the lines of stability and security in areas of conflict rather than the more grandiose visions of some that democracy can emerge in these regions.

There also are drawbacks and limitations attending a containment strategy. The domestic political appeal of containment may be limited; any official declaration that the US government is treating terrorism, de facto, as another security problem is likely to be greeted with derision from the political opposition as well as large segments of the populace that, while opposing the war in Iraq, have supported steadfastly many, not all, of the Bush administration's broader counterterrorism efforts such as the war in Afghanistan. Perhaps even more important is that it may be impossible to "contain" an organization with the diffuse nature, broad reach and messianic sense of history demonstrated by al Qaeda and its adherents. It is not that they are omnipotent so much as their "footprint" that does not depend on holding territory or cities nor does it lend itself to conventional containment strategies. For example, those responsible for the 2004 Madrid train bombing had few, if any, ties to other terrorist organizations, pursuing independent and locally financed operations through the sale of drugs. The disruption of planned attacks in the United States as well as President Bush's 2007 directive to the executive branch that it develop capabilities to detect, disrupt and interdict attacks in the US using improvised explosive devices, indicates that confronting terrorism successfully may require something more aggressive than containment. As with its predecessors, the Obama administration is likely to discover that its most carefully thought out options can dissolve in the cauldron of chaotic world events.

IRAQ, AFGHANISTAN AND PAKISTAN

Individually and collectively, no group of nations has been both more important and troubling for the Bush administration's struggle with Islamic fundamentalism than Iraq, Afghanistan and Pakistan. The costs of prosecuting hostilities in the first two countries has been painful in terms of human losses, excessive in their financial dimensions and debilitating to US diplomatic interests in many parts of the globe. Setting aside the question that will continue to preoccupy historians and commentators for years regarding the merits of the Iraq and Afghanistan campaigns, President Obama will find the far reaching implications of his predecessor's policy choices in those nations impossible to ignore. By any measure the war in Iraq has been extraordinarily unpopular in America as reflected in countless national opinion polls and demonstrated in 2006 by the significant political losses suffered by the Republican Party in the mid-term congressional elections and, of course, the election of Barack Obama and a new coterie of Democrats to Congress. The Democratic Party's foreign policy platform identified a quick but responsible drawdown and end to the war as a major policy priority while Republican John McCain, although acknowledging that significant tactical mistakes have been made in Iraq, was prepared to continue investing American troops and treasure in Iraq until some level of confidence can be reached that a significant withdrawal of US forces won't lead to the collapse of the to date largely dysfunctional Maliki government. Despite its current angst about the course and conduct of the war, is it possible that future public perceptions of the war are likely to revolve around whether US forces are withdrawn as part of a peace settlement or as a result of "war fatigue?"

The competing US political parties had profoundly differing ideas about how to proceed in Iraq but they agreed largely that a central element of US policy must be the insistence that Prime Minister Jawad al Maliki find a governing style with a modicum of effectiveness and credibility that is accepted by the major factions in Iraq. The unexpected but welcomed passage in February 2008 of three pieces of legislation that address various concerns of Sunnis, Shiites and Kurds could be a long overdue start in that direction.

- A provincial powers law sets the stage for elections later this year that could result in regional autonomy for such groups as pro-American Anbar sheiks.
- A partial amnesty for prisoners, 80 percent of whom are Sunni, was passed.
- A $48 billion national budget was passed that allocates government revenue to the provinces, including Kurdistan [10].

In addition, the US military commitment is seen by most, not all, in Washington as finite, implying that even as the Bush-Petraeus "surge" strategy pays substantial military dividends in tamping down violence in parts of the country, the time bought by this strategy will only look in hindsight as well spent if the Iraqi security forces develop far more robust capabilities for protecting the populace than they have demonstrated to date. George Bush displayed almost endless patience in trying to cajole (and occasionally goad) the Iraqi leadership into taking the steps requisite to achieve this goal. It's unclear that president Obama will be so accommodating but his options also will be limited by the practicalities of not wanting to be perceived as "cutting and running" without some plan for managing the possible chaos that would follow such an action. Improved local conditions, as well as growing Iraqi interest in establishing a timetable for US troop withdrawals, also may play a significant part bringing a semblance of stability to this war torn nation. Anti-American Shiite cleric Moqtada al-Sadr in late February 2008 extended his self-imposed cease fire for six months, a possible reflection of his calculation that his long-term influence might best be achieved through participation in rather than confrontation with other Iraqi factions and the national government [11]. Such decisions, albeit in the right direction, are fragile and the early months of the new administration are likely to test its capability to solidify whatever political gains can be achieved by such fledgling cooperation. One of the truisms of political life is that the rhetorical promises of campaigns seldom provide fully formed and unambiguous policy solutions when the reality of governing commences.

Afghanistan poses both similar and different challenges for the Obama administration. As in Iraq, assessing the prospects for success in Afghanistan begins with recognition that the administration of Hamid Karzai has crafted something considerably less than the rallying point for the establishment of a functioning and credible government. Without the achievement of good governance, the unity of the Afghan people and improved economic conditions, no amount of outside assistance is liable to substantially improve the situation in Afghanistan.

The challenges in Afghanistan don't end there. Throughout 2008, most observers assessed that while NATO forces were not losing they were not winning either in the face of resurgent Taliban forces that continue to use the rugged tribal areas of Pakistan as a sanctuary. As noted, among NATO members who have committed forces to Afghanistan there exist significant differences regarding how those military resources, human and material, can be applied. Bearing the brunt for most of the front line fighting in southern and eastern Afghanistan have been US, UK and Canadian units. Germany also has sent troops to Afghanistan but the German parliament has placed severe limits on where those troops and equipment can be deployed, notably in northern Afghanistan far removed from the major fighting. The pressing nature of this situation is underscored by a broad consensus among senior military commanders that the alliance needs perhaps as many as 25,000 more forces throughout the region and particularly to the most unstable regions [12]. US Secretary of Defence Robert Gates in early 2008 went so far as to say that even Germany's modest efforts to train Afghan police officers had been "disappointing" and that NATO risked becoming a "two tiered" organization [13]. Alliance management issues are not the unique province of the current era. The NATO Summit in April 2008 yielded modest progress on the troop issue, mostly because France committed to sending 700-1000 combat forces to eastern Afghanistan to buttress a new round of troop deployments promised by President Bush. Nonetheless, there exists within the alliance a profound de facto difference over the fundamental question of "what is worth fighting for?" During World War II, General Dwight Eisenhower, the supreme allied commander, spent considerable personal time soothing the egos and brokering competing visions of military strategy between US General George Patton and his British counterpart, Sir Bernard Montgomery. Unlike this historical analogy, underlying the current dispute is the perception in parts of official Washington that some alliance members don't believe the war in Afghanistan is worth the sacrifice of blood or treasure. That is a troubling sign for any alliance that claims to represent a long-term commitment to the collective security of its members. Some NATO members want to enjoy the protection of the alliance umbrella but seem to have little enthusiasm for paying the dues of membership.

An example of intra-alliance problems are differing perceptions over how to deal with Afghanistan's expanding poppy fields. They are the source of livelihood for many Afghans, by far the largest source of heroin entering the West, and the vast proceeds from drug sales fund the Taliban [14]. George Bush assigned to Kabul in 2007 as his ambassador William Wood, who oversaw US efforts in Colombia to eradicate drug fields by aerial spraying [15]. Wood has taken a similar tack in Afghanistan, earning the nickname "Chemical Bill." His aggressiveness has raised the concerns of Gordon Brown's UK government, as well as some elements of the US bureaucracy, including the Department of Defense, that crop destruction through spraying is not a long-term solution to winning the support of the local populace. The Obama administration will be challenged to develop adequate programs that give Afghan peasants reason to move away from their most lucrative source of income.

In some significant ways the problems of Afghanistan emanate from Pakistan. Pakistan served in the 1980s as a staging ground for US covert operations in Afghanistan against the Soviet Union. The irony is not lost on US policymakers that Pakistan now serves as the same type of staging ground and conduit for the Taliban to strike at coalition forces in Afghanistan. Pakistan's largely lawless and geographically imposing tribal areas that border Afghanistan have proven a reliable safe haven for insurgent forces. Since its initial military operations in Afghanistan in late 2001, the Bush administration has sought to use its massive economic support to Islamabad, in the order of $10 billion since it took office, as well as a mix of public and quiet diplomacy to goad the Musharraf government into committing Pakistani military forces to the tribal areas to directly confront the Taliban. The now-deposed Musharraf government claimed to have dispatched over the past few years 100,000 troops to interdict Taliban and al Qaeda elements. In addition, small numbers of US military assets have undertaken unilateral combat actions in Pakistan. Both approaches have produced some successes but not nearly enough to significantly compromise or contain insurgent operations into Afghanistan.

More needs to be done but it also needs to be done differently by the Obama administration if the real and underlying challenge of Afghanistan, nation building, is to be a success.

One of the more creative proposals for doing so is contained in the work of Ashley Bommer, a former Clinton administration official. Beginning from the widely held assessment that Pakistan can't resolve the insurgent problem alone, Bommer believes "an effective counterterrorism strategy requires a global ground response to forge a cooperative relationship with the tribes that harbor the insurgents" [16]. Along the more than 1,000 mile border dividing Afghanistan and Pakistan are about 60 major tribes, with local power held by tribal chiefs. Bommer's idea is to improve the lives of those in the region whose way of living is fundamentally unchanged compared to their forerunners hundreds of years ago. Under Bommer's proposal a Global Tribal Fund would be established to identify local resource and infrastructure needs such as roads, education and health care, while pursuing a parallel strategy that unites the tribes and equips and trains their men so they "can resist domination by the insurgency" [17]. The myriad challenges of implementing such a strategy are apparent, but Bommer's assessment that the urgency of the situation requires creative approaches can't be dismissed. The new administration will do well to devote considerable policy focus to this issue and, absent significant improvements, may be compelled to do so. In addition, the Bush administration said very little about the long-term prospects for permanent stability in Afghanistan or the resources required to achieve that outcome. The American public may be much more demanding of the Obama administration in seeking its long-term vision for this war torn nation.

Pakistan's problems begin but do not end in the tribal areas. Among the many challenges of developing an effective strategy for countering the Taliban in the tribal areas few, if any, surpass those posed by the internal turmoil wracking Pakistan's central government. The late December 2007 assassination of Mrs. Benazir Bhutto was one of many reminders that violence, corruption and broad public disenchantment seem almost ingrained in the Pakistani landscape. The parliamentary elections in February 2008 at first blush ushered in new parliamentary leadership prepared to take on the pressing challenges of governing in Pakistan. In the months after those elections then President Musharraf stated his refusal to "go gently into the good night" but the election results were by any standard a stunning repudiation of Musharraf's time in office. Musharraf's Pakistan Muslim League party, known as the PML (Q), won only 42 of a possible 268 parliamentary seats and nineteen of his ministers suffered defeat. The political parties that oppose Musharraf's PML (Q), the Pakistan's People Party (PPP) led by Bhutto's widower, Asif Zardari, and Pakistan Muslim League or PML (N) under the leadership of former Prime Minister Sharif, emerged victorious and vowed publicly to work together against Musharraf. While such an alliance based on a common revulsion of Musharraf's brand of politics is possible and has been set in motion with the formation of a coalition government, profound differences also exist between the two rising parties. A mutually agreed upon path forward is liable to be fragile and may well be short-lived. Simmering tensions with India, while hardly a new occurrence, only add to the pressure on Islamabad.

The fragility of Pakistan's political establishment surfaced dramatically in August 2008 as this chapter was being finalized. In mid-August, President Musharraf was forced from office days before plans to impeach him were to have been set in motion. What followed, all too predictably, was an open squabble and then rupture between the ruling factions over who would fill the vacated presidency with Mrs. Bhutto's widower, Asif Zardari, openly expressing interest in—and ultimately filling the position-- while his former political partner and one-time prime minister, Nawaz Sharif, collapsed the governing coalition in protest over Zardari's decision to do so [18].

In addition, reports that began circulating as early as the first months of 2008 and continued through the year that Pakistan's new coalition government was considering negotiations with militants carrying out suicide attacks in Pakistan, creating considerable unease in Washington. Deputy Secretary of State Negroponte's March 2008 visit to Islamabad was greeted with near hostility by the ruling parties, doing little to allay Washington's fears about the future direction of Pakistan [19]. Under these circumstances the new US president likely will be left with a political situation perhaps even more fragile and complex than what confronted the Bush administration.

In addition to the Machiavellian nature of Pakistan's political scene, Pakistan remains a nuclear weapons state. Those assets remain under the protection of the military and security services and there was no immediate threat to them. Nonetheless, Western experts well understood that within those organizations with custody of the weapons were elements sympathetic to Islamic fundamentalism. Assertions by both the US and Pakistani governments of the security of Pakistan's nuclear weapons notwithstanding, the combination of nuclear weapons in a politically troubled Muslim state on the front lines of the war on terrorism at any time could erupt into the new administration's worst nightmare. US technical assistance to the Pakistan military probably has improved the security of the nuclear assets. Nonetheless, every day dozens of Pakistani scientists and military officers continue to have access to those assets and it is that access or insider threat that has been shown in other countries such as Russia to pose a distinctly vexing security problem.

SECURING NUCLEAR WARHEADS, MATERIALS AND RADIOLOGICAL SOURCES

The breakup of the Soviet Union in 1991 and concern about attendant economic collapse led to the creation of a series of US government programs administered by the Departments of State, Defence and Energy to secure vast amounts of nuclear weapons and materials deemed to be at risk of threat or diversion [20]. For example, within Russia some 600 metric tons of fissile material (highly enriched uranium or Plutonium-239), enough to make thousands of nuclear devices, required security upgrades such as improved fences, alarms and sensors in the wake of the social and economic collapse that followed political disintegration. In the mid-1990s, there occurred several successful smuggling cases in which small amounts of fissile material were removed from Russian institutes and smuggled into Europe and subsequently recovered underscored the real, not hypothetical, nature of the problem [21]. At that time the US government's nonproliferation goal of preventing these and similar materials from falling into the hands of so-called rogue nations such as Iran or North Korea was of paramount concern. In an age of global terrorism those assets also must be kept from subnational and terrorist organizations.

Both US political parties agree on this objective; political adversaries Bill Clinton and George Bush both spoke during their presidencies in strikingly similar terms of the calamitous results of nuclear weapons or nuclear materials as well as radiological materials (which would be used for making radiological dispersion devices or dirty bombs) falling into terrorist hands. Members of both political parties in Congress have been consistently generous in providing the executive branch funds to execute these programs. Since their beginning in the early 1990s under the Nunn-Lugar legislation (named for the sponsoring US senators), about $10 billion in US funds have been appropriated under what is known by the umbrella term Cooperative Threat Reduction (CTR).

The results have been mixed. The Department of Defence has worked cooperatively with its former Russian adversaries to deactivate or destroy over 6500 nuclear warheads and 560 intercontinental ballistic missiles and 142 long-range bombers [22]. These successes have been tempered with the far more checkered record in the Department of Energy's (DOE) programs to secure fissile and radiological materials in Russia. After a series of successes in 1999-2003, more recently bureaucratic ineptitude and Russian suspicion of what senior officials at the Russian Federal Ministry for Atomic Energy (Rosatom) have termed DOE's "nuclear tourism" in which myriad visits to sensitive Russian facilities by US laboratory personnel led to few results have brought the program to a crawl. As a result, in late 2008 there remained by insider estimates at least 200-250 metric tons of fissile material lacking adequate physical security, enough material to make several thousand weapons. That is a poor return on the time and money invested in this program. Moreover, a similar program to secure with DOE funding radiological materials in Russia encountered, after a promising start, similar managerial gaffes of sufficient magnitude that the General Accountability Office (GAO), the congressional investigatory arm, in 2007 issued a stinging critique of the program that, in essence, confirmed that the program was failing, requiring a significant course correction. DOE has yet to hold accountable those managers who have created these problems [23].

It is against this backdrop of missed opportunities and failure that President Obama will have to decide how, and whether, to move the programs forward. Within parts of the US government and among some in Congress, sentiment exists to remove the programs from DOE and consolidate them entirely within the Department of Defence. Such a move has considerable merit given DOE's sustained poor performance.

The new administration also will have to confront a much different Russian government than what existed when these programs began in the early 1990s. At that time, the Yeltsin government embraced cooperation with the US in many areas, including the CTR programs, in part because of considerable financial need. Under former President Vladimir Putin and his hand-picked successor, Dmirty Medvedev, Russia has become and may remain much more confrontational politically with the US as well as much more financially independent than during the Yeltsin era. It remains in the US interest to see that the considerable amount of still poorly secured materials receive security upgrades, but the new president and Congress may begin questioning whether Russia, at the very least, shouldn't assume a much larger share of the financial burden for doing so.

WINNING MUSLIM-AND EUROPEAN-HEARTS AND MINDS

By any measure, the US investment in fighting Islamic fundamentalism has been extensive and even exhaustive. The loss of over 4,500 US soldiers and expenditure of nearly $1 trillion dollars in direct funding for the Iraq and Afghanistan wars will reverberate in the American consciousness for decades to come. Barack Obama, confronted with the stark reality of those figures—which don't reflect Iraqi losses--the domestic and international unpopularity attending them, and the recognition that terrorism as a tactic may remain a prevalent aspect of the political landscape for years to come, may feel compelled to ask whether US resource commitments have been used creatively and are allocated properly. Given the forgoing, the answer may be in the negative.

If the new administration judges that the Bush administration's assessment, as well as the views of various outside experts is correct that Islamic fundamentalism seeks to establish a caliphate or rule of Islamic law throughout the Middle East, it may find that it needs to focus even more political and economic attention in that region. Ultimately, the fundamentalist vision may be far too grandiose to have much prospect of major success, but there is such fragility among some of the secular Arab states that new US thinking regarding how to bolster these states is appropriate. As with most issues in the region, the challenges of doing so are at once multiple and complex. The US long has relied on and supported politically moderate Arab states, in large measure because of America's continuing dependence on Middle East oil. That situation is unlikely to change in the short-term, representing a constraint on US policy options in the region. Nonetheless, it is in America's continuing interest to support those regimes for reasons beyond those related to energy issues. For example, moderate Arab states, if they act cohesively, represent a foil to possible Iranian expansion plans in the region, particularly if Iran succeeds in acquiring nuclear weapons with the attendant political advantages conferred to nuclear states.

American policy through the past several decades has been reluctant to engage in hard discussions with the Arab states on their future course. By the standards of the developed world, many of the Arab states in the region lag in political development, relying heavily if not exclusively on dynastic rule. Economic and social development also lags in many Arab countries as does educational and health care opportunities. To be sure, change is coming to the region but in almost all indices of national development such as the forgoing, the Arab states do not rank in the top twenty five globally. This has been termed by some as a failure of modernization [24].

History is replete with examples of governments that fell by ignoring the will and welfare, human rights and social needs of its populace. The Arab states are hardly immune from these problems. Challenges exist in these areas throughout the Arab world as demonstrated by the persistent level of support generated by the Muslim Brotherhood in Egypt, a political organization whose roots go back decades. While any new administration might be inclined to work cooperatively with its counterparts in the moderate Arab world, US policy at least for some indeterminate period of time will be constrained by the broad perception in the Arab world—including large segments of the general populace—that American credibility has been badly tainted by the invasion of Iraq while American policy continues to tilt in favor of Israel. Under these conditions it is unrealistic to expect that American influence in the region will rise perceptibly or quickly. Nonetheless, Washington is unlikely to stand on the policy sidelines given its strategic and economic interests in the region.

If the United States is to regain its moral voice in the Obama administration it can begin by conveying the belief that terrorism is not the byproduct of poverty as much as it is the result of alienation and a sense of injustice on the part of youth living in the Arab world. If this 'diagnosis" is accurate, it becomes axiomatic that a "cure" is for Washington to encourage and, whenever possible assist, Arab governments in the development of programs and policies that provide their youth reasons to be hopeful for the future and reason to believe they have a genuine role in shaping it. This message must come from the indigenous governments themselves; the hard lesson from the Bush years is that democracy, social development and commitment to human rights can seldom be exported from Washington successfully. How efforts at modernization are carried out is likely to vary from country to country as astute observers of the Arab world have described, but for the United States an overall long-term consistency of approach is likely to yield the longest term dividends [24].

THE DOMESTIC CHALLENGE OF BUILDING A RESILIENT SOCIETY

When viewed through an historical lens, America's greatness is most clearly seen not in its government but in its citizens. Since the founding of the republic, Americans traditionally have taken quiet pride in possessing self-sufficient qualities that eschewed broad governmental intervention. Although that self-image began to change slowly from reality to mirage in the wake of the government's intervention in almost every aspect of American life in the Great Depression of the 1930s, a "can do" spirit still permeates the American self-image in many respects. What has changed in the relationship between the people and their government has been the broad expansion of government in the creation of the national security state, the vast apparatus of US governmental departments and agencies that emerged after World War II when the US confronted the Soviet Union. As noted above, those entities did not protect the American public from the events of September 11, 2001. The Bush administration's response, rather than drawing upon the resources of the public, chose to again expand the mechanisms of government and give it even more sweeping powers of surveillance and intervention in private lives.

In undeniably significant ways the US government must maintain the leading role in developing and implementing a national counterterrorism strategy. Only the national government can marshal the resources required to carry out elements of this strategy abroad. Nonetheless, at the same time the dynamics of confronting terrorism have changed remarkably from the threat perceptions extant during the Cold War. Today a US airport, urban financial center or suburban shopping center can become the locus for terrorist activities in ways never imagined in the past. Given America's size and the complexity of its infrastructure it is an impossible task for the federal government to provide comprehensive protection against these threats. Some local communities such as Seattle, Washington and Charlotte, North Carolina have taken it upon themselves to develop community-based models for responding to such threats. This could be an important trend and a process that is replicated in many American communities in coming years.

But the new president's focus in the war against terrorism will remain fixed overseas, probably on Pakistan which continues to be a potential source of any future attack against the United States. Is such an attack imminent? As noted, since September 2001 the United States has defended its borders successfully against another terrorist attack. At the same time, a quick review of history shows that terrorist attacks against America (and Great Britain and Spain) occurred shortly after changes in presidential administrations in America—1993 and 2001-- as well as in 2004 in Madrid and 2007 shortly after Gordon Brown became Great Britain's prime minister. The timing of these attacks almost certainly was not coincidental. Future attacks, if and when they occur, will reflect the capabilities and limitations of the attackers but also tell us a great deal about the counterterrorism policies developed by the next administration and its allies.

REFERENCES

[1] Louise Richardson, *What Terrorists Want*. New York: Random House, 2006, pp. 23-27.
[2] *The 9/11 Commission Report: Final Report of the National Commission on Terrorist Attacks Upon the United States*. New York: W.W. Norton and Co., 2003.
[3] See, for example, "National Strategy for Combating Terrorism", released by the White House, February 2003 and available at www.whitehouse.gov/news/releases.
[4] Dale Russakoff and Dan Egen, "Six Charged in Plot to Attack Fort Dix," *The Washington Post*, May, 9, 2007, p.A1.
[5] Details on the July 2005 attacks can be found, inter alia, at www.globalsecurity.org in the homeland security section.

[6] Con Coughlin, "Gordon Brown has a New Plan to Beat Terror" January 23, 2008. www.spectator.co.uk.
[7] This discussion draws upon the work of Georgetown University Professor Daniel Byman. See, for example, his "US Counter-terrorism Options: A Taxonomy" in *Survival, The IISS Quarterly*, Volume 49, Number 3, Autumn 2007. p.121.
[8] Ibid., p. 127.
[9] Ibid. p. 128.
[10] Press release from the Embassy of the United States in Iraq, February 28, 2008.
[11] Sudarsan Baghavan and Amit R. Paley, "Sadr Extends Truce in Iraq," *The Washington Post*, February 23, 2008. p. A1.
[12] Craig Whitlock, "Germany Rebuffs U.S. on Troops in Afghanistan," *The Washington Post*, February 22, 2008. p. A10.
[13] Craig Whitlock, "Bush Vows to NATO: U.S. Will Add Troops," *The Washington Post*, April 5, 2008. p. A9.
[14] Jim Hoagland, "Poppies vs. Power in Afghanistan," The Washington Post, December 23, 2007, p. B7.
[15] Ibid.
[16] Ashley Bommer, "Hearts and Minds on the Durand Line," *The Washington Post*, February 18, 2008, p. A17.
[17] Ibid.
[18] Candace Rondeaux, "Governing Coalition Collapses in Pakistan," *The Washington Post*, August 26, 2008. p. A1.
[19] Jane Perlez, "Pakistan to Talk with Militants, New Leaders Say", *The New York Times*, March 22, 2008, p. A1.
[20] Jack Caravelli. *Nuclear Insecurity: Understanding the Threat from Rogue Nations and Terrorists*. Westport, Connecticut: Praeger Security International, 2007.
[21] Ibid., p.17.
[22] Ibid., p. 54.
[23] Ibid., See chapter three.
[24] This idea is reflected in the writings of several noted scholars, particularly Bernard Lewis. See *The Crisis of Islam*. New York: Modern Library, 2003.

In: Strategizing Resilience and Reducing Vulnerability
Editors: Peter R.J. Trim and Jack Caravelli

ISBN 978-1-60741-693-7
© 2009 Nova Science Publishers, Inc.

Chapter 2

EXAMINING THE LINKAGES BETWEEN NATIONAL SECURITY FRAMEWORKS AND SECURITY SECTOR REFORM (SSR): THE NEED FOR 'VALUE-BASED' STRATEGIC PLANNING

Ann M Fitz-Gerald

ABSTRACT

The debate surrounding "Whole of Government (WGA)" approaches to security and development issues has brought about a number of innovative programmatic instruments and other processes supporting policy development. Arguably, the growth in options for programmatic engagement supporting overseas assistance has developed at a faster pace than the development of strategic approaches that should be providing programmatic direction. There is an emerging trend towards improved macro-strategic planning in support of second order security and development programmes, and this can be placed in the context of a strategic multilateral approach to security and development planning. Building a strong foundation upon which national security planning processes can be based is important and can be assisted through the articulation and codification of national interests and core values, which should provide the central pillar for a national security strategy process.

INTRODUCTION

The review and formulation of a national security framework has become regarded as a necessary exercise for informing more specific, second tier security policies and programmes. Unquestionably, the terrorist attacks of 11 September 2001 on the World Trade Centre and the Pentagon forced the US Government to revisit its thinking on immediate threats to US borders and towards the use of appropriate policy instruments to deal with such threats – thinking which informed the subsequent 2002 US National Security Strategy. Similarly, the Canadian Government's decision in 2004 to develop its first National Security Policy illustrated how others were also revisiting these ideas. In December 2003, the national security fervour escalated to a 'multilateral' level with the European Union which approved its first European Security Strategy. Lastly, in March 2008, Prime Minister Gordon Brown's Labour Government also adopted its first National Security Strategy having operated without one for all of its years of active overseas defence, diplomatic and development interventions.

The fervour driving the review of national security processes has developed due to several reasons. Firstly, there have been significant changes in the global strategic environment which has seen a range of new trends and phenomena including terrorism, migratory issues, climate change, and a spread of global diseases such as HIV/AIDS. Secondly, what have become known as "Whole of Government (WGA)" approaches to security and development challenges now demand greater policy coherence between security issues at the programmatic and macro-strategic levels of Government. Lastly, the trend for donor countries to 'get their own structures in order' has carried subsequent implications for their own overseas assistance programmes. Not surprisingly, more efforts are now being made to encourage the development of – and the subsequent use of – the strategic national security frameworks of aid recipient countries.

Whilst all three of the phenomena outlined above are important, this chapter will focus on the latter two, with an emphasis on achieving policy coherence for both national and international planning. This is not to downplay the importance of the changing strategic environment but to simply recognise that the subject warrants a chapter in itself and that much good work in this area has already been undertaken by many leading international think-tanks.

In commenting on the degree of policy coherence across the national security structures of some donor governments – and the degree of coherence between bilateral responses to a range of donor interventions and the recipient country's strategic security priorities – the lack of 'bedrock' for establishing strategic national security priorities becomes apparent. While this chapter highlights the utility of initially engaging with individual security sector programmes which open up further dialogue supporting broader national security processes, it critiques the latter process for not addressing the core foundations of these broader processes. The chapter will end by outlining a reasonably straightforward strategic planning framework which ensures that this level of foundational analysis is addressed.

"WHOLE OF GOVERNMENT" APPROACHES AND LINKAGES WITH NATIONAL SECURITY PLANNING

Whole of Government (WGA) approaches became popular just before the turn of the century when policymakers recognised the utility of looking at global issues and trends from a consolidated defence, diplomacy and development perspective. Until recently, the Government of Canada described the phenomenon to be '3-D' (Defence-Diplomacy-Development) in effect, until its work in countries like Haiti saw the contribution from the wider security domains such as the Canadian prison authorities and the Canadian Public Health Agency.[1] Similarly, in the late 1990s, the UK Government referred to the coming

---

[1] Based on an interview with personnel from Foreign Affairs and International Trade, Canada, April 14, 2007.

together of its security-relevant departments as being 'joined-up'. A study commissioned by the Organisation for Economic Cooperation and Development (OECD) in 2006 provided an overview of a range of national WGA approaches. In providing the rationale behind WGA approaches, the study observed that:

> [...] interventions in Afghanistan and Iraq have revealed the limitations of traditional diplomatic and military interventions. Experiences in Bosnia and Herzegovina, and Kosovo have taught security actors that predominantly military responses are insufficient for multidimensional state-building and post-conflict peace-building processes.[2]

"Whole of Government" approaches have brought significant benefits to processes supporting policy development. The shared knowledge and experience that supports analysis, planning and programmatic formulation has come with positive spin-offs for the implementation of programmes at the operational level. Whilst some analysts have argued about the ongoing cultural, legal and bureaucratic challenges for the "Whole of Government" model,[3] it is the view of the author that such teething problems have, in part, been outweighed by the benefits accrued and by the way in which such challenges have also become drivers for policy change.

Where the "Whole of Government" debate becomes interesting for national security is in exploring the strategic mandates which inform "Whole of Government" security strategies.[4] "Whole of Government" approaches link largely with programmatic responses; more specifically, programmes which fall under the auspices of one or more Cabinet level functions of Government. Due to the proliferation of organisational structures, strategies and projects which have developed as a result of the WGA fervour, questions have been asked regarding the mechanisms used to distinguish between priorities across a range of possible policy areas. The UK Government organises its WGA approach under the theme of Conflict Prevention. To this end, a Conflict Prevention Fund (CPF) is available to fund both security and development-type projects and programmes which have some link to conflict prevention goals and objectives. Other countries have taken similar approaches to creating financial instruments available to support the implementation of programmes and activities, in a way that is considered to be coherent with joined-up policy priorities. The Dutch Government's Stability Fund and the Canadian Government's Global Peace and Security Fund serve as good examples of such financial instruments.

However, a lack of strategic framework supporting the UK's overarching approach to Conflict Prevention meant that, until the UK Government adapted its first National Security Strategy in 2008, there was no macro-strategic level policy/strategy framework which informed the high number of joined up priorities supporting security and development interventions. As a result – and as confirmed in a review undertaken in April 2008 on the UK

---

[2] OECD-DAC report, Whole of Government Approaches to Fragile States, Governance, Peace and Stability Programme, April 2006, p.18
[3] For example, see Stewart Patrick and Kaysie Brown's account of a number of national contexts in Greater than the Sum of its Parts? Assessing Whole of Government Approaches to Fragile States, International Peace Academy, New York, 2007.
[4] The author recognises that there are a large number of WGA approaches that also support domains unrelated to traditional security issues.

Government's spending on SSR through the Global Conflict Prevention Pool[5] - pooled SSR funding has often been used without adequate consideration of its contribution to conflict prevention[6]. A recent paper published by the London-based think-tank DEMOS stated that it remains questionable as to which of the three UK Government 'joined-up Departments' is accountable for the Government's work on conflict prevention.[7] The report further argued that 'the lack of leadership and accountability on shared policy areas greatly weakens the ability of government to respond to the challenges it faces.[8] In referring more broadly to the wider donor community, the 2006 OECD-DAC study on WGA approaches observed that, in the case of engagement in fragile states:

> [...] the lack of a clear objective means that the process is more complicated, as different actors will have different perspectives on (and stakes in) dealing with fragile states. [...] Perspectives range from counter-terrorism to governance, conflict prevention and peacebuilding, or trade promotion. The rationales for engaging in fragile states may differ and, at times, come into conflict. A key challenge for [WGA] engagement in fragile states, therefore, is to balance these different rationales and perspectives.[9]

Although some literature on pooled funding suggests that such approaches can encourage policy coherence and provide a socialising role among agencies in helping participants understand the perspectives of their counterparts[10], other views have recorded that overall, the schemes funded by these instruments are relatively small and the "project-by-project" approach of the instruments is not ideally adapted to the chronic and structural problems of fragile states.'[11]

The arguments above underscore the fact that, even with "Whole of Government" approaches – and thus taking a broader approach to policy and planning for security and development – a direct linkage is required between the way in which donor governments engage in fragile states and the higher macro-strategic national priorities this engagement supports. The OECD report goes some way to recognise this connection by observing that "in the absence of a dialogue on what a joined-up approach means for the various actors, and how this relates to their role in supporting national interests, the risk of maintaining existing approaches remains."[12]

---

[5] In April 2008, the UK Government took the decision to merge the African Conflict Prevention Pool (ACPP) and the Global Conflict Prevention Pool (GCPP) into the Conflict Prevention Pool (CPP).
[6] Nicole Ball and Luc van de Goor. Promoting Conflict Prevention through Security Sector Reform. Pricewaterhouse Coopers LLP, April 2008, p. iii.
[7] Charlie Edwards. National Security for the 21st Century. DEMOS Publication, December 2007, p.71.
[8] Ibid, p. 71.
[9] Van de Goor, op cit, p.23
[10] Patrick and Brown, op cit, p 134
[11] Picciotto, R., C. Alao, E. Ikpe, M. Kimani and R. Slade (2005), "Striking a New Balance Donor Policy Coherence and Development Cooperation in Difficult Environments", background paper commissioned by the Learning and Advisory Process on Difficult Partnerships of the Development Assistance Committee of the OECD, Paris, p.37, as quoted in OECD's Whole of Government Approaches to Fragile States, a DAC Reference Document, 2006, p. 26.
[12] Ibid, p. 22

WGA POLICY INSTRUMENTS SUPPORTING OVERSEAS INTERVENTIONS

The WGA approach underscored the importance of the 'security-development nexus', and a range of new policy instruments which were targeted at this joined-up area. Within the wider security domain these instruments included areas such as rule of law, socio-economic development and SSR, the latter of which has been an area of growing importance and will be used as an example in this section.

Although the concept of SSR only appeared in 1999 following work undertaken by the UK's Department for International Development (DFID) on the linkages between high rates of military expenditure, poverty and incidence of conflict, SSR-type programmes have been around for years. The post-conflict transitional justice issues heard in the Nuremburg Trials of 1945-1949; the efforts by the US Government in 1967 in Vietnam to support the rural political, economic and security development using the Civil Operations and Revolutionary Development Support (CORDS) programme; and the defence reform programmes which spearheaded the drive for the post-1989 new Central and Eastern European democracies towards euro-Atlantic integration, all involved elements of present day SSR thinking. However, through the efforts of the bilateral and multilateral donor community, SSR thinking now comes with a terminology and policy language of its own.[13]

SSR has served as the entry point for a range of different types of interventions in transitional societies. Following the 1999 NATO bombing campaign in Belgrade, bilateral and multilateral donor-funded efforts to develop the Serbian security sector have been a priority for the country. Since the initial UN-OAS (Organisation for American States) post-conflict intervention in 1995 – and despite one further short-lived conflict in 2004 - the efforts of the United Nations Mission in Haiti (MINUSTAH) to support the rebuilding of the country's wider security sector remain ongoing today. Since the first free and fair elections were held in post-conflict Sierra Leone in 2002, donor efforts have been geared towards building a more effective and appropriate security sector to enable national development. Elsewhere in Bosnia, Afghanistan, Iraq and Sudan, international donor funded programmes continue to support the training and equipping of new security forces in parallel with the development of the relevant Government ministries overseeing their conduct.

The popularity of WGA policy tools like SSR in leading bilateral and multilateral donor assistance also applies to countries undergoing transitions of different types and not necessarily emerging from conflict. Heavily indebted countries seeking to support their Millenium Development Goals (MDGs) are often forced to review their excessively-resourced security institutions based on a new current strategic environment. On the other hand, in forecasting its possible re-prioritisation of security sector priorities, at the time of writing, the Government of Botswana has launched the debate on national security requirements in recognition of the need to review its changing security environment and the role of its security forces. This comes at a time when there is great uncertainty surrounding the short-medium term pressures along its Eastern border with Zimbabwe. Even developed countries and leading powers like the United Kingdom have recognised the need to review their security institutions based on changing dynamics. For example, based on a newly

---

[13] For more information on the terminology used to describe international SSR concepts, see OECD-DAC's Security System Reform and Governance: DAC Guidelines and Reference Series, 2005.

declared 'peace dividend' in Northern Ireland, the decision by Tony Blair's Labour Government in August 2004 to disband 2,500 soldiers from the three remaining Royal Irish Home Battalions provides an example of a UK 'homegrown' Disarmament, Demobilisation and Reintegration (DDR) programme in the context of SSR.

Along with the popular use of SSR as a policy instrument also comes the need to look more carefully at the strategic national security structures that SSR programmes seek to support. Due to the sheer breadth and depth of SSR programmes – which can involve parallel programmes across all government security actors, as well as key oversight bodies such as Parliament and civil society - the concept has often become inadvertently elevated to something more strategic than a security policy instrument and programme area. As a result, in the absence of more visionary planning objectives and due to the development of a reasonably large and 'mature' community of SSR practitioners, strategic planning often becomes driven by SSR. It is important to note that instruments like SSR require strategic guidance for informing issues concerning the prioritisation and sequencing of the many possible projects and programme areas.

This phenomenon was recognised in Uganda during the 2002-2004 efforts by the Government of Uganda's Ministry of Defence's (MOD) Defence Reform Unit to undertake a Defence Review. By initiating a strategic threat assessment exercise to support the Defence Review, Ugandan authorities learned that only a very small percentage of the existing threats to Uganda required a military response. The different nature of threats – and the policy responses they warranted – helped attract wider Government and civil society buy-in to the process. This subsequently led to the development of a Security Policy Framework, a Defence Policy and a *White Paper on Defence Transformation*.[14]

One could argue that the donor-supported SSR intervention in Serbia in 2002 was also triggered by a demand from the defence community. This became evident during an SSR scoping study when the author learned that the Serbian MOD was keen to progress with its defence reform agenda as well as with its first draft of the country's national security strategy. As information on the MOD-authored draft National Security Strategy became available to the other security branches across the Serbian Government, other departments gradually became interested in the wider approach to security reforms and accepted that they had a role to play. The cases of both Uganda and Serbia illustrate the benefits of accepting a degree of risk and engaging initially with the defence community in order to open up further dialogue, expose the full range of national security issues for the country and encourage wider stakeholder buy-in across the security community.

With the UK-led post-conflict intervention in Sierra Leone initially prioritising the DDR of former combatants, as well as the development of a better-prepared army and police force, donor efforts also targeted intelligence reform. If undertaken in a comprehensive and analytically rigorous way, good intelligence can assist in informing the foundations of a national security framework. It can also provide ongoing analysis that evaluates linkages between security and development and which can therefore assist in the prioritisation of further reforms. The creation of the Government of Sierra Leone Office for National Security (ONS) was useful in informing options for further donor funding. Between 2005 and 2007,

---

[14] For a comprehensive overview of the processes supporting these outputs, see Sabiti Mutengesa and Dylan Hendrickson, "State Responsiveness to Public Security Needs: The Politics of Security Decision-Making" in CSDG Papers, Number 16, June 2008.

the ONS was also instrumental in developing the first Government of Sierra Leone National Security Review.

The cases of Uganda, Serbia, Sierra Leone and many others illustrate the utility of SSR programmes as a lever to encourage recipient countries to begin thinking about their broader, more strategic national security requirements – and thus expedite the degree of pan-national 'buy-in' to the process. This may require the need to balance the pursuit of the perhaps 'less overt' programmatic engagements with the bolstering of change drivers which will quickly recognise the linkages between the strategic and programmatic levels.

TOWARDS A MORE STRATEGIC APPROACH TO SUPPORTING OVERSEAS SECURITY INTERVENTIONS

Notwithstanding the need to use programmatic entry points at the initial stages of some wider SSR programmes, there is now an emerging trend towards improved macro-strategic planning in support of second order security and development programmes. This section will review some of these efforts.

The 2006 OECD-DAC Handbook on Security System Reform[15] served as a good first effort in providing SSR practitioners and policymakers with a comprehensive guide which offered useful guiding principles, methodologies and lessons identified from elsewhere. The purpose of the Handbook was to ensure that donor support to SSR programmes was both effective and sustainable.[16]

In presenting a useful methodology for an SSR assessment process, the Handbook advises on a range of approaches to research and data consolidation. It also prioritises the requirement to survey the needs of the local people as people's perceptions of security and justice provide a baseline against which progress in a security and justice development programme can be measured.[17] It discusses the utility of household surveys and focus groups to generate baseline data on people's security and justice needs. It also draws on the World Bank's Voices of the Poor report which developed a comprehensive methodology for assessing the views and needs of local people in developing countries, which includes conducting Participatory Poverty Assessments.[18]

The approach taken by the Handbook falls firmly in line with the OECD-DAC's general principles supporting successful SSR engagements.[19] These principles include 'local ownership' and the 'sustainability' of SSR processes – two aspects that cannot be pursued unless the basic needs of the people are correctly identified. These methodological steps in the OECD-DAC's overall assessment framework are, therefore, a positive step towards understanding the foundations for national security.

Another example of a strategic multilateral approach to security and development planning is the Poverty Reduction Strategy Papers (PRSP) process. The PRSP process served

---

[15] OECD-DAC, The OECD-DAC Handbook on Security System Reform (SSR): Supporting Security and Justice, OECD-DAC Publications, 2007.
[16] Ibid, p. 3
[17] Ibid, p. 44
[18] Ibid, p.44
[19] OECD-DAC Guidelines, op cit, p. 22

as an overarching strategic donor-driven approach to national development and has more recently opened itself up to addressing security dimensions of its conventional development focus. The PRSP was initially set up as a national programme for poverty reduction as a foundation for lending programmes with the International Monetary Fund (IMF) and the World Bank and Heavily Indebted Poor Countries (HIPC) debt relief. It is meant to lay out a policy framework and agenda for tackling poverty which has been agreed in a participatory way and which is nationally led and owned.

Similar to a range of other instruments used by the development community, organisations driving the PRSP process (predominantly International Financial Institutions) have had neither the mandate nor the competencies to involve themselves with more delicate – and often defence and arms-related – security tasks and activities. However, as the PRSP processes in Sierra Leone, Uganda and Afghanistan now illustrate, the strategic approach has begun to embrace inter-related security and development priorities. The contrast between the 1997 and the 2004 Ugandan PRSP strategic priorities in Table 1 below provides evidence of this development.

Table 1. A comparison of key priorities in Uganda's 1997 and 2004 PRSP programmes[20]

Uganda's 1997 PRSP Strategic Priorities	Uganda's 2004 PRSP Strategic Priorities
Primary Health Care	Economic Management
Rural Feeder Roads	Production, Competitiveness and Incomes
Primary Education	Security, Conflict Resolution and Disaster Management
Provision of Safe Water	Good Governance
Modernization of Agriculture	Human Development

Therefore, in some national contexts, the more contemporary approach supporting PRSP processes can provide a more overarching and 'strategic rubric' to inform programmes like SSR, particularly in the absence of a national security strategy which has enjoyed a full debate within civil society and Parliament. However, notwithstanding its ability to weave together a variety of national goals, the PRSP still suffers from occasional criticism of being too donor-driven.[21]

There are also examples of more progressive SSR approaches that have been led in part by top-level national security strategy processes. This applies to the recent experiences of countries like Jamaica, Kosovo (albeit described as an Internal Security Sector Review (ISSR)), Ukraine and Botswana. All processes have included step-by-step approaches to identifying national security issues and priorities. The demand for such a process in Ukraine was driven by the need to carefully review its post-independence national security priorities with a view to potential NATO and EU accession. Similarly, the conceptual underpinnings of the Kosovo ISSR methodology were based on the perceived threat analysis generated by the

---

[20] Taken from: Uganda's Poverty Reduction Strategy Paper, IMF (2005), IMF Country Report, August 2005, pp.5-6.

[21] For example, see the report published by Ghananian economist, Charles Abugre which examines how Poverty Reduction Strategies are acting as barriers to policies benefiting the world's poorest people. Found at http://www.wdm.org.uk/news/archive/19992001/PRSP_critique.htm#wrapper

first stage of the process and the Copenhagen criteria which, given the aspirations of Kosovo to be a part of the European community, became a necessary political benchmark for the development of Kosovo's institutions, as well as background for formulation of security policy.

Jamaica's national security review process was initiated in 2003 and supported by the Governments of the UK, Canada and the US. Following an iterative process which lasted over almost three years, a "National Security Strategy for Jamaica" was published in May 2006. The process was championed across the Jamaican Government by the then Minister for Security, Dr Peter Phillips. Unfortunately, due to a sudden change of Government in Jamaica's 2007 general elections which led to the removal of Dr Phillips from his Cabinet post, the national security 'champion' disappeared and the policy process lost momentum.

The phenomenon of leaving the development of national security agenda dependent on the efforts of either individual people and/or individual organisations is widespread. Lessons have been learned from a number of other national experiences, including the Government of Canada's decision to move the 'custodialship' of the 2004 National Security Policy from the Government's Privy Council Office to the Canadian Security and Intelligence Services (CSIS). Senior defence analysts and a number of Canadian academics have suggested that relegating national security to a Ministerial portfolio has resulted in the incomplete and only partial international strategic analysis supporting national security. One analyst commented that:

> [...]due to the current obsession with Homeland Security, borders and immigration issues, the Canadian Integrated Threat Assessment Centre is being driven by internal security concerns affecting our immediate borders, which do not consider the linkages between – for example - crime on the streets of Toronto and the opium in Afghanistan, or our overseas aid policies in Africa and the injection of foreign health workers in Canada and how this export of social capital might be linked to conflict in Africa.[22]

In a speech delivered to the UK Government's Conservative Party conference in Blackpool on 2 October 2007, Dame Neville-Jones offered a similar observation related to the need for Executive level 'buy-in' for a national security agenda:

> [...]when damage to a pipeline in Russia can put up the price of heating in Redditch; when cartoons in Denmark can set off riots in Pakistan; when opium from Helmand can end up on the streets of Huddersfield it's crazy to put foreign and domestic security policy in separate boxes.[23]

For those countries which did draw on national security frameworks either prior to, or in parallel with, the roll-out of SSR programmes, the general pattern of national security processes is recognised as including an environmental analysis, a threat assessment, the identification of assets and organisations available and required responses. In the case of Kosovo, this approach (consisting of 8 steps) meant that most of the subsidiary steps were carefully grounded in European Union (EU), UN Missions in Kosovo (UNMIK) or OECD

---

[22] Based on discussions with Professor W D Macnamara, Ottawa, Canada, January 2007.
[23] See transcript of Dame Pauline Neville Jones' speech delivered in Blackpool at http://www.conservatives.com/tile.do?def=news.story.page&obj_id=139235

processes. In the case of Jamaica, the process did not become sufficiently resilient against political change. A similar 8-step process is currently being followed by the National Security Secretariat of the Government of Botswana. However, at the time of writing, this process is still ongoing.

The next section will argue for the importance of establishing a foundation on which national security planning processes can be built which – to a certain extent – the above-mentioned 'staged' processes are lacking. It will also argue that building a strong foundation can be assisted through the articulation and codification of national interests and core values, which should provide the central pillar for a national security strategy process and around which an analysis should be developed. This will enhance the political resilience and longevity of the national security interests articulated, and will go some way in inviting only occasional and proportionate changes based on environmental shifts and the way in which policy instruments can be used to respond.

CORE VALUES AND NATIONAL INTERESTS: THE FOUNDATIONS FOR NATIONAL SECURITY PLANNING PROCESSES

Core values which serve as the basis for national interests and goals would normally be extracted from a state's constitution or – at the very least – be re-produced in strategic policy papers (e.g. defence, foreign affairs). Such references can then be used to remind the national electorate and Government of the ways in which strategic tools of government will be employed to defend, protect, pursue and project such core interests and values.

In addition to the national examples described above, most countries undertaking national security reviews invariably start with a 'threatist-based' approach or with an initial strategic environmental assessment. Often, there is a complete disconnect between the national interests mentioned in constitutional documents and the key pillars which set out a country's national security framework. This trend often leads to three general outcomes.

First, a tendency develops across the executive offices and government departments to use second and third-order derivatives of core values. This lends to the increasingly evident distinct policy priorities of individual Government departments due to the flexibility of being able to choose amongst a number of loose foundational principles; this leads to a lack of coherency across government policy. The use of second and third order derivatives of core values also masks the whole notion of shared common values, which is the strength of western democracies. The way in which universal core values such as rule of law and social justice then become interpreted and documented as 'tolerance' (in the case of the UK), and 'respect and responsibility' (in the case of Canada) – is quite useful in illuminating the national understanding and culture surrounding national security experiences. However, there is also the need for some common terms in English.

The second outcome resulting from a lack of codification is that values become used without logic for justifying interests. Due to a widespread lack of knowledge with regard to what these values and interests represent, strategic-level decisions in Government may rarely become challenged due to the absence of higher-level guidelines that would serve as the basis for such challenges. These challenges are central to the roles of Parliament and civil society in a mature and active democracy. For example, at the time of writing, many would argue that the UK Prime Minister has yet to provide a clear and concise reason – which is easily understood by the wider electorate – as to why Britain sent troops to Iraq in 2003. Neither policymakers nor civil society have the means to challenge such decisions as and when they are being taken due to an unclear understanding about what justifies and legitimizes such decisions.

The third outcome which arises due to a lack of codified guiding principles is the production of international security analysis which lacks focus. The provision of clearly defined interests and values is essential in providing the bedrock for the further development of policy, for challenging policy and for crafting a strategic assessment that is tailored to a specific set of issues, from which a strategy – in the form of a set of policies – can develop by way of responding to the varying impacts of global trends. Analysis supporting national security frameworks must include international strategic trends described in terms of their impact on the nation's people and national assets overseas as well as at home. Just like a corporate strategy, where a macro and micro environmental assessment becomes shaped around organizational objectives and core competencies, a strategic assessment supporting a national security strategy should be geared around a set of issues or national priorities.[24]

In summary, the separation of 'values' from 'interests' remains artificial as values form a country's interests. The UK Government's March 2008 National Security Strategy refers to the UK 'core values' as including human rights, the rule of law, legitimate and accountable government, justice, freedom, tolerance and opportunity for all. Immediately following the publication of the strategy paper, defence and security analyst Paul Cornish argued that:

> […]these values are mentioned in a strangely passive and defensive way, almost as if the most that should be done with these immense ideas is to protect them from marauding terrorists and criminals […]. Saddest of all, these values appear to constitute little more than the 'normality' to which, we are told, the government's security strategy will enable us to return 'as soon as possible' after some harm occurs. The problem with mere normality is that it isn't usually all that interesting and inspiring and might not be worth defending in extremis.[25]

Arguably, the document would have benefited from a full and frank national debate on what constitutes British values. Having announced the initiative in July 2007 with a view to publishing the document only a few months later, a national debate could not be accommodated. The UK requires first principles to be laid down and codified; first principles to which the majority of the population can subscribe; principles which can bind Britons together in times of need, and principles which can allow questions to be asked when policy decisions go wrong.

The UK is therefore at a point where it must bring three levels of analysis together in terms of clarifying the linkages between universal core values, British core values and national interests. Prior to the publication of the UK National Security Strategy, Britons were accustomed to hearing loose reference to 'what was in our national interest' and the expression of principles like tolerance but without rooting these interests to the core values

---

[24] The three outcomes identified are also discussed in greater detail in Ann M Fitz-Gerald "A UK National Security Strategy: Cultural and Institutional Challenges" in *Defence Studies*, Vol 8, Issue 1, March 2008, pp.4-25.

[25] Paul Cornish, "The National Security Strategy of the United Kingdom: How Radical Can Britain Be?", Chatham House, Expert's Comment, 26 March 2008, found at: http://www.chathamhouse.org.uk/media/comment/nss/

from which they are derived. At the January 2008 Chatham House conference on Defence and Security Futures, Sir David Omand spoke about the importance of 'healthy communities'[26] – which, subject to a full debate, could constitute a British national interest that the Government might seek to protect, pursue and promote in the future through the appropriate use of available policy instruments.

TOWARDS AN IMPROVED PLANNING MODEL FOR NATIONAL SECURITY. THE SOPHISTICATED TO THE SIMPLE

General principles and ideas embraced by the wider school of strategic planning and strategic management can be applied to developing the foundations for national security using a simple approach which minimises academic granularity. There is arguably a need for such simple approaches, particularly when broader national security processes follow on from programmatic entry points; and perhaps when programmatic expertise still dominates the main planning effort.

Such approaches are often initiated following the identification of a relevant national stakeholder group. Those tasked with facilitating a wider national security dialogue might start by challenging a group of national stakeholders to brainstorm what they feel their country is all about in the world they live in (and why they feel that the world they live in is different from the world that others live in); what it is that the country and people pride themselves on and what might represent the unifying forces within a society. Should this be a difficult discussion to initiate, facilitators could also draw on the universal values of western democracies if only to encourage stakeholders to think more deeply about their own notions of 'social justice', 'individual freedoms' and 'rule of law'. These universal values often provide a 'common language' and a platform for further discussion. Planners should not underestimate the time taken to complete this initial phase discussion of first principles. However, a full and frank debate is important, and the exercise itself can be extremely fulfilling in terms of providing stakeholders with some 'guiding points' and in engaging wide buy-in for the articulation and agreement of these points. For example, in undertaking research for this chapter, interviews with national authorities of one country reported that their own national interpretation of 'social justice' would prioritise 'religious tolerance' across their multi-ethnic society.

Drawing on the ideas developed by Donald F Nuechterlein[27], policymakers could then discern between those levels of interests which might be categorised as perhaps being, say, 'vital', 'essential', 'major', 'peripheral', or 'humanitarian' interests. These levels of interests will depend on the national goals, but will collectively address the strategic 'why' question.

For example, as the first and over-riding national interest of a country is to provide for the security of the nation, its people, their assets and their values - all of which a country would fight and die for – this then could be described as a 'vital interest'. A second vital interest may be the assurance of economic well-being, as we would indeed be prepared to

---

[26] In a presentation delivered by Sir David Omand at the Chatham House conference "Defence and Security Futures: Possibilities and Practicalities", February 21-22, 2008.

[27] See Donald Nuechterlein. America Recommitted: A superpower reassesess its role in a turbulent world. Kentucky University Press, 2001.

fight and die for ensuring the maintenance of energy and food supplies as well as essential raw materials (hence, as Macnamara would suggest, the Japanese rationale in 1941 for launching a surprise military attack on Pearl Harbour as a result of the Anglo-American naval blockade which continued to strangle Japan's economy and indeed survival[28]).

Following the identification of national interests (even if more refinement is required), the planning process could then progress to a strategic environmental assessment which identifies trends, issues, risks and threats. The use of a variety of 'descriptors' for this stage of brainstorming is helpful in encouraging the widest possible participation and also for identifying the positive as well as the negative trends. Thought could then be applied to assessing the impact of these trends, issues, risks and threats on the core values and interests identified earlier.

In assessing the impact, planners could consider the different policy goals affected. As policy goals relate to the way in which a Government intends to protect, promote, pursue and defend the national interests articulated, this step is fundamental for illustrating the different policy *areas* affected in relation to each policy *goal* affected. This can have a subsequent effect in terms of how policymakers may consider refining – or even narrowing down or 'clustering' – key national interests.

For example, if the national interests of a country included 'religious tolerance', one policy goal which might further support this national interest might be to 'promote a community focus'. Depending on the degree to which an issue, threat or trend impacted on this policy goal, a number of different policy areas may become affected. For example, it is highly likely that a 'community focus' policy goal could be subsequently reflected in policy areas such as defence, internal affairs, social, and economic policies. By observing how policy goals become mainstreamed through the individual policy areas, better guidance can be provided as to how a Government may respond to a specific issue using a given set of policy instruments. If a Government finds itself unable to respond to the way in which certain policy areas are affected, it may wish to add to – or amend – its existing set of policy instruments.

By spending the requisite time on identifying core values and national interests – and thereby establishing the foundations for national security planning – the resulting strategy becomes more robust, comprehensive and resilient. Values and interests should be reasonably enduring and should outlive political change. This is not to say that national interests should not be periodically reviewed, as these may change over the longer-term due to significant changes in, for example, the population and ethnic composition of a country.

Undoubtedly, a country's strategic environment can also change both incrementally and significantly. The terrorist attacks of 11 September 2001 underscored this point. However, such changes can occur at a time when values and interests remain constant and thus when a country's reaction to strategic environmental shifts should be observed only in terms of how policy instruments are used in a different way than may have previously been the case.

Lastly, with values, interests and a strategic environment held constant, a change of government will undoubtedly lead to changes in policies. However, with little or no change in macro-strategic issues, the degree of policy change is often felt more in the 'letter' of the policy and not in the practice.

---

[28] Based on discussions with Professor W D Macnamara, Queen's University School of Business and Centre for International Relations, 27 March 2007.

CONCLUSIONS

This chapter has highlighted the important link between national security frameworks and security policy instruments, including SSR. It described trends supporting national security planning in donor countries where greater policy coherence is being pursued. It also discussed the trend towards undertaking more informed donor-funded security interventions under the guise of a broader national security process.

In both cases, the absence of a strong foundation for national security becomes apparent. This is due to a lack of codification and articulation of important first principles which should underpin the national security priorities of a country. In addition, there is also a tendency for more strategic approaches to national security planning to begin with a 'strategic environmental assessment' even in the absence of foundational pillars around which such an assessment should be based. Notwithstanding progress across the multilateral and bilateral community in moving towards a more strategic approach to national security planning, a careful, timely and inclusive debate on core values and national interests should serve as a mandatory first step in the planning process. Failure to do so could render the months of planning which follow to be partially flawed, and can expose the process to political vulnerabilities.

In this context, the paper ends by presenting a simple planning process for generating core values and interests, and a discussion of how such principles might inform policy goals and individual policy areas. It reminds the reader that perfection should not be sought in defining these terms. Indeed, the methodology presented allows for an iterative process to cater to the further refinement of the key principles, which should change only over the longer term.

In: Strategizing Resilience and Reducing Vulnerability
Editors: Peter R.J. Trim and Jack Caravelli
ISBN 978-1-60741-693-7
© 2009 Nova Science Publishers, Inc.

Chapter 3

DEALING WITH DISASTER – PARADOX AND PERCEPTION

Robert Hall

ABSTRACT

The perception of risk is changing. While some executives are becoming more risk averse in the face of a growing array of both traditional and new threats, others are taking advantage of the opportunities presented to exploit fresh arenas while, at the same time, mitigating the associated risks. The real challenge is how best to capitalize on the upside of risk. It is therefore appropriate and timely to examine how to seize the opportunities, especially in the race to occupy the 24/7 media space in time of crisis, to overcome collective fear by developing trust, and how all this could lead to greater resilience when effective leadership is generated from the centre.

AN UNCERTAIN WORLD

While catastrophes, both natural and man-made, have plagued human societies for time immemorial, they have taken on a new complexion in recent times. A more populous, globalized, technologically advanced world may have many positive benefits, but it also has introduced diverse vulnerabilities and complex interdependencies. A hurricane in New Orleans can affect the world's oil price by shutting down oil-drilling platforms in the region, while a terrorist attack in New York can change the politico-military stance of a superpower against regimes on the other side of the world. Such local or 'tactical' events now have assumed far greater international or 'strategic' resonance. As a result, many of us have become evermore affected by disasters and absorbed by their consequences.

Modern communications have done much to broadcast the enormities of disasters in real time. At the same time, broadcasts have conveyed a perception that there are more disasters in the world, which is probably untrue: we just know more about them and pay more dearly for their consequences. With a barrage of graphic images coming from a myriad of painful causes, people have understandably become more fearful in their daily routines – regrettably, they may also have become sanitized to some of the pain.

Governments have devoted considerable resources in an effort to reassure their troubled populations. The financial costs are sizeable, whether measured in terms of improved intelligence gathering, more law-enforcement personnel, or enhanced building security. In terms of clean-up, the price is also high. The aftermath of the anthrax attacks in the US in 2001 is reported to have cost roughly US$1 billion for the five lives lost.[1] A similar cost equation could be applied to the consequences of the Hatfield rail derailment in the UK in 2000. Such levels of response to major disasters are clearly untenable for any country to sustain on a repetitive basis. Yet in spite of the spending, there is little sign of public concerns to major risks being assuaged; some might say that there is even an exaggerated sense of insecurity today.

In this new security paradox, ideas and practices around resilience, recovery and continuity have become plentiful. A 2007 survey of 1,257 managers by the Chartered Institute of Management, for example, revealed that 73% believed that business continuity was important in their organization. [2] Business continuity embodies the concepts of preparation and planning which, while appearing to be proactive, are – in reality – more about being better able to cope with the repercussions than in addressing and removing the root causes. All too often, the scale and efficacy of the measures fail to recognize the new parameters around which we all now operate. Furthermore, people all too often view pronouncements from official sources with a degree of scepticism and mistrust, thereby increasing the climate of fear and uncertainty.

Unfortunately, the situation is unlikely to change significantly in the foreseeable future. Identification and analysis of the issues will perhaps provide some indication of a better way forward, so that the paradigm becomes less apparent and perceptions become clearer. However, even with such introspection, it may continue to be the case that when ideas and reality collide, then people will find it difficult to adjust their behaviour to suit the new situation – a symptom, identified by psychologists, of cognitive dissonance.[3]

This chapter draws on previous work by the author that looked at how the information overload is simply giving people more things to worry about; yet the more time that is spent on planning and preparation for disasters, the more vulnerable the population feels. [4] This dilemma is simply going to intensify and needs to be addressed through structural and psychological adaptation.

THE RATIONALITY OF RISK

Scientists and professionals do their best to focus on measurable, quantifiable attributes of risk e.g. probability and impact, while many in the public pay much less attention to these, and respond primarily to value-laden perceptual attributes which the expert community tends to ignore e.g. unfamiliarity, loss of control. People get upset, angry or frightened about a host of risks which if examined in the cold light of day are far from real or rational. This human element has been described as the outrage factor. [5] Catastrophic risks provoke a level of outrage that chronic risks do not trigger. Hence, we are appalled at the terrorist bombing in central London on 7 July 2005 when 52 people were killed but hardly bat an eyelid when

2,946 people are killed on UK roads in 2007. Yet the figures reveal that, in spite of our fears, we are individually far more likely to be killed travelling in a car than in a terrorist incident.

In the same asymmetric vein, most business people see risk in a behavioural rather than mathematical sense. They, like most of us, fear losses more than we value gains. Put simply, we are much more willing to take risks to avoid losses than they are to obtain gains; put another way, we experience the potential pain of losing £1,000 more deeply than we prize the pleasure of a gain of £1,000. This leads to loss or risk aversion, and is increasingly a feature of the commercial world. In fact, a recent survey by Lloyds of London showed that 'one fifth of companies forego otherwise promising business opportunities because of [political] risks.'[6]

Yet if business is to move ahead in an increasingly complex working environment then it is essential that risk-averse behaviour is managed and the opportunities in any situation are unlocked. This does not necessarily mean adopting a risk-seeking behaviour but it does infer realizing the potential for making capital out of the circumstances so as to place a company ahead of its risk-averse competitors. It is about recognizing the 'upside', namely the insight to see risk others do not and unlock the opportunities others cannot. A good example of the two positions can be seen in the actions of two companies – Nokia and Ericsson – following a fire at the Philips semi-conductor plant in Albuquerque (US) in 2000. While Ericsson delayed remedial action by two weeks and so lost US$400m in potential revenue and suffered a 14% drop in share price, Nokia arranged for alternative supplies within days, cornered the surplus semi-conductor market, and went on to prosper. Ericsson was eventually forced to exit phone manufacturing and was bought by Sony soon afterwards.[7] Here, one company was able to take advantage of the dangers presented through a correct assessment of the risks while the other was too slow to capitalize on the consequences. Realizing the upside of risk can confer confidence, strength and resilience to a business.

THE COMMUNICATION OF RISK

In the same way that the power of computing has doubled its capacity but halved the time to do so (Moore's Law), the world of information has followed suit. Information Technology has today built a global stage and the media are ever more dominant actors. Media channels race to fill our visual space 24/7 and, consequentially, do much to shape our lives. Satellite news broadcasts, text and photo messaging, as well as television and video streaming have all contributed to an information blizzard. For example, the BBC apparently received in the hours following the four explosions in London on 7 July 2005, over 1,000 images, 3,000 texts, 20,000 e-mails and 20 video clips. [8]

This capability marks a profound shift in both reporting and responding. The making of news is no longer in the hands of a few but available to the many. The inescapable fact is that the mobile phone has given individuals direct and unfiltered access to the airwaves in a way that was unimaginable only a decade ago. For the authorities trying to keep up with events and the stream of pictures, not to mention mustering the emergency services, then maintaining control and conveying authority have become real problems. What is clear is the disproportionate effect of the moving image (over text). This gives the medium added resonance – and lasting impact. In a way, the omnipresent media has become a vehicle for not just assessing our societal engagement but also judging our moral conscience.

In a dynamic and fast-evolving environment, a captive audience begins to make its own assessments – believing what the media announces – and takes action ahead of any official statements. The latter can appear to be belated and sometimes out of touch in such circumstances. Yet without the expert pronouncement or access to the in-depth briefing, the general audience is not well placed in the early stages of an unfolding disaster to decide what information is relevant and what part can be disregarded. Real-time challenges do not always give either the listener or the broadcaster the luxury to sort, select and verify in a calm and considered way. Regrettably, accuracy and authentication are not only the first casualties in the race to keep up with the pace of fast-moving events.

The volatility of the situation can frequently lead to information denial by the authorities. It is clearly better to say nothing than generate or feed a rumour. The latter is commonly seen as the road to time wasting, confusion and, potentially, further vulnerability. The casual word may also boost the general perception of fear. However, in the disaster scenario – with dramatic pictures and volleys of questions appearing from all quarters – then it is increasingly difficult to wait for clarification and confirmation. So much so, that the traditional 'golden hour' appears to be giving way to the modern 'black hole'. The conundrum cannot be readily resolved. Yet one factor features above all others; that is trust – trust in established organisations and in the voice of authority. Gaining trust depends on an understanding of people's fears and in conveying a collective confidence to overcome those demons. Like leadership itself, it is all about instilling in people the will to do something they would otherwise choose not to. It is also about developing a relationship by way of radar rather than loudhailer.

FEAR AND TRUST

In today's unstable and unpredictable world, we increasingly face situations for which no script has been written. A mass-casualty terrorist attack, a wide-ranging tsunami, or a rapidly spreading pandemic are all alarming and devastating events. It is the unexpected and unknown elements which generate fear, so much so that certain events can lead some sectors to terrorise themselves far better than any terrorists. People may be more aware but they are also more easily scared. The 'culture of risk' has encouraged us, both societally and individually, to become risk averse. [9] Expectations of a safe environment, and litigation to follow if proved otherwise, make for a cautionary orientation which all too easily becomes a zero-risk mentality. Fear is also a cultural phenomenon – the reactions of New Yorkers to 9/11 were visibly different to Londoners after 7/7. This can partially be explained by the latter's long involvement in the terrorist campaign in Northern Ireland and the first foreign assault on the former's homeland since the Second World War. Nevertheless, both incidents saw a downturn in metro/tube travel and an increase in car usage.

The level of risk compared to the degree of fear frequently can get out of kilter. The numbers killed on public highways compared to terrorist acts demonstrates the point. Proportionality in approach and striking the right balance are eminently sensible catch phrases but unlikely to catch on. In fact, public perceptions tend to be at odds with the real nature of the risks. [10] The reason for this – according to some academics – is that people tend to make judgements about risk based on emotional feelings and intuitions, about whether something is good or bad, rather than a dispassionate calculation of costs and benefits. [11] Judgements are holistic rather than analytical, focusing on pleasure and pain rather than logic, and on free associations rather than deductive connections. All this highlights the importance of images and narratives i.e. the media in shaping perceptions.

The fact that Londoners are more used to seeing pictures of bombings from Irish republican terrorists, as well as suffering the disruption to daily routines which a long-term terrorist campaign invariably brings, perhaps goes some way to reinforcing these conclusions. Clearly, a population is adaptable and can prepare itself to be more resilient to extreme circumstances. Many companies have learnt this lesson and market data show that a business which can demonstrably recover from a disaster can actually go on to increase its share price as confidence is enhanced in the market place. [12]

There is also a large body of research, dating back to the Second World War, which shows that far from panicking, people in the throes of a disaster behave more rationally and with greater social responsibility than would be expected – certainly, to a degree that officialdom or the media give them credit for. The issuing of gas masks to the UK population in advance of the outbreak of war in 1939 was, for example, not met with hysteria and revolt but with realism and pragmatism. The 'blitz mentality' can be a positive attitude in the face of adversity.

ENHANCED RESILIENCE

The conclusion is that effective resilience is actually about attitude – so called mindset – which is based to a large degree on trust in the governing authorities. It is about the community being imbued with clarity of purpose, and an understanding of the nature, scale and potential of the dangers. Technical fixes, whether they be based on vaccines, barriers, cameras or guns, are not sufficient by themselves; they may be more comfortable for authorities to introduce as practical responses to a perceived threat – and do engender an extra degree of confidence – but they do not build a residual level of psychological resilience. CCTV, for instance, may be well received by the public but has been shown not to result in any measurable decrease in either crime or terrorism. In the face of suicide bombers then cameras are likely to provide more an evidential tool than a deterrent; deterrence does not have a place in the world of the suicide bomber; for him or her, there are no escape options.

All too often, government emergency programmes tend not to consider ordinary people on the assumption that they will be incapacitated with fear. For reasons already outlined, not to mention a large degree of political squeamishness, the authorities tend to withhold information for fear of scaremongering. Worries about large numbers of deaths and injuries tend to deter discussions. Applying the precautionary principle also has the consequence of emphasising worst-case scenarios, thereby encouraging a tendency to over react to events. However, while some major natural disasters may clearly generate horrific scenes, most serious incidents have lower than expected lethality rates – for example, deaths from vCJD total 164 (UK), the SARS pandemic in 2002/03 killed 774, and the sarin attack in Tokyo in 1995 resulted in 11 deaths. [13]

If authorities are to prepare realistically for all eventualities, there is a need to involve individuals and communities; local people can be highly effective during emergencies and are invariably the first to be on the scene. This means explaining plans and procedures beforehand – albeit in outline – as time will surely not allow during. The London Mass Evacuation Plan (formerly Operation SASSOON) is a step in the right direction but one must ask how many of the general public know what to do from this document, namely how to proceed and to where. [14] What is more, the authorities' over-reliance on top-down control is inappropriate to deal with any rapidly evolving emergency situation. Tactical fluidity simply does not lend itself to bureaucratic involvement – the military learnt this lesson the hard way from the modern battlefield. Nonetheless, there is a need for strong leadership at senior level in an effort to pull communities together in the face of potential major disruptions to everyday routines.

The requirement for senior leadership, in turn, needs a clear 'voice of authority' upon which people can rely upon and rally around. Such a voice should have a degree of independence to avoid political interference; 'experts', whether that be a senior police officer or a medical professional, are generally more trusted than politicians. Clearly, the events surrounding the lead-up to the Iraq war have made people less likely to believe in announcements from officials. A cynical mistrust of leaders is not the attribute required at a time of real national crisis. Similarly, leaders need to develop a higher level of trust in people; both may be surprised in the outcome. With the world facing a flu pandemic then there is no time to lose. Besides prophylactics and plans, public confidence needs to be strong and robust in the face of potential panic.

STRUCTURAL CHANGES

To avoid the traditional British 'ad-hocery' of pulling such experts together to suit a particular crisis – admirable though it may seem – then the role of a permanent crisis-management department, with a public-facing director, deserves serious consideration in the light of the new challenges.

The relevance of the US Federal Emergency Management Agency for the UK should be examined in this regard: the failings of FEMA after Hurricane Katrina should be seen as a spur not a spoil. A similar organisation could usefully take on some of the daily responsibilities of the British Home Office in emergency planning, and the temporary crisis-control functions of the Cabinet Office Briefing Room A (COBRA). It would require the authority to bring together the activities of several departments in time of crisis. Senior government oversight could still be maintained but tactical control could be independent. Resurrection of an organisation such as the Civil Defence Corps – a group of local people with local knowledge prepared to handle the consequences of a nuclear war in the 1950-80s – is an idea also worthy of merit. This concept will naturally need time, resources and training to be effective. Above all, the structure needs a clear intelligence and analysis input on the dangers that are around and that may appear over the horizon. An Indicators and Warning unit, collecting and assessing data from a wide variety of sources over the short, medium and long term, should be an integral part of the operation, providing valuable advance notice of impending disasters (whenever possible). A model could be the Joint Terrorism Analysis

Centre (JTAC) which currently collates information on terrorism threats and advises on threat levels. (See Figure 1 for a possible organizational framework of emergency planning and response.)

Any structural changes must be accompanied by policy changes. The introduction of a national security strategy for the UK, announced in March 2008, is a positive and welcome step towards achieving an overarching, holistic plan. [15] Yet the plan must have the requisite teeth to set standards and encourage compliance. Making the new British Standard on Business Continuity (BS 25999) mandatory, rather than optional as at present, for Category 1 responders such as Local Authorities and certain Category 2 responders like water companies would, for example, be valuable. [16] This would require a change in the legislation enshrined within the Civil Contingencies Act (2004). [17] However, any policy amendments must overcome the fundamental difference in approach and objectives between the public and private sectors: the former broadly exists to restore functionality and control, while the latter is there to maintain profit. Hence, any generic prescriptions on policy or plans do not necessarily or easily translate across the public-private boundary.

WAY FORWARD

The scale and range of risks to a modern and networked society are considerable and growing. If we are to respond to the modern challenges in an effective and efficient manner then we need to look afresh at existing practices and current organizations – they seem ill-suited to dealing with fast-moving events cast in the spotlight of the world's media. Communities and businesses also needs to take a fresh look at their perception of risk and come to accept that dangers cannot be removed altogether but can be rationalized in terms of frequency and impact; this is the true measure of risk. In fact, if handled appropriately, risk is an enabler that can release opportunities that were previously hidden or hindered.

But the direction we collectively take will very much depend on the lead we are given by politicians and other people in authority. If they are seen to organize potential responses in an imaginative and holistic way, providing measured briefing design to alert but not alarm, then it is more likely than not that society will respond to the challenges. A national security strategy is a useful first step in this direction but it must be translated and cascaded into practical measures that organizations and individuals can apply and test in their everyday lives in readiness for a major catastrophe..

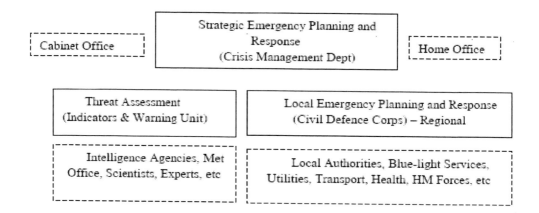

Figure 1. Framework for Emergency Planning and Response.

REFERENCES

[1] 'Little Progress in FBI Probe of Anthrax Attacks', *The Washington Post*, 16 September 2005. Figure quoted from a FBI report.
[2] See www.preparingforemergencies.gov.uk/business/bcm_report2007.pdf
[3] Dixon N F, On the Psychology of Military Competence, New York: Basic Books, 1976.
[4] Hall R, 'Is too much knowledge a dangerous thing?', Survive, Second Quarter 2006. The author thanks Ian Holland & Co for permission to reproduce part of that work.
[5] Sandman P, see various articles on Outrage factors at www.psandman.com
[6] Lloyd's of London 360° Report 'Under Attack? Global Business and the Threat of Political Violence', April 2007.
[7] Cleary S and Malleret T, 'Global Risk: Business Success in Turbulent Times', Palgrave, 2007.
[8] Gowing N, 'Managing Information Asymmetry', RUSI Conference, London, 15-16 November 2005.
[9] Furedi F, Culture of Fear: Risk-Taking and the Morality of Low Expectation, London: Continuum, 2002.
[10] Durodie B, 'Perception and Threat: Why Vulnerability-led responses will Fail', *Security Monitor*, Vol 1, No 4, November 2002.
[11] Flynn J, Slovis P, Kunreuther H, 'Risk, Media and Stigma: understanding public challenges to modern science and technology', Earthscan, 2001.
[12] Knight R and Pretty D, 'Protecting Value in the Face of Mass Fatality Events', Oxford Metrica, 2005.
[13] For vCJD figures, see http://www.cjd.ed.ac.uk/figures.htm For SARS figures, see WHO website: http://www.who.int/csr/sars/country/table2004_04_21/en/
[14] An outline description of the London Mass Evacuation Plan can be found within the London Strategic Emergency Plan at http://www.london prepared.gov.uk/downloads/emergplanv5.pdf

[15] For details of the UK's National Security Strategy, see: http://interactive.cabinetoffice.gov.uk/documents/security/national_security_strategy.pdf
[16] For details on BS 25999, see: http://www.bsi-global.com/en/Standards-and-Publications/Industry-Sectors/Risk/Business-continuity/
[17] For details of CCA, see: http://www.ukresilience.info/preparedness/ccact.aspx An update of the CCA is underway in a 2-3 year programme called the Civil Contingencies Act Enhancement Programme (CCAEP).

In: Strategizing Resilience and Reducing Vulnerability
Editors: Peter R.J. Trim and Jack Caravelli

ISBN 978-1-60741-693-7
© 2009 Nova Science Publishers, Inc.

Chapter 4

THE GROWING COMPETITION FOR WATER: AN EMERGING GLOBAL FLASHPOINT

Marc Glasser

ABSTRACT

The prospects for conflict over water are escalating. Water is one of the most basic elements required for life, and it is a finite resource. The demand for water is increasing while the world is reaching maximum water exploitation. The competition for water will have worldwide consequences and far-reaching impacts in such areas as economic growth and limits, security, food production, poverty, sanitation, politics, and terrorism. Water supply and demand issues can have local, national and international ramifications. Accordingly, water management solutions in some cases require local, national and international collaboration and cooperation involving an array of stakeholders. Inadequate action may produce significant water conflicts, which could result in demonstrations, riots, mass migration, political instability, regime change, terrorism, and armed conflict. In most cases, there are no simple solutions to achieve equilibrium between global water supply and demand competition. Even when solutions can be agreed upon, they can require significant cooperation, effort, resources, and time.

INTRODUCTION

A billboard near the venue of the Fourth World Water Forum held in Mexico in March 2006 proclaimed, "The next world war will be fought over water" (Lane, 2006, p. xiii). Perhaps this is an overstatement, but irreparable water conflicts are indeed a growing threat. The competition for water will affect many countries. For example, it has been estimated that more than 50 countries on five continents could soon be caught up in water disputes unless they move rapidly to establish agreements on sharing water resources (Global Policy Forum, n.d.). A *Middle East Institute* report argues that water scarcity is a natural scientific problem and a political issue, which will lead to water wars. The report cites powerful nations like Turkey and Israel that have regional superior economic and military power that gives them greater access to water, inciting violent conflict with poorer nations such as Iraq and Syria (Jägerskog, 2008). Additionally, in the Middle East and North Africa region the population has more than quadrupled since 1950, to 364 million and is expected to reach nearly 600 million by 2050. By 2050, the amount of fresh water available for each person, already limited, will be reduced by 50 percent (Martin, 2008). The declining water resources could inflame political tensions further in an area already primed for terrorist activities and recruiting.

Water conflicts affect not only food production and the economy, but also regional stability, national security, diplomacy, armed conflict, and terrorism—because water is life.

Although supply and demand for most natural resources and commodities present serious concerns (Brown, 2008), potable water is one of the few resources without which a human cannot survive for more than a few days (USGS, 2007). Whereas many societies would certainly be stressed by a week without petrol, a week without water would have severe consequences for humans, animals, agriculture and society as a whole, perhaps igniting serious water conflicts.

THE CHALLENGES OF MEETING GROWING GLOBAL WATER DEMAND

As a result of uneven distribution, water is scarce in some countries (World Water Council, 2005a). On a global scale, the water situation may not seem so alarming. However, the world's supply of available fresh water will shrink as the rising population increases demand. For example, the world's population tripled during the 20th Century, and the use of renewable water resources has grown six-fold. Moreover, it is expected that within the next 50 years the world population will increase by 40% to 50%. This population growth will be accompanied by industrialization and urbanization, further increasing both demand and environmental consequences (World Water Council, 2005b).

Half of the fresh water available for human use globally is being used. At the current rate of increase in consumption, fresh water consumption will reach 90% of the worldwide supply by 2030. Availability will not be uniform across regions of the world. Two thirds of the world population will experience chronic shortages of safe drinking water by 2030 (Lindell, Perry and Prater, 2007).

In addition, resource challenges, including water supply challenges, will be amplified and will extend well beyond 2030, further straining society. Consider that by 2050, the number of humans on Earth is expected to rise from 6.7 billion to more than 9 billion. U.S. Central Intelligence Agency (CIA) Director Michael Hayden stated that "Most of that growth will occur in countries least able to sustain it, a situation that will likely fuel instability and extremism, both in those countries and beyond" (as quoted in Warrick, 2008). The United Nations Development Programme has estimated that by 2025, about one in two Africans will be living in countries confronted with water stress or water scarcity (Hobbs, 2004).

Water demand will be further exacerbated by the total global growth of the middle class. The growing middle class in Southeast Asia, India, and China will join the West in consuming far more than the minimum 20 to 50 litres of water per day necessary per person. It probably comes as no great surprise that Americans lead the world in water consumption at

400 to 600 litres per day per person. The movement from poverty or lower classes to the middle classes yields more flush toilets, washing machines, and dishwashers. For many people, diets shift from grain to meat-heavy consumption; rearing a cow requires a thousand times more water than the equivalent average for grain. Agriculture is the world's top user of water (80% in some countries), and it is often used inefficiently (Schulte, 2007).

We need not wait for 2025, let alone 2050, to experience significant water supply and demand challenges. In many parts of the world, water is already consumed faster than the natural hydrological process can replenish it. Almost everywhere, water resources are under huge stress from human use. Consider the following American and European examples.

On June 4, 2008, following two consecutive years of below-average rainfall, very low snowmelt runoff and the largest court-ordered water transfer restrictions in state history, the governor of the State of California proclaimed a statewide drought and issued an Executive Order to deal with the crisis. The Executive Order addresses water conservation, upgrading of water infrastructure, and multiparty (bipartisan in this case) legislative solutions (State of California, 2008). Water issues that affect California's £15 billion agricultural industry will in turn affect the Gross Domestic Product of the state, which as of 2007 would be the world's eighth largest economy if it were a separate country (Associated Press, 2007; Schwartz, 2007).

The Atlanta, Georgia, region, with its 5 million people, continues to feel the effects of the extreme drought that has gripped the Southeast U.S. for the past two years. Despite weeks of heavy rainfall during the spring of 2008, Lake Lanier, chief source of water for most parts of the Atlanta area, was more than 4 metres below normal in May and only a few centimetres from the lowest level on record for that month (Bluestein, 2008).

The U.S. Department of Agriculture reported that in parts of Texas, Oklahoma, and Kansas, the three leading grain-producing states, the underground water table has dropped by more than 30 metres. As a result, wells have gone dry on thousands of farms in the southern Great Plains, forcing farmers to return to lower-yielding dryland farming. Although this mining of underground water is taking a toll on U.S. grain production, irrigated land still accounts for only one fifth of the U.S. grain harvest, compared with close to three fifths of the harvest in India and four fifths in China (Brown, 2008).

As reported by the British Broadcasting Corporation (BBC), in May 2008, the Spanish government was hoping to pre-empt a summer crisis by importing water by tanker (Ball, 2007). The local water authority invested more than £80 million in measures to import drinking water and to build desalination and water purification plants. Spain is not alone in its crisis; its neighbour Portugal, which in 2007–2008 suffered its worst winter drought since 1917, was expected to encounter similar problems (Ball, 2007).

Furthermore, while economists rightly hailed the large number of people in China and India who have climbed out of poverty in recent years, many people in these countries are living on "borrowed water" (Lane, 2006, p. xiii). Economic growth and agricultural productivity of the North China Plain and the Indo-Gangeti Basin have led to a reduction in groundwater levels and the drying up of rivers. Sustaining these improved lifestyles will involve the use of water resources from elsewhere to produce food and manufactured goods (Lane, 2006).

As indicated previously, direct water shortages can contribute to economic and political instability. Other secondary or cascading ramifications can also contribute to economic and political instability, mostly in less developed countries. These include the increased spread of infectious diseases through the reliance and consumption of unsafe drinking water, and forced migration to areas where water (safe or unsafe) exists (Lindell, Perry and Prater, 2007).

Cascading ramifications are not limited to less developed countries. For example, nuclear reactors across the Southeastern United States could be forced to reduce output or temporarily shut down, because drought is drying up the rivers and lakes that supply power plants with the cooling water they need to operate. Utility officials say such shutdowns probably would not result in power blackouts; however, millions of Southerners could experience significantly higher electric bills if the region's utilities are forced to buy expensive replacement power from other energy sources and companies. In 2008, 24 of the country's 104 nuclear reactors were in areas experiencing the most severe levels of drought. Because of the year-long dry spell gripping the Southeast, the water levels on lakes and rivers in the region were getting close to the minimums set by the U.S. Nuclear Regulatory Commission (NRC). There were fears that the water could drop below the intake pipes altogether or that the shallow water could become too warm to use as coolant. If either of these situations materialized, the affected nuclear power plants would have to power down. Extending or lowering the intake pipes may not be as simple as it may first appear, nor would it necessarily solve the problem. These pipes, which are usually made of concrete, can be more than 5 metres in diameter and extend over 1.6 kilometres. Modifications to the pipes and pump systems, and their required backups, can cost millions and take several months. If the changes are extensive, they require an NRC review that itself can take months or longer (Associated Press, 2008).

OVERPUMPING OF AQUIFERS

Worldwide, scores of countries are overpumping aquifers as they struggle to satisfy their growing water needs. The drilling of millions of irrigation wells has pushed water withdrawals beyond recharge rates, in effect leading to groundwater mining. The failure of governments to effectively manage water and limit pumping to the sustainable yield of aquifers means that water tables are now falling in countries that contain more than half the world's people, including the big three grain producers: China, India, and the United States. For example, a groundwater survey released in Beijing in August 2001 revealed that the water table under the North China Plain, an area that produces over half of the country's wheat and a third of its corn, is falling fast. The survey reported that under Hebei Province in the heart of the North China Plain, the average level of the deep aquifer was dropping nearly 3 metres per year. Around some cities in the province, it was falling twice as fast. As the deep aquifer is depleted, the region is losing its last water reserve. A World Bank study indicates that China is mining underground water in three adjacent river basins in the north: those of the Hai, which flows through Beijing and Tianjin; the Yellow; and the Huai, the river south of the Yellow. One cubic metre of water weighs one tonne. Because it takes 1,000 cubic metres of water to produce one tonne of grain, the shortfall in the Hai basin of nearly 40 billion cubic metres of water per year means that when the aquifer is depleted, the grain harvest will drop by 40 million cubic metres—enough to feed 120 million Chinese (Brown, 2008).

With regard to India, Brown (2008) reported that:

as serious as water shortages are in China, they are even more serious in India, where the margin between food consumption and survival is so precarious. To date, India's 100 million farmers have drilled 21 million wells, investing some $12 billion in wells and pumps. In a survey of India's water situation, Fred Pearce reported in the *New Scientist* that 'half of India's traditional hand-dug wells and millions of shallower tube wells have already dried up, bringing a spate of suicides among those who rely on them' (p. 71).

India's grain harvest, squeezed by both water scarcity and the loss of cropland to nonfarm uses, has plateaued since 2000. A 2005 World Bank study reported that 15% of India's food supply is produced by mining groundwater. Stated otherwise, 175 million Indians are fed with grain produced with water from irrigation wells that will become dry (Brown, 2008).

Pakistan, a country with close to 168 million people, is also mining its underground water. Observation wells near the cities of Islamabad and Rawalpindi in the fertile Punjab plain show a fall in the water table between 1982 and 2000 that ranges from 1 to nearly 2 metres a year. In the province of Balochistan, water tables around the capital, Quetta, are falling by 3.5 metres per year. Six basins throughout the province have exhausted their groundwater supplies, leaving their irrigated lands barren. Sardar Riaz A. Khan, former director of Pakistan's Arid Zone Research Institute, expects that within 10 to 15 years virtually all the basins outside the canal-irrigated areas will have depleted their groundwater supplies, depriving the province of much of its grain harvest (Brown, 2008).

Pakistan has approximately 163 million Muslims (CIA, 2008). The vast majority of Muslims in Pakistan and elsewhere are peaceful and not involved in or connected to extremist Muslim causes or terrorism. However, Pakistan has a large population of young, poor Muslims, and the country is geographically close to Al Qaeda strongholds in Afghanistan. Perhaps Al Qaeda could capitalize on all these vulnerabilities by disrupting critical water supplies in order to destabilize Pakistan or increase recruitment. An additional concern is that Pakistan is believed to possess approximately 50 nuclear weapons (Caravelli, 2007).

Iran, a country of 71 million people, is overpumping its aquifers by an average of 4.5 billion metric tonnes of water per year, an amount of water equivalent to one third of its annual grain harvest. Under the small but agriculturally rich Chenaran Plain in northeastern Iran, the water table was falling by 2.8 metres a year in the late 1990s as a result of new wells being drilled both for irrigation and to supply the nearby city of Mashad. Villages in eastern Iran are being abandoned as wells go dry, generating a flow of water-related refugees (Brown, 2008).

Neighbouring Saudi Arabia, a country of 25 million people, is as water poor as it is oil rich. Relying heavily on subsidies, it developed an extensive irrigated agriculture based largely on its deep fossil aquifer. After several years of supporting wheat prices at five times the world market level, the government was forced to face fiscal reality and cut the subsidies. Saudi Arabia's wheat harvest dropped from a high of 3.7 million metric tonnes in 1992 to 2.4 million metric tonnes in 2007, a 34% decrease. Some Saudi farmers are now pumping water from wells that are 1.2 kilometres deep. Recognizing its hydrologic limitations, in early 2008 the Saudi government announced plans to phase out wheat production entirely by 2016 (Brown, 2008).

In neighbouring Yemen, a nation of 22 million, the water table under most of the country is falling by roughly 2 metres a year as water use outstrips the sustainable yield of aquifers. In western Yemen's Sana'a Basin, the estimated annual water extraction of 224 million cubic metres exceeds the annual recharge of 42 million cubic metres by a factor of five, causing the water table to drop 6 metres per year. World Bank projections indicate that the Sana'a Basin—site of the national capital, Sana'a, and home to 2 million people—may be pumped dry by 2010. Yemen's population is growing by 3% a year. Yemen grain production has fallen by two thirds over the last 20 years; the country now imports four fifths of its grain supply (Brown, 2008).

According to Brown (2008), this unmanageable food scarcity could certainly lead to massive water-related conflict:

> Since the overpumping of aquifers is occurring in many countries more or less simultaneously, the depletion of aquifers and the resulting harvest cutbacks could come at roughly the same time. And the accelerating depletion of aquifers means this day may come soon, creating potentially unmanageable food scarcity (pp. 74–75).

DESALINATION

Cooley, Gleick, and Wolff (2006) offer the following definition of desalination: "Desalination refers to the wide range of technical processes designed to remove salts from water of different quantities" (p. 52). When thinking about the possibilities of desalination, the famous line from The Rime of the Ancient Mariner by Samuel Taylor Coleridge comes to mind: "Water, water, everywhere, Nor any drop to drink." According to the World Water Council (2005a), "Seventy percent of the earth's surface is covered by water. Ninety-seven percent of this water is contained in oceans, hence salty and unsuitable for drinking or irrigation. Of the remaining 3 % of freshwater, only 0.3 % is found in rivers and lakes, the rest being frozen" (World Water Council, 2005a, Freshwater Resources section). Some have been led to believe that aquifer depletion, water-related food scarcity, and the overall water supply shortage could be overcome by simply building water desalination plants. It is not that simple.

The two major problems associated with desalination are cost effectiveness and environmental issues. The minimum cost of desalination in large-scale plants is still above £0.50 per cubic metre, much higher than the typical cost of urban water. In most parts of the world, alternatives such as cleanup of local water sources, regional water transfers, conservation, wastewater recycling, and implementation of smart land-use policies are more economically viable than the current desalination process. Some believe that desalination costs are dropping rapidly. For the time being, however, ocean desalination will be affordable only in coastal regions that have serious water shortages or significant public subsidies (Cooley, Gleick and Wolff, 2006).

According to the International Desalination Association there more than 13,000 desalination plants operating worldwide, producing more than 49 billion litres of water a day (Kranhold, 2008). Desalination is an important water supply option in energy-rich, arid, water-scarce regions of the world. *Water-scarce regions* are those where the natural availability of fresh water is insufficient to meet demand from traditional water supply options and where water transfers from elsewhere are implausible or not economically viable (Cooley, Gleick and Wolff, 2006).

Despite major barriers to desalination, interest has grown rapidly as technology has improved, water demand has increased, and desalination costs have decreased. Desalination viability has increased for areas experiencing both water scarcity and political concerns about water reliability and independence, as is the case in Israel and Singapore. Viability has also increased in California and other areas with rapidly growing populations, poorly regulated land use, and ecosystem degradation. Recently, Israel and Singapore have built very large reverse osmosis plants, and more than 20 large desalination facilities along the California coast have been proposed. Extensive desalination development continues in the Persian Gulf. Perhaps someday, desalination will be the Holy Grail of water supply policy makers and consumers. However, that someday is not here yet (Cooley, Gleick and Wolff, 2006).

SANITATION AND QUALITY-OF-LIFE ISSUES

Water supply and demand issues extend beyond fresh drinking water. Water demand is and will be stressed by other basic quality-of-life issues such as water required for food preparation and for sanitation, including bathing and human waste processing. The United Nations (UN-Water, 2008) estimated that 88% of the global burden of disease is attributable to unsafe water supply, lack of sanitation, and hygiene and mainly affects children in developing countries. Every day, this situation contributes to the deaths of 5,000 children from largely preventable causes, including diarrhoeal diseases and parasites.

United Nations (e.g., the Millennium Development Goals, World Water Day, World Water Week, The Water Decade, 2008 International Year of Sanitation, World's Water Crisis, Global Water Partnership and African Drought Risk and Development Network)
Water Council
UNESCO
UNICEF
WHO
Earth Policy Institute
European Drought Centre
U.S. Environmental Protection Agency
U.S. Department of Interior
U.S. Food and Drug Administration
National Drought Policy Commission (U.S.)
National Integrated Drought Information System (U.S.)
WaterCAMPWS (Congress for Water Purification Science and Technology in the 21st Century)
United States Strategic Water Initiative (USSWI)
Association of Metropolitan Water Agencies (U.S.)
Western States Water Council (U.S.)
Pacific Institute

Figure 1. Agencies, Programmes, and Initiatives Addressing Water Issues

Public defecation is standard practice in much of the developing world. The Yamuna River, once a lifeline to New Delhi, is an open sewer used by those without toilets. In addition, about half of the waste that goes through New Delhi's sewage system is dumped raw and untreated into the river. A lack of sanitation and clean water has contributed to making diarrhoea the world's number 2 killer of children (Schulte, 2007). "They have water to drink. That's not the problem," said Andrew Hudson, director of water governance for the United Nations Development Program. "They don't have safe water to drink" (quoted in Schulte, 2007, p. 2).

Already there is more wastewater generated and dispersed today than at any other time in the history of our planet. In 2002, an estimated 2.6 billion people—more than two out of six people on the planet—lack adequate sanitation (WHO/UNICEF, 2005). As water sanitation improves, so do local health conditions, and people generally live longer, stay healthier, and become more productive as a result (Schulte, 2007). Additionally, natural hazards research has repeatedly shown that localities composed of well-nourished and healthy individuals and households have the capacity to resist extreme events and the resilience to recover quickly (Bailkie, Cannon, Davis, and Wisner, 2005).

CLIMATE CHANGE

Scientists have pointed out that temperature probably influences our lives more than any other climatic factor, and human society is especially vulnerable to large, long-term temperature changes (Brecke, Lee, He, Zhang, and Zhang, 2007). Most experts believe that climate and temperature change will significantly impact water conditions. For example, at the local level in arid parts of the Southwestern United States, which includes such large metropolitan cities as Phoenix, Arizona, and Las Vegas, Nevada, climate change is represented by increasing air and water temperatures, changing precipitation patterns and stream flow intensity, less snow pack, earlier snowmelt and runoff, an increase in the number and severity of events such as storms and flooding, and intensified drought conditions (Southern Nevada Water Authority [SNWA], 2008d). The snowmelt and runoff in this case is from the U.S. Rocky Mountains and the Colorado River. The river begins as snowmelt in the Rocky Mountains, and the snowmelt travels through a series of tributaries into the river for over 2,200 kilometres, where it empties into the Gulf of California. Seven Western states (California, Nevada, Arizona, Utah, Colorado, New Mexico, and Wyoming) and Mexico share the water, which serves about 25 million people in the United States alone (Ritter, 2007; SNWA, 2008b; U.S. Department of the Interior, 2008a).

On a global scale, food production in many regions of the world, including many of the world's most agriculturally fertile and productive regions, is being impacted. For example, increases in warm weather can result in decreases in rainfall and decreases in rainmaking monsoons in some of the poorest regions of the world. These changes can affect water supply and quality and can also cause crop damage, crop failure, and lower yields. Conversely, some areas are experiencing increases in heavy precipitation, which can cause agricultural soil erosion, water runoff contamination and flooding (Chen, Levy, and de Sherblmin, 2007; Schulte, 2007).

An assessment of climate impacts on water resources in Russia indicates an increase in average water availability, but also a significantly increased frequency of high runoff events in much of central Russia, and more frequent low runoff events in the already dry crop-growing regions in the South. These results suggest that the increasing frequency of extreme climate events will pose an increasing threat to the security of Russia's food system and water resources (Alcamoa, Droninb, Endejana, Golubev, and Kirilenko, 2006). As mentioned above, falling water tables are already adversely affecting harvests in some countries, including China, which rivals the United States as the world's largest grain producer.

POVERTY

It should not be a surprise that in many parts of the world the impoverished are most affected by inadequate water management. For example, in some of India's slums the poor must wait for water to arrive in trucks, and this water is more costly than piped water. In the slums of Jakarta, Indonesia, the poor pay 5 to 10 times more for water than the wealthy (Schulte, 2007).

When discussing water management, it is also necessary to consider water mismanagement and its effect on livelihoods, especially in less developed countries and areas where there are few opportunities that are not agriculturally based. Subsistence livelihoods provide income, food, shelter, clothing, and consumables, as well as reserve and emergency resources. Poor water management can exacerbate poverty, vulnerabilities, and other inequities (Bailkie, Cannon, Davis and Wisner, 2005).

The concluding chapter of the *UN World Water Development Report* states that:

> those affected most by the water crisis are the world's poor. It is they who suffer most immediately from unsafe water, lack of sanitation, food insecurity and from the effects of pollution and a degraded environment. Without representation or any voice in social, economic and political affairs, they are often powerless to improve their situation. This position of powerlessness only reinforces the vicious cycle of poverty, poor health, insecure livelihood and vulnerability to risks of every kind (UNESCO, 2003, p. 504).

Such improvements will promote resiliency and mitigate and perhaps prevent other poverty-related deficiencies and disasters by tackling their cause (Bailkie, Cannon, Davis and Wisner, 2005). Additionally, this empowerment would help restore a sense of pride, decrease humiliation, and fuel ambition. Humiliation and stifled aspirations are two of the greatest terrorist recruiting tools. Removing these tools will benefit almost everyone except terrorists and their foundations (Friedman, 2003). Furthermore, humiliation and defeat can be powerful political tools for promoting anger. Greater economic opportunities, reduced inequities, and empowerment can avenge past defeats and remove anger as a political tool (Tolchin and Tolchin, 2002). The next section will discuss terrorism in more depth.

TERRORISM

Critical water supplies and their infrastructure are appealing targets for terrorists. This is not a new phenomenon. There is a long history of intentional attacks on water resources as a target and a tool of war and terrorism. Recorded attacks on water systems date back more than 4,500 years. Urlama, King of Lagash from 2450 to 2400 BC, diverted water to deprive the neighbouring city-state of Umma of water (Gleick, 2006). Other examples include the intentional jamming of the Tigris River in an effort to prevent the retreat of rebels seeking independence from Babylon around 1700 BC (Hatami and Gleick, 1994). During the Eighty Years' War, the Dutch flooded the land in order to end the Spanish siege of the town of Alkmaar in 1573, and they used the same tactic in 1574 to protect the city of Leiden in South Holland. This tactic was used frequently and became known as the Dutch Water Line.

More recently, a series of events in India, Pakistan, the Persian Gulf, and the Middle East have reaffirmed the attractiveness of water and water systems as terrorist targets (Gleick, 2006). In 2003, both of Baghdad's major water pipelines were attacked. A Saudi Arabian magazine reported that Al Qaeda does not rule out the poisoning of drinking water in American and other cities (Associated Press, 2003; Waterman, 2003).

Modern societies depend upon complex and interconnected infrastructure for reliable supplies of potable water and effective wastewater treatment. There is no substitute for water; too little or too much water can lead to death, damage, interruptions, or contamination in a community of any size. This fact is obvious to terrorists, as it is to most people, and terrorists have utilized their imagination when conceiving and executing terrorist attacks, as dramatically demonstrated by the September 11, 2001, attacks.

Many important water facilities, such as dams, reservoirs, pipelines, and wastewater treatment plants, are easily accessible to the public and therefore vulnerable. Some of these water facilities (e.g., dams) are tourist attractions that offer tours to the public, and many reservoirs are open to the public for recreational activities. Pipelines can be exposed for long distances, and as with other water facilities, are located in urban and rural areas.

As part of the U.S. response to the events of September 11, 2001, the Public Health Security and Bioterrorism Preparedness and Response Act of 2002 was passed by Congress and signed by President Bush. The Act, also known as the Bioterrorism Act of 2002, amends the Safe Water Drinking Act of 1974 and requires local vulnerability assessments and emergency response plans for all community water systems serving 3,300 or more people (U.S. Food and Drug Administration, n.d.). The 3,300-user benchmark is significant, as the U.S. water industry is highly fragmented. Of the more than 50,000 municipal water utilities in the country, 84% serve fewer than 3,300 customers (Gleick and Morrison, 2006). Anyone intending to harm the United States would thus have to disrupt either multiple small water facilities or a major facility to have a significant impact.

The Bioterrorism Act of 2002 does not mandate specific security measures to reduce vulnerabilities; however, other federal resources are available for guidance (some of which are addressed in this chapter). Additionally, almost every state has considered amendments to its U.S. Freedom of Information Act (FOIA) to exempt security information (e.g., vulnerability assessments) related to drinking water systems from public disclosure under a FOIA request. At least 36 states have enacted such legislation in the last few years, bringing to 46 the number of states that appear to afford such protections to water system security information (Atkins and Morandi, 2003). FOIA is a law ensuring public access to government records, unless they can be lawfully withheld from disclosure under one of the nine specific exemptions; Exemption 3 of the statute provides new protection for information pertaining to the nation's critical infrastructure (National Security Archive, 2008; U.S. Department of Justice, 2003).

In December 2003, Homeland Security Presidential Directive-7 (HSPD-7) designated the U.S. Environmental Protection Agency (not the U.S. Department of Homeland Security) as the federal lead for the water sector's critical infrastructure protection activities. However, all activities are carried out in consultation with the U.S. Department of Homeland Security and the Environmental Protection Agency's water sector partners (U.S. Department of Homeland Security, 2008). According to the Web site of the U.S. Department of Homeland Security (2008):

> The Water Sector is vulnerable to a variety of attacks through contamination with deadly agents, physical attacks-such as the release of toxic gaseous chemicals-and cyber attacks. If these attacks were realized, the result could be large numbers of illnesses or casualties and/or a denial of service that would also impact public health and economic vitality. Critical services such as firefighting or healthcare and other dependent and interdependent sectors, such as Energy, Transportation Systems, and Agriculture and Food, would be negatively impacted by a denial of service from the Water Sector.

U.S. water security was important before the September 11, 2001, terrorist attacks, and improving security of the U.S. drinking water and wastewater infrastructures has since become an even higher priority. Protection includes vulnerability assessments, security awareness programmes, threat-level based protocols, access control, intrusion detection, information protection, emergency response plans and security training and support (U.S. Environmental Protection Agency, 2004, 2006, 2007).

Motives for attack be can be economic as well as political. The most traditional form of water system terrorism involves physical infrastructure attacks on water supply dams and pipelines. A terrorist equipped with a relatively small conventional explosive may not be able to cause serious structural damage to a massive dam constructed from rock, earth, or concrete. However, even minor structural damage can cause a major interruption in hydroelectric power. Therefore, it is worthwhile to assess such risks and possible counter measures to reduce these risks. Many First World water systems incorporate redundancies and backups but still have particularly vulnerable points such as pumping plants, treatment systems, and single large pipelines. Other concerns include the hacking of automated computer systems that control major valves, pumps, and chemical processing.

Chemical and biological contamination attacks are also a concern. For example, as a result of contamination due to an improperly functioning water treatment plant and pollution discharges upstream, an outbreak of Cryptosporidium in Milwaukee in 1993 killed more than 100 people and affected the health of at least 400,000 more (Addiss et al., 1994). In addition, the outbreak cost millions in lost wages and productivity. This outbreak, albeit unrelated to terrorism, helps demonstrate the possible effects of an intentional attack (Addiss et al., 1994; Gleick, 2006).

It is true that most biological pathogens cannot survive in water and that most chemicals require very large volumes to contaminate water systems to any significant degree.

Furthermore, the primary focus of a water treatment system is to destroy biological pathogens and reduce chemical concentrations, and therefore such hazards are likely to be neutralized after being subjected to chlorination, filtration, ultraviolet radiation, ozonation, and other common treatment methods (Gleick, 2006). However, any attack would most likely instill fear and terror, as Gleick (2006) pointed out:

> Analysis and historical evidence suggests that massive casualties from attacking water systems are difficult to produce, although there may be some significant exceptions. At the same time, the risk of societal disruptions, disarray, and even overreaction on the part of governments and the public from any attack may be high (p. 2).

Proper and appropriate safeguards can significantly reduce the risks of an event occurring, as well as the consequences if it does occur. Just as imagination fueled the destruction of the twin World Center Towers on September 11, 2001, imagination could facilitate the prevention of terrorist attacks. Additionally, imagination can and must be used to improve water technology to not only improve the safe water supply but also to reduce costs and increase availability. Finally, the physical and procedural security safeguards addressed in this section of the chapter address symptoms only. We must understand there are more complicated, direct, and efficient measures to reduce further terrorism risks and vulnerabilities such as those discussed in the section on poverty. Empowerment, economic opportunities, and the reduction of inequities will address the root causes of terrorism.

LEARNING FROM PAST DISASTERS

To address water conflict issues effectively, it is necessary first to examine a wealth of general and specific information. Simply stated if, we do not learn from past disasters we will have to repeat those lessons at great cost in multiple ways.

Our water conflict problem has many challenges, especially considering it is generally a slow-onset disaster with no quick fixes and that time is running out. There are volumes of credible scientific information about the world's looming water issues. Before we can act, we must learn from history and from experience. In the United States and most other areas, the sad fact is that many times we fail to learn from past disasters.

A U.S. study analysed input from a variety of sources (e.g., interviews, documents, and focus group reports) mostly from the perspective of first responders such as expert emergency incident managers who were mostly chief-level officers from major U.S. municipalities. All participants had significant senior level management experience dealing with large-scale incidents such as Hurricane Katrina; the 2003 Columbia space shuttle crash; the 2001 anthrax and ricin attacks in Washington, DC; the September 11 attacks on the World Trade Center and the Pentagon; the 1995 bombing of the Murrah building in Oklahoma City; and the 1994 Northridge earthquake (Donahue and Tuohy, 2006). Although these incidents are not directly related to water problems, they highlight lessoned learned from the mismanagement of other emergency situations.

Although the perspectives of these incident managers may differ from those of some high level policymakers (who in many cases are in the best position to effectively promote water supply and demand solutions), these identified lessons, in general, can be applied to water conflict management. Additionally, the study's context was in terms of fast-onset disasters (e.g., earthquakes, bombings, hazardous material incidents, for example) rather than slow-onset disasters such as drought and famine. Most water conflicts are a result of slow-onset elements and disasters. However, in general terms, some of the major areas identified in this report offer insights into the challenges arising from water supply and demand. In the broadest terms, and applicable to this chapter, the report identified the following: problems of uncoordinated leadership, weak planning, and resource constraints; and the need for motivation for change and learning and teaching (Donahue and Tuohy, 2006). Some of these points will be incorporated into our practical recommendations for water management solutions.

To effect change, it is necessary to go beyond simply increasing individual awareness and promoting behavioural change on multiple levels. As Donahue and Tuohy (2006) pointed out in their conclusion, "Enduring change needs to address the structure, system, and culture of an organization so that patterns of behaviour can be adjusted" (p. 21). The report also concluded that "The fact that challenges to learning lessons persist, despite regular experience with them, is a serious concern" (pp. 20–21), and this observation is certainly applicable to water supply demand issues. One of our challenges is not to fail to learn from or see the negative consequences associated with this slow-onset disaster before it is too late. Averting this slow-onset disaster will require changes that can take years to plan for and implement. For example, funding allocation, environmental impact studies, and large infrastructure construction may require years if not decades. Furthermore, in order to convince the public and policy makers regarding what actions are needed today and beyond, we must communicate the consequences of prolonging, neglecting, or insufficiently responding to the water supply and demand challenges at the micro, meso, and macro levels. In short, we must communicate the possible catastrophic effects of not learning from today's and future disasters: specifically, that today's water crisis vulnerabilities, if not mitigated, can lead to irreparable water conflicts.

In examining U.S. disaster history, the most fundamental lesson is the danger of "hubris, denial, and complacency" (Butler, 2007), and this seems to be the case with worldwide water supply and demand issues. It is imperative that we educate people in the United States and other developed countries that wealthy countries must look beyond their abundance, realize what is happening elsewhere, and unite behind a single effort to develop effective and efficient water management and promote changes in water use habits.

There are indications that we are learning from our experiences, as demonstrated in the following quote: "Water managers everywhere, particularly in the American Southwest, have come to understand that their communities' futures depend on cooperation with their neighbors more than ever before" (Mulroy and Katzer, 2008). In general, absent unifying U.S. national water policy, denial and complacency has been minimized in the protection of critical U.S. water infrastructure at the federal, state and local level. On December 7, 2007, at the Colorado River Water Users Association's annual meeting in Las Vegas, Secretary of the Interior Dirk Kempthorne signed an historic and wide-reaching agreement that addressed the management of the Colorado River (U.S. Department of the Interior, 2008b). This agreement is an excellent example of complicated water-related issues involving multiple parties with competing demands collaborating and agreeing on one best solution. This process parallels what we must do on a global level. "This is the most important agreement among the seven basin states since the original Colorado River Compact of 1922," said Kempthorne, noting that his decision memorializes "a remarkable consensus" not only to solve current problems but also to prepare ahead of time for future droughts or surpluses without resorting to disruptive litigation (p. 1). This agreement implements new operational guidelines to meet the current eight-year drought in the basin and, potentially, low-water conditions caused by continued drought or other causes in the future. The rules, which took effect immediately, will be in place through 2026 and supersede the original 1922 agreement.

This agreement was made possible through collaboration, coordination, and negotiation among parties who were willing to concede some demands in order for all seven states to agree. Basically, the U.S. Department of the Interior has warned that if the seven states did not agree on an updated compact, the Department would determine the compact. This agreement was hammered out by the states involved with the encouragement and support of the Department. Over the four-year negotiation period, the states did the real heavy lifting. The main motivation for this agreement was twofold: the need to update the agreement, and the wish to avoid a complex and lengthy legal battle. As Pat Mulroy, the General Manager of The Southern Nevada Water Authority stated, "We had to succeed.... We could spend the next 20 years in the Supreme Court. In the meantime, we'd all be sucking air" (as quoted in White, 2007).

The 2007 Colorado River agreement is an outstanding example of a complicated, far-reaching, multifaceted water issue solution encapsulated into one workable framework. Unfortunately, there is no corresponding U.S. national water policy. *The 9/11 Commission Report* found that "Terrorism was not the overriding national security concern for the U.S. government under either the Clinton or the pre-9/11 Bush administration" (National Commission on Terrorist Attacks Upon the United States, 2004, p. 10). Although federal government policies affect water management issues at the local, state, and regional levels, currently it is beyond the U.S. government's role to originate or manage a unified national policy or plan for U.S. water management or even a national emergency supply.

Although Bill Richardson, governor of New Mexico (an arid Southwest U.S. state), called for "a national water policy" while campaigning for the 2008 Democratic presidential nomination (Brean, 2008c), the United States has not come close to instituting a comprehensive national water policy. Some in the United States would argue that federal action should not diminish state rights, which are protected under the U.S. Constitution. As the National Drought Policy Commission upholds the principle of state rights, it is not synonymous with a national water policy or coordinated emergency response.

The Commission is under the U.S. Department of Agriculture, and its members include the Secretary of the U.S. Department of Agriculture and senior executives from the U.S. Department of the Interior, U.S. Department of Commerce, FEMA (Director, Human Services Division), The U.S. Army (Civil Works), and the U.S. Small Business Administration, as well as the Intertribal Agriculture Council; state, city, and local water authorities; farm credit banking interests, and farmer representatives (National Drought Policy Commission, 2000). The National Drought Policy Commission (2000) is:

> an advisory commission to provide advice and recommendations on the creation of an integrated, coordinated Federal policy designed to prepare for and respond to serious drought emergencies [and to] conduct a thorough study and submit a report on national drought policy (p. i).

The foreword of the Commission's report states that:

> none of our recommendations should be construed as diminishing the rights of states to control water through state law, as specifically directed by the National Drought Policy Act, nor as interfering in any way with state, local, and tribal sovereignty (p. i).

The Commision was created under the National Drought Policy Act to advise Congress on how to:

- Integrate federal drought laws and programs with ongoing state, local, and tribal programs into a comprehensive national policy to mitigate the impacts of and respond to drought.
- Improve public awareness of the need for drought mitigation.
- Achieve a coordinated approach to drought mitigation and response by governments and nongovernmental entities, including academic, private, and nonprofit interests" (National Drought Policy Commission, 2000, p. v).

Additionally, this report identified the three federal entities with the greatest federal responsibilities when drought occurs: the U.S. Department of Agriculture, the Bureau of Reclamation, and the U.S. Army Corps of Engineers. Please consult Figure 2.

The Environmental Protection Agency focuses primarily on the five goals of Clean Air and Global Climate Change, Clean and Safe Water, Land Preservation and Restoration, Healthy Communities and Ecosystems, and Compliance and Environmental Stewardship, as well as supporting security initiatives (U.S. Environmental Protection Agency, 2007, 2008).

The Federal Emergency Management Agency (FEMA) assists in preventing and responding to major water-related disasters such as hurricanes, floods, and tsunamis, and (to a much lesser extent) droughts.

Other federal protection agencies include the Food and Drug Administration (U.S. Department of Health and Human Services) as it relates to the Bioterrorism Act of 2002, Department of the Interior, Sandia National Laboratories Security Risk Assessment Methodology for Water Utilities (RAM-W), National Weather Service (e.g., weather tracking and warnings), the National Drought Mitigation Center, and the National Drought Policy Commission under the U.S. Department of Agriculture.

Figure 2. U.S. Agencies Addressing Water Issues.

The state rights argument would not preclude having a U.S. Strategic Water Reserve or a plan for a national emergency water supply. Perhaps some classified plan exists, but that is highly unlikely because of the complex nature and the sheer number of entities involved. The United States did learn its lesson from the 1973–1974 oil embargo. As a result, the government instituted the Strategic Petroleum Reserve, which is the largest stockpile of government-owned emergency crude oil in the world, but there is no water equivalent. The Strategic Petroleum Reserve provides a powerful response option should a disruption in commercial oil supplies threaten the U.S. economy. The reserve is currently authorized to a capacity of one billion barrels (U.S. Department of Energy, 2008b). As of August 2008, the petroleum reserve consisted of more than 707.2 million barrels (U.S. Department of Energy, 2008a) which it is estimated to provide approximately 58 days of import protection (U.S. Department of Energy, 2008c).

Will there have to be a "triggering event" resulting in the establishment of a national U.S. water policy, a response plan, and a reserve capability? Will other countries or regions have to experience other triggering events to take action? Perhaps, as illustrated below with regard to Southern Nevada Water Authority and other Colorado River users, solutions can be pursued in hopes of avoiding a catastrophic "lessons learned" event. As in this example, usually there are no simple solutions.

No Simple Solutions

The era of simple solutions is over; the challenges facing the West in the coming decades are daunting. To meet this challenge, attitudes have to change. The future of all our communities depend on it (Mulroy and Katzer, 2008, p. 4).

The above quote, although made in the context of the U.S. West, applies to almost anywhere in the world that has water issues. Just as any area experiencing water issues has more than one problem, there is no single supply-and-demand silver bullet or panacea for water issues.

We cannot simply build desalination plants, conserve water, implement financial incentives, or turn public utilities over to the private sector to conquer our water-related issues. In most situations it is necessary to combine and integrate various options as part of an integrated water management program.

In spite of their other assets, many parts of the western United States either already do not have enough water or will not have enough water to support the current and growing needs of agriculture, industry, and residential consumers. The report of the Western Governors' Association (2006) anticipates some of the tough decisions that will have to be made in this region and elsewhere:

> New uses to accommodate growth must largely rely on water obtained from changes to existing uses of surface and ground water, with limited opportunities to develop new supplies. In many instances, this will result in the reallocation of water to "higher valued uses" with accompanying third party impacts that must be considered, such as adverse consequences for rural communities and the environment (p. 3).

As the majority of water issues have their greatest impact at the local level, each locality has a unique solution that shares common elements with other comprehensive water management programs. Water management programs must consider the local historical, economic, and political framework and implement their solutions accordingly. As mentioned previously, the highly fragmented U.S. water industry comprises more than 50,000 municipal water utilities, 85% of which are publicly owned. In other countries, such as the U.K. and France, private ownership dominates. Therefore solutions that are appropriate for a municipal water utility in the United States may not apply to privately owned utilities in France or the U.K.

Beyond the local level, there are multifaceted and interrelated regional and global interactions and consequences. Successful water management programs must be specifically tailored to individual local venues, while concurrently addressing water issues related to the larger framework. Supply and demand, water rates, public opinion, governmental regulation and oversight, and other local, regional, and global market forces will drive future water industry trends (Gleick and Morrison, 2006). The following paragraphs present the example of a community that is proactively addressing the formidable water challenges it faces.

The U.S. Southwest desert city of Las Vegas, Nevada, has a metropolitan area population of more than 2 million residents (McCarthy, 2007). It has been one of the fastest growing communities in the United States for the last two decades (Miller, 2007); between 2000 and 2006, its population increased more than 29% (U.S. Census Bureau, 2007). The average annual rainfall for the area is 11.4 centimetres (National Weather Service, 2000) and therefore does not constitute a significant supply factor. A further source of water stress is that the Las Vegas area receives nearly 90% of its water supply from one source, the Colorado River (SNWA, 2008a).

The local water authority has implemented many successful water conservation incentive programs. As a result of these programs, Between 2002 and 2007 a reduction of consumptive water use by over 56 billion litres annually was realized as a result of these programs (SNWA, 2008b). Conservation programmes include mandatory schedules for lawn watering; incentives for residential and commercial property owners to replace lawn grass with much more water-efficient landscaping, ordinances banning front lawns in some new neighbourhoods; and tiered water pricing, whereby residents are billed at increasingly higher rates when their consumption exceeds specified levels (Sweet, 2008c and SNWA, 2008d). Even more impressive, the Las Vegas area experienced a 20% reduction in water use from 2002 to 2006, even though its population increased by more than 300,000 in the same time period and tourist visitation grew to approximately 40 million annually (White, 2007).

Southern Nevada Water Authority's long-term water resource management plans include striking an agreement with Arizona, California, or Mexico for participation in a water desalination plant (Brean, 2008c; Sweet, 2008a). The Southern Nevada region is highly motivated to address its water supply and demand issues because the area could outgrow its supply of Colorado River water in 5 to 8 years in spite of its conservation efforts (Brean, 2008c; White, 2007). Also of concern is a report by the Scripps Institution of Oceanography at the University of California-San Diego, which listed multiple Lake Mead scenarios. Among the most dire predictions were that Lake Mead stood a 10% chance of running dry by 2014 and a 50% chance of being dry by 2021. These figures are based on the assumption that by 2050 the Colorado River will experience a 10% to 30% drop in the amount of runoff it receives from snowmelts from the Rocky Mountains (Brean, 2008c). Similar drops have actually taken place in the recent past, but not in 2008, as discussed below.

Las Vegas and other parts of the U.S. Southwest have been in a drought situation since 1999. Lake Mead (largest man-made reservoir in North America where approximately 97% of the water in it comes from the Colorado River; Brean, 2008b and SNWA, 2008c) was expected to drop 1.8 metres in 2008 (Mulroy and Katzer, 2008), even though the Rocky Mountain snowmelt and runoff was expected to be 122% of normal (Brean, 2008a). Because of rising global temperatures, many expect that the Rocky Mountain snowmelt will evaporate in ever greater amounts, resulting in less water flowing into the Colorado River and Lake Mead (Archibold and Johnson, 2007).

Options other than conservation are being pursued in the Western states. Water projects that are planned or underway reflect the largest expansion in the region's quest for water in decades. For example, a proposed reservoir just north of the California–Mexico border would prevent excess water from passing to Mexico and a proposed 402-km pipeline costing between £1 billion and £1.75 billion would direct water from northern Nevada to Las Vegas (Archibold and Johnson, 2007; Brean, 2008d).

Although the Western region of the United States faces serious water problems, American money and know-how can at least temper some of the impacts, but many parts of the world do not have these options (Schulte, 2007). Even in America, time may be running out. For example, Tim Barnett, professor and author of the controversial study published in February 2008 by the Scripps Institution of Oceanography, stated that if global climate models are anywhere close to correct, "we've got a real problem coming." According to Barnett, the time line is so short that preventing global climate change before the predicted water shortages become reality is impossible and it is therefore necessary to plan for how to deal with the inevitable deficits when they arrive (quoted in Sweet, 2008b).

Other challenging issues, usually more prevalent in the developing world, include political corruption, incompetence, and industrial contaminants flooding waterways (Schulte, 2007). Especially in poorer countries, meeting water challenges is not as simple as turning over public water utilities to the private sector to increase efficiency. In some drought-stricken African countries, even the threat of privatization has sparked uprisings by those who fear that privatization will lead to more indebtedness and poverty. Social unrest and political violence can also arise from resentments over the profits made by private companies while local citizens remain destitute. Viable private utilities can encounter strong opposition and negative consequences even in places where inefficient governments are incapable of providing adequate water supply (Tolchin and Tolchin, 2002). The economic and political ramifications of privatization are complex and regionally specific (Gleick and Morrison, 2006).

However, the private sector plays an important role, especially in developed countries such as the U.K and France, whether independently or part of a private–public partnership. The private sector is also actively engaged in advancing water-related technologies. For example, The United States Strategic Water Initiative (USSWI, 2008) was established to enhance U.S. competitiveness in water purification science and technology. Its purpose is to advance the science of water purification and accelerate the implementation of innovative U.S. technologies that deliver, increase, and protect fresh water supplies. USSWI augments the work of associations, agencies, and companies that serve the water sector by increasing the number of technological solutions they employ in their activities. USSWI collaborates with water associations, suppliers, users, practitioners, and government officials to promote public and private investment in water purification research and accelerate the implementation, commercialization, and adoption of technologies that emerge from such research.

Experts tend to agree that usually the main problem is the lack of water management rather than the lack of water. In some cases, such as in the U.S. West, the reverse is true. Whereas the Western states have mobilized to address water problems arising from population increases and drought, other parts of the world facing similar or less dire challenges do not have the motivation or resources to respond in the same manner. Those reading this chapter, as well as others, are obligated to our current and future generations, to our own and other societies, and to life on Earth to raise awareness and facilitate action. As mentioned previously, many organizations and professionals are taking steps toward these goals. However, we must reach a much wider audience. Not only must average citizens be informed, but they must also be motivated to demand reform and take action. They must become agents of change through such activities as altering consumption patterns and influencing policymakers and politicians to support comprehensive water supplies, both national and international. Our actions must also include improving water management; funding management and infrastructure programs; and improving, incorporating, and advancing water technologies and processes such as desalination, brackish and wastewater treatment, and water conservation measures. We must also support new, imaginative innovations. For example, we may be able to employ the same methods used to find oil to tap significant but previously unknown water supplies (Gleick and Morrison, 2006).

Practically speaking, in most areas of the world, water and politics cannot be separated.

> The way water and politics interact is critical for decisions on and implementation of water reforms. Politics, defined here as the process through which relations of power are constituted, negotiated and reproduced, is indeed in the background of all public decisions and action. Although obvious to water practitioners, this political component has not received sufficient attention so far. On the contrary, the international discourse often exerts a strong depoliticizing effect by focusing on neutral concepts, which avoid controversies being developed and properly addressed (World Water Council, 2004, Preface section).

The World Water Council (2004) has initiated, in partnership with the International Union for Conservation of Nature (IUCN), a Water and Politics programme that aims to raise awareness of the importance of political issues in water reforms and to identify how politics can be a tool for the water community.

Practical solutions, perhaps best administered under one globally orchestrated comprehensive programme, include improving water management, allocating resources and infrastructure initiatives, and developing local water resources through means such as clean-up of local water sources, regional water transfers, waste water recycling, and smart land-use policies. Solutions at all levels need coordinated leadership and strong planning, while incorporating individual accountability (e.g., by limiting corruption and ineffective management), promoting the importance of change and outcomes, and illustrating the consequences of not changing. In some parts the world, practical solutions to the current water crisis will require short-term fixes to alleviate immediate and projected shortages until the long-term water management system is operational. Looking to the future, practical solutions include research and technological advancements in desalination, brackish and wastewater treatment, and emerging and future technologies to alternately reduced costs and increase use worldwide. Finally, all practical solutions must be promoted through innovation, transparency, collaboration, and partnerships that consider beyond immediate needs.

People in the developed world have an even greater responsibility. They will have to change their attitudes, beliefs, behaviour, sense of entitlement, and—most importantly—consumer patterns with regard to water expectations and usage. They must do this not only to set an example for the developing countries with respect to water expectations and usage, but also to lay the foundation of expectations and usage for the world's future generations.

CONCLUSION AND RECOMMENDATIONS

The subject of water conflict is vast and multifaceted. However, we must act to promote water resiliency strategies and solutions and reduce water conflict vulnerabilities. The solution must be part of one globally orchestrated, comprehensive, and integrated water management programme that addresses such issues as supply and demand, sanitation, quality of life, climate change, poverty, security, terrorism, and associated issues in an era where simple solutions are no longer available. Other important issues include politics, economics, energy, food production, policy making, deteriorating infrastructures, raising awareness to facilitate action, and learning from past disasters. This chapter has discussed many related challenges. Perhaps the following U.N. "water security" definition will help us gauge when we know we have met these challenges:

> The human right to water entitles everyone to sufficient, affordable, physically accessible, safe and acceptable water for personal and domestic uses. While uses vary between cultures, an adequate amount of safe water is necessary to prevent death from dehydration, to reduce the risk of water-related disease and to provide for consumption, cooking, personal and domestic hygienic requirements (Wouters, 2005, p.169).

There is no escaping that tough supply and demand choices will have to be made. Two thirds of the world population will experience chronic shortage of safe drinking water by 2030 (Lindell, Perry and Prater, 2007). By 2050, the number of humans on Earth is expected to rise from 6.7 billion to more than 9 billion. Most of that growth will occur in countries least able to sustain it, fueling instability and extremism in those countries and beyond (Warrick, 2008). In many parts of the world, water is already consumed faster than can be naturally replenished (Brown, 2008). Experts believe that climate change will further decrease the fresh drinking water supply and food production (Alcamoa et al., 2006; Brown, 2008).

In 2002, 2.6 billion people lacked adequate sanitation (WHO/UNICEF, 2005). Improvements in sanitation will result in improved local health conditions, longer lives, better health, and more productivity (Schulte, 2007).

We know that those most affected by the water crisis are the world's poor. It is they who suffer most immediately from unsafe water, lack of sanitation, spread of infectious diseases, food insecurity, forced migration, and the effects of pollution and a degraded environment. Moreover, poverty is the common denominator of many vulnerabilities. Without representation or any voice, the poor are often powerless to improve their situation. This position of powerlessness only reinforces the vicious cycle of poverty, poor health, insecure livelihood, and vulnerability to risks (UNESCO, 2003, p. 504).

In the poorest parts of the world, adequate water management will enhance prosperity and diminish poverty. Increased incomes will allow access to previously unobtainable water as well as other material goods and services which go beyond water issues, thus promoting resiliency and mitigating or perhaps preventing other poverty-related deficiencies and disasters (Bailkie, Cannon, Davis and Wisner, 2005). Additionally, this empowerment will help reduce feelings of humiliation and stifled aspirations, two of the greatest terrorist recruiting tools (Friedman, 2003).

The competition for water will affect global prosperity and security. Global water issues are challenging and changing our world. It is up to us to determine what that change will be; however, water supplies are finite and time to act is limited. The future will be determined by local, regional, and global acts of commission or omission.

The Romans are generally credited with perfecting the early aqueducts that delivered water to their cities (Wilson, 2007). We can be remembered as the generation that globally delivered water and sanitation to the have nots, or we can be the generation that drowned in water conflicts.

REFERENCES

Addiss, D. G., Blair, K. A., Davis, J. P., Fox, K. R., Gradus, M. S., and Hoxie, W. R. (1994). A massive outbreak in Milwaukee of Cryptosporidium infection transmitted through the public water supply. *New England Journal of Medicine*, 331, 161–167.

Alcamoa, J., Droninb, N., Endejana, M., Golubev, G., and Kirilenko, A. (2006). A new assessment of climate change impacts on food production shortfalls and water availability in Russia. *Global Environmental Change*, 17, 429–444.

Archibold, R. C., and Johnson, K. (2007). An arid west no longer waits for rain. *New York Times.* Retrieved August 10, 2008, from http://www.nytimes.com/2007/04/04/us/04drought.html?ex=1176436800anden=f12713286b06e375andei=5070andemc=eta1

Associated Press. (2003, May 29). Water targeted, magazine reports. *Associated Press.*

Associated Press. (2007, January 12). California world's sixth-largest economy? Not anymore. *International Herald Tribune.* Retrieved August 10, 2008, from http://www.iht.com/articles/ap/2007/01/12/business/ NA-GEN-US-California-No.-8-Economy.php

Associated Press. (2008, January 23). Southern drought could force nuclear plants to shut down. *AccessNorthGa.com.* Retrieved August 10, 2008, from http://www.accessnorthga.com/detail-pf.php?n=206119

Atkins, C., and Morandi, L. (2003). *Protecting water system security information.* Retrieved August 10, 2008, from http://www.oe.netl.doe.gov/documents/ Water_Security.pdf

Bailkie, P., Cannon, T., Davis, I., and Wisner, B. (2005). *At risk: Natural hazards, people's vulnerability and disasters* (2nd ed.). New York: Routledge.

Ball, S. (2008, August 11). Spain suffering worst drought in over a decade. *BBC Weather.* Retrieved August 10, 2008, from http://www.bbc.co.uk/weather/world/news/ 20022008news.shtml

Bluestein, G. (2008, May 20). Spring rains ease but don't end drought in the Southeast. *Associated Press.*

Brean, H. (2008a, April 15). Colorado River flow: Snowpack delivers on promise. *Las Vegas Review Journal.* Retrieved August 10, 2008, http://www.lvrj.com /news/ 17729769.html

Brean, H. (2008b, February 13). Study gives 50-50 odds Lake Mead will dry up by 2021. *Las Vegas Review Journal.* Retrieved August 10, 2008, from http://www.lvrj.com/news/ 15581197.html

Brean, H. (2008c, January 29). Utility officials water down pipeline fears. *Las Vegas Review Journal.* Retrieved August 10, 2008, from http://www.lvrj.com/news/ 14688207.html

Brean, H. (2008d, April 14). Water story makes big splash: Doomsday predictions for Lake Mead, Las Vegas get world's attention. *Las Vegas Review Journal.* Retrieved August 10, 2008, from http://www.lvrj.com/news/17654274.html

Brecke, P., Lee, H. F., He, Y., Zhang, D. D., and Zhang, J. (2007). The political cost of failure in the Katrina and Rita disasters. In *Proceedings of the National Academy of Sciences of the United States of America* (Vol. 104). Retrieved August 10, 2008, from http://www.pnas.org/content/104/49/19214.full

Brown, L. R. (2008). *Plan B 3.0: Mobilizing to save civilization.* New York: W.W. Norton.

Butler, D. (2007). Focusing events in the early twentieth century: A hurricane, two earthquakes, and a pandemic. In C. B. Rubin (Ed.), *Emergency management: The American experience 1900-2005* (pp. 11–48). Fairfax, VA: Public Entity Risk Institute.

Caravelli, J. (2007). *Nuclear insecurity: Understanding the threat from rogue nations and terrorists.* Westport, CT: Praeger Security International.

Central Intelligence Agency (CIA). (2008). Pakistan. In *The World Factbook.* Retrieved August 10, 2008, from https://www.cia.gov/library/publications/the-world-factbook/geos/pk.html

Chen, R. S., Levy, M. A., and de Sherblmin, A. (2007, July). What does climate change mean for the hazards community? *Natural Hazards Observer, 31*(6), 10–12.

Cooley, H., Gleick, P. H., and Wolff, G. (2006). With a grain of salt: An update on seawater desalination. In P. H. Gleick (Ed.), *The world's water 2006-2007: The biennial report on freshwater resources* (pp. 1–28). Oakland, CA: Island Press.

Donahue, A. K., and Tuohy, R. V. (2006). Lessons we don't learn: A study of the lessons of disasters, why we repeat them, and how we can learn them. *Homeland Security Affairs, 2,* 1–28.

Friedman, T. L. (2003, September 25). Connect the dots. *New York Times.* Retrieved August 10, 2008, from http://query.nytimes.com/gst/fullpage html?res= 9F02E7DE143DF936A1575AC0A9659C8B63

Gleick, P. H. (2006). Water and terrorism. In P. H. Gleick (Ed.), *The world's water 2006-2007: The biennial report on freshwater resources* (1–28). Oakland, California: Island Press.

Gleick, P. H., and Morrison, J. (2006). Water risks that face business and industry. In P. H. Gleick (Ed.), *The world's water 2006-2007: The biennial report on freshwater resources* (pp. 145–167). Oakland, CA: Island Press.

Global Policy Forum. (n.d.). Water in Conflict. Retrieved August 15, 2008, from http://www.globalpolicy.org/security/natres/waterindex.htm.

Hatami, H., and Gleick, P. (1994). Chronology of conflict of water in the legends, myths and history of the ancient Middle East: Water, war, and peace in the Middle East. *Environment, 36,* 6–15.

Hobbs, J, (2004, May 15). Do 'water wars' still loom in Africa? *Inter Press Service News Agency.* Retrieved August 10, 2008, from http://www.ipsnews.org/africa/interna.asp?idnews=23759

Jägerskog, A. (2008). Water and Conflict in the Middle East, *The Middle East Institute Viewpoints, No. 7 (June),* 1-5.

Kranhold, K. (2008, January 17). Water, water, everywhere *The Wall Street Journal.* Retrieved August 10, 2008, from http://webreprints.djreprints.com/1879490638701.pdf

Lane, J. (2006). Forward. In P. H. Gleick (Ed.), *The world's water 2006-2007: The biennial report on freshwater resources* (pp. xiii–xiv). Oakland, CA: Island Press.

Lavelle, M, (2007, June 1). Water woes. *U.S.News and World Report.* Retrieved August 10, 2008, from http://www.usnews.com/usnews/biztech/articles/070527/4water_print.htm

Lindell, M. K., Perry, R. W., and Prater, C. (2007). *Introduction to emergency management.* Hoboken, NJ: John Wiley and Sons.

Martin, A. (2008). Mideast Facing Choice Between Crops and Water. *New York Times.* Retrieved July 22, 2008, from http://www.nytimes.com/2008/07/21/business/worldbusiness/21arabfood.html.

McCarthy, A. (2007, December 5). Las Vegas area population reaches 2 million. *Las Vegas Now Eyewitness News.* Retrieved August 10, 2008, from http://www.klas-tv.com/Global/story.asp?s=7453765

Miller, T. (2007, November 9). Las Vegas looks ahead as growth boom hits a bump. *Online NewsHour.* Retrieved August 10, 2008, from http://www.pbs.org/newshour/ vote2008/july-dec07/vegas_development_11-09.html

Mulroy, P., and Katzer, T. (2008, July 6). The era of simple solutions is over. *Las Vegas Sun.* Retrieved August 10, 2008, from http://lvsun.com/news/2008/jul/06/era-simple-solutions-over National Commission on Terrorist Attacks Upon the United States. (2004). *The 9/11 Commission Report: Final report of the National Commission on Terrorist Attacks Upon the United States: Executive Summary.* Washington, DC.

National Drought Policy Commission. (2000). *Report of the National Drought Policy Commission: Preparing for drought in the 21st century.* Retrieved August 10, 2008, from http://govinfo.library.unt.edu/drought/finalreport/fullreport/reportdload.htm

National Security Archive. (2008). *The Freedom of Information Act (FOIA).* Retrieved August 10, 2008, from http://www.gwu.edu/~nsarchiv/nsa/foia.html

National Weather Service. (2000). *Monthly temperature and precipitation normals,Las Vegas, Nevada (1971-2000).* Retrieved August 10, 2008, from http://www.wrh.noaa.gov/vef/motemps.php

Ritter, K. (2007, December 14). 7 states, U.S. Interior Department sign historic Colorado River water pact. *Forecast Earth.* Retrieved August 10, 2008, from http://climate.weather.com/articles/colorado121407.html

Schulte, B. (2007, May 27). A world of thirst. *U.S.News and World Report.* Retrieved August 10, 2008, http://www.usnews.com/usnews/news/articles/070527/ 4hotspots_print.htm

Schwartz, N. (2007, December 29). Climate change expected to transform the land, lifestyles that made California famous. *North County Times.* Retrieved August 10, 2008, from http://www.nctimes.com/articles/2007/12/30/news/state/16_06_0212_29_07.txt

Southern Nevada Water Authority (SNWA). (2008a). *Colorado River.* Retrieved August 11, 2008, from http://www.snwa.com/html/wr_colrvr.html

Southern Nevada Water Authority (SNWA). (2008b). *Conservation achievements.* Retrieved August 11, 2008, from http://www.snwa.com/html/wr_conservation_achievements.html

Southern Nevada Water Authority(SNWA). (2008c). *Lake Mead.* Retrieved August 11, 2008, from http://www.snwa.com/html/wr_colrvr_mead.html

Southern Nevada Water Authority(SNWA). (2008d). *SNWA Resource Plan 2008.* Retrieved August 11, 2008, from http://www.snwa.com/html/wr_resource_plan.html

State of California, Office of the Governor. (2008). *Governor proclaims drought and orders immediate action to address situation* [Press release]. Retrieved August 11, 2008, from http://gov.ca.gov/press-release/9796

Sweet, P. (2008a, March 21). Desalination gets a serious look. *Las Vegas Sun.* Retrieved August 11, 2008, from http://lasvegassun.com/news/2008/mar/21/desalination-gets-serious-look

Sweet, P. (2008b, June 5). Scientist: Warming bodes ill for water. *Las Vegas Sun.* Retrieved August 11, 2008, from http://lasvegassun.com/news/2008/jun/05/scientist-warming-bodes-ill-water

Sweet, P. (2008c, April 8). Water: The more you use, the more you'll have to pay. *Las Vegas Sun.* Retrieved August 11, 2008, from http://lasvegassun.com/news/2008/apr/08/water-more-you-use-more-youll-have-pay

Tolchin, M., and Tolchin, S. (2002). *A world ignited: How apostles of ethnic, religious, and racial hatred torch the globe.* New York: Rowman and Littlefield.

UNESCO. (2003). *UN world water development report: Water for people, water for life: Part VI. Fitting the pieces together.* Retrieved August 11, 2008, from http://www.unesco.org/water/wwap/wwdr/wwdr1/pdf/chap23.pdf

UN-Water. (2003). *The 1st UN world water development report: Water for people, water for life.* Retrieved August 11, 2008, from http://www.unesco.org/water/wwap/wwdr/wwdr1

UN-Water. (2008). *UN-Water welcomes International Year of Sanitation 2008.* Retrieved August 11, 2008, from http://www.unwater.org/iys2.html

USGS. (2007). *Water trivia.* Retrieved August 11, 2008, from http://ct.water.usgs.gov/education/trivia.htm

USSWI. (2008). *U.S. Strategic Water Initiative.* Retrieved August 11, 2008, from http://www.watercampws.uiuc.edu/index.php?menu_item_id=244

U.S. Census Bureau. (2007). *50 fastest-growing metro areas concentrated in West and South.* Retrieved August 11, 2008, from http://www.census.gov/Press-Release/www/releases/archives/population/009865.html

U.S. Department of Energy. (2008a). *Strategic Petroleum Reserve inventory.* Retrieved August 14, 2008, from http://www.spr.doe.gov/dir/dir.html

U.S. Department of Energy. (2008b). *Strategic Petroleum Reserve - Profile.* Retrieved August 14, 2008, from http://www.fossil.energy.gov/programs/reserves/spr/index.html

U.S. Department of Energy. (2008c). *Strategic Petroleum Reserve - Quick facts and frequently asked questions.* Retrieved August 14, 2008, from http://www.fossil.energy.gov/programs/reserves/spr/spr-facts.html

U.S. Department of Homeland Security. (2008). *Water sector: Critical infrastructure and key resources.* Retrieved August 11, 2008, from http://www.dhs.gov/xprevprot/programs/gc_1188399291279.shtm

U.S. Department of the Interior. (2008a). *Colorado River programs and projects.* Retrieved August 11, 2008, from http://www.doi.gov/issues/colorado.html

U.S. Department of the Interior. (2008b). *Secretary Kempthorne signs historic decision for new Colorado River management strategies.* Retrieved August 11, 2008, from http://www.doi.gov/issues/colorado.html

U.S. Department of Justice. (2003). Homeland Security law contains new Exemption 3 statute. *FOIA Post.* Retrieved August 11, 2008, from http://www.usdoj.gov/oip/foiapost/2003foiapost4.htm

U.S. Environmental Protection Agency. (2004). *Water security: Vulnerability assessments.* Retrieved August 11, 2008, from http://cfpub.epa.gov/safewater/ watersecurity/home.cfm?program_id=11

U.S. Environmental Protection Agency. (2006). *Water security: 14 features of active and effective security.* Retrieved August 11, 2008, from http://cfpub.epa.gov/safewater/watersecurity/14features.cfm#features

U.S. Environmental Protection Agency. (2007). *Water security.* Retrieved August 11, 2008, from http://cfpub.epa.gov/safewater/watersecurity/index.cfm

U.S. Environmental Protection Agency. (2008). *2006 - 2011 EPA Strategic Plan.* Retrieved August 11, 2008, from http://www.epa.gov/ocfo/plan/plan.htm

U.S. Food and Drug Administration. (n.d.). *The Bioterrorism Act of 2002.* Retrieved August 11, 2008, from http://www.fda.gov/oc/bioterrorism/Bioact.html

Warrick, J. (2008, May 1). CIA chief sees unrest rising with population. *Washington Post.* Retrieved August 11, 2008, from http://www.washingtonpost.com/wp-dyn/content/article/2008/04/30/AR2008043003258.html

Waterman, S. (2003, May 28). Al-Qaida threat to U.S. water supply. *UPI.com.* Retrieved August 11, 2008, from http://www.upi.com/Top_News/2003/05/28/Al-Qaida_threat_to_US_water_supply/UPI-89541054166129/

Western Governors' Association. (2006). *Water needs and strategies for a sustainable future.* Retrieved August 11, 2008, from http://www.westgov.org/wga/publicat/ Water06.pdf

White, G. (2007). In Vegas, wasting water is a sin. *ajc.com.* Retrieved August 11, 2008, from http://www.ajc.com/news/content/metro/stories/2007/11/24/vegas_1125.html

WHO/UNICEF Joint Monitoring Programme for Water Supply and Sanitation. (2005). *Water for life: Making it happen.* Retrieved August 11, 2008, from http://www.who.int/water_sanitation_health/monitoring/jmp2005/en/index.html

Wilson, C. (2007, May 27). Pipelines and lifelines. *U.S.News and World Report.* Retrieved August 11, 2008, from http://www.usnews.com/usnews/news/articles/070527/ 4hotspots.aqueducts_print.htm

World Water Council. (2004). *Proceedings of the workshop on water and politics: Under standing the role of politics in water management.* Retrieved August 11, 2008, from http://www.worldwatercouncil.org/fileadmin/wwc/Library/Publications_and_reports/proceedings_Water_Politics/proceedings_waterpol_full_document.pdf

World Water Council. (2005a). *Water at a glance.* Retrieved August 11, 2008, from http://www.worldwatercouncil.org/index.php?id=5

World Water Council. (2005b). *Water crisis.* Retrieved August 11, 2008, from http://www.worldwatercouncil.org/index.php?id=25

Wouters, P. (2005). Water security: What role for international law? In F. Dodds and Pippard, T. (Eds.), *Human and Environmental Security: An Agenda for Change* (166-181). London: Earthscan.

In: Strategizing Resilience and Reducing Vulnerability
Editors: Peter R.J. Trim and Jack Caravelli
ISBN 978-1-60741-693-7
© 2009 Nova Science Publishers, Inc.

Chapter 5

A STRATEGIC VIEW OF SECURITY

Nick Edwards, Peter R.J. Trim and Jack Caravelli

ABSTRACT

A range of events, such as terrorist actions, the disruption of food chains and conflicts over who owns both the supply of water and access to water, have been of concern to policy makers. Furthermore, the after effects associated with natural disasters, has placed the word security firmly in the public domain. It is relevant to stand back and pose the question: What does security entail? Another question that comes to mind is, Who is responsible for security? Making the general public safe is a key part of a government's national security strategy, but managers within organizations are becoming aware that they too need to view the subject of security more fully and place it within the context of business continuity. Senior managers are becoming aware that they need to take greater responsibility for putting in place risk assessment systems that help to reduce the level of threat facing an organization.

INTRODUCTION

Identifying areas of vulnerability can, therefore, no longer be viewed as just the priority of government, it is becoming, and rapidly so, the priority of corporate security personnel. Indeed, those in the public and private sectors are concerned with a range of issues and factors including: energy security, personnel security and physical security. This means that adequate risk management systems need to be in place that take into account broader subject areas such as business continuity; disaster recovery; legislation, compliance and governance; and resilience. In order to ensure that the organization can reduce the level of vulnerability, staff need to ensure that they have the skills to deal with catastrophic risk and that they are prepared to participate in information sharing.

KEY POINTS FOR STRATEGIC THINKERS

As regards physical security, it is essential that managers get to grips with the relationship between physical security and the technical aspects of security. For example, for data to be held securely, it needs to be held in a safe place and it needs to be encrypted. The examples of data going astray and/or getting into the wrong hands underline the importance, not only of adequate physical security measures and who has responsibility for them, but the need for the procedures documented to be strictly adhered to. This raises the question: Are those involved with physical security fully aware of the threats posed by electronic commerce? This question is relevant to managers both in the public and the private sectors, and something that politicians are becoming increasingly concerned about.

The international standard for Business Continuity (ISO25999) is now being adopted more widely. As is the case with ISO27001 which is for Information Systems Security (Infosec), this standard embraces a common sense guidance and does provide a framework for users to ensure a holistic approach. The Cabinet Office/Civil Contingencies Secretariat is promoting the benefit of BS27001 compliance to local government authorities, utilities and the commercial enterprises that support them. It is essential also, that central government embrace BS27001 procedures as this will ensure that there is commonality and will result in a firmer business continuity architecture being developed. This should have the advantage of ensuring that the appropriate auditing and governance mechanisms are in place.

Disaster recovery requirements and practices are often considered together with matters relating to business continuity. However, we know from experience that disaster recovery and business continuity should be considered together but that disaster recovery requires different skills. The foot and mouth crisis of 2001 and the floods of 2007 made it clear to the UK government that the experience and capabilities of the military were needed to ameliorate and then help resolve the situation. For example, it is clear from the floods of 2007 and the ensuing review by Sir Michael Pitt that greater resilience needs to be built into the UKs Critical National Infrastructure. Sir Michael was responsible for producing a report that ran to 500 pages and cited 92 recommendations (www.cabinetoffice.gov.uk/thepittreview). What is clear is that UK resilience is heavily dependent on a multi-layered supply chain and that various management models, such as the just-in-time approach, need to be viewed rigorously with respect to fuel supply deliveries. A third/fourth tier supplier is actually vital to the Critical National Infrastructure and needs to be given attention. The education/training divide has been given attention in the sense that Cranfield University launched its Resilience Centre at Shrivenham in July 2004. Staff at Cranfield University are well placed to provide advice relating to resilience issues to commerce and industry, and government. Coincident with the establishment of the UK Resilience Centre at Cranfield University are two projects which have a high degree of relevance. The OASIS project seeks to establish a civil crisis management methodology to achieve inter-operability across Emergency Services in key EU countries and NATO. DEMOCRITUS seeks to integrate teams to be able to respond to emergencies and crises within and outside the EU.

On the information communications technologies front, it is noticeable that we are moving rapidly to converged Internet protocol networks. Whilst this can bring benefits for many organizations some may need to assess their vulnerability and establish what is effectively a single point of failure. For example, alternate routing for critical voice and/or data networks may be needed and this will result in new skills being developed

THE NEED FOR EFFECTIVE RISK MANAGEMENT

It can be suggested that the term risk management has been around for some years now and it is not always well understood. If risk management is to be successful, it is essential that managers and policy makers are fully aware of the fact that new threats are emerging and that the word vulnerability needs to be viewed as multi-dimensional. Managers may find it relatively simple to establish vulnerabilities but they may well find it difficult to establish the level of threat to their management and computer systems, if that is, they are not keeping a watchful eye on both industry trends and potential environmental hotspots. To produce a comprehensive threat assessment requires sound intelligence relating to the capabilities and intentions of those who are determined to disrupt or destroy an infrastructure. Making systems secure and robust is the key challenge confronting senior managers and policy makers, and because of this, management development programmes need to be introduced to stop managers becoming complacent. It can also be suggested that when entering into a partnership arrangement with another organization, the issue of trust and trustworthy behaviour is paramount. It is for this reason that those involved in negotiating a partnership arrangement and/or establishing a security culture, fully understand the importance of an organizational resilience value system (Lee and Trim, 2006, p.737-739) and understand that the term resilience is multi-faceted (Sheffi, 2005).

The UK Centre for the Protection of National Infrastructure (CPNI) provides excellent advice on its web sites with respect to helping managers to protect against electronic attacks. Unfortunately, many companies that could benefit from this advice are either unaware of CPNI and/or do not take full cognisance of the advice offered. It can be said that CPNI is limited largely to providing advice to Critical National Infrastructure first and second tier providers and its breadth of advice is somewhat curtailed – in part due to staffing and funding issues. Managers will have to seek advice as and where they can, for example, via the British Computer Society (www.bcs.org/security), the Information Assurance Advisory Council (www.iaac.org), ISAF (www.theisaf.org) and Get Safe Online (www.getsafeonline.org).

The existing legislation in the security field is complex and not always easy to follow or comply with. Sir Michael Bichard, led the inquiry into the lessons to be learned consequent upon the Soham murders. The report (www.bichardinquiry.org.uk) outlined the difficulties that police forces and other authorities have in interpreting the 1998 Data Protection Act. This underlines the need for those in senior managerial positions in local and central government, and directors with board level responsibility in industry, to fully comprehend the various aspects of data protection and other issues highlighted in the 2000 Regulation of Investigatory Powers Act.

COMPLIANCE AND GOVERNANCE

Compliance with the provisions of Sarbanes Oxley and Basel II may also be seen as onerous and difficult. Good governance at board level and a strong embedded culture of security policy implementation and compliance within organizations is what is needed if that is an organization is to be classified as resilient. Many companies pursue this route and there are many organizations in business to help them to do so. For example, many of the companies in the UKs FTSE 500 belong to the Information Security Forum (ISF) (www.securityforum.org). ISF members club together to share ideas on security policies, procedures and experiences, which ultimately is for the benefit of all the member organizations. Informal groups such as B2-ORM and E-COM-SEC share information on the implementation of Basel II compliant operational risk management and on e-commerce security.

It is unlikely that individual businesses will ever be able to cope with the results of catastrophic risk such as Hurricane Katrina which ravaged part of the south coast of the US in 2005. However, government departments do need to consider the consequences of such catastrophes and lessons can and should be learnt from significant but non catastrophic events such as the floods in the UK in 2007. The Pitt Review makes a number of helpful recommendations but as regards overall control, it has to be noted that responsibility remains largely unresolved. In the event of an equivalent catastrophe, the British government would certainly call on military assistance (as happened with the foot and mouth crisis of 2001), but it can be said that the military is under resourced. Disaster and emergency work is costly and often, the actual costs are far above the anticipated costs. Although the many Army, Air Force and Royal Navy units rely very heavily on TA (Territorial Army) volunteers, the TA equipment budgets are very severely constrained.

THE INTERNATIONAL ENVIRONMENT

Of all the problems facing the developed and developing world, continuity of energy supply is probably the most pressing. Although the importance of such aspects as energy, water and food supply lines have long been recognized as significant aspects of the Critical National Infrastructure, it can be said that the inter-relation of these aspects has been poorly understood and not properly addressed. It is now clear that ensuring energy supply to the UK is a high priority and some critics would suggest that the nuclear energy issue should have been discussed more openly and placed in context much earlier than it has. Countries without sustainable energy supplies, will need to look more firmly at alternative energy sources and also, will need to carry out risk assessment that incorporates scenario analysis, as countries such as Russia and Iran, seem to want to link energy supplies with political influence. Emerging economies such as China have seen this problem coming and whilst being assiduous in cultivating deals with other countries for energy supply (and raw materials) have taken action to ensure that its indigenous supplies of coal, oil and gas are well protected. It can also be noted that China is committed to nuclear power development and will remain so for the foreseeable future.

DEVELOPING A SECURITY CULTURE

It can be argued that information assurance underpins everything we do. We need to have confidence not only in the information we have or share but also in the way we share it. We need to know that the people with whom we share information will take great care of it and only share this information with others with our agreement. More worrying, are the human errors that result in computer discs being lost or stolen; lap top computers being stolen or offered for sale over the Internet; and computer memory sticks that are mislaid. To this one can add hard copies of material that are left on trains and in public places, and unscrupulous individuals who engage in industrial espionage activities. Encryption is a necessity as regards protecting sensitive data, but unfortunately, criminal syndicates have also understood this and have successfully recruited computer specialists to work for them, which has made it hard for law enforcement officers to break into their systems and to obtain incriminating evidence.

Security lapses will occur sceptics argue because of human error. The solution appears to be to develop, through education and training, a psyche among professional staff which forces them to automatically think in terms of devising and implementing a security culture in the organization that employs them. The ISO27001 standard has been widely adopted across the globe and UK government departments and their sub-contractors all need to adhere to the strictures and the spirit of this sensible and not ever onerous standard, if that is, a security culture within the organization is to be forthcoming.

We have seen examples where large organizations and government departments have been given incorrect information and/or there have been failures of communication between one department/section and another. This can lead to minor annoyance, frustration or activist behaviour. The Gloucestershire floods of 20th July, 2007, highlighted the fact that Severn Trent's Mythe Pumping Station was not on the appropriate Risk Register. It is possible that senior managers at Severn Trent knew of this potential vulnerability and the ramifications associated with a single point of failure. But for whatever reason appropriate action was not taken in time. The same can be said for the Electricity Board with respect to the Gloucester sub-station at Walham. Sir Michael Pitt stated in his report that it was intolerable that citizens should be put at such risk.

Even if we get the security technology right and all the required procedures are put in place, we will still be faced with the problem that people make mistakes through insufficient training or experience, carelessness or misinformation. There is also the real danger of the 'insider' threat. A disgruntled employee or ex-employee intent on reeking havoc represents a constant threat and it can be argued that people today have a different psyche as regards crime and criminal behaviour. This needs to be fully understood by security and law enforcement representatives, if that is, safety and security measures are to prove adequate.

In a world that has come to rely on information and information sharing we should recall that the founding fathers of computer security (Compusec) embraced the principles of confidentiality, integrity and availability. It could be that we need to add the epithet 'appropriate' ahead of these three qualities. Thus the amount of confidentiality needed will vary from situation to situation, depending for instance, on the transaction being undertaken. Government departments have Senior Information Risk Owners in place and they need to ensure that security procedures are always followed. Security must be seen as part of the business process, embedded at its heart and part of the business process. An overarching security culture needs to be established that is embedded in the belief system of the workforce.

OTHER CONSIDERATIONS AND THE WAY FORWARD

Lord Hurd of Westwell stated in 1998 when discussing European Defence issues "What is needed now is less pecking away at procedure and more concentration on substance". A newly invigorated and fully empowered body building on the strengths of CPNI could lead UK plc towards a much more safe and less vulnerable future.

Risk and vulnerability are clearly linked and it is with this in mind that one can suggest that the subject of economic intelligence needs to be thought through more carefully. Herzog (2008) has provided some useful insights into the subject and paid some attention to regional development and security. This is important in the sense that a failing state may become the base from which a terrorist group or criminal gang unleash disruptive activities, which are aimed at destabilizing the government(s) of a country/countries. Terrorist networks in particular pose very real threats to government, commerce and industry, and research into their structural forms, as undertaken by RAND (Lesser et al., 1999), are to be applauded.

However, a deeper understanding is necessary. For example, Czinkota et al., (2005, p.588) have stated that "Terrorism is a contingency, or it leads to the emergence of other contingencies. Its consequences occur particularly in the social, economic, political, legal, and institutional contexts of the external environment. It influences buyer psychology, consumption, and purchasing patterns". Dealing with actual and potential terrorist threats is likely to consume additional amounts of time of the intelligence, security and law enforcement agencies. Indeed, an edited work by Merkidze (2007) has provided insights into terrorist threat assessment and it is clear that a multi-dimensional approach needs to be taken to the subject. The advantage of such an approach is that it would allow the work of the various intelligence agencies worldwide to be brought into harmony. No doubt this is something that our political masters can reflect upon.

Canton (2008, p.487) states that "A paradigm shift must occur if intelligence analysis is to do better. Analysts, their managers, and the bureaucracies in which they work, must embrace the active management of uncertainty-what analysts do in response to what they don't know on key issues of policy interest. Analysts who treat uncertainty with the same care and attention they currently give to substance develop clear guidance for how they can strengthen the depth and quality of their insights. They have a powerful tool to help them avoid cognitive biases and other traps caused by missing, ambiguous, or otherwise limited information".

Bearing the above in mind, it can be suggested that policy makers need to review issues relating to information and communications technologies. For example, Kshetri (2005) has looked in some detail at asymmetry associated with information and communications technologies, and has made a valuable contribution to developing our national security knowledge base. The links between national security and corporate security have been highlighted by Trim (2000, 2001) and Trim (2003, 2005) has also focused attention on issues of importance relating to organized criminal syndicates and terrorist networks.

Li et al., (2005) have broadened our understanding of the role that super-empowered individuals and groups have on the environment, and it is essential therefore that business leaders and our political leaders engage in an open and ongoing dialogue about implementing national strategies to counteract the actions of those that are determined to create damage and disruption.

It is for these reasons that policy makers need to think through how organizations can become less vulnerable than they are, and this may mean redefining what business security represents or having a wider view of the subject (Suder, 2006). Spich and Grosse (2005, p.468) state: "Business security can be defined as a defensive strategy and state of organizational readiness to assure and protect (but not guarantee) the functional integrity of the organization's operational systems against purposeful, wilful and intentional attempts by agents (inside or outside) to disrupt, damage, dismantle or destroy them. The goal and purpose of a security strategy and policy is to protect the firm against the ability of an "enemy" to put the capabilities of the firm's responsiveness to security threats into doubt, to create uncertainty about its ability and willingness to maintain its strategic advantage, use its core competencies fully, or maintain its overall competitiveness".

One point that needs to be remembered is that when senior managers embark on strategy formulation, they avoid making superficial analogies (Gavetti and Rivkin, 2005). One way in which this can be done, is by senior managers within organizations adopting a more holistic approach to security formulation and implementation. The GISES model advocated by Trim (2005) can be used as a basis within which to place government-industry working relationships (Trim, 2002).

As regards the inter-relation of issues, it has been noted that Iran in particular has been of concern to western intelligence agencies because of its energy policy and in particular, its nuclear and missile programmes (Caravelli, 2008, p.98). However, from a security context, Iran cannot be considered in isolation. For example, as well as US and Iran relations, one also has to think in terms of EU and Iran relations, and how Russia comes into the equation. It is also necessary to predict how events in the Middle East are likely to influence geo-political relations, and how this translates into military expenditure. Looking more deeply into the energy security issue, it is necessary to contemplate how nations may develop sustainable energy sources, and how energy prices are translated into national economic gains or losses. Once all this has been ascertained, it will be possible to have a better understanding of how the subject of energy is integrated into the broad field of international affairs.

Conclusion

Security and safety are closely linked terms, and there can be no doubt that as we embrace more fully the wonders of electronic commerce and industry, that various threats will manifest from time to time that need to be dealt with quickly and effectively. As well as paying attention to the highly organized groups of computer hackers and crackers, terrorist networks and organized criminal syndicates, it is necessary to remain vigilant as regards potential internal security weaknesses that need to be eradicated through the development of a robust security culture. Indeed, insider threats are most likely to consume a great deal of attention of senior managers in the years ahead, and it is necessary that a resilience psyche is built into the organization's value system. As well as an organization appearing vulnerable, it is true to say that a government and indeed a nation is vulnerable. Hence the necessary investments need to be made in order to ensure that a nation's Critical National Infrastructure can withstand any attack unleashed upon it.

The challenges for business, the focus of this chapter, will unfold in both the UK and US in a changing political context. President Obama has now taken office and the pending British general election timetabled for 2010, will no doubt, focus the minds of political analysts and strategists. Political change will almost certainly lead to revised threat perceptions vis-à-vis the external environment. As a consequence, political relationships will be realigned and the priorities of government, and commerce and industry, will be reassessed as business leaders place more emphasis on business continuity planning. A new wave of terrorist attacks, such as that which greeted new US administrations in 1993 and 2001, the Spanish in 2004 (the Madrid train bombing) and the British in 2007 may reinforce that directions already underway and described herein, are indeed built upon and communicated more forcibly to the general public.

REFERENCES

Canton, B. (2008). "The active management of uncertainty", *International Journal of Intelligence and CounterIntelligence*, 21 (3), pp.487-518.

Caravelli, J. (2008). *Nuclear Insecurity: Understanding the Threat from Rogue Nations and Terrorists*. Westport, Connecticut: Praeger Security International.

Czinkota, M.R., Knight, G.A., Liesch, P.W., and J. Steen. (2005). "Positioning terrorism in management and marketing: Research propositions", *Journal of International Management*, 11, pp.581-604.

Gavetti, G., and Rivkin, W. (2005). "How strategists really think: Tapping the power of analogy". *Harvard Business Review*, 83 (4), pp.54-63.

Herzog, J.O. (2008). "Using economic intelligence to achieve regional security objectives", *International Journal of Intelligence and CounterIntelligence*, 21 (2), pp.302-313.

Kshetri, N. (2005). Information and communications technologies, strategic asymmetry and national security, *Journal of International Management*, 11, pp.563-580.

Lee, Y-I., and P.R.J. Trim. (2006). "Retail marketing strategy: The role of marketing intelligence, relationship marketing and trust", *Marketing Intelligence and Planning*, 24 (7), pp.730-745.

Lesser, I.O., Hoffman, B., Arquilla, J., Ronfeldt, D., and M. Zanini. (1999). *Countering The New Terrorism*. Santa Monica, California: RAND.

Li, S., Tallman, S.B., and M.P. Ferreira. (2005). "Developing the eclectic paradigm as a model of global strategy: An application to the impact of the Sep.11 terrorist attacks on MNE performance levels", *Journal of International Management*, 11, pp.479-496.

Merkidze, A.W. (2007). (Ed). *Terrorism Issues: Threat Assessment, Consequences and Prevention*. New York: Nova Science Publishers, Inc.

Sheffi, Y. (2005). *The Resilient Enterprise*. Cambridge, Massachusetts: The MIT Press.

Spich, R., and R. Grosse. (2005). "How does homeland security affect U.S. firms' international competitiveness", *Journal of International Management*, 11, pp.457-478.

Suder, G.G.S. (2006). (Ed). *Corporate Strategies Under International Terrorism and Adversity*. Cheltenham: Edward Elgar.

Trim, P.R.J. (2000). "The company-intelligence services interface and national security". *International Journal of Intelligence and CounterIntelligence*, 13 (2), pp.204-214.

Trim, P.R.J. (2001). "A framework for establishing and implementing corporate intelligence". *Strategic Change,* 10 (6), pp.349-357.

Trim, P.R.J. (2002). "Counteracting industrial espionage through counterintelligence: The case for a corporate intelligence function and collaboration with government". *Security Journal*, 15 (4), pp.7-24.

Trim, P.R.J. (2003). "Public and private sector cooperation in counteracting cyberterrorism". *International Journal of Intelligence and CounterIntelligence,* 16 (4), pp. 594-608.

Trim, P.R.J. (2005) "The GISES model for counteracting organized crime and international terrorism". *International Journal of Intelligence and CounterIntelligence*, 18 (3), pp.451-472.

WORLD WIDE WEB ADDRESSES

British Computer Society (www.bcs.org/security)
Get Safe Online (www.getsafeonline.org)
Information Assurance Advisory Council (www.iaac.org)
ISAF (www.theisaf.org)
Information Security Forum (ISF) (www.securityforum.org)
Sir Michael Bichard report into the Soham murders (www.bichardinquiry.org.uk
Sir Michael Pitt's report can be viewed at www.cabinetoffice.gov.uk/thepittreview

The Cabinet Office web site also deals with the Business Continuity Standard BS25999 which CO/Civil Contingencies Secretariat is actively promoting.

The international standard ISO27001 can be viewed at www.bsi-global.com/ISO/IEC27001

In: Strategizing Resilience and Reducing Vulnerability
Editors: Peter R.J. Trim and Jack Caravelli

ISBN 978-1-60741-693-7
© 2009 Nova Science Publishers, Inc.

Chapter 6

OPEN SOURCE SOFTWARE, INFORMATION ENTREPRENEURS AND ISSUES OF NATIONAL SECURITY

Peter R.J. Trim and Yang-Im Lee

ABSTRACT

This paper focuses on the usage of open source information and software, and makes reference to the information entrepreneur and the growing demand associated with information services. The development of networked communities is highlighted and attention is given to the work of computer hacker groups. The problems facing law enforcement officers, intelligence and security officers, and corporate intelligence and security officers are referred to. Various arguments for counterintelligence are put forward and a pro-active approach to security work is advocated. The paper makes clear the fact that greater co-operation is needed between staff from both the public and private sectors, and makes the case for an effective intelligence and security monitoring system to be put in place.

INTRODUCTION

Facilitating technology such as the Internet is having an increasingly important influence on an individual's work routines and their social activities. It is evident that school children, university students, government employees, professional staff and practising managers, are embracing connectivity and interactivity on an increasing scale and are participating in on-line, information exchange within integrated community networks. Indeed, on-line chat rooms and opportunities for blogging are being embraced by individuals from all social groups and as a consequence a new psyche associated with information availability that could lead to new forms of activism is emerging. It is also noticeable that young adults in particular are less aware of the dangers associated with releasing data and information onto the Internet and it has been suggested that young adults may pose a security threat to society if their behaviour goes unchecked. Changing behaviour or making young people act appropriately in the workplace is something that employers are being forced to address.

Emerging technologies are likely to be embraced speedily by a technology hungry public and will provide a stimulus vis-à-vis the development of networked communities, some of which are likely to derive pleasure from carrying out inappropriate acts. These networked communities allow individual's to both consult and indeed offer information and advice on a wide range of issues [1, p.97]. What is clear, is that facilitating technology is supportive of the concept of sustainability in the sense that on-line communities are forming tightly knit, knowledge rich and interdependent advice oriented associations. This can be considered a natural process, however, it is now clear that computer literate individuals are discovering ways in which to increase their personal value through identifying ways in which to market data, information and knowledge. Indeed, various individuals are identifying gaps in the market that need to be served and are preparing to meet the challenge. These market opportunities centre around open source information utilisation and the deployment and development of open source software. It is no surprise to note, therefore, that we are witnessing the rise of the 'information entrepreneur'. An information entrepreneur is somebody who realises that an unmet need exists that can be satisfied through a product/service offering and at the same time does not have any inhibitions about supplying data/information in a form that is acceptable to an end user or middleman (information broker).

An emerging trend is evident. Computer literate individuals will in the future be more able to become self employed through identifying, selecting, screening, analysing and interpreting data and information that is made available on the world wide web, and which can be packaged and produced in a certain form that is acceptable to a variety of customers of information services. Information entrepreneurs as the packagers of information can be called, are finding it relatively easy to derive a living from such activity without too much time and effort expended on the process. By forming relationships with information providers and users, based on continuity of supply and quality of delivery, information entrepreneurs are increasingly able to devise and implement niche marketing strategies that result in marketable products and services and ultimately, brand recognition. As regards the open source software that is freely available and which can be down loaded from the world wide web, it is clear that individuals possessing specific methodological skills and approaches will be able to analyse and interpret huge amounts of data and information, and package it for a client base that is located world wide. An important consideration is of course, whether the data/information contained on the world wide web is valid, reliable and is generalisable. And in some cases, the issue of whether the material on the Internet should be freely available or whether it has been placed there because of an ulterior motive, needs to be borne in mind. Sensitive and confidential data and information does from time to time find its way onto the world wide web and may originate from a disgruntled employee intent on causing an employer/previous employer harm. The 'insider threat' as it has become known is more likely to absorb increased amounts of senior management's time in the years ahead as disillusioned employees seek revenge for not being promoted or simply make a calculated risk and decide that the punishment associated with a particular criminal act is not worth worrying about [2].

As regards the quality of the data and information available, it can be assumed that information entrepreneurs will consult more than one source, and will make every effort to ensure that the original source of the data and information are deemed credible. This is important from the stance of trust and the fact that the information provided has been repackaged and classified as generalisable. One can assume that those involved in providing information broking services will adopt a rigorous approach to searching, checking and validating the various data and information sets available, before the data is analysed and interpreted, and packaged in the form of a report. The key point to note, is that information is viewed as a commodity and because this is the case, questions do not need to be asked regarding its source and how it was obtained.

This paper focuses attention on a number of issues relating to open source software usage and in particular, places the subject matter in a security context. For example, attention is paid to how facilitating technology is producing information entrepreneurs, how people and organisations are being connected in network arrangements, and how customers are exercising collective action. Reference is made to networked communities and in particular those groups that are involved in criminal activities. Various national security issues are highlighted and a link is made with the work of the intelligence and security services. The need for senior managers to authorise counterintelligence activities and be involved in the development of an intelligence and security monitoring system is made clear.

PLACING DATA, INFORMATION AND OPEN SOURCE SOFTWARE IN CONTEXT

Ljunberg [3, p.208 and p.209] has indicated that: "An open source project is a loosely coupled community kept together by strong common values such that software should be free At the core of open source movements lies a culture that encourages people to contribute and share, ie getting credit for good contributions is what brings status and influence". An interesting point to note is that the contributors do in fact place their trust in those who are members of their community and this means that they place trust in the world wide web itself [4, pp.6-9]. Prestige, an individual's intellectual development, knowledge sharing and knowledge transfer seem to be the main reasons why people become part of an open source software development community. It is also worth noting, according to Dahlander and McKelvey [5, p.619], that opportunity costs (the mobilisation of resources and incentives for example), also play a part with respect to encouraging individuals and organisations to participate in open source software development.

It can be argued that open source software is available because of the skill of software designers; a benevolent attitude exhibited by computer industry experts; an established information highway infrastructure; and a legal framework that allows ideas to be turned into original products that are then made freely available to individuals world wide. To this one can add a supportive community of governments that are happy to openly promote connectivity and interactivity, from the perspective of how a higher quality of life can be provided through greater choice and openness (transparency of operations). There will, through time, be modifications in software technology development, and this will create further opportunities for information entrepreneurs because one can assume that the users of information will become more demanding in the years ahead. Information entrepreneurs and information brokers will become more sophisticated and more demanding as they seek to differentiate their products and services, and open up new markets. This will result in a higher level of expectation and a commitment to customer relationship management. Indeed, Baker [6, p.56] has suggested that in order that an organisation can develop a profitable relationship with its customers, marketing staff in the supplier organisation will need to produce products and services that are perceived as being of value to the customer. The current demand driven era, which is underpinned by a new approach to consumerism, is forcing information entrepreneurs to set new goals of attainment. This will require them to perform at higher levels of achievement and to differentiate the products and services on offer. It will also force computer software engineers to think in terms of producing the next generation of open source software and to establish how new open source software products and services can be made available on the Internet. These developments will continue to fuel the aspirations of information users, and as a consequence the cycle will continue and result in information users becoming more dependent upon information suppliers. As a result, competition among information entrepreneurs will increase and so too will the opportunity for stolen data and information to find its way onto the world market.

INFLUENTIAL INTER-ORGANISATIONAL NETWORK ARRANGEMENTS

As regards network arrangements, Nivet [7, p.9] has stated that: "Networks and collective action are essential ingredients of informal norms". The Internet, is therefore, a device for connecting people and organisations, in the form of networks of people who exercise collective action. Indeed, from an inter-organisational perspective, it is important to note that a layered-network organisation is information-processing oriented [8, p.148]. There are extensive vertical connections across and also among the organisation's layers and these connections reach out into the external environment [8, p.149]. The inter-organisational connections also reach out into government web sites, trade association databases, custom designed industry databases, databases owned by banks and stockbrokers, market research consultancy databases, databases owned by news corporations which include data contained in reports and newspapers, and databases and web sites emanating from academia for example. It is clear also, that as staff in an organisation become more dependent upon external information sources, that first, senior management need to have a forward thinking approach and establish how an organisation is structured to receive and make use of data and information; and second, identify and put in place the tools and techniques that are needed to analyse and interpret various forms of data and information. Ultimately, it may be necessary for senior management to commission the design and development of software packages that can be used to package information into formally structured reports. As regards, transmutating organisational structures, it is useful to note that Child and McGrath [9, p.1138] have indicated that managers are confronted with the need to maintain flexibility, and this is another reason why senior managers need to establish how the organisation should be structured to make the most appropriate use of data and information, purchased from external sources. One reason why senior managers need to establish appropriate organisational structures, is first to avoid duplication (personnel, operational duties and data and information utilisation) and second, to create an effective counterintelligence operation that allows corporate intelligence and corporate security staff to implement actionable programmes that counter, in a speedy manner, immediate and anticipated threats [10]. Threats can manifest in the form of changes in government legislation, a competitor's retaliatory actions, a new technology that has been developed at a secret laboratory, and pressure from the general public (this may be in the form of a pressure group), and may result in activists mounting an attack via a consumer association. Adequate corporate intelligence enables staff in the organisation to deploy open source software in order to collect and analyse issues and situations at speed, and the findings can be stored in the company's computer system. Custom made computer software packages can be developed in-house to carry-out more sophisticated analyses of the information that is contained in the company's corporate intelligence databases, but these are likely to be company and industry specific.

It is also useful to note that networking has a positive impact on innovation in various types of organisation [11, p.148]. It can be argued, that marketing intelligence and corporate intelligence officers are concerned with all types of intelligence work (both internal and external) and that the main objective is to provide the marketing strategy decision-making process with authentic, factually based data and information that assists strategists to establish a sustainable competitive advantage. Marshall and Brown [12, p.105] have indicated that in order to achieve sustainability, it is necessary for an organisation to have a supportive culture and also, an articulated and shared vision.

Preece et al., [13, p.3] have indicated that an 'on-line' community may also have a physical presence or may exist through physical connections. This is an important point because terrorist groups and organised criminal syndicates use various ways in which to communicate on an intra-group and inter-group basis. Indeed, it is possible for on-line communities to adapt open source software for their own particular needs [13, p.5]. As society embraces the concept of electronic government, government will need to ensure that various assistance is available to a diverse audience (especially from the stance of language utilisation associated with a multi-cultural society where distance, religion, gender and language can result in the isolation of individuals). There are computer packages available to assist with the translation of documents into a foreign language, but special software is needed in order to run them. It is essential, therefore, that performance support tools are available via a learning centre site and that adequate attention is given to developments such as wireless technology and courseware [14, pp.355-357]. As regards courseware, it is important to realise that one needs to think in terms of global reach and some of the data and information may appear unacceptable to some governments (reference to corruption, incompetence and human rights violations for example). Policing such developments will witness resources being applied in terms of monitoring, inquiring and following through when necessary. Developments in mobile technology are also expected to play a useful role. Mobile technology allows a government to make information available to a number of publics at "any time, anywhere, on any device" [15, p.467]. This can be placed in context when one considers that according to Sharma and Gupta [15, p.468]: "The goal of government is to develop a citizen-centred, network-centred, mobile computing oriented flexible environment that can allow citizens, businesses and other stakeholders to access the content whenever they need it, in whatever form they need it".

Buzan [16, p.205] has suggested that as international society becomes stronger, international relations become dominated by "a dense web of shared rules" and a "mature anarchy" is formed that represents "a system of strong states (in terms of high levels of sociopolitical cohesion), embedded in a well-developed international society (a dense network of mutually agreed norms, rules and institutions)". Provided that facilitating technology is fully embraced, information entrepreneurs can customise information services. Issues such as who pays for the service will arise, and so too will what material can be distributed and whether translation services need to be incorporated [17, pp.197-203]. Alternatively, some data and information may be repackaged and provided free of charge, and a fee levied on more sensitive data/information. It is also possible to deduce from this that some information entrepreneurs, who wish to protect their brand identity, will no doubt double check the validity of the data and information they are supplying. As a consequence, they will establish a network of trust with alternative data and information suppliers, and this will act as a catalyst for new sources and forms of data and information supply.

NETWORKED COMMUNITIES

Von Krogh and von Hippel [18, p.1149] have stated that: "Open source software development projects are generally Internet-based networks or communities of software developers. The software they develop is made freely available to all that adhere to the licensing terms specified in the open source project". This quotation reinforces some of the points made in the above, and what is of interest, is that one can think in terms of inter-related groups or communities. For example, one can extend the concept of community to include computer hackers, crackers and politically oriented on-line activists; and a wide ranging counterintelligence group. The counterintelligence group is composed of the law enforcement services, intelligence and security services, private security companies, specialist computer consultancies, and a range of other service providers (research laboratories, university departments, international institutions and legal experts for example), who are concerned with disrupting the activities of the criminally oriented. One growing area of concern is the ability of computer hackers to form operational groups, that contain computer virus ideas people and world wide web screeners; computer virus designers, co-ordinators, and implementers; public relations liaison staff or network facilitators (those that network with other computer hacker groups and share and exchange information); and computer virus warriors (those that engage in spreading computer viruses, and undertake hacking and cracking activities). The more sophisticated the computer hacker group is, the better organised it is and the more able it is to identify potential members and develop partnership associations and work with them. Computer hacking regional conferences (some of which are virtual) will become more frequent and new ways will be found to obtain and share data and information. Those intent on carrying-out acts of computer hacking will also devise ways to protect themselves against the actions of law enforcement officers. Law enforcement officers will become more involved in identifying and arresting computer hackers and crackers, and will also spend large amounts of their time disrupting the activities of those involved in criminal activities. The cost to the public and commerce and industry is expected to rise as new ways are found to counteract the activities of those involved in criminal activities.

What is clear from the above, is that there are a number of tribes/camps in existence: the developers of open source software; the promoters of open source software; information entrepreneurs/information brokers; information users; computer hackers and crackers; government officers; and private security personnel; and this will warrant new approaches to information assurance. To this can be added organised criminal syndicates and international terrorist groups. Thus what is emerging, is a world in which the services of computer hackers and crackers is seen by some to be annoying and by others to provide business opportunities (sensitive and confidential data and information can be stolen and traded at a profit), and this is of concern to the various law enforcement officers and intelligence and security officers, who are charged with guarding the data and information of companies that are classified as strategic national assets. Specialist computer companies, and a variety of companies that produce similar but different marketable software, and independent industry commentators (journalists, consultancy companies and trade associations), are also to be considered part of the community that is either directly or indirectly involved in the production or utilisation of open source software. There are also a range of government regulatory bodies and government appointed observers that are part of the community. Furthermore, researchers employed by think tanks that are involved in discussions about the current and future development of open source software should not be ignored. As well as legally binding rules that have been produced and enforced by government bodies, it is important to note that there are various technical standards for digital behaviour, and these have been produced by a range of organisations, institutions and companies [19, p.72].

NATIONAL SECURITY AND CORPORATE INTELLIGENCE

The fact that open source software development communities are not managed by an individual and do "not share a common employer" [20, p.1179] is worrying in itself. As well as government officials, industry representatives and university research teams [21] being involved in the development of knowledge, various terrorist groups and organised criminal syndicates are also actively involved in the acquisition of knowledge in order to develop further their platform of activities.

In order to counter the activities of terrorist groups and organised criminal syndicates, the US government has encouraged the development of information sharing analysis centers (ISAC), which are expected to work closely with government agencies, and in so doing will build trust based relationships that are aimed at information sharing [22, p.9]. Indeed, a framework has been developed for organising and prioritising efforts that are aimed at protecting the nation's cyberspace and as well, guidelines are provided that both individuals and organisations can follow in order to provide more adequate cybersecurity [22, p.22]. Smith and Dickson [23, p.45] have indicated that with respect to international partnership arrangements, even when the partners are judged to be equal, it is necessary for senior staff from the partner organisations to travel to attend meetings as this ensures that a common collaborative language is maintained. Other factors that come into play in collaborative arrangements are self-interest and competition [24, p.54 and p.61].

Intelligence and security officers are aware that nowadays, there is a huge amount of data and information available via open sources, and this may present various problems. For example, intelligence officers have to continually develop their tradecraft and are using their expertise in conjunction with the military and law enforcement agencies. Owing to the fact that data and information is now abundant, there are issues of quality control, and Treverton [25, p.103] has reported that intelligence officers are confronted with a large amount of unreliable information and that policy makers, because they lack time, will become more dependent on information brokers. Treverton [25, p.104] has stated: "Now, openness, is blurring the distinction between collection and analysis. ...... The Web is rich in sources but short on reliability". Over time, search engines will improve and help provide first-cut assessments of reliability".

Intelligence officers have access to data, information and images from human operatives, satellites and on-line news providers. They can and do monitor the various information service providers through time. Intelligence officers do need to gather data and information at speed, and the Internet provides a mechanism that allows for this. The Internet also facilitates information sharing in the sense that because a lot of information is available and is not "classified", and can be grouped and analysed, the interpretations can be considered to be 'neutral'. The findings can be packaged in the form of a newsletter and then transmitted electronically to the members of the receiving group and to "friendly personnel" (those outside the inner circle but deemed to benefit from the information sharing process). This is part of the information/knowledge sharing and exchange process, and the service packages provided can be enhanced through time. Additional but different newsletters can be devised and exchanged. The newsletters (both in hard copy and in electronic form) are more likely to include information that relates to a single theme, and are likely to cite original sources. What is important to note, is that electronic newsletters can be distributed quickly and provided the information is relatively up to date, should allow the receiver to undertake their own open source research activity into the topic of interest. This will widen the intelligence base of the information user as it will encourage/stimulate them into identifying additional experts and information suppliers in a specific area of activity. Electronic newsletters are useful devices as they provide a mechanism for building additional networks. They also stimulate developments in technology vis-à-vis information storage and retrieval, and result in custom designed data bases being designed and used.

Both electronic and physical forms of networking reinforce the relationship building process that underpins inter-group and intra-group activity. As a result, trust based, exchange oriented relationships are formed that allow for the development of an information and knowledge based intelligence community (IKBIC). Various IKBICs will be formed and will transmutate into multi-dimensional information and knowledge based intelligence communities (MIKBICs), as other more specialised groups and communities are formed to replicate and initiate projects.

There is a great deal more to intelligence than simply providing an interpretation of a situation or event. Intelligence officers are required to explain assumptions, outline antecedent conditions and highlight possible outcomes/occurrences, and will in the years ahead draw on experts from both academia and the private sector [25, p.133]. Drawing on the knowledge and expertise of various individuals and organisations will become essential if information users want to develop a holistic appreciation of evolving and future (predictable) events. Whereas government representatives and practising managers in commerce and industry require answers and solutions to specific problems, it is academics who can provide deeper insights into why the world is as it is, through undertaking research, possibly in the form of longitudinal studies. This should allow information users to identify various trends and activities, and to match outcomes and provide explanations. It should also allow public-private partnerships to be formed that are focused on solving recurring security problems through the deployment of integrated intelligence systems and processes [26].

Although there are formal bilateral and multilateral agreements in place that allow certain nation's to participate in intelligence sharing and exchange, it should also be noted that law enforcement officers, and intelligence and security officers, form one-to-one relationships with their counterparts in similar organisations overseas. These one-to-one relationships are based on trust and need to be reinforced through time in situations where trust is limited or political differences exist (between participating nations), and relationships become strained. It is a reasonable assumption to suggest that certain individuals may be denied information and access to other individuals in the extended network. This is normal in social networks, indeed, Assimakopoulos and Macdonald [1, p.100] have indicated that in social networks, "individuals (or other actors) generally know only their own connections and do not have an overview of all the connections that make up the system". However, intelligence and security work is very different. There are times when security and intelligence officers find it essential to leave their closed world and enter into the public domain, mostly by going undercover. It is also true to say that during the course of their work, intelligence and security officers, do find it necessary to liase with legal representatives, academics and government officers, as well as selected journalists. They are also required to make instant decisions regarding a range of issues, and they are also becoming more actively involved with trade associations and industry groups. This is not surprising to learn vis-à-vis the activities of some governments that establish overseas industrial espionage activities; fund terrorist groups; and have connections (either direct or indirect) with criminal syndicates. Adding to this the increased risk associated with insider orchestrated crime means that it is becoming increasingly easy for disgruntled employees to download doctored software and introduce it into the company's computer system with severe consequences.

COLLABORATION INVOLVING GOVERNMENT, INDUSTRY AND ACADEMIA

As regards collaboration involving industry and academia, it can be noted that in the UK, there have been a number of policy initiatives since the 1970s and areas of research that have been deemed important to specific industries have been funded [27, p.9]. If one engages in discussions about the world order and the future security strategies of various nations, the discussions become complex and inconclusive. There are many reasons for this. One can cite a number of factors such as a nation's stage of economic development; the political ideology that underpins the policy decision-making process; multi-faceted arguments for and against technology transfer; human rights violations; corporate security issues; and government initiated strategic alliances between companies that are based in different parts of the world. To this can be added movements in foreign direct investment and preferential trading agreements. This all seems complex enough, without having to dwell on issues of culture and religion for example. It can be argued that there are different approaches to teaching the subject of strategic studies, and these differences should be made public in order that more interpretation can be made of the subject matter. Staff based at different universities can form working relationships with staff at other universities and this can result in staff and student exchange programmes. A number of issues relating to intelligence and security degree courses and programmes of study have been highlighted by Shultz et al., [28] and placed in context. Furthermore, as regards corporations and the issue of competitive intelligence, it is interesting to note that senior managers are taking this activity seriously and are deploying a number of management intelligence focused frameworks [29]. Those involved in competitive intelligence work follow a strategic orientation and tend to think in terms of following a wide brief [30]. It can be argued that there is commonality between government oriented intelligence work and corporate intelligence activities [2]. Companies of all shapes and sizes, in a range of industries, are recruiting ex-intelligence and security specialists to advise on issues of business continuity. Key concerns confronting senior managers are issues of adequate threat analysis and assessment, and reducing a company's vulnerability. It has to be said that open source software is providing a means to not only analyse large amounts of industry data, but also, is proving a mechanism by which future threats (carried out by on-line activists) can be identified, monitored and disrupted when necessary. Sometimes, a common problem emerges that witnesses corporate security, intelligence and security officers, and indeed law enforcement personnel, coming together to work on country specific problems. For example, one only has to read about the economic and political complexity of countries such as Nigeria [31] to understand that in this day and age it is necessary for corporate intelligence officers to work with government intelligence officers owing to the fact that events are changing the dynamics of strategic intelligence. Intelligence work needs to incorporate the actions of overseas governments and overseas companies, and needs to embrace open source intelligence.

Friedman et al., [32, p.116] are right to state that: "Open source electronic systems have increased the quantity of material available while decreasing the amount of time needed to find and acquire that material". The data and information that is available in the form of commercial on-line services, in CD-ROMS and on the Internet, accounts for about 60 per cent of the information and the other 40 per cent, is in the form of paper and other forms [32, pp.116-118]. The various bulletin boards and self interested groups that share/exchange information over the Internet are proliferating and it would seem that people are becoming conditioned to communicating with each other via the Internet. It is relevant to point out that from an organisation's point of view, searching, downloading and screening data and information from the Internet is not necessarily expensive, compared with hiring external information providers and employing a large number of analysts, but a trade-off does have to be made. For example, not all the material placed on the world wide web has relevance or is useable. Indeed, there is a lot of disinformation and the hackers, crackers and activists (sometimes referred to as hacktivists), are able at times to disrupt computer links. Furthermore, intelligence analysts will in many cases still need to verify a fact/event by two separate sources, otherwise there is the possibility that the reporting process may be inaccurate and this may have consequences for the decision-making process if those analysing intelligence findings do not take precautions to ensure that the data and information being accessed is accurate, reliable and valid. So the question of robustness of information is central and needs to be constantly addressed.

A COLLECTIVIST APPROACH TO INTELLIGENCE AND SECURITY, AND THE NEED FOR COUNTERINTELLIGENCE

Vegh [33, p.72] has highlighted the work of on-line activists and it is clear that information disseminated via the Internet can consolidate organisational activism and mobilize support. Dissident on-line communities can be formed that focus their attention on specific political campaigns, and ultimately upon carrying out certain actions that are aimed at doing damage or causing maximum disruption [33, p.73]. Corporate security staff and law enforcement personnel should monitor these developments and interactions, in order to identify future threats. Sometimes, web sites of companies and indeed government departments can be hijacked and disinformation put out by the hacktivists. This has happened to several UK companies and is of concern to government officials because in times of economic instability, companies can be at a higher level of risk when shareholder value is eroded and a loss in investor confidence results in the panic selling of shares. Ultimately, a company in such a situation may be acquired by another company or may collapse and exit the industry.

Cyber conflicts/cyber wars have been evident in the past, some are continuing, and others can be predicted. The question facing government policy makers and advisors is: What measures need to be put in place to counter the work of cyber warriors? Additional questions can be posed: Should the solution be a joint one (solved through government-industry collaboration)? Should managers become less protective and share data and information with companies and organisations both in and outside the industry in which the company competes? It might be argued that as open source software becomes more widely available, there is less need for companies and governments to engage in industrial espionage, however, during times of economic downturn one can assume that acts of industrial espionage will intensify as rival companies try and reduce the gap between themselves and their competitors. A collectivist approach would seem appropriate, the problem remains however: Will an isolated and small scale attack be refocused into an all out attack if government is seen to handle the situation in a heavy handed manner? As regards cyber attacks unleashed on companies, it can be stated that web site defacements, e-mail campaigns and virtual sit-ins; are different in context to cybergraffiti [33, p.85]. It may be necessary for company and government representatives to be aware of this, but it is correct to say that coordinated attacks can, if given maximum publicity, have the desired effect [33, pp.85-89]. It is because of the likelihood that companies, government agencies and a nation's critical infrastructure will be prone to attack from time to time that the call for public-private sector co-operation to defeat acts of cyber terrorism are made [34].

In order to counter the acts of terrorists and extreme right wing groups, it is necessary for law enforcement, intelligence and security staff to monitor the activities of extremist political groups, and this may mean working with various ethnic groups in society and also, monitoring the on-line ethnic groups/communities. Indeed, those undertaking monitoring activities and conducting surveillance, will need to ensure that they operate within the law and ensure that an individual's human rights are not violated.

Gandy [35, p.28] has made reference to the fact that data mining, which is an applied statistical technique aimed at extracting "meaningful intelligence, or knowledge, from the patterns that emerge within a database after it has been cleaned, sorted and processed", is possible owing to the development of computer databases. Marketing staff in particular are keen to use data mining because it allows them to segment customers and establish customer relationship management programmes for example [35, p.33]. The US government has in recent years come up with initiatives to identify and capture suspected terrorists using data mining tools and analysis aids, linked to an integrated information base [35, p.35]. There are also initiatives in commerce and industry to use data mining approaches to identify possible unsavoury individuals and at risk companies. An issue that surfaces here is the right of privacy and what might be called anti-discriminatory policy. Gandy [35, p.41] is right to suggest that: "People tend to be outraged when they discover, or are informed that, they have been discriminated against. There is some value, therefore, in supplying the press with egregious examples of individuals, or communities, or classes of people, who have been victimized by data mining, and by the use of profiles based on irrelevant attributes like race or ethnicity".

Herman [36, pp.319-320] has raised many issues and questions relating to how the UK and the US view intelligence and security work, and has suggested that more attention needs to be paid to career planning and central staff support, the key being to avoid forming a unified national intelligence agency owing to the fact that operating units need a degree of independence, strategy and planning. Lahneman [37, p.621] has addressed the issues of information becoming knowledge, and knowledge sharing, and has suggested that "Creating databases is not enough". Indeed, managing knowledge and sharing knowledge, has to be thought of from the perspective of organisational change, and issues that surface are appropriate forms of leadership and organisational restructuring [37, pp.623-630]. One has to remember that intelligence analysts and marketing intelligence officers work within legal constraints. The USA Patriot Act that came into being in October 2001, allows "roving" or "multi-point" wiretaps to be used and makes other provisions that allows the law enforcement agencies to make interceptions [38, pp.16-17]. This is evidence of the fact that we are now entering a period of rapid and continual change, and that open source information and software are creating new opportunities but also, giving rise to new problems that require government-industry co-operation.

THE CASE FOR AN EFFECTIVE INTELLIGENCE AND SECURITY MONITORING SYSTEM

Trim [39] has indicated that it is necessary for government agencies to establish a monitoring system that gauges adequately the effectiveness of security measures, especially initiatives in the area of homeland security. This will allow intelligence and security officers to track events and predict disruptions. However, it is unrealistic to suggest that government agencies possess sufficient resources to devote time and effort to comprehensive risk assessment, analysis and the prevention of all types of attack. Although Sheffi [40, p.167] is correct in stating that "monitoring systems can also provide past data to help catch near misses and developing patterns of disruption", it has to be remembered that developments in open source software development can be likened to an expanding universe, and as a consequence, a fully operational and effective monitoring system would need to be composed of individuals from government agencies, research institutes, trade associations, university laboratories, and of course, a range of companies involved in the development of computer software.

Policy advisors need to bear in mind the fact that once an individual is in possession of a source code, the innovation is no longer limited to the owner/originator [41, p.49]. Furthermore, businesses have embraced open source software [42, p.231] and von Hippel and von Krogh [43, p.210] are right to suggest that "open source software has emerged as a major cultural and economic phenomenon". So where does this leave us? It is clear that a robust government designed monitoring system needs to be put in place that eradicates (as far as possible), the work of computer hackers and crackers; terrorists and criminals. Intelligence and security officers will need to remain vigilant and establish if an open source software community has been penetrated by individuals who are determined to acquire knowledge that can be used to disrupt and cause harm in any way. As regards key industries such as the defence industry, it is clear that a person may be cajoled into providing sensitive information without knowing that the person that is being given the source code is a representative of a terrorist group or is a representative of an 'unfriendly' overseas government. The key point to note is that by transferring information and knowledge, it is possible that representatives of an overseas government/company, obtain an advantage that allows them to close the technological gap on the leaders in the field. It is also possible that during an economic recession when a company makes certain skilled people redundant, an overseas based company can recruit those made redundant and harness their brain power to reduce the technological gap further.

Bearing the above points in mind, it can be suggested that information usage needs ultimately to be placed in the context of knowledge creation, and this requires that policy makers think in terms of how value is created within organisations and how the knowledge development process facilitates trade between nations and results in trading arrangements that are underpinned by the concept of mutuality [44]. This line of thought is embedded in economic theory and information sharing is of benefit to both public sector and private sector organisations, in the sense that it plays a pivotal role in economic development.

CONCLUSION

It is clear from the above that open source information and software, are accelerating the process of information usage. It is also clear that new information markets and exchange processes are being established, and that information entrepreneurs are stimulating demand for all types of data and information. Although the government appears to be supportive of developments in information availability and utilisation, it has to be said that law enforcement officers in particular are finding it increasingly difficult to safeguard the public vis-à-vis the activities of criminally oriented computer hacker groups. Ultimately, the issue of national security will arise as criminal syndicates become more able to achieve their objectives, possibly by working more closely with international terrorist groups and networks. What is clear, is that senior managers in a variety of organisations, will need to invest more in the way of resources in the area of corporate security. Senior managers will need to monitor the overt and covert operations of organisational criminal syndicates and competitor organisations, as they may be intent on causing damage to the company and its operations. By investing in counterintelligence operations, both company personnel and government officers can ensure that issues such as counterfeiting, smuggling, and stealing sensitive company secrets for immediate use or to order, are dealt with in a timely and appropriate manner. It is also true to point out, that legally administered open source software can enrich the lives of various individuals, because it allows individuals to search for data and information on the world wide web, and once found, to use it and benefit from it. The benefits associated with open source software are numerous and can be placed in various contexts: individually oriented and personal; professionally oriented and work based; and family oriented and leisure enriching.

REFERENCES

[1] Assimakopoulos, D., and Macdonald, S. (2003) 'A dual approach to understanding information networks', *International Journal of Technology Management*, Vol 25, No. 1/2, pp.96-111.

[2] Trim, P.R.J. (2008). 'Effective communication and persuasion for behaviour change', *The Malicious Exploitation of Information Systems Conference,* Master Class Session (7th November), University College London, University of London

[3] Ljungberg, J. (2000) 'Open source movements as a model for organising', *European Journal of Information Systems*, Vol 9, No. 4, pp.208-216.

[4] Stewart, K. J. (2003) 'Trust transfer on the World Wide Web', *Organization Science*, Vol 14, No. 1, pp.5-17.

[5] Dahlander, L., and McKelvey, M. (2005) 'Who is not developing open source software? Non-users, users, and developers', *Economics of Innovation and New Technology*, Vol 14, No. 7, pp. 617-636.

[6] Baker, S. (2003) *New Consumer Marketing: Managing a Living Demand System,* Chichester, John Wiley and Sons.

[7] Nivet, J-F. (2004) 'Corporate and public governances in transition: the limits of property rights and the significance of legal institutions', *The European Journal of Comparative Economics*, Vol 1, No. 2, pp.3-21.http://eaces.liuc.it

[8] Achrol, R.S., and Kotler, P. (1999) 'Marketing in the network economy', *Journal of Marketing*, Vol 63 (Special Issue), pp.146-163.

[9] Child, J., and McGrath, R.G. (2001) 'Organizations unfettered: organizational form in an information-intensive economy', *Academy of Management Journal*, Vol 44, No. 6, pp.1135-1148.

[10] Trim, P.R.J., and Lee, Y-I. (2008). 'A strategic marketing intelligence and multi-organisational resilience framework', *European Journal of Marketing*, Vol 42 No 7/8, pp.731-745.

[11] Pittaway, L., Robertson, M., Munir, K., Denyer, D., and Neely, A. (2004) 'Networking and innovation: a systematic review of the evidence', *International Journal of Management Reviews*, Vol 5/6, No. 3/4, pp.137-168.

[12] Marshall, R.S., and Brown, D. (2003) 'The strategy of sustainability: a systems perspective on environmental initiatives', *California Management Review*, Vol 46, No 1, pp.101-126.

[13] Preece, J., Abras, C., and Maloney-Krichmar, D. (2004) 'Designing and developing online communities: research speaks to emerging practice', *International Journal of Web Based Communities*, Vol 1, No. 1, pp.2-18.

[14] Bose, R. (2004) 'E-government: infrastructure and technologies for education and training', *Electronic Government*, Vol 1, No 4, pp.349-361.

[15] Sharma, S.K., and Gupta, J.N.D. (2004) 'Web services architecture for m-government: issues and challenges', *Electronic Government*, Vol 1, No. 4, pp.462-474.

[16] Buzan, B. (1995) 'Security, the state, the "new world order," and beyond', in R.D. Lipschutz (Ed.), *On Security: New Directions in World Politics*, New York, Columbia University Press, pp.187-211.

[17] Macdonald, S. (1998) *Information for Innovation: Managing Change from an Information Perspective*, Oxford, Oxford University Press.

[18] Von Krogh, G., and von Hippel, E. (2003) 'Editorial: special issue on open source software development', *Research Policy*, Vol 32, pp.1149-1157.

[19] Jarvenpaa, S.L., Tiller, E.H., and Simons, R. (2003) 'Regulation and the Internet: public choice insights for business organizations', *California Management Review*, Vol 46, No. 1, pp.72-85.

[20] O'Mahony, S. (2003) 'Guarding the commons: how community managed software projects protect their work', *Research Policy*, Vol 23, pp. 1179-1198.

[21] Beesley, L.G.A. (2003) 'Science policy in changing times: are governments poised to take full advantage of an institution in transition? *Research Policy*, Vol 23, pp.1519-1531.

[22] USGAO. (2004) *Critical Infrastructure Protection: Improving Information Sharing with Infrastructure Sectors*. GAO-04-780. (June). Washington, D.C., Unites States General Accounting Office.

[23] Smith, H.L., and Dickson, K. (2003) 'Geo-cultural influences and critical factors in inter-firm collaboration', *International Journal of Technology Management*, Vol 25, No. 1/2, pp.34-50.

[24] Coles, A-M., Harris, L., and Dickson, K. (2003) 'Testing goodwill: conflict and cooperation in new product development networks', *International Journal of Technology Management*, Vol 25, No. 1/2, pp.51-64.

[25] Treverton, G.F. (2001) *Reshaping National Intelligence in an Age of Information*, Cambridge, Cambridge University Press.

[26] Trim, P. (2004) 'Corporate intelligence and national security: partnerships and future direction', *The First CAMIS Security Management Conference*. (20th October). London, Birkbeck College, University of London.

[27] Howells, J., and Nedeva, M. (2003) 'The international dimension to industry-academic links', *International Journal of Technology Management*, Vol 25, No. 1/2, pp.5-17.

[28] Shultz, R.H., Godson, R., and Quester, G.H. (Eds.). (1997) *Security Studies for the 21st Century*, Washington, D.C., Brassey's.

[29] Prescott, J.E., and Miller, S.H. (Eds.). (2001) *Proven Strategies in Competitive Intelligence: Lessons from the Trenches*, New York, John Wiley and Sons.

[30] Hussey, D., and Jenster, P. (1999) *Competitor Intelligence: Turning Analysis into Success*, Chichester, John Wiley and Sons.

[31] Inamete, U.B. (2001) *Foreign Policy Decision-Making in Nigeria*, Selinsgrove/London, Susquehanna University Press/Associated University Presses.

[32] Friedman, G., Friedman, M., Chapman, C., and Baker, J.S. (1998) *The Intelligence Edge,* London, Century Limited/Random House Limited.

[33] Vegh, S. (2003) 'Classifying forms of online activism: the case of cyberprotests against the World Bank', in M. McCaughey and M.D. Ayers (Eds.), *Cyberactivism: Online Activism in Theory and Practice*, London/New York, Routledge, pp.71-95.

[34] Trim, P.R.J. (2003). 'Public and private sector cooperation in counteracting cyberterrorism', *International Journal of Intelligence and CounterIntelligence*, Vol 16, No. 4, pp.594-608.

[35] Gandy, O.H. (2003) 'Data mining and surveillance in the post-9/11 environment', in K. Ball and F. Webster (Eds.). *The Intensification of Surveillance: Crime, Terrorism and Warfare in the Information Age,* London, Pluto Press, pp.26-41.

[36] Herman, M. (1997) *Intelligence Power in Peace and War,* Cambridge, Cambridge University Press.

[37] Lahneman, W.J. (2004-2005) 'Knowledge-sharing in the intelligence community after 9/11', *International Journal of Intelligence and CounterIntelligence*, Vol 17, No. 4, pp.614-633.

[38] Hitz, F.P., and Weiss, B.J. (2004) 'Helping the CIA and FBI connect the dots in the war on terror', *International Journal of Intelligence and CounterIntelligence*, Vol 17, No. 1, pp.1-41.

[39] Trim, P. R. J. (2005) 'The GISES model for counteracting organized crime and international terrorism', *International Journal of Intelligence and CounterIntelligence*, Vol 18, No. 3, pp.451-472.

[40] Sheffi, Y. (2005) *The Resilient Enterprise: Overcoming Vulnerability for Competitive Advantage*, Cambridge, Massachusetts, The MIT Press.

[41] Krishnamurthy, S. (2003) 'A managerial overview of open source software', *Business Horizons*, Vol 46, No. 5, pp. 47-56.

[42] Appelbe, B. (2003) 'The future of open source software', *Journal of Research and Practice in Information Technology*, Vol 35, No. 4, pp.227-236.

[43] Von Hippel, E., and von Krogh, G. (2003) 'Open source software and the "Private-Collective" innovation model: issues for organization science', *Organization Science*, Vol 14, No. 2, pp. 209-223.

[44] Jerbic, M. (2009) 'The economics of information, security and information security', *The Cyber Security Economics of Information Security Special Interest Group*, Internet lecture (2.20 to 2.50pm on 27th January), Regus London Victoria, London.

In: Strategizing Resilience and Reducing Vulnerability
Editors: Peter R.J. Trim and Jack Caravelli

ISBN 978-1-60741-693-7
© 2009 Nova Science Publishers, Inc.

Chapter 7

COLLABORATIVE SECURITY: POINTERS FOR GOVERNMENT REPRESENTATIVES AND CORPORATE SECURITY PERSONNEL

Peter R.J. Trim

ABSTRACT

International criminal organizations are forming working associations and alliances with international terrorist groups and these networks are becoming increasingly imaginative in the way they share knowledge and transmit data and information to each other. As a consequence, government officials and corporate security experts need to develop closer links between the corporate sector and relevant government departments in order to counteract the threats posed. Senior managers in the partnership arrangement need to find unique solutions to recurring problems and one way that this can be achieved is through a transparent organizational culture that facilitates information sharing. Policy makers also need to think in terms of integrating homeland security objectives in their country with homeland security objectives in other countries, if that is, a collectivist approach to security is to be adopted.

INTRODUCTION

Governments around the world are becoming increasingly concerned about the level, intensity and diversity of organized criminal activities and the fact that criminals are highly mobile and appear to cross borders with ease. Although the general public want the law enforcement agencies to be both robust and visible, it has to be said that criminal activity is multi-faceted and involves individuals, organizations and unscrupulous government officials. The issue of how best to serve the general public, bearing in mind resources are limited and there is no unified, worldwide police force and judicial system in place, focuses the mind of the policy advisor.

It has been acknowledged that law enforcement officers and intelligence officers need to work more closely together; share information and utilize the benefits of technology; if that is, they are to thwart the actions of criminals. Technology is used to track, monitor and record unlawful activity, and what needs to be borne in mind is that those involved in monitoring the work of organized criminals and terrorist networks (a growing percentage of whom are using the Internet in order to establish cells and fake front companies that engage in money laundering activities), need to introduce innovative intelligence policies, if that is, they are to keep control of the situation.

It is true to say that serious crime will continue to focus the attention of senior police officers and their political masters. However, as criminals and terrorists become more sophisticated, the ways in which the authorities deal with them will come under greater scrutiny (especially ethical issues incorporating human rights for example). Furthermore, policing and intelligence methods do need to become more specialized and focus more on crime prevention. The ability to monitor trends, identify changing patterns of criminality; and predict possible terrorist outcomes; are essential intellectual qualities that need to be developed through time. Areas of concern continue to be counterfeiting, the trafficking of drugs and individuals, money laundering, motor industry theft, computer hacking and cracking, and terrorist activities for example.

The chapter is structured in the following way. First, attention is paid to the topic of Europol and the public interest and this is followed by a section entitled organizational culture and organizational learning. Next, the topic of interoperability is addressed and is followed by the situation facing small companies. Attention is then given to the collectivist approach to security and a conclusion is provided.

EUROPOL AND THE PUBLIC INTEREST

European liaison officers based at Europol, collect, pool, process, analyze and interpret data and provide guidance to participating police forces (Watson, 2005). By harmonizing investigative techniques, it is possible to accumulate expertise and when necessary, ensure that police forces in different parts of the world that are working simultaneously on a case of investigation find unique solutions to recurring problems. Although the police and security service (also assisted by other law enforcement personnel) are able to disrupt criminal activity as well as arrest criminals, there is an increasing issue which is that international criminals are forming working associations and alliances with international terrorist groups and these networks are becoming increasingly imaginative in the way they share knowledge and transmit data and information to each other. As a consequence, information is needed relating to different types of criminal activity and perceived threats, but because terrorism is viewed differently from government to government, and the priorities of governments differ, one cannot suggest that there will be a uniform approach to the problem. It has to be said that a European FBI is needed in order to integrate more firmly the work carried out by the police forces based in Europe (Trim and Caravelli, 2007, pp.142-143). The question should not be is a European FBI necessary but what law enforcement initiatives need to be introduced in order to allow law enforcement officers, security and intelligence officers, and staff based in other relevant organizations (including the corporate sector) to work more closely together in order to seek and receive information and assistance from police forces abroad. Placing this in an international context is vital owing to the fact that both China and Russia have a number of problems (criminal gangs for example) and the pressure associated with rapid economic development is likely to give rise to anti-government feeling and actions as people become displaced from the land and/or witness their assets being taken from them and redistributed. Furthermore, as the opportunities present themselves, counterfeiting and money laundering are likely to intensify as criminals focus their attentions on brand leaders and move swiftly to benefit from expanding markets.

Caravelli (2008, p.15) has provided a unique insight into one of the major problems associated with the post-Cold War era that is haunting security and intelligence officers today: "Worries about Russia's deepening financial instability also spilled over into the security arena, becoming linked to Washington's concerns about the security of Russia's vast nuclear arsenal. Outsiders could not easily penetrate that closed and tightly monitored world while insiders with access to materials that could be sold for quick profit-a situation that would soon become a major security threat-were intimidated from doing so". This raises many questions relating to how open governments are prepared to be about situations that can be considered very high risk and how cooperative security officials will be, if they consider that the publicity surrounding an event/situation may have adverse affects on the country's image and its standing in the world. It also raises issues and concerns regarding how senior managers in the corporate sector respond to geo-political threats. Indeed, Wernick (2006, p.68) has indicated that "terrorism is among the top concerns in the boardrooms of multinational companies". It is not surprising to note, therefore, that corporate security experts are advocating closer links between the corporate sector and relevant government departments.

Watson (2005) has indicated that whereas Interpol was created to facilitate the sharing of information between EU states, Europol was established in order to assist the integration of EU policing activities and this suggests that Europol has a political dimension to it. Watson (2005) has outlined the fact that Europol staff have been heavily involved in drug enforcement and are increasingly sharing information relating to terrorist actions, and as a consequence there is enhanced cooperation between EU states, the USA and the Russian Federation. Watson (2005) has provided some useful insights into future security and intelligence policy by stating that: "The creation of Europol can be seen as a unique milestone in the creation of international policing bodies. This is due, in part, to its close association with the European integration process, and the fact that its origins are political, as opposed to functional. Indeed, unlike Interpol, which was established in order to facilitate the sharing of information between states – an obvious need, Europol can claim no such immediate legitimacy. However, although it may be true that to begin with, law enforcement within the EU had not demanded the establishment of such a body, it has still managed to grow and increase its remit. Further, in association with other EU bodies, including EuroJust, Europol has managed to calve a distinct and increasingly relevant 'niche' in the policing field.

This can be seen by the fact that at first, its only function was to share data on drugs and drug runners. Since then it has established a number of other functions, which permeate into virtually every area of legitimate police concern. The Europol Convention has thus created a robust and expanding strata within the sphere of international police cooperation. It is also clear that …. in particular the terrorist outrages of September the 11th 2001, Madrid and most recently London, massively helped the argument for Europol. Not only is there a clear need to share information between EU states, but there is also a perceived requirement to liaise with other interests, most notably the USA and the Russian Federation, via a collective 'European' voice.

Despite this there has been considerable unease about these developments – and from across the political spectrum. Not only are there serious implications for human rights, but in addition, Europol has become a highly publicised example of the changing nature of international security, and the place of the Nation State within an increasingly globalised world. Nevertheless Europol is a logical and necessary reflection of the Europeanisation process, which includes the reduction in border controls between EU states, as well as the closer ties developing between its various members. Further, the benefits of liaison, the ability to exploit computer systems, and the need to establish workable protocols are all legitimate goals."

Ultimately, working partnerships will be formed that that result in increased opportunities for finding unique solutions to recurring problems. Although the police, security and intelligence services (also assisted by other law enforcement agencies) are able to disrupt criminal activity (and in the case of the police force arrest criminals), there is an increasingly urgent issue to address. International criminals are finding ways of working with international terrorists groups and as a consequence information is needed relating to the context and infrastructural aspects of different types of criminal activity and threat. However, because the priorities of governments differ, it has to be said that a European FBI is needed in order to integrate more firmly the work carried out by the police forces in Europe. The question should not be is a European FBI necessary but what law enforcement initiatives need to be introduced in order to allow law enforcement officers, and security and intelligence officers, to work more closely together in order to seek and receive information and assistance from other police forces abroad.

Western society in particular needs to weigh very carefully issues of human rights and data protection, against the threats posed by counterfeiting, acts of industrial espionage and terrorist actions, if that is, the current quality of life is to be maintained. What is clear, is that future cooperation involving law enforcement agencies, and security and intelligence agencies, both at home and abroad, is likely to intensify as the potential threat level rises and the nature and degree of potential damage associated with a threat manifesting is made clearer. The issue of fair trials abroad is something that can and does receive a lot of media attention and is a particular area of future concern as related publicity, if handled badly, may well result in activist action on a world wide basis.

ORGANIZATIONAL CULTURE AND ORGANIZATIONAL LEARNING

Law enforcement agencies, security and intelligence agencies, and central government bureaucracies, have varying types of organizational culture. An open and transparent organizational culture is most likely to facilitate partnership development and result in manageable working arrangements between partner organizations. Hence it is essential for an organizational review to take into account the internal operating systems that exist/are to be implemented and how changes in the external environment impact on a partner organization. By embracing the organizational learning concept, it is possible for senior managers to develop a transformational leadership style that ensures that an organizational review and audit is managed proactively. Should a range of management systems be put in place, this should be done in such a way that the organization's performance is enhanced.

Managing change in a constructive and transparent fashion is far from easy, especially when it requires that managers and those lower down the hierarchy are required to attend a series of staff development programmes. In order to obtain the support of organizational members, it is essential that individual staff have a clearly defined role to play and that they are rewarded accordingly. Keeping staff loyal to the organization is a key challenge, especially when some individuals may be of the opinion that they are not valued highly. Senior managers need to ensure that staff adopt a long-term approach to management problem solving, and devise working practices and routines that are future oriented (embrace advances in technology for example). Senior management need to ensure that the necessary management development support mechanisms are in place to assist individual staff development, and management development needs to be approached from the perspective of theory building. It can also be suggested that individual learning programmes need to be tailored to career development opportunities. International project groups can be used to foster information sharing and knowledge transfer between partner organizations.

Lee (2005) has indicated that the organizational learning concept can be used to promote the organization's value system and can at the same time facilitate incremental change. As regards the implementation of transformational change, Lee (2005) suggests that senior managers need to distinguish between leadership and strategic leadership, and adopt a dual leadership approach, in order that junior managers can devise and implement new management models that result in improved decision-making processes. The main advantage of this approach is that it should result in more open communication and an acceptance of what is known as institutionalizing organizational learning, which can facilitate government to government co-operation; government to organization co-operation; and organization to organizational co-operation (Lee, 2005). Lee (2005) has stated: "In order that an organization improves its level of performance, it is necessary for top management to make strategic decisions that provide it with a clearly defined direction. By embracing the concept of organizational learning, top management can encourage staff to improve their knowledge and skill base through time. However, problems do occur and a major problem is how top managers can encourage their staff to learn on a continuing basis, and to co-operate with staff outside their immediate department. The learning process is not just about acquiring knowledge and skills, it is also about developing a vision that is based on understanding the values that are promoted by top management. Hence, staff at various levels throughout the organization need to identify with the organizational value system and embrace incremental change. This is necessary if an organization is to adapt to a changing international environment and at the same time undergo a change in organizational culture.

Attention needs to be given to national cultural value systems and how these value systems influence organizational value systems. Top managers employed by global organizations do need to distinguish between leadership and strategic leadership, and manage through a dual leadership approach. By adopting a dual leadership approach, managers will be able to devise and implement new management models and processes that result in integrated decision-making mechanisms that improve the decision-making process".

INTEROPERABILITY

Interoperability is key with respect to managers in Europe developing a coherent equipment and systems policy and getting people to think in a strategic and holistic manner. Attention also needs to be given to information requirements, because policy makers need to think in terms of how information gaps are to be identified and how their immediate and long-term objectives are to be realized. Furthermore, it is necessary to think in terms of how systems can be put in place to facilitate information flows and in particular, ensure that as few as possible interruptions occur as this will save time. It can also be pointed out that if delays do occur, then lost opportunities are likely to result.

Spender (2005) has indicated that owing to the fact that many agencies are in existence that focus on various criminals and their activities, it is not surprising to learn that a Network of Enabled Capability (NEC) of interoperable systems and databases is needed in order to facilitate intelligence work. The need exists to "review the sharing of information between departments and governments" and this means that more attention has to be paid to interoperability assurance for government projects (Spender, 2005).

With respect to the issue of homeland security, government policy needs to be clear and acceptable; information exchange requirements need to be planned; and investment in technology and technological systems need to be based on integrated procurement (Yates, 2005). Furthermore, it is useful for policy makers to think in terms of integrating homeland security objectives in their country with homeland security objectives in other countries, if that is, world wide working relationships are to be developed between governments and the various law enforcement, security and intelligence agencies. By identifying who the stakeholders are, it is possible to devise training and management development programmes that ensure that officers have the skill, knowledge and confidence to manage change and set new standards of performance. Government needs to be committed to producing architectures that facilitate interoperability and information sharing, and any shortfalls identified can be rectified in a proactive and timely manner.

THE SITUATION FACING SMALL COMPANIES

In order to counteract the various threats posed, senior managers in international firms have authorized an increase in corporate security expenditure (Wernick, 2006, p.68). However, this is not likely to be mirrored by small companies, or if it is, it will be on a much smaller scale. Galpin (2005) has paid attention to the vulnerability of small companies. He has noted that small companies occupy a single site, and in the case of a minor disruption may not be that affected that extensively but in the case of a major disruption, may well find it impossible to continue trading. For example, if the building within which the small company is based is totally destroyed, and all the staff are killed, then it is very possible that the company would no longer exist. Therefore, Galpin (2005) has questioned why small companies need to engage in business continuity planning. Although senior management in a small company may have installed various forms of physical security (uniformed guards and CCTV for example), none of these would deter a suicide bomber (Galpin, 2005). Owing to the fact that managers in small companies have limited budgets, it could be argued that managers do not have the resources to invest in information back-up facilities that are many miles away from the company (and also the possible area of impact) and this is of concern to politicians.

THE COLLECTIVIST SECURITY APPROACH

Law enforcement, security and intelligence officers, will continue to focus their efforts on what type of security threat is likely to manifest in the years ahead. Indeed, Caravelli (2008, p.155) has indicated that: "Political problems require a political approach that reflects nuance and sophistication as well as the last resort-application of force. The threat of radical fundamentalism almost certainly will remain a pre-eminent challenge to U.S. national security for the foreseeable future". As well as focusing attention on hot spots overseas, one must remember that the U.S., like countries in Western Europe, is still a target. Ervin (2006, p.176) has put this in context: "The importance of getting homeland security-related intelligence right should now be apparent to all. We had the "dots" before the last attack; it's just that no one connected them in time. The Department of Homeland Security's Intelligence unit was supposed to fix that, but even its own leaders give it a grade of no better than five or six on a scale of ten. Given the ability and the determination of terrorists to strike again, can we really afford to have only a 50-50 chance of stopping them?"

In order to produce effective countermeasures, various intra-organizational forms of working need to be established. Should this be the case, it can be argued that security will not be the priority of a few, but will in essence be viewed from a society perspective. A collectivist approach to security does, therefore, need to be placed within the context of international relations. Corporate security staff have a very distinct role to play as regards the collectivist security approach because security managers and directors of corporate security are known to have a military, police or intelligence background. This equips them adequately to assume the role of first responder and their background, experience and network of contacts suggests that they have a psychological commitment to the nation. First responders are, therefore, by definition, an integral component of society's security architecture and can be called on to perform certain duties in the event of a major disaster/emergency.

It can also be suggested that a growing percentage of security and intelligence work is now being outsourced and two questions emerge: Who polices what private security companies do? And how are industry security standards to be protected? One of the key issues here is industrial espionage and the fact that unscrupulous overseas governments can and do establish front companies with the intention of obtaining sensitive data and information. This suggests that a collectivist approach to security is needed that is reasonably flexible and holistic, and which bridges the gap between the public-private divide (maintaining law and order and corporate security objectives).

Law enforcement, security and intelligence officers, need to ensure that as well as a comprehensive architecture being developed that facilitates partnership development between the various intelligence and security agencies, government departments, law enforcement agencies, and various organizations in the public and private sectors, attention is also given to specific organizational architectures that embrace organizational change. The reason for this, is that the concept of knowledge management (however defined) needs to be fully embraced if that is a collectivist security approach is to be embraced on a long-term basis.

Trim (2005a) has stated that: "The international environment is complex and becoming increasingly unpredictable. It can be suggested, therefore, that the elimination of risk and the reduction of uncertainty should not be the priority of a few, but that a collectivist approach to security and intelligence work needs to be adopted. The concept of security does need to be placed in different contexts as governments, organizations, and individuals based in different parts of the world view problems, threats and vulnerabilities differently. This suggests that academics, government representatives and experts in the public and private sectors need to come together in order to rethink what security is and how security and intelligence studies can be developed in order to raise the profile of security and intelligence officers. Placing the subject matter in a broader context, is useful vis-à-vis making public the work of the law enforcement agencies and it can be argued that national governments need to adopt a similar view to disasters and emergencies. This is because of the fact that international organizations and institutions may in the years ahead need to play a different role from the one they play at present. It also means that organizations around the world need to devise ways in which to share relevant information and to co-operate more fully in times of crisis.

In order to fully comprehend the problem of providing security to a growing world population, it is necessary to think in terms of sustainability. However, the factors influencing change are themselves complex and deep rooted. Being able to predict a threat is necessary but so too is being able to predict the consequences associated with the outcome of a threat materializing. Owing to this, it is necessary for intelligence and security experts and their advisors, to think in terms of developing a comprehensive architecture that facilitates the development of partnership arrangements throughout the public and private sectors that provide open communication that allows relevant information to be shared. This being the case, the work of organized criminal syndicates and international terrorist groups can be counteracted".

The Global Intelligence and Security Environmental Sustainability (GISES) Model (Trim, 2005b) can be used to focus the attention of policy makers and their advisors on ways in which to disrupt and destroy criminal-terrorist network arrangements. The GISES model embraces the concept of knowledge management, proactive leadership and teamworking. By adopting the GISES model, it is possible that intelligence and security work will be viewed as mainstream, and that the profile of security and intelligence officers in both the public and private sectors, will be raised.

Turning attention to companies operating in an ever increasingly complex business environment, it can be suggested that senior managers need to devise robust business continuity plans, which should ensure that the subject of risk is addressed adequately. Senior managers or more specifically a business continuity manager, can explain why risk reduction strategies need to be placed in the context of reducing an organization's vulnerability. There is a clear need for senior managers to ensure that corporate security objectives are in line with government objectives vis-à-vis national security and this means that business leaders and top government officials need to be aware that various bodies of knowledge (management and political science for example) are drawn on and interpreted from an interdisciplinary perspective. This is especially important in the context of a failing state and all the ramifications associated with the government of the failing state not being able to maintain law and order.

The Global Intelligence and Security Environmental Sustainability (GISES) model (Trim, 2005b) should make it possible for governments to adopt a range of security and intelligence initiatives, which can be linked with theory building. The Anti-Terrorist Business-Politico (ATBP) model (Trim and Caravelli, 2007) is a case in point. For example, the ATBP model can be used to focus the collaborative efforts of those involved in fighting terrorism (corporate security specialists, law enforcement officers, security and intelligence officers, politicians and military personal for example). Furthermore, it can also be used to direct policy at the highest political level and assist intra-government and inter-government communication and cooperation. Viewed as a generic model, it can assist inter-government decision-making and enhance the operational capacity of security and intelligence officers. The ATBP model can be deployed by high level security and intelligence decision makers to counter a range of specific threats that are of international concern, and has a high degree of flexibility which suggests that it can be adapted as required. Those that deploy the model will be able to formulate and implement security and intelligence action plans that deal with both the immediate threat itself and the consequences and ramifications of an incident. Hence the ATBP model is a tool to be used by those advising high level political decision-makers on various aspects of security and intelligence.

It is important that politicians, government policy advisors, and senior military personnel, working with law enforcement, security and intelligence officers, re-evaluate the concept of international security. Dannreuther (2007) has raised many questions about what the term international security encompasses and how the subject should be interpreted. A collectivist approach to international security, assumes that those at the apex of the political strategic decision-making process are willing and able to share information about potential high level threats and then commit resources to eradicate the foreseen problem(s). But this may not be the case. The pressure associated with being the world's policeman is enormous and so too are the resources needed to undertake, what often is a thankless and continuing task. Security threats can be considered multi-faceted and multi-dimensional, and the ever growing cooperation between organized criminal syndicates and terrorist networks suggests that no one nation is equipped to undertake the role of being the world's policeman.

The illegal trade in secrets is expected to grow as some nations compete ever harder to dominate certain industries. The sale of secrets, solutions and technologies, and the honey trap approach, are real and likely to become more engrained in day to day life. To counteract this situation, a greater and sustained effort is needed to identify future vulnerabilities and put systems in place to ensure that the countermeasures are both timely and effective.

As well as government, companies will be required to invest more heavily in security, and this raises questions and concerns relating to who owns a nation's critical information infrastructures. Hyslop (2007, p.3) has focused attention on many issues relating to critical infrastructure and has advocated a partnership approach owing to the fact that "The processes of today are not in the sole hands of any Government, they are in the hands of a number of different partners".

CONCLUSION

So what does this mean for government? One interpretation is that government and the various policy advisors, will work more closely with law enforcement agencies, security and intelligence agencies, and the military, as well as independent think tanks and university research teams, in order to identify future potential threats and at the same time, establish ways in which to deal successfully with them. This suggests that there will be a redesigning of security and intelligence activities. It also suggests that new methodological approaches will be developed to study the subject of international security.

Security and intelligence work is highly demanding and requires that those involved have intellectual, linguistic and technical capabilities. They also need stamina and a diplomatic disposition. Those that climb the hierarchy and assume positions of responsibility need to be good at managing change. They also need to be viewed as good role models with respect to producing innovative ideas and management processes. By providing new insights into terrorism and the work of organized criminal syndicates, policy advisors will be better able to devise long-term solutions that encompass enhanced co-operation between security, intelligence and law enforcement officers. Another advantage of this approach, is that it should be easier to build firmer links between government agencies and institutions and organizations in the private sector.

REFERENCES

Caravelli, J. (2008). *Nuclear Insecurity: Understanding the Threat from Rogue Nations and Terrorists*. Westport, Connecticut and London: Praeger Security International.

Dannreuther, R. (2007). *International Security: The Contemporary Agenda*. Cambridge: Polity Press.

Ervin, C.K. (2006). *Open Target: Where America is Vulnerable to Attack*. Basingstoke: Palgrave Macmillan.

Galpin, C. (2005). "How a small organisation responds to increased security risk post 7/7 in the real world." *The Second CAMIS Security Management Conference: Managing Complexity and Developing Partnership Initiatives*, Birkbeck College, University of London (23rd September).

Hyslop, M. (2007). *Critical Information Infrastructures: Resilience and Protection*. New York: Springer.

Lee, Y-I. (2005). "A strategic model for facilitating inter-organizational and intra-organizational development." *The Second CAMIS Security Management Conference: Managing Complexity and Developing Partnership Initiatives*, Birkbeck College, University of London (23rd September).

Spender, H. (2005). "Coherent information interoperability is essential for integrated homeland security." *The Second CAMIS Security Management Conference: Managing Complexity and Developing Partnership Initiatives*, Birkbeck College, University of London (23rd September).

Trim, P.R.J. (2005a). "The global intelligence and security environmental sustainability model: Counteracting organized crime and international terrorism". *The Second CAMIS Security*

Management Conference: Managing Complexity and Developing Partnership Initiatives, Birkbeck College, University of London (23rd September).

Trim, P.R.J. (2005b) "The GISES model for counteracting organized crime and international terrorism". *International Journal of Intelligence and CounterIntelligence*, 18 (3), pp.451-472.

Trim, P.R.J., and Caravelli, J. (2007). "Counteracting and preventing terrorist actions: A generic model to facilitate inter-government cooperation". In: *Terrorism Issues: Threat Assessment, Consequences and Prevention*. Merkidze, A.W. (Ed). New York: Nova Science Publishers, Inc., pp.135-152.

Watson, N. (2005). "Europol: Form, function and implications." *The Second CAMIS Security Management Conference: Managing Complexity and Developing Partnership Initiatives*, Birkbeck College, University of London (23rd September).

Wernick, D.A. (2006). "Terror incognito: International business in an era of heightened geopolitical risk". In: *Corporate Strategies Under International Terrorism and Adversity*. Suder, G.G.S. (Ed). Cheltenham: Edward Elgar Publishing Limited, pp.59-82.

Yates, S. (2005). "What should be Government's role in preparing a business response to disruptive major events?" *The Second CAMIS Security Management Conference: Managing Complexity and Developing Partnership Initiatives*, Birkbeck College, University of London (23rd September).

In: Strategizing Resilience and Reducing Vulnerability
Editors: Peter R.J. Trim and Jack Caravelli
ISBN 978-1-60741-693-7
© 2009 Nova Science Publishers, Inc.

Chapter 8

ISOMORPHIC LEARNING IN BUSINESS CONTINUITY: A REVIEW OF HOW THE "LESSONS IDENTIFIED" WERE SHARED AFTER THE 7TH JULY, 2005 TERRORIST INCIDENTS

Kevin Brear

ABSTRACT

This chapter sets out the case that the employment of Isomorphic Learning is appropriate in the discipline of business continuity and then seeks to establish how the business continuity lessons identified from the events in London of the 7th of July, 2005 were collected and then disseminated in the industry. The chapter describes the methods of research and some of the barriers encountered, but then also reports on some of the successes and positive outcomes. Some of the lessons identified during the research process are reported in the chapter and it is shown that much of the available information was held in silos (stovepipes) and not shared with the wider industry. The implications of that latter approach are discussed and suggested solutions are offered.

INTRODUCTION

"On the 7th July 2005, four bombs were detonated in central London. Seven people were killed on a train at Aldgate station. Seven were killed at Edgware Road. Twenty-four were killed at King's Cross/Russell Square. Fourteen were killed on a No. 30 bus at Tavistock Square. Seven-hundred people were treated for injuries. Hundreds more suffered psychological trauma, which for many people, persists to this day and has irrevocably changed their lives" (Barnes et al., 2006:6).

The events of the 7th July caused widespread disruption to London's transport system and to many other areas of society. One of the groups that suffered disruption on that day was the business community. Many organisations within the business community had previously undertaken a number of measures to protect their operations from disruption and the generic term for this activity is business continuity management. On the 7th July and immediately afterwards, a number of businesses were forced to enact business continuity plans or to invoke special measures to maintain business operations. These activities were met with varying degrees of success. In some organisations, a review took place after the events, to measure the level of that success. A number of debriefs and conferences also took place, a number of articles were published, a number of research surveys were conducted and some of the results were then published.

At one of the events held to review the response measures, the British Bankers Association conference entitled *A half day seminar, examining lessons learnt from 7/7*, a delegate, who was a senior business continuity manager within a large financial organisation, stated that his organisation had been unprepared to deal with the loss of mobile telephone communications in the immediate aftermath of the explosions. Another delegate, who was a business continuity consultant, stated in response that he was surprised that the first delegate had not absorbed the "lessons learnt" following the attacks on the World Trade Centre on 9/11 and the subsequent problems with mobile phones in New York after that incident.

The events of the 11th September 2001 were widely reported and the business continuity issues from those events were also reported and have formed the basis of a number of reports and documents. The subject of business continuity "lessons learnt" being communicated was considered worthy of further exploration by the author and the decision was made to review the methods of collection and subsequent dissemination of the business continuity lessons identified from the 7th of July events.

The author formulated a research proposal and discussed it with Tony Moore of Cranfield University and the method of approach was reviewed. Moore stated that "lessons learnt" was a common misnomer that was frequently used in business continuity circles and that a truer descriptor should be "lessons identified". Moore suggested that a lesson was only truly learnt once remedial action had been taken to prevent a reoccurrence of the same error and that numerous academic works had shown where the same errors had been repeated time and time again. This view is apparently supported by Toft and Reynolds (2005:66).

The effectiveness of transmission of the business continuity lessons identified was not examined, but merely the methods in which the lessons were collected and disseminated. It was felt that the measure of the absorption of the communications could form a subject for further research.

The study was conducted using a number of data collection methods, firstly through personal observation, secondly through attendance at conferences and seminars, thirdly through collection of material published in an assortment of media and finally through unstructured interviews. The study identified that there appeared to be a large number of information sources available and this will be reflected in the review of the material obtained. The information sources were similar to those as suggested that might be anticipated in previous research (Toft & Reynolds, 2005).

The research revealed that the lessons identified appeared to be held within a number of silos and that there did not appear to be a single point of reference where a collection of the lessons identified could be reviewed. One of the objectives of the research was to gain a wider collection of the information with a view to publishing the conclusions through a number of sources. The research also revealed in the literary review that there appeared to be a gap between academic learning and the business world (Mittelstaedt, 2005:133) and a possible solution to the gap was identified.

LITERATURE REVIEW

Isomorphic Learning

The underpinning premise to the study was that of isomorphic learning, as espoused by Toft and Reynolds (2005) in their book *"Learning from Disasters"*. Toft and Reynolds stated that learning from disasters could have value in preparing for future unwanted events. Toft and Reynolds suggested that errors can be found to be repeated in a number of different disasters' reports and provide examples to support that argument. Toft and Reynolds (2005:65) whilst specifically looking at disasters and using information gained from public inquiries and other sources identified that, at some level, patterns can be found in disasters and they quote Lagadec "…the disaster must not be seen like the meteorite that falls out of the sky on an innocent world; the disaster, most often, is anticipated, and on multiple occasions." Toft and Reynolds (2005:66) argued that if disasters have patterns within them then it may be possible that there may be patterns within what is learnt from those disasters.

Toft and Reynolds (2005:30) built upon the previous work conducted by Turner (1997) into the causation and evolution of disasters. Turner (1997:71) developed a model for disasters, in which he theorised that each disaster has six clearly identifiable stages. This model was called the Disaster Sequence Model (see Table 1).

Table 1. The six stages associated with a disaster

Stage I – notional normal starting points.
(a) Initially culturally accepted beliefs about the World and its hazards.
(b) Associated precautionary norms set out in laws, codes of practice, mores and folkways.
Stage II – the incubation period, the accumulated set of events that are treated as "everyday" problems within a socio - technological system and the relevance of those precursors is not recognised.
Stage III – a precipitating event, of such an attention grasping nature that the event is recognised to be outside the arena of the events in Stage II.
Stage IV – onset, the inability to deal with the situation with the normally available responses or resources becomes apparent.
Stage V – rescue and salvage, special arrangements are implemented to assist in the recovery from the event.
Stage VI – full cultural readjustment, an inquiry or assessment of the aetiology of the event is carried out.

Source: (Turner, 1997:71)

Turner's model envisaged that the knowledge gained from the Stage VI (1997:77) activities would be incorporated into the organisational culture to attempt to prevent a re-occurrence of a similar set of circumstances or at least produce strategies to mitigate the effects of such a re-occurrence.

Turner and Pidgeon (1997:173) comment upon the work of Toft and Reynolds in relation to the development of the theory of Isomorphic Learning and state:

"…The subsequent research by Brian Toft was designed to explore this critical issue of cultural adjustment for a disaster, focusing in particular upon a sample of major fires and explosions that had occurred in the UK. The account of man-made disasters …was based solely upon reports from official inquiries. Toft on the other hand supplemented documentary sources with direct interviews with a sample of individuals and organisations who had been involved in the incubation periods underlying the selective events. His work starts from the observation that while there are indeed similarities in the preconditions to major accidents and disasters, learning requires a priory some recognition of the similarities between past and present experience. A first point is that this task is far from easy where, as is the case with most complex socio-technical system failures, both the past and the future situation are dynamic and highly ill-structured. A second point is that such learning is complicated by the need often to draw lessons from samples of very few, or singular incidents and events".

Pidgeon et al., (1992:97) also acknowledge the apparent advantages of studying past failings and identifying the lessons by stating:

"There is now ample evidence that the behavioural causes of accidents and disasters involve not just individual slips and lapses, but also, as demonstrated by Turner (1978), patterns of management and organisational failings such as failures of communication, information handling, coordination and error diagnosis".

Toft and Reynolds (2005:72) stated that there are at least four ways in which organisations can be viewed as displaying similar isomorphic properties, the first, "event isomorphism"; this is where two events with different causes may lead to the situation where they both present similar hazards. Toft and Reynolds (2005) provide the example where a train signal is passed at danger because of a driver error and a second example where another train passes a signal because of a fault in the signal wiring. In both cases, the trains involved are placed at risk of being involved in a collision, by being on the wrong section of track, at the wrong time.

Toft and Reynolds (2005) state that the second type is "cross-organisational isomorphism" and this concept relates to the area of organisational activity where two very different organisations are engaged in similar activities or industries. Toft and Reynolds (2005) supply the example of two airline companies, both operating out of two different countries with the consequences of two separate cultures and regulations, however, both companies could be using similar aircraft and operating systems for those machines. The two companies could also be engaged in similar goals and objectives for each organisation.

The third type is identified as "common mode isomorphism" and relates to the situation where any number of disparate organisations are using similar tools, equipment or substances in their daily activities. Toft and Reynolds (2005:73) provide the example of polyurethane foam furnishings and the dangers associated with it, when the substance is burnt. Toft and Reynolds (2005) report that the substance has been extensively used in aircraft upholstery, domestic furnishings and vehicle interiors and so consequently many disparate organisations have been exposed to similar hazards.

The fourth type of isomorphism suggested is "self-isomorphism" and this type relates to large conglomerates and organisations that are split into smaller operating cells, each smaller cell facing similar hazards and operational challenges.

The definition of lessons identified will be harder to categorise and may even prove to be impossible to actually define. The manner in which post incident analysis takes place after a disaster or major incident is the key to this consideration. Hood and Jones (2002:75) consider this area:

"After some types of events, a judicial inquiry may take place; an example of this would be the Fennel inquiry (1988) into the events of the Kings Cross Underground Station fire. As a direct result of some of the recommendations from the conclusion of that inquiry, London Underground Limited went through a paradigm shift in its approach to fire risk reduction in its stations".

Some organisations engage in debriefs after the event in order to identify areas of weakness and strength and this allows management to develop best practice when facing similar challenges in the future. These debriefs are usually held internally and the results may or may not be shared with other stakeholders or interested parties. Finally, lessons may be learnt from internal reporting procedures of incidents and analysis of those reports. This process is widely used within the airline industry and is endorsed and regulated by national governments (Hood and Jones, 2002:79).

It has to be recognised that there are a number of barriers to Isomorphic Learning and these are perhaps best encapsulated by the views of Turner (1997:64):

" ... the problems of obtaining adequate intelligence, of avoiding transmission of the wrong information, of avoiding its dispatch to the wrong people, avoiding distortion in transmission, avoiding the failure to operate on messages when this is expected, not relying too much on informal networks created for other purposes and avoiding ambiguous communications…Since the recipient may be swamped by too much information, those attempting to communicate should beware of avoiding responsibility for selective communication by adopting the expedient of providing all the information, instead of looking at the problem from the recipients point of view, and attempting to make clear what it is thought he or she needs to know".

Business Continuity

Having established what is meant by the term isomorphic learning, consideration should now be given to the term business continuity and what is meant by that term. There is currently no industry wide accepted definition for business continuity, but Woodman (2006:1) provides a definition from *Emergency Preparedness,* the UK government guidance on part one of the Civil Contingency Act, November 2005, and states that business continuity management may be defined as:

"A Management process that helps manage the risks to the smooth running of an organisation or delivery of a service that it can operate to the extent required in the event of a disruption".

Barnes and Hiles (2005: xvii) state: "many attempts have been made to define business continuity planning and, in truth, we have probably yet to arrive at the perfect, succinct definition. The task of definition is made more difficult as a result of the wide range of different terminology used either in different parts of the English-speaking world, or by professionals operating at different levels of development (because this management practice, like so many others, takes its lead from the USA and has evolved at different speeds, and for different reasons, around the world)...business continuity management is the development of strategies, plans and actions which provide protection or alternative modes of operation for those activities or business processes which, if they were to be interrupted, might otherwise bring about a seriously damaging or potentially fatal loss to the enterprise. Business continuity planners deal with the consequences of the business threatening "what-if" scenario- what if our operations are destroyed by fire or flood? What if a negative media story drives our clients to our competitors? What if the data base upon which we depend for our sales is stolen or attacked by a virus? What if our offices are innocent victims of a terrorist attack? The list of potential threats is unending!"

As Barnes and Hiles (2005) stated there was a need for a more holistic definition for Business Continuity and the definition contained within the United Kingdom British Standards Institute BS25999-1:2006(2.3) standard document attempts to fill that apparent void and currently states that the definition for Business Continuity Management is a:

> "Holistic management process that identifies potential threats to an organization and the impacts to business operations that those threats, if realized, might cause, and which provides a framework for building organizational resilience with the capability for an effective response that safeguards the interests of its key stakeholders, reputation, brand and value-creating activities".

NOTE: Business continuity management involves managing the recovery or continuation of business activities in the event of a business disruption, and management of the overall programme through training, exercises and reviews, to ensure the business continuity plan(s) stays current and up-to-date.

Having established the underpinning theories behind isomorphic learning and reviewed some of the considerations in business continuity management, it would seem appropriate to establish any links between these two concepts. Borodzicz (2005:85) states:

> "Business continuity management is a new area of professional activity, but also an area of academic study and research, which aims to facilitate the mitigation of emergencies, crises and disasters in organizations. ...Many university management and business schools are beginning to recognise the importance of business continuity in their curricular, but coverage is still patchy at best. Where courses are offered these are normally options, rather than core, and often restricted to very specialised master degrees. This is surprising, as it is hard to imagine a management activity that is not closer to the heart of corporate life".

In his book *Risk, Crisis and Security Management,* Borodzicz (2005) devotes an entire chapter to business continuity management, including a section entitled *Identifying and assessing known risks*, in which he sets out a number of methods for hazard identification and risk assessment. At no point within the chapter does Borodzicz make any reference to the works of Turner and Pidgeon (1997), and Toft and Reynolds (2005), and he makes no mention of the potential use of experience gained from previous business continuity events to prepare for the challenges of future events. However, elsewhere in the same book, Borodzicz (2005:26) does make reference to the work of Toft and Reynolds (2005) and reports that isomorphic learning has value in relation to the study of disasters and he states:

> "...for an industry to be able to learn from the experience of managing these types of risk, individual organizations need to be able to learn from the experiences of each other. Cumulatively, Toft and Reynolds would argue, the same disasters keep recurring because what little is learnt from them is passed only to managers in the organization concerned".

The apparent omission is perhaps exacerbated when, in reviewing guidance on the establishment of in-house security systems, again within the same book, Borodzicz (2005:70) states:

> "There may be much "reinvention of the wheel" as already tried and tested risk management procedures are developed. These might subsequently have been easier to identify if there had been greater cooperation available within the industry to capitalize on the isomorphic system learning highlighted by Toft and Reynolds (1994). As suggested by Toft and Reynolds, intrinsically similar systems of operation will have similar risks; for criminals these systems offer similar opportunities. An adequate risk communication context should be developed in order to capitalise on this knowledge between security organizations."

Some academics have also apparently attempted to link the concept of isomorphic learning with the business world and in his book *"Will Your Next Mistake be Fatal?"* Mittelstaedt (2005:5) states:

> "The objective is to learn to recognise the patterns of mistakes that precede most business disasters and take actions to eliminate the threat or to reduce the incident to something that does not require full-scale crisis management. These patterns of mistakes and potential responses are surprisingly similar across physical and business disasters and across industries. This should make it easier to learn how to deal with dangerous situations, but we rarely take the time to see the parallels in what appear to be unrelated experiences. If we did take the time, it might help us to learn and to change our behaviour. We can learn to see patterns, and patterns can help us to anticipate, prevent, minimise, or to control the potential exponential down side for most crisis, accident, or disaster scenarios."

In his book, Mittelstaedt (2005) makes no reference to the previous works of Turner and Pidgeon (1997), and Toft and Reynolds (2005), although he seems to reach similar conclusions to Toft and Reynolds, and it should be noted that rather than employing the term isomorphic learning, Mittelstaedt has developed his own term which he describes as *Managing Multiple Mistakes* or *M3*. Although, Toft, Reynolds and Mittelstaedt appear to have reached similar conclusions through their research, it should be noted that this appears to have been done independently and in isolation of each other's works. Mittelstaedt (2005: 44) appears to have recognised the value of the application of his theory in commercial business, but neither he nor Toft and Reynolds (2005), have proposed the use of the theories in business continuity management activities. The links between the academic study of emergency and disaster management and business activities have also apparently been recognised by Lakha and Moore (2003). In their book *Tolley's Handbook of Disaster and Emergency*

Management: Principles and Practice, Lakha and Moore (2003) apparently acknowledge the links between business continuity and emergency and disaster management studies. Business continuity is given prominence within the book by being the subject of the first chapter and rather than providing generic guidance or approaches, Lakha and Moore (2003) set out seven separate approaches to business continuity management from around the world. Lakha and Moore (2003: 32) do not indicate a preference for any of the seven systems and merely conclude that there appears to be a need to rationalise the seven approaches. None of the seven approaches mentioned make mention of the use of using lessons identified from previous business continuity events to prepare for future business continuity events, having said that, Lakha and Moore (2003: 306-327) devote large sections of the book to the concept of identifying lessons for the future through the study of previous disasters and unwanted events. Lakha and Moore (2003) make no specific reference to isomorphic learning or to the works of Turner and Pidgeon (1997), and Toft and Reynolds (2005).

It has been shown that there appears to be a quite limited amount of published material in relation to the linking of business continuity and the academic study of risk crisis and disasters. Despite this apparent lack between the two disciplines there appears to be consciousness at some level within some business continuity publications that recognises the value of identifying lessons from previous events and publishing those lessons. In their book, *The Definitive Handbook of Business Continuity Management* Barnes and Hiles (2005:295), publish a list of case studies and they state:

> "…disasters range from small fires, to large infernos, floods, explosions, hurricanes, human error. Many lessons can be learnt from the experience from those unfortunate to have experienced disaster and live to tell the tale. It is hoped that these lessons, drawn from the presentations at survive conferences, articles in Survive Magazine, cases from the Survive database and experiences from authors from the main text of this volume, will provide valuable guidance in enabling disaster recovery and business continuity plans to be drawn up."

Between the pages 296 and 351 of the same volume, Barnes and Hiles (2005) report a number of events including storms, earthquakes, terrorist attacks, floods, hurricanes, fires, crimes and power failures. The incidents reported were each done so in a non standard format and each incident was reported in an individual style, the lessons identified are in some cases shown at the end of the incident report and are in some cases buried in the main text of the incident report. In the case of the Chicago floods report (2005:306), the business continuity lessons identified were reported in just five lines of text. In the same incident report it stated that the floods affected at least 200 buildings, 250,000 people and that the estimated cost in lost productivity was US$1.5 billion.

In their book *Business Continuity Management: A Crisis Management Approach,* Elliott et al., (2004:3) apparently acknowledge the potential links between business continuity and isomorphic learning and they state:

> "…broadening of business continuity reflects the underlying assumption that crisis incidence or business interruptions are systemic in nature, comprising of both social and technical elements. Such a view has been well developed within the field of crisis

management (Turner, 1976; Turner and Pidgeon, 1997; Schrivastava, 1987; Smith, 1990; Pauchant and Douville, 1993; Perrow, 1997)".

Although the book makes no specific connection between isomorphic learning and business continuity, it does contain the following quotation from Mellish (Elliott et al., 2004:189):

> "...during the fuel crisis J Sainsbury invoked a continuity plan developed for dealing with the threat of the millennium bug. Although J Sainsbury experienced difficulties because they were without supplies to their 230 petrol stations, more significant was the sharp increase in demand for staple products like bread, milk, baby food and nappies. Demand for many goods was reaching Christmas levels, placing excessive strain upon unprepared suppliers who were also short of fuel supplies."

RESEARCH METHODOLOGY

Techniques

The author selected a research methodology that incorporated four basic strands; the first strand was personal observation. As a result of employment within the City of London Police, it was possible to observe issues that arose in the response to events of the 7th July 2005 from the Corporation of London Business Coordination Centre. The primary function of the centre is to act as an information conduit between the emergency services dealing with a major incident and the City of London business community. This facility was developed from the response by the Corporation of the City of London to the St. Mary Axe terrorist bomb attack of 1992 and the Bishopsgate terrorist bomb attack of 1993 (Coaffee, 2003:150). This first strand was augmented by being in a position of trust and access was granted to information sources that were not available to other researchers or the general public. This access was undoubtedly an advantage, but brought with it a number of ethical issues that required resolution and this area will be reported within the "ethical issues" section. A change of career, but within the same disciplines of incident management and business continuity, provided access to more closed source material which again was an undoubted advantage with associated ethical issues that had to be addressed. The resolution of this area will also be reported within the ethical issue section.

The second strand of research took the form of attendance at conferences, seminars, presentations, briefings and similar events. This section proved to be an extremely rich source of material but once again as some of the events were closed, further ethical issues arose that had to be addressed.

The third research strand took the form of research of published material. The majority of the published material was available within the public domain. The material was gathered from internet websites, publications, reports and surveys. Some of the published material was not available within the public domain and access was gained as a consequence of employment position. This again created ethical issues.

The final strand took the form of unstructured, one to one interviews, with a number of individuals from a wide spectrum of stakeholders. The various stakeholders included business continuity professionals, emergency responders, business leaders, media members and others that may not be identified because the description of their role could lead to their identity being discovered. This area created the greatest number of ethical issues which will also be reported.

Ethical Issues

The first ethical issue relates to the obtaining of material through employment sources. Senior managers within the City of London Police and Lloyds TSB plc granted permission for material to be used provided it did not identify the source of the material or break any rules of confidentiality or of national security. The ethical issues in relation to published material are more clearly defined, in that if the material is published in the public domain then it is verifiable. However, some of the material obtained was not security classified or restricted within the terms of the Freedom of Information Act (2000), but the material was published on password protected websites and access to the websites concerned was granted to authorised persons only. This material will be commented upon within the "unpublished data" section of the reported data. The final issue around published material lies in the subject matter of copyright privileges and where necessary, permission was obtained to reproduce information from such material. The issue of reporting conferences and seminars is aligned to the ethical issue arising from the one-to-one interviews and where delegates have provided presentation material for publication and distribution to the other delegates this may be referenced, as it is within the public domain. However, where delegates have asked personal questions or made personal statements the material will not be referenced to protect the identity of the respondents. This policy is also extended to all persons who gave responses in the one-to-one interviews. All respondents were told that responses given may be used within an academic dissertation with the University of Leicester but an undertaking was also provided that any information given would be reported in such a way that it could not be used to identify the individual or the organisation that they worked for. This methodology followed the approach used by Coaffee (2003) in gathering research material for his book entitled *Terrorism, Risk and the City: The Making of a Contemporary Urban Landscape.* The issue of providing identities also led to the situation where it may not be possible to identify a respondent at a conference or event even by job description because the respondent may be the sole member of that profession at that event. Some events were also so small in nature that it could be possible to identify respondents and in such case reference would be made to the type of event and no reference will be made to the date, location or name of event to protect the identity of the individuals.

The policy of providing anonymity to respondents could also ensure compliance with the requirements of the 1998 Data Protection Act and the issue of publishing any attributed comments was addressed by obtaining the required consent from the respondent.

The last and arguably perhaps the most complex ethical issue related to the apparent discovery of regulatory issues within some organisations. This problem was most clearly identifiable in those organisations that are regulated by the Financial Services Authority (FSA). The Financial Services Authority regulates some 25,000 UK financial firms (http://www.fsa.gov.uk) and provides guidance to the regulated firms in relation to the way in which business activities are conducted. It should be noted that the FSA and its partner agencies, the Bank of England and HM Treasury (the tripartite) uses the term *"Major Operational Disruption"* as a term to describe a large scale business continuity event.

Much of the research was only achievable with the cooperation and assistance of senior members of staff from within the tripartite agencies and the relationship was viewed as completely symbiotic. The tripartite staff provided guidance that confidentiality must be maintained with any cooperating firm and that any minor issues discovered should be dealt with by providing advice and guidance. It was also decided that any more serious issues could be dealt with by providing similar advice and guidance and incorporating the business continuity lessons identified into future Market Wide Business Continuity Exercises and Tests.

Limiting Factors

Aside from costs and time factors, the main limiting factor was the inability to locate all of the information from all of the possible sources relating to the 7th July 2005. This was anticipated and was considered to be an issue to be aware of during the research activities. In general, the difficulties encountered in obtaining information during the research stage followed the pattern as described by Turner and Pidgeon (1997:163).

1) Information buried amongst other material.
2) Information distributed amongst several organisations.
3) Limited information available to two parties.
4) Prior information wilfully withheld.

Data

Some of the data collected from the research will be reported in this chapter under the name of the parent organisation that harvested and disseminated it. It was felt appropriate to use this method of reporting as some organisations engaged in more than one collection process and more than one method for the dissemination process. The published data is reported in an edited format.

Business Continuity Institute

The Business Continuity Institute is an international organization that represents the interests of business continuity professionals. The Institute is based in the United Kingdom. As of the 18th of April 2008, the Institute had over 4,000 members located in 75 countries around the world.

After the events of 7th July 2005, the Business Continuity Institute commissioned a group of consultants called Link Associates to conduct a survey into the response to the events from the perspective of business continuity professionals. The results of survey were published in the September of 2005, in a report entitled *Information and Communications Survey Report 7th July 2005*.

The report states in the introduction that:

"The comments and information provided has been analysed to provide feedback on what worked well, what didn't work well, where problems with procedures occurred and the lessons learnt within organisations."

The report stated that it was based on the responses from less than 80 organisations of which some were not based in London and some were not directly affected by the events of the 7th July. The report does not specify any figures for the number of organisations in either of the latter two categories. The survey for the report was advertised to the membership of the Business Continuity Institute and not outside that survey pool. The survey when published did not contain specific information on the lessons identified from the survey, but contained five sections that provided generic observations on such things as human resources, switchboards, communications, news sources and response plans. The report provided general statements such as *"the BBC is a good source of information"* and *"ensure that your business continuity plans are up-to-date"*. The report was published in electronic format and was initially placed in the password protected members area of the Business Continuity Institute website. The Business Continuity Institute did not publish any other material on the lessons identified from the 7th July 2005.

Continuity Central

Continuity Central is an independent website that specifically concentrates on the business continuity industry. The website is United Kingdom based but has a membership that is drawn from around the world and has a large number of members from North America. Soon after the events of the 7th July 2005 the website editor published an appeal requesting that members provide experiences from the response to the events of the 7th July and to share any business continuity lessons identified with the other members. Several responses were published on a web page on the Continuity Central website at the end of July 2005 and this web page was deleted from the website soon after without explanation. Continuity Central then advertised that a further survey would be conducted into the events of the 7th July 2005. The second survey was conducted in collaboration with a company called ICM, which is a provider of disaster recovery services. Disaster recovery is the term used for contingency work space and is usually centred on the arrangements for providing a suitable environment and facilities to support computer operations. The results from the second survey were published in July 2006 to coincide with the first anniversary of the terrorist attacks. The second survey was responded to by 161 organizations and no definition was given as to whether the organisations were directly impacted by the events of 7th July or the geographical location of the responding organisations. Analysis was provided of the type of organisations that responded and the report stated that 24.6 per cent of the organisations that responded to the survey were from the financial sector. Other organisations that responded included those from the retail industries communication suppliers, energy providers and the emergency services. The report was published within the opening section of the Continuity Central website and was not disseminated outside the confines of that website; although it was made available to download electronically (Appendix 1). In the "lessons learnt" section of the report a number of direct quotes were made from the survey without any accompanying explanations or clarifications (July the 7th 2005: *looking back for the future*: 6).

Continuity Forum

Continuity Form is a "not for profit" organisation that supports the business continuity industry. Continuity Forum did not conduct any specific surveys into the response to the events by its members, nor did it hold any conferences or seminars, or publish any reports on the subject. Two articles were published on the organisation's website (http://www.continuityforum.org) that contained personal observations of the events. A third article was published that contained a synopsis of the conclusions of the survey conducted and originally published by Continuity Central and ICM. Although Continuity Forum did not conduct its own survey into the relevant events, it did collaborate with the Chartered Management Institute and the Civil Contingencies Secretariat to produce the 2006 Business Continuity Management report written by Woodman. The report does not contain any specific lessons identified relating to the 7th July 2005, but does contain a section entitled *Lessons from experience* (Woodman, 2006:6) and states:

> "Managers whose organisations had invoked their BCP were asked to comment on the key successes or learning points that they had drawn from the experience".

The importance of communication was highlighted by one manager in a large retail company: "the communication plan is a critical element which needs to be initiated quickly. Rumour and speculation can quickly cause chaos." Another senior public sector manager said the key lesson was to "Communicate, communicate, communicate with stakeholders, staff, emergency services and the press."

Others highlighted the need to make sure all employees are engaged in the BCP. "Ensure that staffers refresh their knowledge of contingency plans frequently. Revise plans in light of actual implementation and feedback. When implemented, our BCP worked seamlessly, minimising down-time and disruption."

Some respondents acknowledged how hard it is to identify every possible threat. One manager in a small security organisation pointed out that "it is not possible to plan for a specific disaster in great detail. Rather it is best to have a plan that identifies how key members of staff can be brought together to respond to a set of pre-defined questions which will enable an appropriate response to be made."

By focusing on the impacts of disruption and accepting the need for flexibility, resilience can be improved. As one manager in a construction company put it "the plan must be capable of revision to cater for unforeseen circumstances."

The survey was based on a sample of 1,150 organisations, of which only 14 per cent were located within London, the majority of the other respondents were located throughout the United Kingdom and 6 per cent of the respondents were located outside the United Kingdom. It should be noted that the survey is conducted annually and that this is the seventh survey and the May 2006 survey covers the period which includes the events of the 7th July 2005.

GREATER LONDON ASSEMBLY

The Greater London Assembly (GLA) formed a committee and the committee was tasked with identifying the "lessons to be learnt" from the events and aftermath of 7 July 2005. The full terms of reference of the committee were (Barnes et al, 2006:150):

"To review and report with recommendations on lessons to be learned from the response to 7 July bomb attacks.
How information, advice and support was communicated to Londoners.
How business continuity arrangements worked in practice.
The role of Broadcasting services in communications.
The use of Information and Communication Technology in aid to the response process."

Paradoxically, in view of the stated terms of reference, the *Report of the 7 July Review Committee* does not provide any details of specific business continuity lessons identified, or how business continuity arrangements worked in practice. However, the report does provide a full overview of the failings of the mobile telephone systems in London on the 7th of July (Barnes et al., 2006:42) and the report then provides recommendations for improvement in this area for the future, if faced with similar mobile telephone issues (2006:90). The report (Barnes et al, 2006:93) also recommends that effective communication systems are established by local authorities, for example Recommendation 45 states:

"...Businesses need further information and advice in relation to business continuity and the welfare of their staff."

Survive

Survive ceased operating after a protracted period of financial difficulties in May, 2007. It was not possible, as a non-member, to obtain openly published material, relating to the business continuity lessons identified, from the Survive Group in relation to the events of 7th July and no such material was published on the public section of the Survive website, however, Survive did host a conference on the 22nd September 2005 entitled *Review of Impact on Businesses of London Bombings*. The conference was attended by 80 delegates and presentations were provided by members of the emergency services, key communications service providers, co-ordinators and information providers and experts in the field of human aspects and disasters. Approximately 5 months after the conference, a leading Survive consultant was asked to supply a copy of the business continuity lessons identified from the 7th July 2005 and he stated in response:

"All of the presentations from the 7/7 Workshop are available in the members section of the Survive website. However, there is no overall summary of lessons learned from throughout the workshop but there is the summary of the discussions...."

It appears that the summary of discussions was not placed on either the closed or open section of the Survive website. However, a summary of discussions was provided to the delegates of the conference, if it was so requested.

The summary (Appendix 2) states that the business continuity lessons identified in the workshop were reported in five broad sections - resources and logistics, human aspects, sources of information, communications and crisis management teams (Needham-Bennett, 2005:1).

The Tripartite

The Tripartite is an alliance between three UK government agencies, the Bank of England, H.M. Treasury and the Financial Services Authority and the agencies work together to support the financial sector during a civil emergency, such as the events of the 7th of July, 2005. Some of the product from the work of the tripartite can found at the Financial Sector Continuity (FSC) internet site (http://www.fsc.gov.uk). The primary functions of the tripartite group may be described as follows (Maddison, 2006):

"The Tripartite priorities during a Major Operational Disruption are to keep the financial markets open and operating and to facilitate an early return to normal trading. This is based on close interaction with key firms and markets, collection and *dissemination of essential information and timely and effective decision making*".

The FSA, on behalf of the tripartite agencies, sent a questionnaire to major financial institutions soon after the 7th of July. The results of the survey were published in the open access section of the FSC internet site in a report entitled *Incident Review - July 7 2005*.

The business continuity lessons identified from the tripartite survey were also published by the Joint Forum of the Basel Committee on Banking Supervision, in a consultation paper, entitled *High-level Principles for Business Continuity*.

Unpublished Data

The research data were gathered during a series of one-to-one unstructured interviews, with a number of individuals from both the private and public sectors. All of the individuals agreed to provide information on the basis that the data would not identify the informants or any organisation that they may be employed by or have a professional relationship with. It was agreed that the information would be used for research purposes and that where possible any lessons identified would be used for educational purposes. The individuals concerned were identified through existing professional links or through identification as part during the research process. The business continuity lessons identified during the course of each interview are reported, where the information reported met the anonymity test. With three interviews the information was so specific that it could lead to the identity of the organisations concerned, or of the informant's identity possibly being established by a reader. It should be noted that all three organisations had the same basic business continuity lesson identified, in that all three organisations found that the deputies of the organisations' leaders were not suitably trained or empowered to deal with the challenges that the events of the 7th of July presented.

Interview 1

A senior manager, employed by international bank, stated soon after events of 7th July:

"We could get no information from our local police, local council or the estate managers. I phoned one of my contacts in the City Police and they provided up- to- date information, although we are not based in their area. A number of things went wrong for us on the day. Firstly, we decided to open our DR centre, but there was no public transport, but we have an arrangement with a coach company to provide emergency transport for staff. The coach company sent us two coaches but they never arrived at our headquarters building because the traffic conditions in London were horrendous. We could not open our DR centre on the 7th July. We could not get our staff home because all the roads to our building were blocked and all the public transport links were closed. We couldn't give accurate messages to our staff and despite advice, some left the building and tried to walk to the nearest mainline train station."

Interview 2

This interview was conducted soon after the events of 7th July, with a local government officer, who stated:

"The company was evacuated and about thirty minutes later they were on the phone, pleading with me to intervene with the police on their behalf, because only after they had evacuated did they realise that they had forgotten to take the data keys and some documents with them that they needed to get their Disaster Recovery centre going. The same company made numerous phone calls to our office over the course of the next four days and they stated that if they could not get back into their office then they would not be able to continue business and this would have a disruptive effect on the UK financial industry."

Interview 3

The respondent was seen about one month after the events of 7th July and he worked as a building manager and stated:

"It was chaos, a policeman ran into the reception area and told the security officer that we had to evacuate immediately. Our normal security guy was off sick and there was a relief officer on duty, instead of informing me, he just activated the building fire alarm to evacuate the building. All of the tenants evacuated from the building and assembled at the fire muster point. It was only then the tenants found out that they were not allowed back in the building and that this was going to be at least for a few days. The tenants were in such a rush to get out that they even left the building unlocked, and I had to go to the police and get a police escort through the cordons back to the building to secure it."

Interview 3 led to interview 4, with some of the tenants affected directly by the events relayed by the respondent to interview 3.

Interview 4

One of the respondents affected by the events of interview 3, worked for a financial firm and the respondent stated:

"We have never had a proper business continuity plan, although there was some stuff that covered just the IT. They (The FSA) have never bothered with us because we are only a small firm and it is not something that we as a business had really considered before. On reflection this may have been an oversight."

The respondent was provided with information and support to compile a simple business continuity plan for his organisation by the researcher.

Interview 5

This interview was conducted with a senior civil servant, who stated:

"They (The FSA) have done a survey and published some information. They have got another eleven A4 sized pages of lessons learnt that they are not prepared to reveal. I have asked them to reconsider this decision, but they are concerned about the commercial sensitivities and that's the end of it."

ANALYSIS

The quality of the collection processes was viewed as an important factor in the analysis of the material produced. The Business Continuity Institute and Link Associates provided a copy of the questionnaire that was furnished to the respondents for their survey, but they were the only organisations to provide the researcher with a copy of the research material that the subsequent reported findings were based upon. The inability to obtain copies of the original questionnaires was seen as a potential barrier to the analysis of the information gathering review, but it should be noted that not all of the data reviewed was published as a result of a formal survey.

The Business Continuity Institute and Link Associates provided a questionnaire that focussed entirely upon communications issues on the 7th of July and so it appeared axiomatic that any business continuity lessons identified from that survey would relate to communications. This was proven to be the case and the subsequent report of the survey indicated that some of the 80 firms that responded to the survey had experienced communications difficulties, both internally and externally. No other business continuity issues were reported. The narrow focus of the survey appeared to be a missed opportunity as it appears that none of the other business continuity lessons identified reported in the other published reports on the subject of the 7th of July, were circulated to the membership of the Business Continuity Institute, via that organisation.

The material published by Continuity Forum, Global Continuity, City and Financial Services conferences, City Security Magazine, Continuity Insurance and Risk Magazine and the Royal United Services Institute appears to be mainly anecdotal in nature and based on the personal observations of the respondents. The information does not appear to have been shared outside of the organisations that collected it, with the notable exceptions of the Continuity Forum and Global Continuity. These two organisations appear to cross publish information from each others' websites and this activity appears to take place in conjunction with Continuity Central and a report of the results from the second Continuity Central/ICM survey into the events of the 7th of July, were also published on the Continuity Forum and Global Continuity websites.

One of the most informative and complete reports into the business continuity lessons identified from the 7th of July was compiled by Needham-Bennett (2005), on behalf of Survive. The Survive report contains a number of recommendations and suggestions for areas of improvement in the field of business continuity and it should be noted that the report compiled by Needham-Bennett was not apparently disseminated outside of the 80 delegates that attended the Survive event on the 22nd of September 2005.

The FSA appears to have undertaken a clear and defined review of the events of the 7th of July 2005 and published a report, on behalf of the tripartite agencies, entitled *"Incident Review - July 7 2005"*. The FSA and tripartite agencies have also undertaken to provide a small number of presentations on the subject at financial sector events and conferences. It should be noted that the business continuity lessons identified by the FSA do not appear to have been disseminated outside of the confines of the financial sector, although the dissemination within the financial sector has been on both a national and international basis.

The business continuity lessons identified from the unpublished material have not been entirely lost, but they have not been effectively disseminated, as may have been anticipated.

However, representatives from the financial company, referred to in interview 1, have made a number of presentations at conferences and events since the 7th of July and none of the issues reported by the informant have been acknowledged in any of the presentations on this subject. Representatives from the company referred to in interview 2 have also provided presentations at conferences and events on the subject of the 7th of July. Again none of the issues reported in the course of interview 2 have been revealed during these presentations.

Information was reported to the FSA in relation to the matter of cordons and access denial and the researcher was invited to join the Scenario Design and Development Group for the 2005, Tripartite Market Wide Exercise. The business continuity lessons identified from the interviews were incorporated into the exercise scenario. The conclusions from the exercise were published in the password protected section of the UK Financial Sector Continuity website. Again the business continuity lessons identified were not apparently published outside of the financial sector.

CONCLUSION

The main premise behind the research was to establish whether it could be possible for an individual to obtain an informed view of the business continuity lessons identified, arising from the events of the 7th of July, 2005. Collecting data for the study involved many hours of research and attendance at a number of events over a period of about one year.

Some of the data identified and recorded was only obtainable as a result of the positions of trust held by the researcher, as a result of employment. It was also established that further data were available that could not be accessed, because of commercial sensitivities or perceived security issues. No data or information was identified for research that was available from either the retail industry or the transport industry, this despite the fact that the transport industry in London was the area that sustained the most physical damage and may have endured one of the longest recovery periods after the events of the 7th of July. No data or information, relating to business continuity lessons identified, has been located by enquiries with some members of the UK tourism industry, relating to the events of the 7th of July.

The study did reveal that a large volume of information was apparently available that related to the business continuity lessons identified from the events on the 7th of July. However, it has been established that the information available was held in "silos" and with one or two noticeable exceptions, the FSA and Continuity Central, there were no apparent efforts to disseminate the information gathered to a wider audience. This follows the pattern identified in the literary review of business continuity publications and works. None of the books published on the subject of business continuity or the books relating to Isomorphic Learning make any apparent attempt to link the two concepts.

There is some evidence to confirm the opinion that the world of academia has attempted to provide some bridges between the discipline of business continuity management and social research in risk, crisis and disaster management. For example Elliott et al., (2004) published *Business Continuity Management: A Crisis Management Approach* and Borodzicz (2005) devoted a whole chapter to the subject in his book *Risk, Crisis and Security Management*. Lakha and Moore (2003) also appear to link business continuity and emergency management with their book *Tolley's Handbook of Disaster and Emergency Management: Principles and*

Practise. However, within the United Kingdom, that appears to be the main links.. The University of Coventry (http://www.coventry.ac.uk) currently offers a Diploma/Certificate in Business Continuity Management, but it is apparently the only university in the United Kingdom to provide any form of academic qualification in the subject, as a distinct and separate entity. Several other universities in the UK, such as Cranfield University (http://www.cranfield.ac.uk) and Leeds University Business School (http://lubswww.leeds.ac.uk), now offer the subject as an optional module, as part of an academic qualification in emergency or resilience management. This position should be compared to the prevailing position within North America, where a number of universities offer academic qualifications in the subject of business continuity. Perhaps one of the most notable amongst those courses is the Masters of Science in Management in the subject of Business Continuity and Emergency Management, offered as an online course by Boston University (http://www.bu.edu).

It is recommended that the academic institutions located within the United Kingdom develop and deliver further courses that may provide academic qualifications in business continuity at undergraduate and postgraduate levels. Further social research would seem to be appropriate in the application of business continuity, but it seems that a period of structured education should be available to the professionals within the industry before any meaningful measures of the application of academic concepts can be conducted amongst those individuals.

REFERENCES

Barnes, P. & Hiles, A. ed., (2005). *The Definitive Handbook of Business Continuity Management*, Chichester: John Wiley & Sons Limited

Barnes, R. Hamwee, S. McCartney, J. Hulme-Cross, P. Johnson, D., (2006). *Report of the 7 July Review Committee*, London: Greater London Assembly

Basel Committee on Banking Supervision, the Joint Forum, (2005). *High – level Principles for Business Continuity Consultative Document*, Basel: Bank for International Settlements

Borodzicz, E.P., (2005). *Risk, Crisis & Security Management*, Chichester: John Wiley & Sons Limited

Boston University Online. (2006). *Master of Science in Management, Specialization in Business Continuity Management and Emergency Management* [internet], Available at: http://www.bu.edu/online/online_programs/graduate_degree/master_management/emergency [accessed on 19/08/06].

British Standards Institute. (2006). *BS 25999-1: 2006 Business Continuity Management Part 1: Code of Practice*, London: British Standards Institute

Buck, G., (2005). On Speaking Terms. *CIR, Continuity Risk & Insurance*, July-August p.24-27. Perspective Publishing *City Security*, (2006). Volume 17. London: City of London Crime Prevention Association

Coaffee, J., (2003). *Terrorism, Risk and the City: The Making of a Contemporary Urban Landscape*, Aldershot: Ashgate Publishing Limited

Continuity Central. (2006). Available at http://www.continuitycentral.com/news02647.htm [internet], [accessed on 26/07/06]

Continuity Central. (2006). *July 7th 2005: Looking Back for the Future,* London: Continuity Central / ICM

Continuity Forum. (2006). Available at http://www.continuityforum.org [internet], [accessed on 19/07/06].

Coventry University. (2006). *Business Continuity Certificate / Diploma course* [Online], Available at http://www.coventry.ac.uk/courses/undergraduate-part-time-a-z/a/1262, [accessed on 19/08/06].

Cranfield University, (2009). *Resilience MSc/PgDip/Pgcert,* Available at http://www.cranfield.ac.uk/students/courses/page1809.jsp [internet], [accessed on 07 / 07 /09]

Elliott, D. and Swartz, E. & Herbane, B., (2004). *Business Continuity Management: A Crisis Management Approach,* Abingdon: Routledge

Fennel, D., (1988). *Investigation into King's Cross Underground Fire,* London: HMSO.

Financial Services Authority Handbook, (2003). *Senior Management arrangements, Systems and Controls (SYSC),* release 026. London: FSA *Freedom of Information Act 2000,* London: HMSO

Global Continuity. (2006). Available at http://www.globalcontinuity.com[internet], [accessed on 26/03/06].

Government Response to the Intelligence and Security Committee's Report into the London Terrorist Attacks on 7 July 2005, (2006). London: HMSO

Hood, C. & Jones, D. ed., (2002). *Accident and Design* London: Routledge.

Hood, C., Jones, J. Pidgeon, N. & Turner, B., (1992). *Risk Analysis, Perception & Management* London: The Royal Society

Financial Services Authority, Bank of England, & H.M. Treasury, (2005). *Incident Review – July 7 2005,* London: The Tripartite

Lakha, R. and Moore, T. ed., (2003). *Tolley's Handbook of Disaster and Emergency Management: Principles and Practise,* London: LexisNexis

Leeds University Business School, (2009). *Academic qualifications in partnership with the Emergency Planning College,* Available at http://lubswww.leeds.ac.uk/wbl/index.php?id=83 [internet], [accessed on 07 /07/09]

Link Associates, (2005). *Information & Communications Survey Report 7th July 2005,* Derby: Link Associates International

Maddison, R., (2006). *UK Market Wide BCM Exercise: Business Continuity and Disaster Recovery in the Financial Services Sector, 5th Annual Conference,* London: City & Financial Conferences

MI5 Security Service (2006), *Protecting Against Terrorism,* London: HMSO

Mittelstaedt, R.E. Jr., (2005). *Will Your Next Mistake Be Fatal? Avoiding the Chain of Mistakes that can Destroy your organization,* Upper Saddle River: Wharton School Publishing

Needham-Bennett, C., (2005). *Review of Impact on Businesses of London Bombings, Workshop - 22 September 2005, Summary of Group Discussions,* London: Survive

Ritchie, D., (2005). *Hand in Hand: CIR, Continuity Risk & Insurance,* July p.20-22, Perspective Publishing.

Survive, (2005). *Review of Impact on Businesses of London bombings Conference,* held on 22nd September, London

The Tripartite Standing Committee on Financial Stability, (2005). *Financial Sector Business Continuity Annual Report,* London: Bank of England, H.M. Treasury, Financial Services Authority.

Toft, B. & Reynolds, S., (2005). *Learning from Disasters,* 3rd ed. Basingstoke: Perpetuity Press Limited / Palgrave Macmillan

Turner, B.A. & Pidgeon, N.F., (1997). *Man-Made Disasters,* 2nd ed. Oxford: Butterworth-Heinemann

University of Lancaster, Faculty of Social Sciences, Committee on Ethics, (1998). *Meeting the Requirements of the Data Protection Act (1998)* [Online], Available at http://www.lancs.ac.uk/fss/resources/ethics/protect.htm, [accessed on 19/08/06].

Woodman, P., (2006). *Business Continuity Management,* London: Chartered Management Institute

APPENDIX 1 CONTINUITY CENTRAL

1) A 'lessons learned' document was produced and changes have been implemented.
2) A review of the control and command network is being undertaken. More responsibility is being devolved to local managers in regional/local offices. Communication issues are being addressed.
3) Additional communications resilience - reduce reliance on mobile phones.
4) Better immediate response required.
5) Catering, accommodation, transport, alternative meeting place for crisis teams, changes to travel policy and procedures for London based staff.
6) Clearer communication to staff of details of event, multiple methods of updating staff, home email address, bureau service to automate text message and e-mail.
7) Clearer guidance as to using the plan.
8) Comms plans out of date. Staff lists out of date. Mobile phones single point of failure.
9) Communication was an issue.
10) Contact strategy - confirmation that people are safe required.
11) Create a more detailed plan taking into account multiple issues (such as primary, secondary, and subsequent places to meet and methods for communications).
12) Creation of a Crisis Communications Plan enabling remote working staff to be able to contact a central point following an incident not affecting our own premises. Methods include: ansaphone, e-mail both intranet and Internet access, direct calling. Also created a Crisis Communications Card with all relevant numbers and addresses to use.
13) Crisis management and communication improvements.
14) Easy access to all employees' home addresses and routes home including what public transport they use. Procedure for employees to ring home saying they are OK to save relatives ringing and clogging our lines. Better communication between teams. Increased training and awareness for all staff as well as Incident Team.

15) Enhancements to communications strategy.
16) Enhancing our methods of communication. Both verbally as rumours were rife amongst staff picking up snippets of information from the media. Generally people rely upon mobile telephones these days and they forgot that their desk telephone continued to work. The other factor that received some attention was how to manage the human resource aspect, people panicked when they could not contact loved ones by mobile contact.
17) Ensuring that all key staff can be contacted.
18) External hosting of critical applications.
19) Formal plan instead of ad hoc arrangement required. The London office is adjacent to the Aldgate incident and staff were directly affected though thankfully not injured. The office was closed for 24 hours.
20) Given that the tube network was out and no buses were available we had to look at ways of getting staff to the DR centre. New maps and walking directions included.
21) HR and facilities plans improved.
22) I developed a separate, simpler plan on how to respond to an emergency not directly affecting my employer.
23) Improve communications.
24) Improved IT processes to detail what can and can't be shut-down in CER as wrong things were turned off; improved procedures for manual start up of generator and improved testing schedule; stern conversation with DR provider; improved comms options.
25) Improvements required for city-wide incidents.
26) Incident and response communication in general, alternatives to mobiles (And update Terrorism Procedures).
27) It highlighted logistical problems which were mainly communications as we have some forty sites in the London area.
28) Less reliance on mobile phones. Process introduced to track staff whereabouts.
29) Main areas were ability to contact staff, requirement for them to contact the office if OK but unable to come in, need for regular communications and how to deliver the messages, dealing with death of an employee - not a short term issue.
30) Mainly the impact of access denial to our site by Police since we are located directly next to the main railway station in Cardiff.
31) Mainly transportation issues. Also helped to review plans of companies directly affected.
32) Make cascade and command and control links more prominent to more potential users. The main feature of this event was emergency responses to external issues, rather than pure BC.
33) Management of contacts and messages.
34) Mobile telephone communications cannot be so heavily relied upon.
35) More comprehensive scoping of services which might be impacted by a remote threat. Comprehensive includes subcontractors.
36) Most of the focus was upon making the plans more robust in respect of accounting for staff.

37) Need for separate space for the different teams. People felt more comfortable managing the incident together, though with hindsight it may have been more effective if they were not.
38) Needed to implement a specific continuity plan for London office.
39) New short term DR office implemented; hardware location moved to outer London; DR office migrated to new office location in outer London; currently considering wider BCP solution.
40) Nothing specific, but we are always updating following testing.
41) Old BCM manager was sacked and new one (me!) employed to review and update BCM process and plans.
42) Our plan relied heavily on mobile contact so we reviewed contact details and ensured we had alternative numbers for critical contacts.
43) Overnight provision. More coordinated technical management procedures. A dedicated command centre.
44) Plan was incomplete and suspended last year. It's now in progress again and due to be completed by end of 2006 for 35 offices. Original implementation was ill thought out. The new plan is being produced with the guidance of a BCI recognised consultant.
45) Put into place emergency comms to contact all staff in an incident.
46) Rather than recall all operational managers to our Hillingdon headquarters where it proved almost impossible to utilise them as a result of gridlocked Greater London roads, we now recall and disperse managers to pre determined sites around London where they are better able to respond to the needs of our business.
47) Review of procedures where threat is to staff beyond phone contact (underground).
48) Revision to the communications plan and our transport and operations plan.
49) Sensing of the issue was good but improvement was possible. Parochial attitude of some key staff (site rather that full business view) realigned.
50) Set up process for staff to contact call centre for the purposes of accounting for staff. Key supplier BC review brought forward.
51) Some changes, more in relation to Incident Management procedures. Introduction of Blackberries to more key staff, upgrade of Incident Room facilities, better process for tracking staff travel.
52) Some slight amends to the roles of particular individuals and not using critical numbers as a helpline as it stops other vital info getting through.
53) Staff communication and awareness.
54) Structure of CMT Communications processes, speed and responsibilities. Communications methods (i.e. loss of mobile). Whereabouts of staff and managers. Decision making process. Local authority contacts. Transport issues.
55) Telecommunications, police liaison, board engagement, crisis management procedures.
56) The plans had previously focused on loss of property and/or facilities. We had not considered invoking them in the event of large scale reassignment of staff though we had looked at loss of staff through flu pandemic! It's about getting people to consider using their plan on every occasion where they may not be able to perform to their normal standard, whatever the cause.

57) The working from home / mobile working capability was found to lack capacity in some areas of the portfolio that we would utilize in addition to 3rd party work space.
58) Travel arrangements, office entry and appointment procedure. International travellers reminded of risk issues.
59) Travel Plans for overseas visitors.
60) We have a number of new staff who did not have a clue what they would have to do. Down to manager of each department to make sure everyone understands all aspects of the plan.
61) We may be unable to rely on mobile phones or VOIP.
62) We need a better one!
63) We needed plans for our retail store operation at the middle level i.e. area / regional level to ensure better coordination when clusters of stores are affected in a geographical area.
64) We were affected by the Birmingham Evacuation on the 9th. The cordon affected all our sites where previously we thought one to be 'safe'. Our short term contingency plans have been modified so that calls are now sent outside of Birmingham city.

APPENDIX 2 SURVIVE

Resources and Logistics

Summary

The consensus of the group was to take a minimalist approach: identifying the problems that staff will face and advising them to make provision themselves to cope with potential difficulties rather than making elaborate plans which may be impractical in the event.

Transport

The discussion focused on the difficulties of getting staff home with such severe disruption to the transport infrastructure. One delegate had tried to get hold of buses on the day but couldn't; one believed that they had an agreement in place with a bus company but they let them down on the day and the question was also raised of where one would bring buses to (even if you could get hold of them) in order to pick up staff.

The consensus was that, given the impossibility of guaranteeing staff that you can provide alternative transport, it is better to be quite explicit about this and make sure that everyone understands that it will be their own responsibility to make arrangements on the day. In particular, staff members with family responsibilities need to arrange an emergency alternative.

There is a separate issue of moving specific personnel to the DR site which was not discussed in detail but most delegate were confident that, had this been necessary they would have managed.

Accommodation

Most delegates agreed that rather than try to book hotel accommodation (much of which will be taken up by the Emergency Services in a large scale disaster) they would simply keep their office buildings open to accommodate staff who cannot return home. It was felt by the majority that it was impractical to stockpile large numbers of camp beds, blankets, pillows etc and that staff would put up with pretty basic facilities in a real emergency.

Food and Water

Many delegates stated that they were already running low on food supplies by the evening of the 7th July and most would have been unable to continue to serve hot food into the 8th July. We were assured that the banks' wine cellars remain well stocked.

Other Resources

There was no opportunity to discuss issues like stockpiling warm clothing and waterproofs in case staff members have to evacuate or make their way on foot for long distances. This was a key learning from the Manchester bombing in 1996 when tens of thousand of people had to be evacuated from the City Centre and were stuck out of doors for many hours with no transport available to get them home – fortunately it was a fine Summer's day.

Human Aspects

The following points were raised by the delegates, subdivided as follows …

1) locating staff
2) supporting staff, including crisis management teams
3) information and planning

Locating Staff

1) Staff, visitors and contractors can be given an electronic tag to monitor their whereabouts in normality. This can also be used in the event of an incident, so that the person's safety can be verified. However, the system must be resilient, and there needs to be a backup.
2) Know when staff are working away from the office/main worksite. If you use a travel company, they will have a log of when people are travelling and where. Set up a system whereby managers know when and where their staff are working away, and make sure that people know why you want this information – i.e. for their own safety and wellbeing as opposed to tracking them for performance management reasons.

Supporting Staff

1) Decide who will respond to different people issues in advance of an incident, and incorporate this into your plan.
2) Do not assume that HR will handle everything (or not be involved at all)
3) Empower people to make on the spot decisions, such as block booking hotels or making purchases.
4) Have an emergency pack of information, such as lists of locksmiths, taxi/coach companies, places where you can access large amounts of cash.

5) If your office space is unaffected and not within a cordon, offer it as overnight shelter for those who cannot get home, if for instance, the transport system is paralysed.
6) Recognise that stress/post traumatic counselling may be needed – and for longer than you think.
7) Find ways of de-stigmatising stress reactions – it is not a sign of weakness.
8) Practical help and support is invariably welcomed – checking that they are OK, letting their loved ones know they are OK, giving them an emergency payment to get home etc..
9) Decide what your stay/go policy will be and how you will respond to those who do not want to follow your instructions.
10) Remember your crisis management teams also need support – they cannot work continuously if they are not given food, drink, rest periods and rotas. They may also need stress first aid.
11) Do not make the crisis management team's job any more difficult that it is already – ensure that they have the training, tools and techniques to do their job well. For those who have to lead such teams, make sure they have the training to help them manage and motivate people under pressure.
12) Remember to tell your staff that they are doing a good job in difficult circumstances – don't just assume they know, or even worse, take it for granted.
13) It isn't just your staff who may be affected in an incident, but their friends, family and community. How you treat your staff will affect them too.

Information and Planning

1) Use a buddy system with other companies in the area, so if your work site goes down, a reciprocal arrangement can be invoked to find work space in each other's work sites.
2) Brief people to stick together in the event of an emergency, so that they can look after each other, and also be kept informed of what is happening.
3) Ensure that those used to provide counselling and employee assistance programmes are involved in plan rehearsals.
4) Ensure that you have "help lines" that staff can contact to ask for updates and further instructions.
5) Encourage staff to phone in to let you know they are safe, if there is an incident in which they might have been caught up.
6) Decide who your essential staff will be in the event of an emergency, and make sure that they know this, and are trained and prepared for the role. Also remember to reassure those who do not fall into this category that they are still important to you!

Sources of Information

The question revolved around the ability to make high quality important decisions based on the information provided on the day and what would the ideal requirement be?

The syndicate identified two distinct forms of information, internal and external.

1) With regard to internal technical information most companies seemed quite happy with the quality and detail of what was reported as happening to their company,

(however it should be noted that no damage to internal communications systems had occurred in this event).

This view changed dramatically to significant dissatisfaction with the lack of any single authoritative 'voice' saying what the nature of the event was.

1) This lack of 'voice' gave rise to staff speculation and their access to the web potentially fuelled speculation.
2) Despite an understanding by companies of the Cabinet Office/COBR imperative not to speculate and to deal in confirmed fact there was a feeling that even negative information to the effect that they were "investigating reports of...." would have been preferable to a dearth of comment and the resultant media lead on events.
3) Concern was expressed that the 'cover story' of power surges lacked credibility. The consensus was that there is always an expert on something in every company and few staff actually believed the power surge announcement.
4) This in itself gave rise to speculation and damaged the potential credibility of both subsequent ongoing HMG announcements and it placed the company in the awkward position of perhaps having to be complicit in what they suspected was an evident cover story.

The companies represented in the syndicate were mainly unaffected by staff loss or difficulty in accounting for them. The consensus view was that the incident was relatively small scale and not too many lessons should be extrapolated in the prediction of resilience in the face of a larger scale incident.

Communications

1) There is a need for timely updating of Emergency lines as several had 'old news' on them and lack relevance.
2) Multiple methods of communication needs to be undertaken to get messages to staff, landlines, emails, text, tannoy, fire wardens, etc..
3) There was concern that there was little evidence that the companies cared for their staff and follow up messages to staff thanking them for their cooperation etc should be made at least by the next day.
4) Options for maintaining communications were discussed and the following proposed:
5) Manx telephone SIM cards
6) Use a different network for outbound calls
7) Pre-prepare scripts for release by email
8) Pre-prepare address lists for release
9) Request staff to restrict internet access but provide alternative means of obtaining information including TVs
10) Set up extra conference bridge lines
11) Use PA systems to talk to staff to reassure even if there is nothing concrete to say
12) Practice the use of alternative communication methods

Crisis Management Team

CMT Activation

This raised the question of "when does an adverse event become a potential crisis?" This was decided to be a very subjective question, but the suggested solution was:

1) Fast access to senior management levels to report emerging issues.
2) Clear ownership of the process and audit of the procedure.
3) Good and resilient communication systems.
4) Early activation of CMT in face of potential threat "easier to go large and stand down assets, than to try and regain lost ground and time after an event".

CMT Working Facilities

1) Good communications.
2) Administrative support to CMT.
3) CMT resilience, enough suitably trained staff to deal with a protracted incident.
4) Facilities to support audit / compliance requirements of CMT activity.
5) Access to assorted information sources and equipment to record information details to provide context of CMT decisions (log keeper?)

CMT staff performance

All CMT members should be trained and exercised.

In: Strategizing Resilience and Reducing Vulnerability
Editors: Peter R.J. Trim and Jack Caravelli

ISBN 978-1-60741-693-7
© 2009 Nova Science Publishers, Inc.

Chapter 9

A JOURNEY TOWARDS RESILIENCE: LESSONS FROM THE BRITISH EXPERIENCE

Andrea C. Simmons

ABSTRACT

Given the breadth of outsourcing and the splintering and fracturing of responsibilities across so many facets of our daily lives, it is important that we are clear where the connections are and how they remain linked together – conceptually, contextually and in relation to the connections people need to make together.

We need clarity on the relationships and understanding as to what our respective remit is in order to ensure that the right people receive the right message delivered in a language pattern that makes sense. The "noughties"[1] have brought with them so many changes and challenges and there are clearly many more to come – we will all need to be ready both intellectually and practically. This chapter will examine the journey from "disaster recovery", through "business continuity" to "corporate resilience" as terms and as operational concepts and then reflect on them with reference to the importance of the individual as well.

INTRODUCTION

This chapter is unashamedly UK focused, for that is the core skill area of the author. However, it is likely that some of the key messages and learning outcomes are relevant throughout the globe. In particular, this need for genuinely effective connections in the 21st century.

---

[1] This is a media coined term to reflect the date references from the year 2000 onwards to date i.e. we've had the swinging 60s, the 70s, the 80s, the 90s and now we are in the 00s.

When presented with this subject to research and write about, the following conundrum arose for me:

- Why is there still anything left to say?
- We know what the risks are.
- We know what to do about them.
- We even know how much it will cost.
- So why is this all still such an issue?

There have been many years of research, study and review of incidents, lessons learnt and awareness raised in the field of business continuity. And yet it has to be accepted that there will always be those for whom the journey is new. There is the next generation to consider, to whom some of these concepts are alien. Thus it is important to posit the current position but also to take the journey further forward through study and learning, in order to provide robust analysis and influence those to whom the information should be seen to be of value.

At minimum, business continuity (BC) is a more commonly understood term than corporate resilience. Time and the maturation of the industry, however, could leave business continuity sidelined in order to allow for new challenges requiring new resolutions. In the recent business continuity management (BCM) standard, BS25999, resilience is mentioned as "the ability of an organisation to resist being affected by an incident"[1]. And risk management in relation to business continuity, is described as "BCM is complementary to Risk Management". Business continuity management deals with keeping an organisation functioning after a period of downtime. The objective of resilience is not to experience downtime at all or, at least, not have it interrupt the business.[2]

So we are on a journey into a new era of managing corporate issues across a range of platforms, many of which are embedded in compliance requirements but also in both internal and external audit regimes that are continually changing in order to address the pace of life as we are now experiencing it, in line with technological and legislative advances that impinge on day to day operations in a way previously not experienced.

INDUSTRY MATURATION

The Information Security industry has been on a journey from *IT Security*, through *Information Security* – where many industry sectors are still struggling to navigate towards – and onwards into *Information Assurance* – where, for example, the UK National Health Service (NHS) has been for some time and where now other government departments (in particular through the Central Sponsor for Information Assurance [www.csia.gov.uk]) have been taking a lead and seeking to influence wider sectors.[3]

---

[2] Source: Ross, S.J. (2006). "Downtime and data loss", Information Systems Control Journal, Vol 5, pp.1-2.
[3] Wikipedia holds the following helpful steer with regards to defining some of these terms :
Information security means protecting information and information systems from unauthorized access, use, disclosure, disruption, modification, or destruction. The terms information security, computer security and information assurance are frequently used interchangeably.

Figure 1. From IT security to information assurance.

All of this, though, needs to be seen in the context of *Information Governance* – which incorporates Information Management, Records Management and related disciplines and is a subset of Corporate Governance. Information Security Governance is also a subset of this discipline, focused on Information Security systems and their performance and risk management.

Similarly, *Business Continuity Management* (BCM) grew out of IT Disaster Recovery and Contingency Planning a decade or so ago. Business continuity management is the organisational means by which integrated strategy is designed, developed, implemented and maintained, to ensure that organisations are capable of *planning for, responding to, coping with*, and *recovering from*, major disruptions to "normal" operations from events across the spectrum. "BCM is about prevention, not just cure." [1] This is definitely heading us in the right direction towards our central theme in this publication - resilience.

> BCM establishes a *strategic* and operational framework to implement, proactively, an organisation's *resilience* to disruption, interruption or loss in supplying its products and services. It should not purely be a reactive measure taken after an incident has occurred BCM requires planning across many facets of an organisation, therefore its *resilience* depends equally on its management and operational staff, as well as technology and requires a holistic approach to be taken when establishing a BCM programme.
> (PAS 56: 2003).

Business Continuity Management was developed into a recognised discipline in the mid-1980s and it appears that, some twenty years on, in the noughties it is growing up. It seems that the significant business continuity planning efforts that were undertaken in order to provide surety of escaping the "millennium bug" was the turning point for maturity. PAS 56[4] appeared in 2003 and it is the first real mention of the term *resilience*. In Thejendra's 2006 book on *Disaster Recovery and Business Continuity*, [2] resilience receives no mention, by way of description or otherwise. So we are on the beginning of the crest of this wave. Resilience needs to be seen to cover the breadth of the disciplines of Business Continuity, Information Security and the cross over with Incident Management (in all its guises).

A further element of the maturation has been the progression from a straight consideration of appropriate computer *disaster recovery* through to ensuring the availability of information systems in all relevant, risk assessed circumstances. Given that the core

---

[4] The BSI originally published PAS56 as a guide which established the process, principles and terminology of BCM. This described the activities in and 'outcomes' of establishing a business continuity management process, and provided a series of recommendations for good practice.

principles of Information Security are based on the triad of an agreed requirement to maintain the CONFIDENTIALITY, INTEGRITY and AVAILABILITY of information systems, combined with a growing understanding that business continuity is about the need to ensure that systems are available as required (and prioritised) by the business, then the synergies start to appear quite obvious and natural.

Figure 2. The link between business continuity, information security and incident management.

All the disciplines mentioned above need to have a grounding in Operational Risk Management in order to be effective. Risk Management is a subject well researched and discussed in many quality journals and publications. It is fundamentally about being able to apply strategies to reducing vulnerabilities of an organisation in order to ensure that potential impacts are managed. Unfortunately, what the Information Security and Business Continuity disciplines appear to be finding regularly is that Corporate Risk Management is done in isolation of the breadth of supporting and related issues that affect the average member of staff. Too many layers between management and workforce can create a chasm of understanding and the forthcoming Corporate Risk Register may not adequately reflect the core information centric risks that may be experienced at any given point.

However, with the persistent focus on issues such as "data breaches", lost laptops and information handled in a somewhat cavalier fashion, we are now beginning to see a shift to something more holistic as an expression of understanding of the breadth and scope of each area and its contingent impact on an organisation's capability to continue operation in the face of many threats, vulnerabilities and opportunities for criminal activities.

Much as the forward looking organisation now includes Corporate Social Responsibility (CSR) and references to their "green" agenda credentials in their annual reports for example, they should equally be including continuity in any mission/vision statement, in order to ensure that it is placed as a key management objective that is visible to all (both internally and externally). Equally, a mature organisation will have at minimum a *Business Continuity Manager* and at maximum *a Resilience Director*.

THE ART OF STRATEGY

The IT industry is full of acronyms and has the capacity to "steal" words and use them for new ends – which in some instances makes something that we have all been struggling to achieve sound new and exciting and can distract on the good work of those stalwarts who continue to ply their trade appropriately within the industry. **Corporate resilience** occurred to me to be something of this ilk, when first I heard the expression in the summer of 2007 at a conference. However, as a philosophy graduate myself, I fully support the need to undergo continued academic study in order that the results of findings can be used to develop strategies and methodologies that can be applied in the real world.

In order to *strategize resilience*, as it were, we need to understand the need and requirement for a strategy[5] that addresses what it means to be resilient. The latter is likely to be different in most cases for most organisations. However, where similarities exist, these need to be shared and communicated in a manner that is likely to embed good practice and thus ensure an element of resilience is built in from the outset rather than bolted on after an incident.

A dictionary definition[6] of *resilience* describes it as "the power or ability to return to the original form, position, etc., after being bent, compressed, or stretched; the ability to recover readily from adversity." In the context of what has already been said in this chapter, the "adversity" would need to have been an identified vulnerability that a risk management strategy has sought to reduce. A threat may have realised the residual risk and a contingency is still required. This is not the place to delve further into risk management as there are so many other resources available.

The point is to provide a few stepping stones to the main point – progressing beyond the strategy to the implementation of understanding that supports resilience and reduces vulnerability. A good place to start, in spite of all the criticism that the UK government receives, is the Civil Contingencies Secretariat where, specifically, there is a resilience website[7]. The Civil Contingencies Secretariat (CCS) sits within the Cabinet Office at the heart of central government. It works in partnership with government departments, devolved administrations and key stakeholders to enhance the UK's ability to prepare for, respond to and recover from emergencies. Whilst the resources are good and valuable, use of the term "emergencies" can inject a sense of panic into proceedings! Irrespective, there is evidence of work being done in joining up various agencies, representative groups and organisations[8] in order to share knowledge and learn lessons from events – more particularly because there have been a number of them in recent times that have stressed and stretched a large number of participants, and which have highlighted the need for a continued and deeper sharing and understanding.

The Civil Contingencies Act 2004[9] (in many ways, in support of which the Civil Contingencies Secretariat was formed), contains an explicit requirement for local authorities (a duty) to provide businesses and voluntary organisations with advice and assistance on business continuity management. This duty aims to ensure local businesses are able to recover quickly from disruptions. A resilient business community supports a resilient country. This is about assessing risks and using these to inform emergency planning; putting those emergency plans in place; putting in place business continuity management arrangements; and sharing appropriate information to better inform others and enhance co-ordination.

As a result of this effective legislative move, organisations in the public sector, now have much greater support for efforts to abide by best practice such as PAS56 – which was

---

[5] A strategy needs to be seen as a comprehensive document setting out the medium to long term arrangements required to deliver a policy or set of policies – in this case, a Business Continuity Plan or similar.
[6] www.dictionary.com
[7] http://www.ukresilience.info/
[8] This manifests itself when reading articles in various relevant publications in the Business Continuity industry.
[9] http://www.opsi.gov.uk/acts/acts2004/ukpga_20040036_en_1

upgraded to be a British Standard in 2006 - as this standard establishes the process, principles and terminology of business continuity management.

Figure 3. The hierarchical process associated with crisis management.

Figure 3 is deliberately stepped rather than "square" to denote some element of hierarchy between Emergency Planning (EP) and Business Continuity (BC), and also to denote that there may, in certain circumstances, be direct links between Disaster Recovery (DR) and *either* business continuity or emergency planning. This is provided by way of seeking to visualize some of the plethora of terminology in this sector of the industry.

All of the above elements need to be considered in order to be able to meet the flow shown in Diagram 1 below.

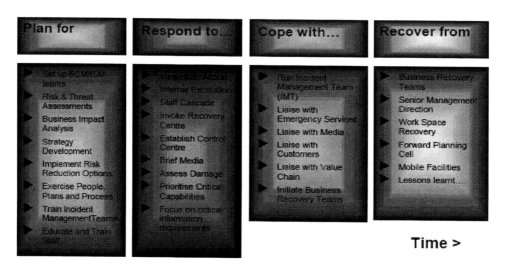

Diagram 1. The processes associated with building resilience.

Either way, successful resilience needs to start from the top of an organisation and be effectively communicated throughout it and beyond – to incorporate key suppliers, stakeholders, and customers for example.

So, *Corporate Resilience* can be seen to be best described as:

> the ability for businesses to continue to function in the face of adverse conditions is key to their corporate viability and credibility. A company that is unable to respond to change will not survive.

As a term, it was coined to describe the mechanism for engaging with the strategic needs of businesses and to reconcile the demand for flexibility, continuity and contingency. Thus it is about recognising that businesses are necessarily resilient (or not) by virtue of their existence. Being (corporately) resilient equates with being a successfully run business or organisation. This means knowing that resilience in a fast changing world is predicated on a lot of corporate uncertainty where it is difficult to know what events might change the business landscape for better or worse.

Thus, corporate resilience becomes a platform to integrate forward planning, reputation management, corporate social responsibility, risk management, governance, ethical and environmental policies and security. It has to be organic, participative and dynamic.

The concept of corporate resilience has wider applicability, especially at the national level but a *common language* and articulation of purpose is a key prerequisite to achieving this, along with an accommodation between the political cycles and resilience strategy. The strengthening of business continuity management, and the widespread adoption of this throughout all the areas that contribute to the social and economic wellbeing of the nation, ensures a certain level of national resilience. However, such a strategy fails to harness the inherent resilience of the 'system of systems' or to deliver a comprehensive and strategic approach to managing risk.[10]

Corporate resilience is achieved through executive level authority orchestrating a delicate balance of risk management measures. There is risk that a dominant element tasked within operational continuity – say, business continuity management – may not only upset the ability of the board to manage the risk and balance organisational objectives but that the professionalisation of the discipline may also introduce a separation between the organisation's operational continuity function and the resilience function of the executive authority.

THE BENEFITS OF EXERCISE

In recognition of the need for resilience to permeate across organisational and geographical boundaries, the UK and US have co-ordinated a series of exercises entitled "Cyber Storm"[11]. The exercises are designed to sharpen and assess participants' ability to

---

[10] Source: RUSI Corporate Resilience Workshop, June 2007, www.rusi.org
[11] Source: Reference to Cyber Storm II can be found here http://www.darknet.org.uk/2008/03/cyber-storm-ii-us-uk-3-others-involved-in-mock-cyberwar/-

respond to a multi-day, coordinated attack and better understand the "cascading effects" such attacks can have.

Results of Cyber Storm I pointed to the need for better coordination between various agencies and for a common framework for communicating among different parties. From a UK perspective, resilience lessons learnt include a number of factors, which have been outlined in Table 1[12]. These highlight ongoing requirements for greater and more open communication – often from a bottom up angle – i.e. there are usually plenty of individuals "on the ground" who have a firm grip on the reality of the situation but they may not be listened to due to hierarchical views of "chain of command" and political machinations surrounding the management of egos. Whilst this is not unusual, *in extremis* the rules need to be allowed to be bent a little to accommodate whatever may be occurring. In many cases, individuals react differently to stressful situations so those who are coping well and making informed, clear decisions, should be allowed to "rise to the top" and take on a leadership role, at the time of an event – and be recognised for having done so afterwards. Reacting in this way would certainly be a manifestation of positive resilience.

Table 1. Resilience requirements

Nationally:	
–	The need for consistency over what services continue to be delivered, balanced against potential regional variations in cases.
–	Consideration of the potential impact of social distancing measures on some services (e.g. those provided by the National Blood Service).
Regionally:	
–	The need for sharing of trigger points and risks with industry, especially critical national infrastructure (CNI) sectors, in order to improve regional planning.
–	Adequate plans to ensure backup and succession planning for key staff.
–	Further consideration of rural recovery measures.
Locally:	
–	Further work with both voluntary and private sectors to better define linkages and the areas of assistance that they might be able to provide.
–	The water needed for cooling the data centres.
–	Generators only cover critical loads.
All levels:	
–	The need for good recovery plans for managing the backlog of routine work.
–	The need to consider increased demands on some services – particularly support and communications.
–	The benefits of good communications between organisations where working together will make the best use of resources.
–	Understanding the practical difficulties and limitations of home working – the increased numbers of people working from home contending with increased internet use (from children at home) resulting in very slow-moving internet traffic.

---

[12] Source: Cabinet Office, www.cabinetoffice.gov.uk

As with any exercise, there were a number of ways to look at the results, several of which are referenced below by way of illustration of the communication point, in particular.

Crisis Management and Co-Ordination

Lessons learned included the following:

i) Channels of communication during a pandemic are complex and there is a need to improve the linkages between established local and regional resilience structures and their equivalents in the National Health Service and to review the process of the collection and collation of daily reports into the centre, together with clarity of the consistent use of data in describing the evolution of the pandemic.

ii) Many aspects of the response to an influenza pandemic fall within the competence of the devolved administrations of Scotland, Wales and Northern Ireland and the exercise highlighted several policy areas where there might necessarily be a difference in approach between administrations.

iii) The exercise demonstrated the need for continuing close liaison between the UK and the Republic of Ireland on pandemic influenza response planning.

iv) There is a need to strengthen and codify central government links with international bodies, e.g. the World Health Organisation and the European Centre for Disease Prevention and Control (ECDC).

Public Advice and Communication

Lessons learned included:

v) During a pandemic, a robust and coordinated communication approach will be necessary, particularly between the national and regional levels.

vi) Post–exercise feedback indicated that many people thought that public messages needed to be refined and that communications from central government departments and agencies needed to be better coordinated to ensure clarity and consistency.

vii) The exercise highlighted the need for better engagement with the public and communities and particularly community responsibility for vulnerable people. There was a need for clearer advice to the public on the use of antiviral drugs, facemasks and other measures and on the stocking of home supplies.

In many ways, the last point reflects an area of concern whereby in particular the UK press can be contributory to a certain level of panic that reduces public capacity to act rationally and calmly. Inflamed tempers are never going to be able to easily tap into the kinds of resilience that are required *in extremis*.

Continuity of Government

If you look at the extent of the split of both responsibilities and activities below, it is clear why it is so difficult to achieve quality, coordinated communication:

i) Department for Business, Enterprise and Regulatory Reform (www.berr.gov.uk)
- Electricity failure (electricity distributors and transmitters)
- Gas and electricity markets/interaction
- Telecoms issues
- Mobiles fail after 1 hour
- Landline congestion
- Broadcasting limited
- Petrol pumps close
- Fuel issues develop
- Priority lists required

ii) Department for Transport (www.dft.gov.uk)

- Rail and underground operations cease
- Network evacuation
- Displaced passengers
- Airport and port closures
- Harbour authorities
- Traffic management
- Urban gridlock
- Fuel distribution
- Abandoned vehicles
- Highways authorities

iii) Department for Environment, Food and Rural Affairs (www.defra.gov.uk)

- Food industry production
- Distribution, retail and storage
- Water industry (pressure failure, quality of product, shortages in supply)
- Sewage treatment and pumping
- Flooding
- Agriculture
- Animal welfare

iv) Home Office (www.homeoffice.gov.uk)

- Public protection
- Civil disruption
- Law and order

- National security
- Police mobilisation
- Airwave failure

v) Department of Health (www.doh.gov.uk)

- Health and safety executive
- Health authorities

vi) Department for Culture Media and Sport (www.culture.gov.uk)

- Use of Sports Halls for Family Assistance Centres (FACs)

It is accepted that you can see the benefits of distribution of activities and responsibilities in terms of resilience – in that you reduce the risk of a single point of failure. However, the tangential difficulty is in the increased likelihood of complexity in full communication as there are so many channels and levels to be circumnavigated. Addressing content and delivery of public messages, seeking and gaining military assistance, addressing priorities and achieving recovery were also considered to require follow up attention after the exercise.

All of the above could be put into educative terms under the umbrella of Isomorphic Learning (IL) which is defined as the facility to learn from the similar experiences of others. It can be particularly important in the context of crises on a wide scale where organisations can benefit from each other's experiences with various types and scale of incidents. Isomorphic Learning is not new[13]. It is an area of study that can be reviewed further in order to develop a greater understanding of some of the human factor elements of the future of corporate resilience.

> "A resilient ecosystem can withstand shocks and rebuild itself when necessary. Resilience in social systems has the added capacity of humans to anticipate and plan for the future."[14]

Ultimately, as with any perceived new initiative, a change in culture is required. The following encapsulates a good mantra for the future:

> "Take notice of other people and learn. You are never too old or too ugly to learn and there is always space to find out new things."[15]

---

[13] Note: Professor Brian Toft spoke about the need to learn from "near misses" as far back as 1992 - http://www.ema.gov.au/agd/EMA/rwpattach.nsf/viewasattachmentpersonal/(C86520E41F5EA5C8AAB6E66B851038D8)~Learning_from_near_misses.pdf/$file/Learning_from_near_misses.pdf

[14] Source: Wikipedia Resilience (Ecology)

[15] Source: Sarah Beeny, Property Developer, Spring 2008 - NatWest Business Sense Magazine

THE PEOPLE CONNECTION

Part of the journey for many has been the appreciation that "systems" cannot, now, be seen to be solely IT systems but rather should be viewed as information systems and thus allow for information (and indeed data) to be considered in all its forms – electronic (server/PC based), print (paper, files, manual for example), or other forms (CDs, discs for example). From the communication challenges referenced previously, we have seen that the system view *has* to include people.

At some stage, there needs to be a realization that you may be over-complacent or going over the top in your resilience planning – i.e. you may end up over emphasizing the need for selection of contingencies for risks that have such a low probability and low impact that your energies would in fact be better spent on addressing obvious high impact issues in a timely manner. One way of assessing this is to compare practices and exchange notes with other organisations. This will also generate useful side-effects such as gaining a transfer of good ideas or enabling collaboration in sharing infrastructure or resources.[16]

Figure 4 outlines the fact that human factors can be aligned with Maslow's Hierarchy of Needs[17]:

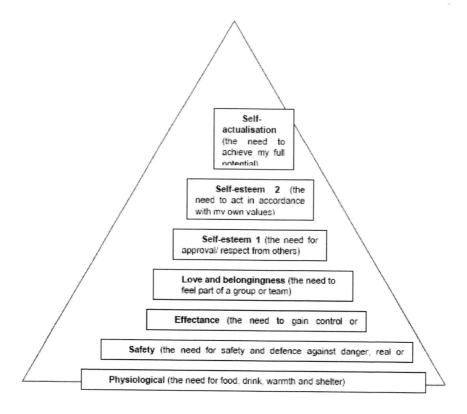

Figure 4. Human factors aligned with Maslow's Hierarchy of Needs concept.

---

[16] Source: David Lacey, August 2007, CW blog
[17] Source: Abraham Maslow's 'Hierarchy of Needs' (1954). New York:. Harper

One approach is to ensure that all teams are positively engaged. Starting off with a process flow view can be valuable as it is an important tool in providing visibility for an organisation with regard to where all the links are with regard to systems and information – both internally and externally. In other words, addressing who needs to know what, when; who needs to receive what information or data from whom, when; and who it needs to be shared with and so on.

Another approach is to ensure that support staff are trained in a way that supports their emotional needs. It is necessary to build an individual's resilience by explaining about trauma and showing that any symptoms are quite normal.[18] This approach will require an understanding and inclusion of emotional intelligence, as has been seen to be effective in new training approaches.

Emotional Intelligence (EI), often measured as an *Emotional Intelligence Quotient (EQ)*, describes an *ability,* capacity, or *skill* to perceive, assess, and manage the *emotions* of one's self, of others, and of *groups*. It is a relatively new area of psychological research. The definition of emotional intelligence is constantly changing.[19]

The journey from Disaster Recovery through Business Continuity to Resilience is a journey of change from an IT centric perspective of corporate requirements through to one where the individual is more important than the server. Hence the view that emotional intelligence is important – in order to place the understanding of the personal role to be played in ensuring resilience across.

Highly intelligent people may lack the social skills that are associated with high emotional intelligence. However, high intellectual intelligence, combined with low emotional intelligence, is relatively rare and a person can be both intellectually and emotionally intelligent.[20] Those who ride this wave are flexible and resilient – if you habitually use your past experience to try to solve today's problems, you are looking in a rear-view mirror. It is quite possible that what you did back then was perfect for back then but is not right for right now.[21]

In this hyper mobile society, there are more strangers. We are operating in a high speed, anonymous, low trust world where we are likely to sue a stranger. In many ways this poses a contradictory challenge as on the one hand, we can make many more connections than was ever previously possible but on the other, we can experience more isolation and disconnectedness. However, you cannot deal with digital age challenges using previously successful analogue processes. So we must be careful to ensure that we are not trying to cope with digitally related continuity incidents by using risk assessment structures, rules and processes designed for a much slower world.

Ensuring wide communication coverage can be easily done in terms of message delivery but it may not be equally feasible to ensure that the message has been received by the right audience, understood in the right way and acted upon appropriately. It is therefore incumbent upon organisations to be cognizant of this mindset when seeking to implement robust resilience programmes as the personal and subjective elements can be put in stark repose depending on the nature of the incident occurring at any one time.

---

[18] Source: www.cirmagazine.com, CIR Mar/Apr 2008
[19] Source: Wikipedia Emotional Intelligence
[20] Source: www.bbc.co.uk
[21] Source: Miranda Kennett, April 2008, First Class Coach, www.managementtoday.com, page 41

Part of the people issue now has to be viewed in the context of the capability to form relationships quickly through technological means. Everyone needs to develop an extensive personal and professional network of trust-based relationships but to take these beyond the digital ephemera and ensure that the networks are supported by sincere real-time connections. This can include taking a proactive view with regard to meetings, membership groups, seminars and conferences – do not just attend, volunteer to help, participate as a panellist or be a speaker. This is both an important professionalism tip but also a potential organisational strength and thus resilience point.

RISK MANAGEMENT

Fundamentally, and operationally, successful resilience will have as its bedrock a deep understanding of risk management in its broadest context.

The Institute of Risk Management (http://www.theirm.org/) and the Business Continuity Institute (http://www.thebci.org/) provide many resources, though the concepts of risk and business continuity are not solely defined by them. The pillars on which risk management needs to be structured and utilised within a resilient organisation include:

i) Moving business continuity from just impact assessment to plotting likelihood and mitigation of all mutating and evolving risks.
ii) The mechanism to combine crisis and risk management, information and corporate security - not just through the prism of either business continuity, risk or security, but together in absolute harmony with enterprise risk management, corporate social responsibility and environmental and ethical polices; thus maturing an holistic view of risk management. This then fully supports corporate governance too.
iii) A process predicated on corporate uncertainty vis-à-vis reputation management, rather than maintenance of an ideal status quo.
iv) A coherent and holistic business strategy that combines accountability, customer confidence, and competitive advantage.
v) A mechanism to advance the reality of corporate uncertainty - where it is not possible to know what events will alter the competitive operating landscape for better or worse and the need to combine, not just compliment a range of existing but discrete activities.

In many cases, exaggerated claims are made about how risk management can be used to manage the future. There is a requirement to balance real versus perceived risks. Over exuberant risk management can be positively counter productive, as it runs the risk of inducing complacency in those it sought to protect. However, can the "perceived" risks exist only in our imagination? Often, Objective Risk Assessment can be seen to be overtaken by the dominance of Perceived Risk Management. We all bring our own perception filters to any discussion about risk, usually from one of four perspectives, as applied to culture theory, which can be expressed through the quadrant view outlined in Diagram 2.

An alignment of employees' feelings in relation to risk can be overlaid with the emotional intelligence view referenced earlier in this chapter, at which point as an organisation there should be a much greater understanding of the drivers of the key players and their support staff so that in the event of an incident, a crisis or a disaster, the organisation will be in a better position to "bounce back" quickly and with the minimum amount of damage or loss of form (ref. elasticity, as it were) – a key sign of maturing resilience.

Diagram 2. An organisational cultural theory perspective

	Low grid	High grid
High group	Egalitarian – Everyone unites in support of a cause, with each individual contributing his/her norms/categories. Examples: environmentalist, ideological, trade unions.	Hierarchical – Everyone serves their place in the system, fulfilling as best they can the duties of the position they hold; seeking out efficiencies. Examples are HR, government/regulators.
Low group	Individualist – individuals act on their own for their own good; make their own norms / categories. Examples: racing car driver, entrepreneur, gambler, maverick. They do not perceive loss – just misuse. They refer to Hierarchy as Big Brother or Nanny State.	Fatalist – individuals act on their own and are out for themselves, but the "rules of the game" are pre-set by "the man." Blank incomprehension!

RESILIENT TOOTHBRUSH[22]

As with any industry shift, there is a tendency to put the new term in front of everything in the hope that it will "fly". We saw this regularly when in the UK, the public sector was avidly following the "e" (electronic) agenda – moving services and processes online in the hope of improving efficiency. This then matured to the "t" (transformational) agenda when presumably there was a realization that actually just applying technology to an existing process without establishing whether the process was correct, appropriate or adequate does not guarantee any tangible improvements or benefits on either side of the transaction equation.

It would be possible to map the requirement to build resilience in from the ground up across the IT technologists OSI model – also known as the "seven stack layer" (as displayed, in reverse order - see Figure 5). In our resilience planning, we need to be able to match this stack with that robust "elasticity" at all of the layers:

---

[22] Source: Ross, S.J. (2008)."The resilient toothbrush". *Information Systems Control Journal*, Vol. 2, pp.1-2.

- Physical Resilience – buildings, locations, geographical boundaries and travel arrangements.
- Resilient Data centres – mirroring between sites for example.
- Resilient networks – no single points of failure.
- Resilient applications.
- Resilient users (as per the People section previously in the chapter).

We must also seek to ensure that the same risk is not realised when it comes to embedding corporate resilience as a movement across organisations in both the public and private sector.

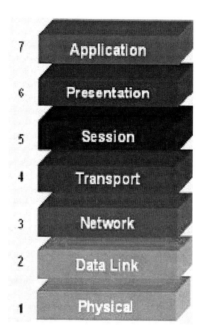

Figure 5. The OSI Model.

POLICY RECOMMENDATIONS

Policy needs to be changed by leadership in order to be driven from the top. We have seen in this chapter that there are a number of vital constituent parts to the maturation journey of business continuity and its siblings through to corporate resilience across an organisation as a whole. In particular, ensuring ongoing stakeholder engagement at all levels needs to be built into the cultural DNA of any organisation – certainly by first identifying the breadth of coverage of stakeholders and then by ensuring that the message creation and delivery is appropriate to suit all possible audiences, all the while being mindful of the process flows of activity and information within and without the organisation and its outsourced providers, partners, contractors for example.

Managing expectation is important too – both externally *and* internally. In all regards, at minimum, consider the time required to:

i) regroup;
ii) redeploy staff;
iii) travel to new location(s);
iv) rebuild (premises and/or plant equipment and machinery and/or PCs, hardware for example);
v) respond to customer enquiries;
vi) respond to press enquiries;
vii) pay employees;
viii) pay creditors and chase debtors.

This needs to be factored into the understanding and risk assessment frameworks in order to better react and ensure the longevity of an organisation and thus the resilience of it within the infrastructure of the economy and society as a whole.

CONCLUSION

There are many real issues ahead for us that will challenge our societies, countries, cultures, governments and businesses no matter where we live or work. No organisation or country can afford to either ignore the risks, or act in isolation when it considers them.

The word resilient means that something cannot be stopped from functioning (or at least not for long) or will have little or no impact from whatever caused the potential interruption. Certainly, resilient human resources can be considered as achievable with cross-training, outsourcing, teleworking, succession management and functional distribution. The benefits of a resilience approach include positioning an organisation to make the most of sudden opportunities – disruptions are not necessarily negative.[23] Ultimately the human factors will be the most significant aspect with respect to thinking, planning, responding and reacting.

REFERENCES

Books

[1] BSI Management Systems, *How to Deploy BS 25999*
[2] Thejendra B.S. (2006) *Disaster Recovery and Business Continuity – A Quick Guide for Small Organizations and busy Executives.* Cambridge: IT Governance Publishing

---

[23] Source: Stuart Anderson, principal consultant at PA Consulting Group, Mar/Apr 2008, CIR - www.irmgazine.com, page 34

Journal articles

Bennett, Dr Simon, (2000). "Learning from "near misses": a case study", *Australian Journal of Emergency Management*, Issue 3 (August), pp. 7-9 [www.ema.gov.au/.../$file/Learning_from_near_misses.pdf]

Power, P. (2008). "Business continuity – the need for a new generation", CIR (March/April), www.cirmagazine.com

Ross, S.J. (2008) "The resilient toothbrush", *Information Systems Control Journal*, Vol 2, pp.1-2.

Turner, E-J., and McGee, S. (2008) "Human resilience and business continuity", *Continuity Journal*, (May) pp.22-24 [www.humanresilience.com]

Electronic Media

*Goodin, D. (2008), "*US, UK and friends have cyber-war party - I'll hose your network, if you hose mine*", San Francisco: The Register. http://www.theregister.co.uk/2008/03/10/cyber_storm_ii_exercises/*

Wikipedia - http://en.wikipedia.org/wiki/It_security

Further Reading

BS25999-1:2006 *Business Continuity Management* – Part 1, Code of Practice, London: BSi British Standards.

BS25999-1:2006 *Business Continuity Management* – Part 2, Specification, London: BSi British Standards

Harris, S. (2003), *CISSP Certification All-in-One Exam Guide*, Second Edition, USA: McGraw Hill Osborne.

Sharp, J. (2008), *Meeting the Requirements of BS 25999*, London: BSi Business Information.

In: Strategizing Resilience and Reducing Vulnerability
Editors: Peter R.J. Trim and Jack Caravelli

ISBN 978-1-60741-693-7
© 2009 Nova Science Publishers, Inc.

Chapter 10

TOWARDS THE HARDENED ORGANIZATION

Maitland Hyslop

ABSTRACT

Business, or more correctly organizational, continuity has developed over time from disaster recovery, through business continuity, to a current emphasis on resilience. It is a logical extension of this progression to seek a hardened organization under certain circumstances. A hardened organization requires certain characteristics not found in resilient organizations. Some of these may be surprising e.g. the type of staff required. In time it is likely that certain particular organizations operating in specific vertical sectors and in a global market will need to become hardened organizations. Hardening an organization is not just about technology. It is also about governance, business strategy, management, marketing, and human resources. At the centre of the hardening approach is an understanding of risk. It is a much more holistic approach than is normally taken by disaster recovery, business continuity, or resilience approaches. The approach to hardening can be based in a number of different business functions. Marketing is one. The impact of a hardening approach on marketing and the key thirteen critical infrastructures is discussed. Hardening an organization can be approached in different ways. An effective way is to start from the CEO, as other approaches have dangers.

INTRODUCTION

Protection from disruptive and potentially lethal events has become an important subject for both states and organizations, particularly when facing either Asymmetric Warfare or Obstructive Marketing attacks. Over the past 25 years the general approach to protection has developed from the means of disaster or business recovery, through 'business' continuity, to a current emphasis on resilience. Looking further ahead it is logical to assume that beyond the resilient organization, and organization is probably a better term than business, lies the 'hardened organization'. This chapter briefly explores the development of the continuity processes of defending both states and organizations, and looks forward to how a 'hardened organization' might develop.

The assumption is made, for the purposes of this chapter, that the term resilience [1] and other related terms are understood. It is important to place in context and define our current terms: hardened, and organization. The context is a democratic, capitalist state. It is also assumed these terms are understood. This context could be more closely defined as those organizations in countries/nation states who might expect to be attacked by either Asymmetric Warfare[2] or Obstructive Marketing [3]. In general these are likely to be the constituent members of the G8 [4], OECD [5] or NATO [6] and their national organizations – be they private [7], public [8] or third sector [9].

THE HARDENED ORGANIZATION

In computing, hardening is the process of securing a system. This work is especially done to protect systems against hostile environments or attackers. Hardened steel is steel which will not deform or degrade. Hardening in martial arts is the process of strengthening the body to withstand various attacks. Hardened shelters are those, particularly in a nuclear conflict context, which will withstand military attacks. Organization is a term that refers to a functional social body that operates, usually, in a defined environment and has a defined boundary. The use of the word 'usually' is because it is increasingly clear that some organizations have 'fuzzy', or poorly defined, boundaries as a consequence of either the personnel involved or process design. This is particularly the case with 'virtual' organizations and those organizations that permit the use of personal digital accessories.

The 'hardened organization' can therefore be defined as a public, private or third sector organization within the context of a democratic and capitalist state which can withstand, and is protected from, Asymmetric Warfare or Obstructive Marketing attacks. The 'hardened organization' differs from the resilient organization in that it is not damaged by an attack and

---

[1] Resilience: the ability to bounce back to an original form.
[2] Asymmetric Warfare: originally referred to war between two or more actors or groups whose relative power differs significantly. Contemporary military thinkers tend to broaden this to include asymmetry of strategy or tactics; today "asymmetric warfare" can describe a military situation in which two belligerents of unequal power interact and attempt to exploit each other's characteristic weaknesses. Such struggles often involve strategies and tactics of unconventional warfare, the "weaker" combatants attempting to use strategy to offset deficiencies in quantity or quality.
[3] Obstructive Marketing: 'Any process, legal or not, which prevents or restricts the distribution of a product or service, temporarily or permanently, against the wishes of the product manufacturer, service provider or customer' Hyslop, MP (1999) quoted in Hyslop,MP (2007) Critical Information Infrastructures, Springer, Boston, USA
[4] G8 Canada, France, Germany, Italy, Japan, Russia, the United Kingdom and the United States: accounting for over 65% of world trade.
[5] OECD The 30 member countries of the OECD are:Australia, Austria, Belgium, Canada, Czech Republic, Denmark, Finland, France, Germany, Greece, Hungary, Iceland, Ireland, Italy, Japan, Korea, Luxembourg, Mexico, the Netherlands, New Zealand, Norway, Poland, Portugal, Slovak Republic, Spain, Sweden, Switzerland, Turkey, United Kingdom, United States. Accounting for over 80% of world data traffic.
[6] NATO: Belgium, Canada, Denmark, France, Iceland, Italy, Luxembourg, Netherlands, Norway, Portugal, UK, USA, Greece, Turkey, Germany, Spain, Czech republic, Hungary, Poland, Bulgaria, Estonia, Latvia, Lithuania, Romania, Slovakia, Slovenia. Defending much of the G8 and OECD.
[7] Organizations generally responsible to Shareholders
[8] Organizations generally responsible to Government
[9] Organizations generally responsible to their Members, or a Charity

therefore has no need, as the resilient organization has, to 'bounce back in its original form' from an attack. It is therefore even more robust than the resilient organization.

The 'hardened organization' represents the pinnacle of a 'business (or organization) continuity' hierarchy comprising:

- Recovery
- Continuity
- Resilience
- Hardening

This hierarchy began life some 25 years ago when it was realised that lost organizational data, in particular, needed to be recovered in order for an organization's operations to continue. This process was started by the banks. In turn it became important, again led by the financial services industry, to plan their business so that business could continue in the event of loss or damage. This was the beginning of the business continuity programmes. Later again it was realised that businesses should not be disrupted at all by flood, fire, data loss etc., and hence the pursuit of the resilient business. As time went on it was clear that not just businesses required such strategies and tactics. These terms became appropriate for all organizations. Recently, for some organizations, it is clear that a 'hardened' approach is appropriate. In all these areas there is a cost/benefit balance. So a sole trader would commit business suicide if he/she tried to harden their business from the start. On the other hand some multi-nationals, big banks and international oil companies are appropriate examples, need to harden all or part of their business.

Please consult Figure1.

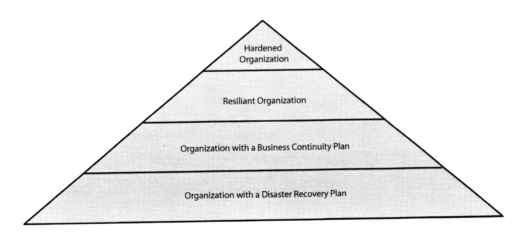

Figure 1. The Hardened Organization Hierarchy.

These are the improving and sequential steps of an organization's ability to withstand attack or disaster (although a hardened organization should never, by definition, suffer a disaster).

This hierarchy has at its base those organizations that rely on some form of business or disaster recovery plan to get back on their feet after some damaging event. Statistically, these organizations have a poor chance of survival, less than 25% according to London Resilience and others [10]. The next stage up consists of those organizations that have a business continuity plan. Yet a business continuity plan does not guarantee safety – as 90% of businesses that lose data are forced to shut down within 2 years.[11] Many of these do have a business continuity plan. The resilient organizations are those that can 'bounce back' after an event. This group accounts for less than 10% of all organizations. At the top is the 'hardened organization', the organization that does not have a problem at all following an event that challenges 'business continuity'.

The essential issues to look at in order to create a hardened organization can be broken down into a number of headings. Please consult Exhibit 1.

Exhibit 1

- Strategy
  o Business
  o Hardening
- Governance
- Risk Management
- Risk Scorecard
  o Leadership
  o Business Design
  o Business Ecosystem
  o Business Environment
  o Performance Measures
  o Knowledge Management
  o Management Processes
  o Organizational Values
- Business Rhythm and Routine
- Internal Processes
  o Finance
  o Sales and Marketing
  o Operations
  o Technical
  o RandD
  o Manufacturing Processes and Fulfillment
  o Service Processes and Fulfillment
- Staff
- Premises
- Company Equipment
- Information Technology
- Paper Records
- External Disruption

---

[10] London Resilience and Northumberland County Council Emergency Planning Department Business Continuity Leaflets 2007
[11] From www.businesscontinuitycentres.com (Accessed 20 February 2008)

- Business Locality
- Insurance

This is a familiar list, but the requirements for 'hardening' each part may come as a surprise to some. In addressing the 'hardening' of an 'organization' this Chapter seeks merely to highlight some of the main points to be covered by a hardening plan. It is not possible to go into great detail here. Some of the issues that must be looked at under these headings are therefore as follows.

BUSINESS/ORGANIZATION STRATEGY

Business Strategy basically comes down to improving profits and cash flow drastically as then everything is possible! The initial fundamentals are:

- Sales Opportunities – these need to be protected and understood from an Obstructive Marketing perspective.
- Customer Service – customer service must be continued under all circumstances, so IT and communication systems need to be sophisticated.
- Business Image – the Brand must be as 'secure' as the rest of the business; it must stand for something and be capable of surviving an attack in its own right. This applies to charities too – where Red Cross and Red Crescent may not be effective third sector 'Brands' in certain religious areas.
- Cost Reduction – cost reduction is not a contradiction in terms for a hardened organization. Often costs can be reduced through 'hardening'. IT systems are one example of an area where this may happen. Additional security prevents costly IT project management mistakes.

Asset and Cash Management – physical and non-physical assets need to be looked at from a slightly different perspective in a hardened organization. Are the physical assets in a position to take up the requirements of another part of the organization? Is cash, particularly in an international context, readily available to keep different parts of the organization going. Can it be safely accessed? Are there potential unknown threats to cash management in an emergency?

In addition a number of considerations have been cited in Exhibit 2.

Exhibit 2

- Taking Stock
  - Identifying market segments and geographical territories – which will survive an attack, or will not have a major impact on core business in the event of an attack. Oil businesses, for example, need to think about this one.
  - Relevant historical analysis – to understand opportunities and threats. Former colonial, and American, businesses need to think about this one.
  - Market forecasts – are they robust enough?

- Customer profitability – will the customers stay loyal?
- Product costs – can they be controlled?
- Total cost impact – can they too be controlled?
* Overcoming Obstacles
- Internal obstacles – do all staff understand the concept?
- External obstacles – is there external support, for example in the supply chain?
* Developing Alternatives
- Organic Growth
- Licensing and Royalty Deals
- Franchising
- Minority Equity Stakes
- JVs and Consortia
- Mergers and demergers
- Majority Equity Stakes
- Take-over and Reverse Take-Overs
- Alternatives within Functions
* Acquisitions
- Acquisition Profiles
- Sticking To The Profile
- Post –Acquisition Management
* Key Ingredients For Success
- Major Business Development Projects
- Effective Organizational Structure
- Sound Decisions
- Motivated Staff

> All Free From Obstructive Marketing Issues

In each of these strategic areas the hardening plan would include an Obstructive Marketing defence plan to cope with potential threats in each area. An Obstructive Marketing defense plan is a plan that predicts the obstacles to a business' marketing plan and devises means of overcoming them.

HARDENING STRATEGY

The hardening strategy is different for each type of organization. Some state/public organizations will need no cost related judgments to be made. Commercial/private and third sector organizations' hardening decisions are likely to be governed by cost and the issue of compliance. It should be noted that very few organizations can consider themselves free from some sort of regulation regarding business recovery/continuity/resilience/hardening planning. Indeed many banks now consider fulsome compliance to be a competitive advantage. This is not the case with motor manufacturers' Tier 1 – 3 suppliers, who, currently, consider it an unnecessary cost. This attitude will no doubt change over time, as regulation and compliance drives down into all sectors of the economy in response to an increased range of threats and real, or perceived, mismanagement issues.

The key to the hardening strategy is the business strategy, and an understanding of how critical strategy is to continuing operations. This is the who, what, where, when and how type of analysis. This analysis should also involve a Strengths, Weaknesses, Opportunities and Threats (SWOT) analysis of the organization and a Boston Matrix (identifying the market position of products/services) approach to products/services in order to better understand the parts of the organization and products that need to be hardened.

Governance is increasingly important to the hardening of an organization.

A selection of Governance advisories that makes a 'hardened organization' approach appropriate are the following:

- Turnbull Guidelines — addresses business continuity, risk management, and appropriate internal controls for companies listed on the London Stock Exchange, which first mandated requirements of this type. Stock exchanges around the globe are watching the impact this has when the compliance date has been reached and what the domino effect will be. (UK)
- Cadbury/Higgs/Nolan reports on Governance in the private and public sectors. (UK)
- Financial Services Agency Guidelines. (UK)
- Solicitors Regulatory Authority Rules. (UK)
- NYSE (proposed) Rule 446—addresses business continuity, risk management, and appropriate internal controls for companies listed on the New York Stock Exchange. NASD has required that all of its members implement risk management and business continuity programmes. (USA)
- Sarbanes-Oxley Act (2002)—requires auditors (internal and external) to provide a detailed report on a company's internal controls to the SEC. This will be published in the annual reports in its entirety. (USA)

Regulations related to privacy, security, risk management, and corporate governance:

- HIPAA (U.S.)—includes seven specific business continuity management points with 2003 compliance by large corporations. Includes federal civil and criminal penalties.
- Expedited Funds Availability Act (U.S.)—requires demonstrated business continuity plans to ensure prompt availability of funds (federally chartered financial institutions).
- Gramm-Leach-Bliley Act (U.S.)—wide range of organizations providing financial services beyond banks (for example, automobile dealers, retail stores, financial planners, tax preparers, and insurance and real estate industries) requiring appropriate controls in place for a strong focus on client privacy. An unusual addition to this act is that it also includes vendors and suppliers to the institutions identified.
- Presidential Decision Directive (PDD) 63 (U.S., 1998 – and later updates)—calls for an effort to ensure the security and continuous availability of critical infrastructures (physical, IT, and telecommunication) by 2003.
- Telecommunications Regulations 2000 (UK).
- Australian Commonwealth Criminal Code (December 2001 update) (Australia)— establishes criminal penalties for officers and directors of organizations that

experience a major disaster and fail to have a proper business continuity plan in place.
- Telecommunications Act of 1996 (USA).
- Foreign Corrupt Practices Act (FCPA) (USA)—addresses internal controls and criminal penalties.

Additional regulations and guidelines:

- Computer Fraud and Abuse Act of 1986, revised 1996.
- Computer Security Act of 1987, Public Law 100-235.
- Federal Financial Institutions Examination Council (FFIEC): Information Systems Examination Handbook.
- Federal Reserve Commercial Bank Examination Manual, Section 4060 Computer Services.
- Federal Deposit Insurance Corporation, BL-22-88: Contingency Planning for Financial Institutions.
- Federal Reserve Board, Policy Statement, SR89-16: Interagency Policy on Contingency Planning for Financial Institutions SP-5.
- Federal Reserve Board, Policy Statement, SR97-15 (SPE): Corporate Business Resumption and Contingency Planning SP-5.
- Federal Reserve Board, Policy Statement, SR98-9 (SUP): Assessment of IT in the Risk-Focused Framework [12]

If your organization is subject to one or more of these Governance approaches then your organization probably needs a 'hardened' approach in one or more areas.

RISK MANAGEMENT

Some of the oldest writings known to historians are concerned with man's wrestle with uncertainty, and over thousands of years he has evolved a number of ways to attempt to handle it, from sacrifices to influence the harvest, to fortune telling such as astrology, to more scientific means such as market research and economic modeling. Risk management concerns itself with uncertainties about the future that could bring down an organization. It is among the most important disciplines of modern management, yet it is poorly understood. It is concerned with statistics and unpredictability, yet most managers, even many trained scientists, do not grasp statistical behavior at the intuitive level. Subconsciously we all confuse a very small probability of a major disaster, with a small disaster.

The formal parts of an organization are those most often emphasized. These are the parts about which we make decisions and over which we have some control. We will sometimes refer to them as the controllable parts of the organization, although we have at best only partial control over them. They include our mission, our organizational structure, our

---

[12] More detail available at: http://ftp.hp.com/pub/services/continuity/info/corp_gov_bca_5983-1677EN.pdf (Accessed: 20 February 2008)

recruitment policy, the systems we use, the hardware we buy, the training we provide, the procedures we enforce, and so on. A fuller picture includes factors over which we have virtually no control, such as national strikes, equipment failures, outbreaks of fire, the weather, the existence and intentions of hostile parties, human frailty and so forth. These uncontrollables, each of which affects many business functions, do not just occur singly, but may arise in combination, and of course the number of combinations is enormous.

It is unfashionable to speak much of these uncontrollables since they make us feel uncomfortable and helpless. Yet every organization on the planet is susceptible to certain combinations of things all going wrong at the same time. As risk analysts we know that we all depend on things over which we have little or no control. These things constitute the essential luck we need to continue functioning. Our job is to arrange things so that we rely on as little of this luck as possible.

This leads us to the following definitions:

- Risk is sensitivity to those things we cannot control.
- Risk Management is the science of understanding and reducing our sensitivity to those things we cannot control.

Understanding risk involves understanding why we depend on things we cannot control, through an understanding of Dependency Relationships. The formal part of the organization can be thought of as being under constant attack by the uncontrollable part. Risk Management is about designing the former to be maximally resilient to the latter. While we cannot control the root causes, the uncontrollables, nevertheless the effects are more under our control through management of the dependency relationships within the organization. Interdependency relationships are unique to the particular organization, and only by coming to terms with the actual relationships in that organization can anything really valuable be done to understand, manage and reduce risks.

Dependency Modeling was developed to capture these interdependencies in a highly visual model so that the consequence of failures could be uncovered in the safe, virtual environment of the computer. Having created the model it is relatively easy to:

- Infer the risk to the organization implied by the model.
- Illustrate the risk graphically in easy-to-understand terms.
- Find which scenarios are the most dangerous to the organization.
- Find variations of the organizational structure which carry less risk.
- Evaluate the effectiveness of any countermeasures.
- Determine which factors are important and which can be ignored.
- Support management proposals with evidence.
- Avoid spending money on measures which are likely to be ineffective.
- Find ways of reducing risk without necessarily spending money.

Using the methodology above also allows us to create an Asymmetric Warfare or Obstructive Marketing Risk Model. The risk model, of course, would be different for each organization looking to deal with Asymmetric Warfare or Obstructive Marketing threats. This modeling is important because it has allowed the concepts of Asymmetric Warfare and

Obstructive Marketing to move from an idea, to a concept, through examples, to a scientific base, to a plan to control them. Clearly, the model has developed from the who, when, where, how and why questions. This is not only a complete cycle – but completes the requirement concerning the ordering experience. Asymmetric Warfare and Obstructive Marketing are therefore sufficiently real for a plan to be constructed to deal with their various risk aspects [13]. As ever, when discussing risk, it is important to emphasize that the benefits of taking a risk are as important as any mitigation of the risk. This is a point often lost on those, particularly in the public sector, who make risk assessments.

Risk Scorecard

The Business risk scorecard would look to include:

- Leadership
- Business Design
- Business Ecosystem
- Business Environment
- Performance Measures
- Knowledge Management
- Management Processes
- Organizational Values

These processes follow Robin Wood's ideas [14]. Proper attention to these issues will, of themselves, result in a resilient organization. The analysis of each area from a hardening perspective will lead to different approaches.

BUSINESS RHYTHM AND ROUTINE

Every business has a rhythm and routine. It is important to understand that maintaining rhythm and routine is part of a hardening process. This is because rhythm and routine breeds a familiar environment in which staffs are comfortable, but not necessarily in a 'comfort zone'. It is also because keeping to routine and rhythm makes sure that time becomes free for more imaginative planning time. Please consult Exhibit 3.

Exhibit 3.

Internal Processes
- Finance
- Sales and Marketing

---

[13] From Hyslop, MP (1999). Op.Cit. These comments also appeared in Hyslop, MP et al (1996) Advanced Inventory Management. Whessoe plc and Hyslop, MP (2008) Advanced Inventory Management, Reiver. These comments on risk and dependency are originally from discussions and documentation on Dependency Modeling accredited to Professor John Gordon and Chris Baker.

[14] Wood, R. (2001), Managing Complexity, Economist Books, London, UK

- Operations
- Technical
- Research and Development
- Manufacturing Processes and Fulfillment
- Service Processes and Fulfillment
- Quality System – Six Sigma or ISO 9000

Staff

- Type, Location, Quality, Training, Age, Susceptibility to Disease e.g Bird Flu, Vaccinations etc, Screening

Premises

- Ability to operate without one or more sites

Company Equipment

- Transportable or able to pick up any new capacity requirements (N.B. This may mean not, for example, being the lowest cost producer but being the producer that can guarantee production).

Information Technology

- Anywhere anytime

Paper Records
- Indestructible storage of key papers

External Disruption

- Minimized, especially in the supply chain

Business Locality

- Robust

Insurance

- Benefits the hardened organization in terms of premiums

The key benefit of a hardened organization is company value…it is clear what happens when a company is not what it is perceived to be (Shell – reserves [15]) or an individual business leader not what he is perceived to be (BP - Lord Browne [16]) – so if a company is all it says it is then there will be clear shareholder value in this – just as there is, within the balance sheet, in maintaining good information systems and a brand. In general, hardening is probably more appropriate for a global company than it is for a local SME. However, the principles involved in hardening the organization are likely to be valid to both. This is an area in which research is required.

HARDENING AND THE MARKETING MIX

Hardening can, of course, be looked at in different ways. So, as an alternative to the approach noted above, a more marketing centric approach could be taken.

Looking at the 'hardening' of an organization by reference to the Marketing Mix is one way of structuring an approach to looking at how a business might harden its activities. Such an approach also has relevance to the public and third sectors. The marketing mix is the combination of marketing activities an organization develops to best meet the needs of its targeted market. Traditionally the marketing mix consisted of just 4 Ps.

For example, motor vehicle manufacturers like Audi produces products that are of the highest quality and fit for the needs of different groups of consumers and:

- Offers a range of cars at value for money prices, depending on the market segmented they are targeted at,
- Sells the cars through appropriate outlets such as dealerships and showrooms in prime locations, i.e. in the right places, and
- Supports the marketing of the products through appropriate promotional and advertising activity.

The marketing mix thus consists of four main elements:

1 Product
2 Price
3 Place
4 Promotion. Getting the mix of these elements right enables the organization to meet its marketing objectives and to satisfy the requirements of customers.

In addition to the traditional four Ps it is now customary to add some more Ps to the mix to give us seven Ps. The additional Ps have been added because today marketing is far more customer oriented than ever before, and because the service sector of the economy has come

---

[15] Shareholders Want To Know Where Shell's Reserves Went Available at www.guardian.co.uk /oil/story/0,11319,1125480,00.html (Accessed 20 February 2008)
[16] Lord Browne Resigns Available at http://news.bbc.co.uk/2/hi/business/6612703.stm (Accessed 20 February 2008)

to dominate economic activity in many areas. These 3 extra Ps are particularly relevant to this new extended service mix.

The three extra Ps are:

1. Physical layout - in the days when manufacturing dominated the UK economy the physical layout of production units such as factories was not very important to the end consumer because they never went inside the factory. However, today consumers typically come into contact with products in retail units - and they expect a high level of presentation in modern shops - e.g. record stores and clothes shops. Not only do they need to easily find their way around the store, but they also often expect a good standard or presentation.

The importance of quality physical layout is important in a range of service providers, including:

- Students going to college or university have far higher expectations about the quality of their accommodation and learning environment than in the past. As a result colleges and universities pay far more attention to creating attractive learning environments, student accommodation, shops, bars and other facilities.
- Air passengers expect attractive and stimulating environments, such as interesting departure lounges, with activities for young children.
- Hair dressing salons are expected to provide pleasant waiting areas, with attractive reading materials, and access to coffee for customers.
- Physical layout is not only relevant to stores, which we visit, but also to the layout and structure of virtual stores, and websites.

2. Provision of customer service - customer service lies at the heart of modern service industries. Customers are likely to be loyal to organizations that serve them well - from the way in which a telephone query is handled, to direct face-to-face interactions. Although the 'have a nice day' approach is a bit corny, it is certainly better than 'a couldn't care less' approach to customer relations. Call centre staff and customer interfacing personnel are the front line troops of any organization and therefore need to be thoroughly familiar with good customer relation's practice.

3. Processes - associated with customer service are a number of processes involved in making marketing effective in an organization: e.g. processes for handling customer complaints, processes for identifying customer needs and requirements, processes for handling orders and so forth.

The 7 Ps - price, product, place, promotion, physical presence, provision of service, and processes comprise a modern marketing mix that is not only particularly relevant in the service industry, but is also relevant to any form of business where meeting the needs of customers is given priority [17].

---

[17] See http://www.thetimes100.co.uk/theory/theory--the-extended-marketing-mix-(7ps)--319.php

ILLUSTRATING HARDENING USING THE MARKETING MIX AND CRITICAL INFRASTRUCTURES

Critical Infrastructures are classified, after Hyslop's (2007) [18] common list, as follows:

- Critical Information Infrastructure
- Energy
- Finance
- Food Supply
- Health
- Government Services
- Law and Order
- Manufacturing
- National Icons
- Transport
- Water
- Waste Water
- People
- Education/Intellectual Property

The 7P's and the 13 Critical Infrastructures allows for the creation of a matrix which helps to suggest the key areas in which infrastructures might best be hardened.

An example is Figure 2.

Figure 2. The Important Marketing Issues In Each Common List Infrastructure As A Means Of Identifying Key Hardening Issues

	Product	Price	Place	Promotion	Physical Presence	Provision of Service	Processes
CIIP	X			x		x	x
Energy	X	x	x	x	x	x	x
Finance	X		x		x	x	x
Food Supply	X		x		x		x
Health	X						
Government	X		x	x	x	x	x
Law and Order	X		x		x	x	x
Manufacturing	X	x	x	x	x	x	x
National Icons	X		x	x	x	x	x
Transport	X	x					x
Water	X	x					x
Waste Water	X	x	x		x	x	x
People	X	x	x	x	x	x	x
Education	X	x	x	x	x	x	x

---

[18] Hyslop, MP (2007) op.cit.

Such a matrix might suggest that all Critical Infrastructures need to make sure their product is hardened. In other words all must continue to be able to deliver their product or service under the most extreme of circumstances. Many require an effective price, and a secure place to be protected against attack. Few really require promoting themselves but more require an appropriate physical presence, an effective and defendable service provision and robust processes to be considered hardened. Much of this is common sense – but this matrix addresses one way in which a hardening process may be constructed.

From such a matrix it has been noted that all Critical Infrastructures need to be able to deliver their product or service under the most extreme of circumstances. Therefore, at a strategic planning level, plans must be put in place to ensure such delivery. The remaining factors are more or less important and therefore different weights would be put upon these factors in developing a hardening plan. Statistical factor analysis would demonstrate rather more clearly than such a brief description how this needs to be weighted. This is one area for further research.

CONCLUSION

Of course these approaches, and particularly such a matrix, are neither exclusive nor exhaustive. They merely suggest that a strategic or marketing approach can be taken to hardening an organization. Strategic and marketing approaches can include a hardening approach without much philosophical or practical difficulty. After all, the issues surrounding strategy or marketing are ones where such issues have to be considered in any event. However, dangerous starting points for a hardening approach might be found in finance, human resources and, potentially, security functions. The movement of call centers to India based purely on a human resource cost approach, or the movement of manufacturing to China based purely on an accounting approach, has frequently been shown to be less than holistic in the approach to protecting the parent organization over the longer term. The security function is, of course, potentially the best place to develop a hardening approach, largely because of the thought processes involved - but until such a function has better visibility at C-suite level there are also dangers in this functional approach. Clearly the best place to start is with the CEO who should realize that the best protection for shareholders/stakeholders/members lies in an organization that can quite clearly withstand the vagaries of the current and future global international environment.

This chapter has sought to introduce the concept of hardening in relation to organizations. Hardening of organizations is particularly important when such entities may be challenged by Asymmetric Warfare or Obstructive Marketing events. It is suggested that hardening represents the latest development of an organization protection and continuity hierarchy that started some twenty years ago by looking at disaster recovery, moved on to continuity and, most recently, concentrated on resilience. The hardening process can be approached in different ways. In this Chapter hardening has been looked at, very very briefly, from a strategic, marketing and infrastructure view. Much more research and practical work needs to be undertaken on the subject of hardening the organization.

In: Strategizing Resilience and Reducing Vulnerability
Editors: Peter R.J. Trim and Jack Caravelli

ISBN 978-1-60741-693-7
© 2009 Nova Science Publishers, Inc.

Chapter 11

ESTABLISHING A SECURITY CULTURE: POINTERS FOR SENIOR MANAGEMENT

Nigel A. Jones and Peter R.J. Trim

ABSTRACT

Now and in the years ahead, senior managers will be required to pay more attention to the human and behavioural aspects of security, and this means paying attention to both internally and externally orchestrated, technical and human threats. In order that the organisation is classified as resilient, it is necessary to ensure that the organisation can absorb shock and continue to operate during an attack or crisis. Furthermore, the other organisations in partnership in an interdependent and networked world also need to be resilient, if that is, the organisational network is to be classified as secure. If an organisation within the partnership arrangement is vulnerable to attack, then the partner arrangement itself will be vulnerable. One way in which to ensure that an organisation is indeed resilient, is for senior managers to establish a security culture that permeates throughout the partnership arrangement. This means that all staff within the organisation need to be immersed in and embrace the organisation's value system, and continually promote security initiatives.

INTRODUCTION

First and foremost, security is about how people behave, whether it is behaviour that enhances security or behaviour that deliberately or accidentally undermines security. This is a basic tenet particularly espoused by those in security who come from a social sciences or human factors background. Perhaps one might say, 'Well, they would say that, would they not?' This chapter will argue that this tenet is however correct and anyone who designs security policy, strategies, technologies or systems needs to think in terms of 'Does my input help people behave more securely or less securely?' And, 'Does it introduce new vulnerabilities or difficulties which human operatives need to work-around?' In posing these questions one immediately finds that the human element is not something that is bolted on to a system but one that runs through it, from the development of applications to security architectures, daily routines and working environments. It is therefore, hard to purchase a 'human vulnerabilities plug-in'. Rather, one has to examine and take account of the human dimension at every level. Unfortunately, this can mean that important human dimensions can be neglected in the design stage of a system and as a result, an error of judgement, act of theft or even sabotage, can cause serious damage to the organisation. In an extreme case, the damage may be so severe that the organisation is unable to recover and ceases trading.

The idea underpinning the title of this chapter comes in the main from various discussions the authors have had with academics, security specialists and senior managers in various parts of the world. Several questions have recurred, namely 'Who is responsible for security?' And, 'Are managers really sympathetic to the human-centric approach to security?' The unanimous reply as always, is that everyone in an organisation is responsible for security and that security must, if the organisation is not to be vulnerable, be placed in an appropriate context in order that a security conscience is evident and manifests in a security culture.

It is crucial at this stage of the argument to indicate that the human dimension is important throughout all the organisation's operating levels and each employee has a role to play, for example to suggest what security initiatives can be put in place so that potential weaknesses are eradicated or to provide early warning of impending problems. Consequently, when security personnel start to think in terms of what specialist security related skills are needed, the role played by the social scientist and psychologist should be firmly in their mind. Indeed, the security manager's tasks are diverse and appear to be growing in complexity. Understanding different mindsets and getting people to accept the views of others and to assimilate security information and values, can be difficult when there are competing pressures and limited time horizons for example. Where there are perceptions of a blame culture or where people are seen as the problem, this can result in conflict and may give rise to further resistance to change.

Posing the question: 'Who is responsible for security?' Assumes that one has also given thought to the question: 'Who is qualified to take responsibility for security within an organisation?' The latter also needs to be viewed from the perspective of 'How will the person designated to take responsibility for security be held accountable for their actions?' A simplistic but highly relevant point.

When posing the above cited questions, it is necessary to make a distinction between 'core skills' and 'specialist skills'. The reader will it is hoped, be enthused by the content of this chapter and will take the necessary steps, either independently or in consort with their peers, to put in place a security system and processes that places the human being at the centre of security design. The tasks to be undertaken are diverse and relate to mobilising the necessary resources, building the necessary internal and external relationships, and putting in place management development programmes to raise the skill base of the employees. This is all necessary if a security culture is to be established that holds people accountable for their actions and which prompts people to commit to caring about and protecting the organisational assets, data and processes. By embedding the ethos of security within the value system of the organisation, it is hoped that the blame culture mentality, which surfaces from time to time, will be replaced by a collective and pro-active approach to problem solving and a more strategic orientation to managing change which goes beyond tactical policy enforcement with a 'big stick'.

The chapter starts by examining some of the drivers that are making security and business professionals engage in thinking about the human dimension. Attention is next paid to the insider threat and how security can be viewed as everyone's responsibility. The collectivist approach to security is highlighted and this is followed by a number of recommendations which will it is hoped provide the necessary basis for putting in place the required skills and competencies to ensure that a security culture is forthcoming. The chapter ends with a conclusion.

DRIVERS AND TRENDS

A number of drivers have been identified that have resulted in a number of threat oriented trends. It is the dynamic nature of these changing threats and their potential impact on an organisation's sustainability that is of concern to industry leaders, government representatives and security specialists. Broadly speaking, the potential impact of a threat needs to be viewed not in the context of a single organisation but in the context of interdependency, whereby organisations are linked through networked interrelationships (suppliers, manufacturers, wholesalers, retailers, trade associations and other stakeholders for example).

In the past seven years, it has become evident that there has been a growing debate among intelligence, security, law enforcement and disaster recovery personnel, about matters of risk and uncertainty and public-private sector co-operation. The terms business continuity and organisational resilience are now in common use and surface continually. With respect to disaster recovery, it can be noted that businesses had opened up a new vulnerability through increasing reliance on information technology (IT) systems[1]. Disaster recovery was, and is focused still, on what to do when IT systems go down. Business continuity built on this by putting the business at the centre of planning rather than the systems themselves. Senior managers started to recognise that business continuity was more than simply IT. Resilience goes further yet, and whilst it is not a term that is in widespread business use, it seeks to convey the idea of resilient organisations having the ability to absorb shock(s), while continuing to operate. The idea of a resilient organisation is therefore one with resilient processes, people and systems, and as a consequence requires more thought at the design and re-design stage (owing to legacy issues) than is the case when something goes wrong.

Coherence, continuity, cost savings and continual improvement throughout the supply chain are advocated by pro-active managers that are keen for their organisation to develop and maintain a sustainable competitive advantage. But what about the threat from within? Malicious action carried out by an employee can increase the organisation's overall level of vulnerability and needs to be placed in the context of the sustainability of the partnership arrangement, increased use of temporary and agency staff as well as more sensitive, critical infrastructure and data in the hands of the private sector.

A range of threat 'vectors' such as physical and cyber attack has led large corporations to examine the relationship between their security strategy and the risk oriented contingency plans of the various components of the organisation. The rise of the Chief Security Officer has been well charted.[2,3,4]

There are however, a number of different approaches to the problem and this is acceptable owing to the fact that the different business models that exist warrant different security oriented solutions. While this is an important point to note, it still needs to said that the different approaches require a high level of understanding (based on analysis and interpretation), up-to-date expertise and an ability to integrate security objectives into tactical, operational and strategic business plans. One large bank has brought the corporate and physical security departments under one roof, and another financial institution has brought them under the remit of the Chief Finance Officer, as he is responsible for all risk within the organisation; financial, business or security. A major oil company, brought together the security and risk departments, but discovered that a number of cultural differences militated against the initial convergence. This resulted in a degree of divergence whilst recognising the value of improved dialogue, even if not organisationally or geographically unified. The improved dialogue between different 'risk disciplines' is becoming established, and although it may not be a universal situation, it can be viewed as a positive step vis-à-vis the development of a security culture within an organisation.

The Chief Finance Officer above, also noted that a distinction could be made between what is managed as opposed to what is protected. This illustrates the fact that risk, viewed in a wider context, can be seen as an active part of doing business rather than simply a defensive measure. This is well understood from a financial perspective where the upsides and downsides of risk have been routinely considered, if not always practiced well given the recent crisis in banking. More work needs to be done in understanding how security and resilience can be discussed from an upside perspective as invariably it continues to be discussed in terms of what could go wrong.

One way to look at the upside/downside issue is, as some experts advocate, is to look more closely at an increasingly regulated environment. Particularly in the financial sector, where the rise of 'governance' as a concept has seen new bodies of knowledge develop such as due diligence, and linked with this is control and audit, which are viewed as necessary in order to have a 'licence' to operate. Whilst there is a downside in the form of inflated costs, one can argue that the upside of this is an improvement in standards and a framework for maintaining corporate reputation. Of course a more cynical reading of this is where the corporation maintains a check-box approach to governance through audits without substantive qualitative changes in security, behavioural propriety or culture. What is clear is that the rise of governance has had a knock-on effect and has produced a raft of regulations, standards, best practices, professional bodies and training courses, producing a fragmented stakeholder landscape, difficult to navigate and comprehend. 'Who is responsible for security and qualified' therefore requires careful consideration. It focuses attention on issues relating to security related education and training; and requires that senior managers think through what needs to be done to make governance truly effective in their organisations. Creating accountability in organisations, instituting suitable processes and raising the knowledge and skill levels of those involved in security are important considerations that need further consideration as part of implementing good governance through an effective security culture.

To illustrate this, it is worth briefly examining the role of governance and regulation in terms of its impact on organisations. A financial organisation listed on the New York stock exchange and operating in the UK is a good example to cite. The company will be subject to legislation which includes the Sarbanes Oxley Act in the US and the UK Data Protection Act amongst many others. Sarbanes Oxley, for example, requires that the organisation establishes a mandate for directors and officers relating to corporate responsibility certification and assessments for each official company financial report. This must include certifications of truth of reporting, disclosure of possible fraud and certification of internal controls. Senior managers within the company must be confident about the security of data stored and the integrity of the data itself. The Data Protection Act requires that data should be subject to "appropriate technical and organisational measures to prevent the unauthorised or unlawful processing of personal data, or the accidental loss, destruction, or damage to personal data"[5].

In order to ensure prudential behaviour this finance company is subject in the UK to the regulatory requirements of the Financial Services Authority (FSA), a non-governmental independent body, which is empowered by the UK's Financial Services Act. The FSA has four strategic statutory objectives:[6]

i) market confidence: maintaining confidence in the financial system;
ii) public awareness: promoting public understanding of the financial system;
iii) consumer protection: securing the appropriate degree of protection for consumers; and
iv) the reduction of financial crime: reducing the extent to which it is possible for a business to be used for a purpose connected with financial crime.

Also of interest to this financial institution is the Basel II requirements which for example demand that risk assessment and risk management procedures must be adequate and up to date, this includes the issue of availability of the information infrastructure.

It is clear therefore that in some way, legislatively or regulatory, the financial institution is obliged to pay attention to the traditional components of information assurance, namely confidentiality, integrity and availability. However, it is up to senior management within the organisation to decide precisely how it will meet these requirements. For assistance they can turn to various standards such as the International Standard for Information Security Management, ISO 27001. This of course states what the standard is, but does not provide detailed guidance on how it should be implemented in any particular organisation. To do this the company can turn to professional bodies which claim to be custodians of best practice and to offer professional development for those engaged in such disciplines as Information Security. The professionalisation of security is a relatively recent phenomenon. In the UK the Institute of information Security Professionals has recently established a full membership scheme with the aim of advancing "the professionalism of information security practitioners and thereby the professionalism of the industry as a whole."[7]

Other disciplines mirror this interrelationship of legislation, regulation and best practice. For example in the resilience domain, where continuity may be mandated by the UK Civil Contingencies Act, best practice guidance is provided by relevant professional bodies such as the Business Continuity Institute, Institute of Risk Management and the Emergency Planning Society. The issue for the employer or professional is to some extent the problem of deciding which qualification to have, or which body to belong to.

All of these bodies are involved in educational and training initiatives that are aimed at shaping formally or informally the skills, competencies and knowledge required by individuals to upgrade their skill base. Indeed, some have formed close contacts with institutions of further and higher education and this is encouraging to note. The UK's e-skills council aims to "ensure the UK has the skills it needs to compete in the global economy" and this is to be achieved by bringing together "employers, educators and Government to address together the technology-related skills issues no one party can solve on its own".[8] This initiative includes skills relating to information and communication technologies (ICT) security.

It is interesting that the e-skills council recognises that there is a need for partnership development in the context of educational security provision and this raises a challenging issue, namely that if one is going to tackle interdependency in resilience and security planning, at the business/institutional level and at the national level, more attention needs to be given to defining the limits of security. The challenge has a number of facets. First, is the issue of de-perimeterization. The Jericho Forum,[9] established in 2003, recognised the fact that business was relying on the secure and resilient flow of data and that there was therefore a dependency upon each organisation in the partnership arrangement to remain secure. The forum described this as the erosion of network perimeters, hence the term 'de-perimeterization'. The second issue is that the network perimeter has been extended into peoples homes through e-commerce. This means that organisations share the risk with their customers. There is therefore, a need to hold a discussion about the division of responsibility for security and the skills and knowledge required by all parties. We will return to this issue later. The third facet seems to indicate a weakness in the governance approaches described above. First and foremost the CEO will take responsibility (or at least should) for problems within their organisation. When an institution undertakes vulnerability assessment of their networks, current practice tests for vulnerabilities within the 'perimeter' of their network and does not consider the impact on other networks. When dependencies are examined at a national level, the issue of accountability and ownership becomes more problematic. The loss of one infrastructure may have an impact on another, but approaches to governance and accountability do not necessarily account for this. The issue of public good and who pays for resilience beyond a specific infrastructure is one which continues to be discussed.

In examining the drivers that produce the trends, the who's responsible and who's qualified debate surfaces. It is clear that a wide range of stakeholders are involved, encompassing the legislative and regulatory processes, the standards, best practice, knowledge and skills axis, as well as the dependency and culture issues. However, even when all these factors have been considered, the standards set and the competencies captured, the problems identified still remain: 'How can security and resilience become part of an institution's approach to business and corporate life?' 'How can security and resilience become embedded in the organisation's value system?' And 'What do senior managers need to do in order to make organisations more secure and resilient?'

People will increasingly need to be able to make sense of this apparent complexity and buy-in to the need for secure behaviours which maintains the integrity of their responsibilities and ultimately their businesses, and even societal resilience beyond their own work. While it is clear that effective governance arrangements can make individual bosses accountable for security, effective implementation will rely on bringing the workforce along with them if security is to be everyone's responsibility. The next section of this chapter examines the issues of implementing effective security and resilience measures in the workplace.

The Insider Threat and How Security Can be Viewed as 'Everyone's Responsibility'

It is fair to say that managers, planners and consultants have hitherto largely focussed on the technical aspects of backup, the physical security of buildings, the logistics of supply chains and the maintenance of office space and less on the human element. This is also true in the security space where the importance of human behaviour continues to be underplayed. Bearing this in mind, it can be argued that the type of threat posed by an insider(s) is not well understood and has not to date been fully appreciated. For example, it is well known that employees are required to memorise a number of passwords and can suffer from memory lapses. The various problems experienced by users of passwords have been cited and it can be noted that both the password and the userID need to be remembered; the password restrictions on a system by system basis need to be remembered; and when a user changes a particular password they need to remember which system it applies to.[10] Taking this a step further, it has been suggested that "security must be designed as an integral part of the system that supports a particular work activity in order to be effective and efficient. Decisions about system and file access must be based on how tasks and the workflow are organised in the real world. For example, in modern organisations, many tasks are assigned to teams, and teamwork and collaboration are encouraged. If users are then given individual passwords, and unable to access each other's files even though they are needed for shared tasks, password disclosure will become common".[11] The issue of good design combined with security awareness is key and needs to be taken seriously by organisational members, if that is, an effective security culture is to be forthcoming.[12]

The monitoring of staff, through surveillance software and other means, is controversial and often unpopular and can be interpreted as the organisation not having trust in the employees.[13] However, security professionals focus their attention on identifying and eradicating threats, and part of their work involves risk assessment and management. It has been noted that: "At the core of risk management in any social or organizational context lies the issue of how social actors discern risks and enter into communication about them and how they may be addressed".[14] It is noted, that as well as face-to-face communication, the email and telephone are effective forms of communication, and so too is teleconferencing.[15] However, in order for the communicator of a message to have influence, they must be perceived as being trustworthy.[16]

The way in which an organisation is structured is important because of how people report to those higher up the hierarchy, and how their peers are held accountable for their actions. Indeed, it can be argued that there are different organisational structural possibilities based on the age of the organisation, the industry dynamics in which it competes, the degree of turbulence in the external environment (meaning that there are additional reporting responsibilities), the degree of internationalisation of the organisation, and the way in which the organisation relates to the various stakeholders for example (organisations/institutions which may or may not have a direct influence on the organisation). The level and degree of integration is also an important factor. For example, a strategic alliance may be constructed in such a way that the organisation reports to a senior management team based in another organisation and/or operates from a different country. This outlines how complex the day to day management situation is and calls into question various management and regulatory issues. It can also be noted that some organisations are tightly controlled and the process of change is implanted on those lower down the hierarchy, normally through the services of an external consultancy.

Another point that is often overlooked but which is of importance is that known as organisational politics. In some organisations, apathy and distrust have resulted in a blame culture which is firmly embedded in the organisational value system. Power and trust are related and manifest in relationships and organisational control. However, it is important to note that organisational structural form can vary and that contingency theory recognises that it is necessary to think in terms of different contexts, if that is, an appropriate organisational structure is to be established.[17] In order to fully appreciate the various management theories and models that exist, it is necessary to understand how they have evolved through time and how they have been absorbed, accepted and rejected/modified. The systems perspective is useful as it requires that a system is viewed "as a set of interrelated and interdependent parts arranged in a manner that produces a unified whole".[18] The cultural perspective view of the firm emerged in the late 1970s and rapidly established itself.[19] Of central consideration was the organisation's cultural value system and how employees fitted into the organisation's environment.[20] Although much debate can be entered into as regards which management theory and/or model is relevant and in what context it is relevant, it has to be said that Dawson is right to point out that when analysing an organisation, it is necessary to take into account a number of issues and factors:

[1] "Organisations are interactive systems, with change in one aspect having repercussions for others, sometimes in an unintended or unanticipated way. Organisations are highly complex systems in which there is a great deal of uncertainty.
[2] There is no one best way to act in organisations: an appropriate path should be taken through paradox and contradiction in a manner appropriate to the context.
[3] Resources are always scarce, and any action is likely to have financial or social costs as well as benefits.
[4] Organisations are arenas for the activities of different interest groups which are linked through patterns of conflict, consensus and indifference.
[5] People in organisations perceive varying sources of opportunities for, and constraints on, possible action.
[6] Activities in, and outcomes from, organisations can be analysed in terms of the level of the individual, group, organisation or society; it is very important to identify the levels that are appropriate to the problems, issues or opportunities with which any practitioner or analyst is concerned".[21]

International companies and especially those in the finance sector, have tended to adopt the matrix system of management, and advances in ICT which have supported the decision-making process have facilitated this development.[22] Whatever organisational structure is decided upon, it should be noted that a company that operates globally will need to ensure that as well as taking into account local factors vis-à-vis management policies and procedures, that careful attention is paid to internal control systems.[23] The need for effective corporate governance is clear for all to see, but some would suggest that it is important to have a logical view as to what corporate governance involves. Indeed, Fahy, Roche and Weiner are convinced that a more holistic view needs to be taken towards the subject and suggest that "Enterprise Governance is based on the principle that good governance alone cannot make an organisation successful".[24] Fahy, Roche and Weiner argue that performance, conformance and corporate responsibility need to be viewed from how they will deliver long-term value in the eyes of the stakeholders.[25] They place their work in the context of an emerging framework, which also takes into account that corporate responsibility is "linked to corporate governance and risk management, as well as 'ethical' environmental and social stewardship, on which its origins are founded".[26] It is important at this point to indicate that the term corporate social responsibly has been defined as: "a commitment to improve community well-being through discretionary business practices and contributions of corporate resources".[27] This needs to be interpreted in terms of the specific attitudes and behaviours required by all stakeholders. Consequently, it is necessary to add a marketing dimension owing to the fact that organisations are involved in establishing a number of partnership arrangements, and these partnership arrangements need to be placed in various contexts (stakeholders can include suppliers, wholesalers, retailers, governments and trade associations for example). What surfaces therefore, is a collectivist view to security, which is based on an understanding that it is in everyone's interest to be aware of and champion heightened security measures, in order to counter the threats posed by both insiders and those external to the organisation, all of whom are determined to carry out an act of theft through industrial espionage or sabotage in the way of hacking into a computer system with the intention of causing damage for example.

THE COLLECTIVIST APPROACH TO SECURITY

There have been various attempts made to make public the need for a collectivist approach to be taken to security. For example, reference to the collectivist approach has been made and it has been suggested that it would be helpful to introduce a criminological perspective and ground security research within a social science context.[28] Trim has added to the body of security knowledge by advocating a broader based approach to the subject, and has also linked the subject of corporate intelligence more firmly with the subject of national security. [29,30,31,32,33] Although the emerging security concepts and frameworks are needed, it should be remembered that senior management must not lose sight of the main point, which is, 'Who is responsible for security?'[34] The question can be placed in a wider context, namely: 'Where are the boundaries of enterprise security responsibility and accountability?'[25] As well as understanding why senior managers need to pay adequate attention to resilience from the perspective of both the insider threat and the threat emanating externally, full attention needs to given to developing management security processes that integrate more fully the needs of stakeholders.[36] If a collectivist approach to security is to be successful, it needs to take into account user expectations. It also needs to take education and training beyond merely making people aware of the need for heightened security measures by influencing senior managers into agreeing that security is a core competence and an important consideration in the design of the work environment, processes and systems.[37] These aspects of strategic management, awareness and good design are developed further below.

An attempt has been made to explain how various aspects of security can be incorporated in a strategic management context, and Trim's SATELLITE (Strategic Corporate Intelligence and Transformational Marketing) model incorporates this approach and goes slightly further by having a clear marketing focus embedded in it.[38] The model specifies the work undertaken through the creation of a Corporate Intelligence Staff Support Group, a Strategic Marketing Staff Support Group, a Corporate Security Management Group, an Internet Marketing Group, a Relationship Marketing Advisory Group and a SATELLITE Advisory Group. It can be used by senior managers to integrate more effectively the work of corporate intelligence staff and staff based in stakeholder organisations (the intelligence and security services, and law enforcement agencies for example). The intelligence-security dimension is made explicit and requires that organisational designers think in terms of devising an organisational structure that ensures that data and information are protected, and the data and intelligence gathering activities undertaken do not result in an unnecessary duplication of effort. It can also be noted that the tasks assigned to people hold them accountable for their actions (owing to the high degree of transparency involved) and because of this the problems associated with inadequate information synthesising are eradicated.

The main advantage of the SATELLITE model is that it brings together in a logical manner, those involved in formulating a security auditing process; those involved in establishing an effective counterintelligence policy; staff charged with developing competitive intelligence models, tools and techniques; staff employed to identify the potential threats relating to e-commerce and e-business; specialist staff charged with establishing policy vis-à-vis the company's Web site; and marketing personnel whose job it is to identify appropriate and effective public relations channels so that the various stakeholders can be kept informed about events/situations.[39] By incorporating the term transformational, it can be noted that there is a clear indication that senior management need to be aware of what is required of them with respect to providing a vision but also in terms of how this vision is translated into organisational values that result in the acceptance of a certain style of leadership. Indeed, senior management can establish a Corporate Security Management Group that is responsible for undertaking risk assessment and the commissioning of special projects that study the various activities/potential activities of organised criminal syndicates.[40] Organised criminal syndicates are becoming increasingly involved in acts of cyber crime and counterfeiting, and their level of operational sophistication is increasing through time. Senior managers are also becoming increasingly concerned about the harmful effects associated with internally orchestrated fraud and acts of sabotage. Bearing these points in mind, it can be suggested that as well as monitoring the external environment, it is essential that managers put in place mechanisms for monitoring the internal environment. They also need to reinforce the fact that security is everybody's concern and this needs to be communicated continually. As well as specifying which security tasks are to be undertaken and when, it is clear that the style of leadership used is about reinforcing the fact that behavioural change may be necessary. Should this be the case, it can be argued that the process of change needs to be planned, communicated at all levels within the organisation and managed in an incremental manner.

However, communication, awareness, and education are not enough on their own. One reason why education and training are so important in helping for example employees to use systems and processes properly is that they can be very complicated to begin with. In other words, training is used as a way of mitigating the complexity of the products and services that are provided to people. So whilst training and education may be seen as something that is added at the end, much more thought needs to be given to designing-in security, and assurance and other so called 'non-functional' requirements up front and early in the design stage. The Cyber Security Knowledge Transfer Network has published papers on privacy engineering and secure software development and both disciplines are examples of where engineering and design needs to be improved.[41,42]

Both papers point out the need for capturing security and privacy requirements at an early stage of the process. Usually requirements are seen as how the system or software will function. Of course it is more problematic to outline what those systems, applications or processes should not do or where concepts such as security or privacy are seen as principles rather than specific functions to be designed. What is clear is that too often the 'cool functionality' is placed ahead of these other apparently mundane requirements. This can be compounded by economic pressures whereby it is more important to get what may be an imperfect application to market first rather than be second or third with a well designed product.[43]

Furthermore, both papers identified the need for security and privacy to be built in and vulnerabilities designed out throughout the life cycle of a programme, for example from requirements which build in the principles of data protection to the secure disposal of systems and data at its end of life. There is no doubt that this principle applies broadly including the design of access controls, authentication procedures, office space and environment. It requires that a common body of knowledge in what may be called security engineering be developed and that professional bodies develop standards and best practice in what it is to be an engineer just like what it is to be a security professional as described earlier. This will involve the take up of a whole system approach to engineering and design that has people and the end user at its centre.

The subject of leadership has been extensively researched and written about over the years and works by authors such as Schein have done much to place the subject in a strategic context as opposed to just an operational context.[44] Our understanding of leadership theory has been enhanced by academics such as Kakabadse, whose interpretation of what transformational leadership involves has provided new insights into what senior managers need to do in order to get their subordinates to carry out change.[45] The transformational leadership style, which is credited with empowering staff, needs to be placed within an organisational learning context, if that is, strategy formulation and implementation are to be effective. Hence, organisational learning, in order to produce the results required, should be viewed more holistically than is the case at present. Senior managers are required to pay attention to what is known as adaptive learning and generative (double-loop) learning, if that is, the knowledge available in-house is to be used to improve the functioning of the organisation.[46] Should this indeed be so, it can be argued that the organisation's value system will produce a task oriented approach to managing complexity and as a result the areas of weakness will be identified and eradicated. Furthermore, senior managers will, in the years ahead, need to take greater note of the potential threats that can manifest in the external environment. Indeed, Sheffi has indicated that senior managers will need to pay greater attention to identifying and prioritizing vulnerabilities than is the case at present.[47] It is useful at this point to highlight the fact that management theory is evolving that can provide deeper insights into how various areas of threat related complexity can be studied and management systems and processes introduced to provide guidelines for organisational change. Organisational change should not be viewed as an isolated topic but needs to placed in the context of strategy development. Indeed, the work of Kaplan and Norton is useful with respect to this as it requires that senior managers devise a strategy map which "describes the process for transforming intangible assets into tangible customer and financial outcomes. It provides executives with a framework for describing and managing strategy in a knowledge economy".[48]

Recommendations

On reflection, it would appear that senior managers will in the future need to take into account more fully, the need to devise an organisational resilience value system that gives rise to mutually-oriented business relationships that are underpinned by trust.[49] However, although it is useful for senior managers to think in terms of security being a core activity, it is necessary to suggest that this may be the case only if a holistic approach is adopted whereby senior management ensure that there is adequate risk assessment and an effective counter-intelligence policy in place.[50] This is unlikely to be achieved, however, unless senior management look more closely at the human resource implications of establishing a security culture.[51] In order that a security culture is developed, it is important that top management take into account the following recommendations: [52] a behavioural and attitudinal view of security culture is adopted that facilitates understandable, achievable and desirable behaviour, otherwise the term security culture can be meaningless;

(i) simple, attention grabbing techniques are used to engage the various stakeholders in the security culture development process;
(ii) ways are found through good design and engineering to make security easy for people to comply with and that the assigned security responsibilities hold people accountable for their actions;
(iii) ways need to be found to make security information easily accessible to staff generally;
(iv) in-house information technology staff and external professionals need to adopt a collectivist approach to security and understand that core skills have a human and behavioural element;
(v) a set of behaviour oriented human vulnerability standards need to be devised, (because there is a current gap in security standards);
(vi) a human vulnerability audit procedure needs to be established; and
(vii) a realistic assessment made from time to time (through an appropriate monitoring mechanism) of how the organisation's security culture is developing.

Conclusion

The years ahead are likely to provide senior managers with many challenges, unfortunately, a number of the challenges that are likely to arise and which become high level threats, and which may result in significant damage to the organisation, will do so because they were undetected. Predicting adequately both the threat itself and the consequences of the threat manifesting, are key challenges for managers. The threat posed by organisational insiders has not as yet been fully realised and quantified, and this is of concern. However, some industry leaders are now embracing more fully this issue and are working hard to put a security culture in place that should allow the various management safeguards to be devised and implemented, which eradicate future potential problems. It is hoped that initiatives in the area of counteracting the unlawful attempts made by insiders will become common practice within organisations and the threats, should they materialise, will be dealt with effectively thus limiting the damage caused to the organisation.

REFERENCES

[1] See http://www.businessresiliency.com/evolution_history.htm accessed on 18 May 2008, for a brief US-centric resilience timeline.
[2] See for example http://searchsecurity.techtarget.com/tip/0,289483,sid%20%20% 20% 2014_gci851563,00.html# accessed on 24 October 2008.
[3] Barrass, N., Briggs, R., and Edwards, C. (2006) *Well Qualified? The Skills, Qualities and Values Needed for Doing Business Securely in the 21st Century*. Demos, London.
[4] Briggs, R., and Edwards C. (2006) The Business of Resilience Corporate Security for the 21st Century. Demos, London.
[5] See for example http://www.legislation.gov.uk/acts/acts1998/ukpga_19980029_en_ 9#sch1-pt1 accessed on 18 May 2008, for UK Data Protection Act Principles.
[6] See http://www.fsa.gov.uk/Pages/about/aims/statutory/index.shtml accessed on 18 May 2008.
[7] http://www.instisp.org/
[8] http://www.e-skills.com/
[9] http://www.opengroup.org/jericho/
[10] Sasse, M.A., Brostoff, S., and Weirich, D. (2001). "Transforming the 'weakest link' – a human/computer interaction approach to usable and effective security", *BT Technology Journal*, Vol 19 No 3 (July), p.124.
[11] Ibid., p.128
[12] Adams, A., and Sasse, M.A. (1999). "Users are not the enemy", *Communications of the ACM*, Vol 42 No 12, pp.41-40.
[13] Cialdini, R.B., Petrova, P.K., and Goldstein, N.J. (2004). "The hidden costs of organizational dishonesty", *MIT Sloan Management Review* (Spring), p.71.
[14] Backhouse, J., Bener, A., Chauvidul-Aw, N., Wamala, F., and Willison, R. (2005). "Risk management in cyberspace", in Mansell, R., and Collins, B.S. (Eds) *Trust and Crime in Information Societies*. Edward Elgar, Cheltenham, pp.349-379.
[15] Ibid., p.355.
[16] Ibid., p.355.
[17] Dawson, S. (1996). *Analysing Organisations*. Palgrave, Basingstoke, p.124.
[18] Robbins, S.P. (2000). *Managing Today*. Prentice Hall, Upper Saddle River, NJ., p.605.
[19] Ibid., p.606.
[20] Ibid., pp.606-607.

[21] Dawson, S. (1996). *Analysing Organisations.* Op. Cit., pp.268-269.
[22] Backhouse, J., Bener, A., Chauvidul-Aw, N., Wamala, F., and Willison, R. (2005). "Risk management in cyberspace". Op. Cit., p363
[23] Ibid., p.363.
[24] Fahy, M., Roche, J., and Weiner, A. (2005). *Beyond Governance: Creating Corporate Value Through Performance, Conformance and Responsibility.* John Wiley & Sons Ltd., Chichester, p.2.
[25] Ibid.,p.2.
[26] Ibid., pp.2-3.
[27] Kotler, P., and Lee, N. (2005). *Corporate Social Responsibility: Doing the Most Good for Your Company and Your Cause.* John Wiley & Sons Ltd., Chichester, p.3.
[28] Backhouse, J., Bener, A., Chauvidul-Aw, N., Wamala, F., and Willison, R. (2005). "Risk management in cyberspace". Op. Cit., pp.370-371.
[29] Trim, P.R.J. (2000). "The company-intelligence services interface and national security". *International Journal of Intelligence and CounterIntelligence*, Vol 13 No 2, pp.204-214.
[30] Trim, P.R.J. (2002). "Counteracting industrial espionage through counterintelligence: The case for a corporate intelligence function and collaboration with government," *Security Journal*, Vol 15 No 4, pp.7-24.
[31] Trim, P.R.J. (2003). "Public and private sector cooperation in counteracting cyberterrorism." *International Journal of Intelligence and CounterIntelligence*, Vol 16 No 4, pp.594-608.
[32] Trim, P.R.J. (2005) "The GISES model for counteracting organized crime and international terrorism." *International Journal of Intelligence and CounterIntelligence*, Vol 18 No 3, pp.451-472.
[33] Trim, P.R.J. (2005) "Managing computer security issues: preventing and limiting future threats and disasters." *Disaster Prevention and Management*, Vol 14 No 4, pp.493-505.
[34] Jones, N. (2007). "Security – who's responsible, who's qualified?" *The Third CAMIS Security Management Conference: Strategizing Resilience and Reducing Vulnerability*, Birkbeck College, University of London, 5th to 7th September.
[35] Ibid.
[36] Ibid.
[37] Ibid.
[38] Trim, P.R.J. (2004). "The strategic corporate intelligence and transformational marketing model". *Marketing Intelligence and Planning*, Vol 22 No 2, pp. 240-256.
[39] Ibid., pp.253-254.
[40] Ibid., p.249
[41] http://www.ktn.qinetiq-tim.net/content/files/groups/privacy/CSKTN_Privacy_SIG_White_Paper_08.pdf accessed on 24 October 2008.
[42] http://www.ktn.qinetiq-tim.net/content/files/groups/securesoft/SSDSIG_softwareSecurityFailures.pdf accessed on 24 October 2008.
[43] For more information on security economics see http://www.ktn.qinetiq-tim.net/content/files/ESRC_econinfsec.pdf accessed on 28 October 2008.
[44] Schein, E.H. (1992). *Organisational Culture and Leadership.* Jossey-Bass, San Francisco.

[45] Kakabadse, A. (2000). "From individual to team to cadre: tracking leadership for the third millennium." *Strategic Change*, Vol 9 No 1, pp.5-16.
[46] Morgan, R.E., Katsikeas, C.S., and Adu, K.A. (1998). "Market orientation and organizational learning capabilities." *Journal of Marketing Management*, Vol 14, pp.353-381.
[47] Sheffi, Y. (2005). *The Resilient Enterprise: Overcoming Vulnerability for Competitive Advantage*. The MIT Press, Cambridge, Massachusetts.
[48] Kaplan, R.S., and Norton, D.P. (2001). *The Strategy-Focused Organization: How Balanced Scorecard Companies Thrive in the New Business Environment*. Harvard Business School Press, Boston, Massachusetts, p.69.
[49] Lee, Y-I and P.R.J. Trim (2006). "Retailing strategy: the role of marketing intelligence, relationship marketing and trust." *Marketing Intelligence & Planning*, Vol 24 No 7, p.739.
[50] Trim, P.R.J. (2005) "Managing computer security issues: preventing and limiting future threats and disasters". Op. Cit., p.502.
[51] Jones, N. (2007). "Security – who's responsible, who's qualified?" Op. Cit.
[52] Ibid.

In: Strategizing Resilience and Reducing Vulnerability
Editors: Peter R.J. Trim and Jack Caravelli

ISBN 978-1-60741-693-7
© 2009 Nova Science Publishers, Inc.

Chapter 12

STRATEGIC TRANSFORMATIONAL MANAGEMENT IN THE CONTEXT OF INTER-ORGANIZATIONAL AND INTRA-ORGANIZATIONAL PARTNERSHIP DEVELOPMENT

Yang-Im Lee

ABSTRACT

By embracing the concept of organizational learning, top management can encourage staff to improve their knowledge and skill base through time. Problems do occur and a major problem is how top managers can encourage their staff to learn on a continuing basis, and to co-operate with staff outside their immediate department. The learning process is not just about acquiring knowledge and skills, it is also about developing a vision that is based on understanding the values that are promoted by top management. Hence, staff at various levels throughout the organization's hierarchy need to identify with the organization's value system and embrace incremental change. This is necessary if an organization is to adapt to a changing international environment and at the same time undergo a change in organizational culture. In order to manage effectively, senior managers need to ensure that the organizational configuration change process is as transparent as possible, and that organizational learning reinforces the strategic marketing approach. The process of institutionalizing organizational learning focuses senior management's attention on the management of change and the qualities associated with leadership. However, senior managers need to make a distinction between transformational leadership and transactional leadership, and take notice of the fact that a dual leadership style can be deployed in a culturally sensitive organizational environment. By embracing the concept of organizational learning, senior managers will be able to implement a leadership style that puts into place relevant management controls and workable partnerships with external organizations. It should also be possible to devise and implement a number of management models and processes that result in a pro-active and integrated decision-making process being established throughout the partnership arrangement.

INTRODUCTION

In order that an organization improves its level of performance, it is necessary for top management to make strategic decisions that provide it with a clearly defined direction and at the same time promote the concept of organizational learning. By embracing the concept of organizational learning, top management can encourage staff to improve their knowledge and skill base through time, and to devise management policies that reduce organizational vulnerability through adequate risk assessment management. However, the key focus of attention is how top managers can encourage their staff to learn on a continuing basis. Furthermore, encouraging staff to co-operate with staff outside their immediate department and organization, and especially with personnel based in partner organizations and government departments, is a major task.

Cooperation is essential if staff are to embrace the concept of the resilient organization and it can be noted that the learning organization concept is not just about acquiring knowledge and skills. Organizational learning is underpinned by a strategic vision that reinforces the core organizational values that are promoted by top management. Hence, staff at various levels throughout the organization need to identify with the organizational value system and embrace incremental change, if that is, they are to develop their full potential and become valuable members of the organization. Being a valuable member of the organization is necessary if an organization is to adapt to a rapidly changing international business environment and at the same time undergo a change in organizational culture, that results in a repositioning strategy being implemented.

In order that an organization obtains a sustainable competitive advantage, senior managers need to ensure that the organization is customer focused and is well placed to counteract the movement of competitor organizations (Montgomery and Weinberg, 1991)(Aaker, 1992, p.167; Slater and Narver, 1994, pp.24-25; Greenely, 1995, p.7; Webster, 1997, p.39). This requires that staff review the organization's strategy when appropriate and evaluate its mission statement in order to ensure that customer value is being delivered. Managers need to be aware of and understand the perceptions of customers and understand such issues as customer motivation and loyalty (McGoldrick,1990, p.1; Davies and Brooks cited in Omar, 1999, p.6; Corstjens and Corstjens, 2000, p.17). Walters (1979), Buzzell and Ortmeyer (1995, p.86), Hines (1996, p.4,633), Lewison (1997, pp.627-629), Siguaw et al., (1998), Dyer et al., (1998) and McIvor and McHugh (2000, p.223) have pointed out that in order for an organization to succeed with its strategy implementation, the organization must be able to build a relationship with its employees, and that a strong organizational culture is underpinned by a shared value system (Bass, 1985; Porter, 1996, pp.70-75; Han et al., 1998, p.31; Harris, 1998, p.368). By establishing clear aims and objectives, senior management will be able to develop an organizational culture that should, in the long-term, result in strong working relationships with partner organizations.

Building working relationships does require that senior managers devise custom made management development programmes for junior managers and also, that they select the most able junior managers and place them on a leadership development programme that incorporates aspects of strategic management. Should this be the case, the concept of organizational learning will be fully embraced and junior managers will be trained to implement change management programmes. They will also become pro-active strategic planners. Flexibility is a necessary quality with respect to managing staff from diverse backgrounds that operate on an inter-organizational and intra-organizational basis, and is something that can be taught through a crafted management mentoring process.

This chapter focuses attention on how managers can utilize the concept of organizational learning so that they can develop and implement an effective partnership oriented strategy. Reference is made to both the transformational leadership and transactional leadership style and how leadership style relates to the learning process at both the employee level and the organizational level. The issue of organizational culture is addressed and attention is given to how the organizational learning concept can provide organizational staff with the necessary strategic knowledge that enables them to devise and implement new management models and processes. Attention is also given to how leadership can be placed within the context of a strategic model of inter-organizational and intra-organizational development.

AN ORGANIZATION'S CONFIGURATION

The author of this chapter has a resource based perspective of strategy development and has linked it with the concept of organizational learning. Figure 1 outlines that an organization is composed of people, strategic processes, cultural traits, structure, systems and procedures. An organization's configuration is a result of how managers within the organization devise and implement the strategy process. In order for the strategy process to be successful, a number of distinct elements need to be in balance and be integrated into a strategic management model. Issues such as how a partner organization fits into the organization's configuration and how staff within the organization make collaborative strategic decisions, are important considerations.

According to Mintzberg (1974), the purpose of organizational structure is to identify and draw boundaries; to distribute different tasks among members; and to co-ordinate organizational activities. Senior managers shape the structure of an organization, in the sense that the strategic management process is responsible for strategic decisions relating to what type of information is required for effective decision making; how much of the information is to be processed and shared across functions and networks; and how the decision-oriented, sharing information activities are carried out (through either formal or informal means) (Vera and Crossan, 2004, p.232). Both the operational activities and the management processes for sharing strategic information have an impact upon how people in an organization adapt to change and how they embrace concepts such as organizational learning.

The organizational configuration change process outlined in Figure 1 plays a key role in providing staff lower down the hierarchy with guidance in the sense that senior managers act as mentors for junior managers, and career progression is determined by an individual's level of intellectual ability. In order to understand what is happening in both the organization's internal environment and the external business environment, it is essential that the decision-making process is as transparent as possible. This being the case, junior managers will be able to develop their intellectual appreciation of how decisions are made and what the calculated risks are; and they can interpret various signals (actions of competitors) in the external business environment.

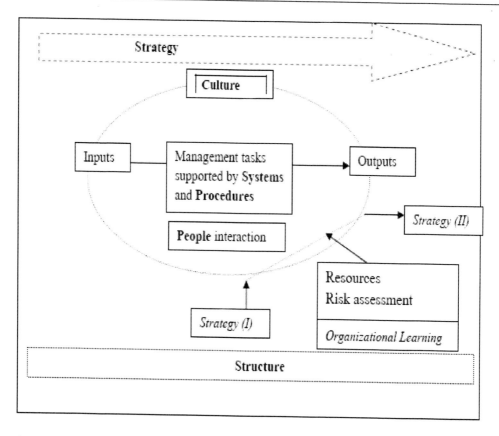

Figure 1. The organizational configuration change process.

The key point to note is that managing change needs to be viewed from a risk reduction perspective, if that is, the organization is to be viewed as less vulnerable than competitor organizations. This is important if potential threats are to be identified and dealt with before they become actual threats, and if the organizational change that occurs makes the organization more resilient. Threats that are evident in both the internal environment and the external environment have to be prioritized, in order that they can be dealt with in a logical order. It is not always possible to deal with potential threats simultaneously, and some threats have more potential to cause damage than others, and this has been recognized.

Returning to Figure 1, it can be suggested that organizational strategists need to establish if the potential threat facing an organization is likely to spill over (if it manifests) and affect partner organizations. For example, a strategy that is implemented (referred to as Strategy (I) in the Figure 1), is the current strategy and will in effect result in a secondary strategy or new strategy (referred to as Strategy (II)) being implemented in due course. In order that the strategy implementation process is successful, organizational strategists need to evaluate the staff development programmes that are in existence; decide upon the appropriate level and intensity of new staff development programmes; and identify what necessary further support is required in order that the knowledge and skill base available in order to produce workable, partner oriented strategies that counteract threats from existing and potential sources, is in place.

When evaluating the staff development programmes, senior managers need to think in terms of current and future investment programmes in human resource management development; and the time and effort needed in order to put in place development programmes that are outsourced. This means that a person centred approach is adopted to staff development and that transparency needs to be viewed from the perspective of peer group decision-making that results in consensus decision-making. As regards the motivation of staff, it is important that all members of staff view partnership development as important and mutually beneficial. The concept of mutuality is grounded in synergistic strategy development (which is evident in Strategy (II)). Connected with the issue of mutuality is loyalty, hence senior managers need to be aware of the fact that junior managers will, provided that their commitment to the organization is recognized and they are rewarded for it, remain highly motivated and goal oriented. If senior managers want their staff to remain loyal to the organization, they need to ensure that they participate fully in the decision-making process and also, that they are viewed as building organizational resilience. In other words, if senior managers provide close control and provide clear direction (Bratton et al., 2005, pp.62-73), staff lower down the hierarchy will be motivated to undertake a threat analysis and contribute to the organizational change process. By doing so, the organization's level of competence will increase and it will be viewed as less vulnerable than previously. Hence it is important for senior management to ensure that an appropriate leadership style is developed as this is essential vis-à-vis the organization's survival.

By reviewing the two major areas of leadership theory, transformational leadership and transactional leadership, and linking these two distinct approaches with the concept of organizational learning, it is possible to explain how senior management can implement the concept of organizational learning through an appropriate management style that reflects the characteristics of a leadership approach. This is the logic that underpins the development of an appropriate organizational culture, and the formulation and implementation of a new organizational strategy (Strategy (II) in Figure 1).

THEORETICAL FRAMEWORK

It is a well known fact that organizational strategists and marketing strategists work closely together on a number of issues. Montgomery and Weinberg (1991) have produced a strategic intelligence system that can be utilized by marketing strategists, and the body of knowledge has developed extensively over the past 15 years. In order to position the organization in the industry, it is essential that strategists scan the external business environment so that both existing and potential threats, are identified. Once this has been done, the threats can be listed in order of priority. Rapid change in the external environment can have a major impact on an organization's strategic direction and can result in lost opportunities for the organization if competitors deploy market blocking strategies. This may result in the organization becoming more vulnerable than it previously was as growth plans are put on hold and new strategic approaches are sought. Viewed from a marketing perspective, it is important to understand what Harvey and Denton (1999, pp.909-910) meant, when they stated that customers are becoming more demanding and as a consequence managers need to think in terms of the company adopting a 'customer focus' in order to produce 'customer satisfaction'. It is customer satisfaction which results in repeat purchases and ultimately customer loyalty, and this is why organizational strategists and marketing strategists need to work together in order to develop both strategic intelligence insights and initiatives (Trim and Lee, 2007).

In order that an organization maintains its level of excellence and meets specific objectives (increasing market share and providing higher returns to shareholders) in the customer driven era, senior managers need to pay attention to how their staff exchange both ideas and knowledge, among individuals and across functions, and how individual staff can work more independently (Appelbaum and Gallagher, 2000, pp.43-44). In order for an organization to enhance its resource based strategy, Appelbaum and Gallagher (2000, p.49) suggest that training "must be designed to help close the gaps between an organization's current reality and its future transformation". This can be interpreted as managers placing learning in a multidimensional context. For example, when managers implement a customer relationship management policy to ensure that the organization is close to its customers and thus through repeat business increases the organization's market share, they need to identify which management training and development programmes are appropriate to provide their staff with the necessary knowledge and skill base, in order to ensure that the momentum can be maintained. Hence the activities of organizational learning need to be integrated with the competitive intelligence process as learning objectives need to be prioritised and ranked accordingly. By ensuring that the organization is customer oriented, it should be possible to harness and utilize the knowledge within the organizational partnership arrangement to good effect. In order for this to be achieved, senior managers need to set realistic and achievable organizational learning objectives that allow the organization to create uniqueness and to turn the knowledge gained into a competitive advantage (Rubin, 1995; Hitt, 1996: 16; Trim and Lee, 2004, p.286).

Morgan et al., (1998, p.357) have suggested that organizational learning needs to be viewed from two perspectives: adaptive learning and generative (double-loop) learning. Adaptive learning is about improving the quality and the efficiency of existing operations and this is done through utilizing the knowledge gained. Generative learning is the next step in the adaptive learning process and this suggests that staff can formulate new practices, perspectives and frameworks; which can then be applied in order to develop the organization's capability.

It is important to note that there are two particular forms of organizational capabilities: utilitarian and psychological (Herbiniak cited in Morgan et al., 1998, pp.358-359). Utilitarian capabilities are associated with the organization learning from the strategic planning process and can be viewed as improving managerial skills and coordination between functions. As regards psychological capabilities, these refer to cognitive benefits, which organizational staff have learned from the processes and mechanisms that are in place and which can be applied in order to identify which managers are committed to achieving the organizational goals set (Morgan et al., 1998, p.359).

THE LINKAGE BETWEEN ORGANIZATIONAL LEARNING AND STRATEGIC MARKETING

In order that managers understand how they can utilize the concept of organizational learning from the organization's strategic development perspective, it is necessary that they understand how the process of learning occurs (both at an individual level and an organizational level). Diagram 1 outlines the process of institutionalizing organizational learning. What needs to be realized is that organizational learning permeates throughout the organization's structure and can be viewed as a process occurring at multiple levels (individual and group level), and how it is embedded within the organization (De Weerd-Nederhof et al., 2002, pp.320-321; Mintzberg, Ahlstrand, and Lampel, cited in Vera and Crossan, 2004, p.225).

At the individual level, an employee learns through being provided with guidance about the company's norms and objectives, and the learning process is enhanced when they exchange information with other individuals. The learning process is reinforced when the individual attends a specific training programme and is provided with various supporting mechanism(s), and is encouraged to develop a learning strategy that ensures that they gain specific skills and knowledge. The process of interaction with other members of staff is important as it allows an individual to internalise knowledge and reflect upon the organization's norms and objectives. Through the process of interaction, it is possible to place the knowledge gained in a wider context. This should allow the individual to establish what the requirements of the job entail and how they can interact with other organizational members in order to achieve the strategic goals set. Some might suggest that the integration of ideas results in internal harmony and this can be a strength. However, it is a well known fact that if senior management are to manage the change management process effectively, it is essential that the knowledge process is managed carefully as individual employees also belong to sub-groups that may be competing with other sub-groups (departments or strategic business units) within the same organizational configuration. An example of intra-organizational rivalry is when two independent subsidiaries compete for a contract to supply the parent company with components.

Bearing the above in mind, it is logical to suggest that senior management need to think in terms of creating a learning environment (McKenna, 1999, p.776) that is distinct from a training environment. Hence it is important that senior managers view learning and training as an investment as opposed to a cost. The reason for this is that "Learning organizations are skilled at systematic problem solving, and each is accompanied by a distinctive mind-set, tool kit, and pattern of behaviour" (Appelbaum and Reichart, 1997, p.234).

What senior managers need to be aware of is that a learning organization can embrace change, and new challenges that manifest in the form of a threat can be dealt with in a systematic manner, without causing undue stress and anxiety. The advantage of this approach is that senior managers will be judged by employees as embracing the concept of organizational learning in order to safeguard them. This being the case, senior managers will keep their position as they protect their employees and the investments made by shareholders by instilling confidence in how the organization is managed. Key indicators of success include an acceptable return on investment, incremental growth and ultimately survival (Trim and Lee, 2004).

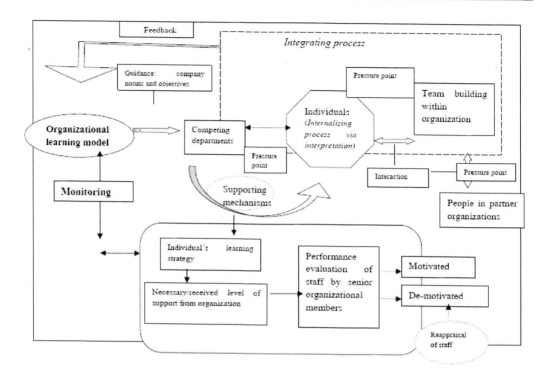

Diagram 1: The process of institutionalizing organizational learning

A DUAL LEADERSHIP STYLE

Studies relating to leadership have usually made a distinction between what constitutes a leader and what constitutes a manager. The differences can in part be attributed to how 'power' within an organization is used and how an individual uses their 'position' in order to achieve something. It is clear that a leader has the capability to exercise power either directly or indirectly, and that power is often exercised through a group (Robbins, 1996, p.412; Shackleton cited in Rosenfeld and Wilson, 1999, p.197).

The above comments come as no surprise when it is suggested that the role of top management is to cope with complexity and to manage the change management process; to devise strategic plans; to define an adequate organizational structure; and to put in place a mechanism for evaluating organizational performance. Andersen (2000, pp.2,281-2,283) has highlighted a number of controversies relating to leadership theory and has addressed the issue of how to transfer a leader's view into a sustainable strategy (i.e. behaviour leadership theory). Behaviour leadership theory revolves around the process of work and how people share ideas. During the process of information exchange, it can be noted that information is interpreted but also, the actions and views of senior managers proves influential with respect to whether something is perceived as positive or negative. Hence interaction is a key element and the interaction process can determine whether a strategy, once implemented, succeeds or whether a change in policy is needed at the operational level. Managers need to be skilful communicators, especially in a time of crisis, and need to find ways to inspire staff if that is, they are to achieve the results expected of them. Transparency is important and so too is holding people responsible for their actions. Therefore, a leader can be viewed as someone who can take charge of a situation and inspire staff to achieve the goals set (Robbins, 1996, pp.412-413; Fincham and Rhodes, 1999, pp.216-217, and pp.243-245; and Hughes et al., 1999, pp.8 and 10).

The above has established that a senior manager needs to be viewed as a leader, if that is the process of change is to be effective. A senior manager also possesses power and can influence matters as a result of creating, through various actions, a momentum for change. Kotter (Robbins, 1996) and Fincham and Rhodes (1999, p.417) have argued that a proactive leadership style is useful as it allows those making strategic decisions to think in terms of anticipating the unforeseen.

By making a distinction between 'leadership' and 'strategic leadership', it is possible for senior managers to adapt a flexible leadership style that can be called a dual leadership style. The dual leadership style can be thought of as an ambidextrous strategic management style that contains the characteristics of transformational and transactional leadership. The ambidextrous strategic management style is becoming adopted as the external business environment becomes more complex due to increasing competitive practice. Senior managers that work internationally and/or have close working relations with overseas partner organizations need to ensure that they adjust their management style in order to deal effectively with people that have a different cultural value system to themselves. Being sensitive to government demands and understanding why a government may intervene in a specific situation is also important, and requires attention.

An ambidextrous management style allows managers to remain proactive and in the case of overseas partner organizations, allows them to think in terms of understanding organizational culture as being underpinned by a specific national cultural value system. This is very important with respect to public sector organizations that are held accountable by government for their actions. The ambidextrous strategic management style is underpinned by the concept of organizational learning, however, the organizational learning approach will only be effective provided employees are determined to upgrade their skill base and develop new knowledge. So the ability to learn and the willingness to learn are key factors. Senior managers may also need to include the employees of partner organizations in the learning programmes and should this be the case, attention will need to be given to the context of institutionalizing organizational learning. The institutionalizing organizational learning process is very complex and needs to be managed strategically if that is, the resources devoted to training and staff development are to yield the returns expected.

Charismatic leadership theory, which is grounded in the transformational leadership approach, is about improving the relationship between a manager and his/her subordinates. It is also about employees being committed to a leader, which is achieved through them identifying the common characteristics that are used as a means of inspiration (Conger and Kanungo cited in Robbins, 1996, pp.436-438; and Hughes et al., 1999, pp.286-290). Charismatic leadership theory demands that communication between the leader and his/her subordinates is open and frequent, and the advantage of this is that people know what the tasks set involve and what is required of them. Hence a senior manager, needs to be perceived as a successful leader in the sense that he/she is able to define matters clearly; have a clear vision of the future; and set realistic goals. It is possible for a junior manager to be trained and become a charismatic leader, and this is an important point as a junior manager needs to embrace organizational development and ensure that the decision-making process is improved through time (Allaire and Firsirotu, 1984, p.210; Oile, 1994, pp.400-404; Robbins, 1996, p.437; Clark, Deveraux, Dawnton, Marcus and Shils cited in Hughes et al., 1999, p.289; Fincham and Rhodes, 1999, p.213). Monitoring staff performance is a necessary function of senior managers and the reader will note from Diagram 1 that a monitoring mechanism is in place to ensure that if any member of staff is identified as de-motivated, then action can be taken to correct the situation.

It can be argued that a good leader, like a good manager, is able to form an emotional attachment with their subordinates. A leader/manager needs to be aware of each individual employee's situation and can provide appropriate advice and assistance when necessary. This should result in a high degree of mutual understanding between staff and result in employees being committed to the organization as a result of them identifying with the organization's value system. It is relevant to point out that although forming emotional attachments can be viewed as positive, that ultimately a transformational leader needs to achieve his/her goals through assisting his/her subordinates to achieve the organizational goals set (Hughes et al., 1999, p.293). By acknowledging this, it can be stated that there are distinct and varied views within the charismatic model of leadership, and care needs to be taken with regards to the implementation of a leadership style.

Burns (Hughes et al., 1999, pp.90-291) suggests that transactional leadership occurs when a leader and his/her subordinates have something to exchange, hence relationships are formed that aim to result in needs being met (loyalty may be rewarded with an increase in salary for example). However, the relationship exists only as long as both the leader and the followers/subordinates understand what the benefits are; what fairness represents; each individual/party feels their commitment is being rewarded; and their needs are met. According to Robbins (1996, p.439), Hughes et al., (1999, p.291), and Bass and Avolio, Conger, Kirkpatrick and Locke (Fincham and Rhodes, 1999, p.234), a transformational leader can articulate problems and set challengeable goals for followers/subordinates, therefore, he/she is able to stimulate followers/subordinates to achieve the organizational goals set through a process of providing individual's with assistance, which is not the case with respect to transactional leadership. The logic that underpins this interpretation is that a transformational leader considers that a subordinate's values need to be in line with those of senior managers and because of this wishes to see that an individual(s) has a career progression within the organization. In other words, transformational leadership provides an opportunity for the creation of a hybrid organizational culture that takes into account the fact that an individual's value system is in harmony with the organization's value system. Should this be the case, then trust will materialise and respect will result.

Kakabadse (2000, p.6) has suggested that leadership is about transforming the way people think within an organization and that a transformational leader needs to listen to individual employees and empower people so that organizational change can occur and the organization can progress. However, it has to be noted that a transformational leader needs to manage his/her tasks adequately and maintain control (also at the operational level), if that is staff are to perform their duties to the standard required.

DISCUSSION

Bearing in mind the above, a number of propositions can be cited. It can be noted that the first two propositions are general in nature and relate to both the transformational and transactional leadership approach.

Proposition 1: When an individual/group of people feel that they are valued and secure, they will have a sense of belonging with the organization and embrace the organizational learning concept, in order to gain knowledge and skills that help improve the organization's performance.

Proposition 2: When an individual/group of people feel a sense of belonging to an organization they are more likely and willing to share information with staff based in partner organizations.

The following propositions relate to the transformational leadership approach.

Proposition 3: Individual employees will identify with the learning organization concept provided the organization's strategy embraces the transformational leadership style, which inspires subordinates to explore ways of solving existing problems in an innovate manner.

Proposition 4: Individuals/groups of people will accept and be motivated to learn when a transformational leader possesses ability to listen to them and is able to communicate with them in a sophisticated manner, by being sensitive to cultural differences.

Proposition 5: A relationship between a leader and a follower/group of people will be established strongly when a transformational leader demonstrates their understanding of each individual's situation and needs.

Proposition 6: Positive communication between an individual/group of people will result in high levels of productivity as a result of the transformational leader allowing staff to think though complex situations in a proactive manner, and carry out a given task without restriction and in full cooperation with staff based in other departments and organizations.

The following propositions relate to the transactional leadership approach.

Proposition 7: Individual employees can identify with the learning strategy concept that is the outcome of the transactional leadership style provided they are set clear work tasks.

Proposition 8: Individuals/groups of people will accept and be motivated to learn when a transactional leader possesses ability to explain to them a task in a clear and matter of fact manner.

Proposition 9: A relationship between a leader and a follower/group of people will be established strongly when a transactional leader interacts with them and explains the task set.

Proposition 10: Positive communication between an individual/group of people will result in high levels of productivity as a result of the transactional leader allowing staff to carry out their given task within their restriction and in the way specified.

Bearing these propositions in mind, it is possible to suggest that in order that people within an organization communicate with each other in a positive and productive manner, a leader/manager needs not only to inspire subordinates but needs to show that he/she understands what factors influence or affect the followers/subordinates communication process. The factors may include: the reporting mechanisms within the organization's structure; the cultural value system of the employees; the individual characteristics of the leader/manager; acceptable modes of behaviour; a certain distinct leadership style; and the intellectual ability of the employees. These factors give rise to the context of an organization's culture and ultimately fashion the type of leadership model that becomes embedded within the organizational machinery.

In order that senior managers charged with managing an overseas operation are viewed as sensitive to local customs, they need to deploy a consistent leadership style that relates to the national cultural value system. Oile (1994, pp.400- 404), Robbins (1996, pp.437-438), Fincham and Rhodes (1999, p.312) and Vera and Crossan (2004) have indicated that a leader can be trained to deploy various leadership styles as required. It is important to note that in order to deploy different leadership styles, not only must the manager have a thorough understanding of the different theories of leadership, but must also be aware of how different national cultural value systems emerge and how cultural traits are incorporated in the decision-making process.

The point being made here, is that if a manager is given responsibility for managing an overseas operation, that he/she is able to comprehend the intricacies associated with comparative national culture as it is important to be seen as non threatening and supportive. A study undertaken by Jung and Avolio (1999) into which of the two leadership styles referred to in this chapter (transformational and transactional), would be appropriate for people from a collectivist or individualistic cultural background, suggested that in the case of a collectivist culture, the transformational leadership style appeared appropriate and in the case of an individualist culture, the transactional leadership style was deemed appropriate. One has to be cautious about making generalizations from research findings because there may be a number of factors, not referred to, which need to be taken into consideration. For example, exceptions to the rule may materialize due to the interventionist policy of central government; the stage of economic development that the country has attained in which the local company is based; the sub-organizational cultures that predominate (an engineering organizational culture is different from a finance oriented organizational culture); and the number of local managers that are in positions of responsibility, who have been educated abroad. In the case of the latter, it can be suggested that an adaptive or hybrid leadership style may be relevant.

The issue of management control is important as people from different cultural backgrounds may have a different perception of what management control is and how the controls are exercised, from the perspectives of strategy formulation and implementation. Furthermore, it is necessary to think in terms of a time frame and in particular, how long it will take to implement the concept of organizational learning. Bearing these points in mind, a limited number of assumptions of a general nature can be cited.

Assumption 1: In order that a manager formulates and implements a strategy successfully, the leader/manager must think through the type of leadership required in a local business context and deploy, if necessary, an adapted leadership style.

Assumption 2: When a manager/leader deploys an adapted leadership style he/she must ensure that there is continuity in the management process and the same leadership style is placed within an inter- and intra-organizational context.

From the above, it is clear that organizational culture is about vision, shared values and beliefs (Dawson, 1992, p.136). Organizational culture is established over a long period of time and is used to differentiate one organization from another (Deal and Kennedy, and Peters and Waterman cited in Young, 1989, pp.188-190; Hofstede, 1996, p.3,822 and 1997, p.5; Morgan, 1997, p.141; Rosenfeld and Wilson, 1999, p.274). Although there are many arguments as to how important organizational culture is, various management writers agree that organizational culture is deeply influential with respect to how an organization is managed and how it performs (Rosenfeld and Wilson, 1999, p.281; Lewis, 2000). If the organizational culture established embraces the concept of organizational learning, it can be argued that the organization will be adaptable with respect to leadership style development, establishing relevant management controls, and workable partnerships. Should this be the case, a strong organizational culture will be forthcoming. Hence the leadership style that emerges and which is deployed will be grounded in the organization's culture and so too will the leadership style exercised by local managers. Bearing in mind the fact that managers are required to be sensitive to events, one can argue that with respect to partnership development, the relationship marketing approach will be adopted. Mourdoukoutas and Papadimitrious (1998), and Porter et al., (2000) have argued that a strong organizational culture is important as it encourages employees to exchange/share information and engage in peer group learning. It can also be argued that collaborative working ensures that the organization benefits from tacit knowledge (Huseman and Goodman, 1999, p.186; Platts and Yeung, 2000, pp.348-349). By encouraging staff to interact with each other in a logical and constructive manner, it is possible for the organization to increase both its level of tacit knowledge and its level of explicit knowledge. As a result, the communication process will be improved and the organization will be able to develop a sustainable partnership arrangement with a limited number of overseas companies.

CONCLUSION

In order to effectively manage a partnership arrangement, staff based in the dominant partner organization need to ensure that the organizational configuration change process provides the organization with an effective strategic decision-making apparatus that manifests in a clearly defined leadership model being exercised. The process can be reinforced by managers developing a robust organizational structure that can withstand various threat related impacts. Junior managers do need to develop their knowledge and skill base, and become expert at taking calculated risks, if that is they are to become strategically influential within an organization. The organizational learning concept can be utilized to provide managers with an understanding and an appreciation of threats emanating from the external business environment, and can be used to develop evidence based strategic intelligence systems. By understanding the role that strategic marketing plays, it should be possible for managers to identify potential threats and to deal with them before they become actual threats. This should ensure that the organization remains customer oriented and the organizational change process builds organizational resilience.

REFERENCES

Aaker, D. A. (1992) *Strategic Market Management*. Chichester: John Wiley and Sons, Inc.

Allaire, Y and M. Firsirotu. (1984). "Theories of organisational culture", *Organisational Studies*, 5 (3), pp.193-226.

Allen, L. A. (1985:51). *Management and Organisation*. Tokyo: Kogakusha Co., Ltd.

Andersen, J. A. (2000). "Leadership and leadership research", pp. 2,267-2,287. In: *The Current State of Business Disciplines, Volume 5*. Dahiya, S. B. (Ed). Rohtak: Spellbound Publications Pvt. Ltd.

Appelbaum, R.S., and Gallagher, J. (2000). "The competitive advantage of organizational learning", *Journal of Workplace Learning: Employee Counselling Today*, 12 (2), pp.40-56.

Appelbaum, R.S., and Reichart, W. (1997). "How to measure an organisation's learning ability: A learning orientation: Part 1", *Journal of Workplace Learning*, 9 (7), pp.225-239.

Bass, B. M. (1985). *Leadership and Performance Beyond Expectations*. New York: The Free Press.

Buzzell, R. D., and G. Ortmeyer. (1995). "Channel partnerships streamline distribution", *Sloan Management Review*, 36 (3) (Spring), pp. 85-96.

Corstjens, J., and M. Corstjens. (2000). *Store Wars: The Battle for Mindspace and Shelfspace*. Chichester: John Wiley and Sons Ltd.

Dawson, S. (1992). *Analysing Organisations*. London: The Macmillan.

De Weerd-Nederhof, P.C., Pacitti, B.J., Da Silva Gomes, J.F., and Pearson, A. W. (2002). "Tools for the improvement of organizational learning processes in innovation", *Journal of Workplace Learning*, 14 (8), pp.320-331.

Dyer, J. H., Cho,. S., and W. Chu. (1998). "Strategic supplier segmentation: The next 'Best Practice' in supplier chain management", *California Management Review*, 40 (2), pp. 57-77.

Fincham, R., and P. Rhodes. (1999). *The Principle of Organisational Behaviour*. New York: Oxford University Press.

Greenely, G. E. (1995). "Market orientation and company performance: empirical evidence from UK companies", *British Journal of Management*, 6, pp. 1-13.

Han, J. K., Kim, N., and R. K. Shrivastava. (1998). "Marketing orientation and organizational performance: Is innovation a missing link?" *Journal of Marketing*, 62, pp. 30-45.

Harris, L. C. (1998). "Cultural domination: The key to market-oriented culture?" *European Journal of Marketing*, 32 (3/4), pp. 354-373.

Harvey, C., and J. Denton. (1999). "To come of age the antecedents of organizational learning", *Journal of Management Studies*, 36 (7) (December), pp. 897-918.

Hines, P. A. (1996). "Strategy and buyer-supplier relationship", pp..4,632-4651. In: *International Encyclopaedia of Business and Management*, Volume 4. M. Warner (Ed). London: Routledge.

Hitt, W.D. (1996). "The learning organisation: Some reflections on organizational renewal", *Employee Counselling Today*, 8 (7), pp.16-25.

Hofstede, G. (1996). "Organisation culture", pp.3,821–3,838. In: *International Encyclopaedia of Business and Management*, Volume 4. M. Warner. (Ed). London and New York: Routledge.

Hofstede, G. (1997). *Culture and Organisations: Software of the Mind. Intercultural Cooperation and its Importance for Survival*. New York: McGraw-Hill.

Hofstede, G. (2000). "Organizational culture: Siren or seacow? A reply to Dianne Lewis', *Strategic Change*, 9 (2)(March-April), pp. 135-137.

Hughes, R. L., Ginnett, R. C., and C. J. Gordon. (1999). *Leadership: Enhancing the Lessons of Experience*. Singapore: Irwin McGraw-Hill.

Huseman, R. C., and J. P. Goodman. (1999). *Leading with Knowledge: The Nature of Competition in the 21st Century*. London: SAGE Publications Inc.

Jung, D. I., and B. J. Avolio. (1999). "Effects of leadership style and follower's cultural orientation on performance in group and individual task conditions", *Academy of Management Journal*, 42 (2), pp. 208-218.

Kakabadse, A. (2000). "From individual to team to cadre: Tracking leadership for the Third Millennium", *Strategic Change*, 9 (1) (January-February), pp. 5-16.

Lewis, D. (2000). "The usefulness of the organizational culture concept: A response to Geart Jon Hofstede's comments", *Strategic Change*, 9 (2) (March-April), pp. 139-141.

Lewison, D. M. (1997). *Retailing*. Upper Saddle River, New Jersey: Prentice-Hall Inc.

McGoldrick, P. J. (1990). *Retail Marketing*. London: McGraw-Hill.

McKenna, S.D. (1999). "Maps of complexity and organizational learning", *Journal of Management Development*, 18 (9), pp.777-793.

McIvor, R., and M. McHugh. (2000). "Collaborative buyer supplier relationships: Implications for organization change management", *Strategic Change*, 9(4)(June-July), pp. 221-236.

Mintzberg, H. (1974). *The Nature of Managerial Work*. New York: Harper and Row.

Montgomery, D. B., and C. B. Weinberg. (1991). "Toward strategic intelligence systems", pp.299-316. In: *Marketing Classics: A Selection of Influential Articles*, Enis, B. M., and K. K. Cox. (Eds). Boston: Allyn and Bacon.

Morgan, G. (1997) *Images of Organisation*. London: SAGE Publications Inc.

Morgan, R. E., Katsikeas, C. S., and K. A. Adu. (1998). "Market orientation and organizational learning capabilities", *Journal of Marketing Management*, 14, pp. 353-381.

Mourdoukoutas, P., and S. Papadimitrious. (1998). "Do Japanese companies have a competitive strategy?" *European Business Review*, 98 (4), pp. 227-234.

Olie, R. (1994). "Shades of culture and institutions in international mergers", *Organisational Studies*, 15 (3), pp. 381-405.

Omar, O. (1999). *Retail Management*. London: Pitman Publishing.

Platts, M. J., and M. B. Yeung. (2000). "Managing learning and tacit knowledge", *Strategic Change*, 9 (6), pp. 347-355.

Porter, M. E. (1996). "What is Strategy?" *Harvard Business Review*, (November-December), pp. 61-78.

Porter, M.E., Takeuchi, H., and M. Sakakibara. (2000). *Can Japan Compete?* London: Macmillan Press Limited.

Robbins, S. P. (1996) *Organisational Behaviour: Concepts, Controversies, Applications*. Englewood Cliffs, New Jersey: Prentic-Hall International Ltd.

Rosenfeld, R. H., and D. C. Wilson. (1999). *Managing Organisation*. London: McGraw-Hill.

Rubin, M. D. (1995). "Reinventing customer management-lessons from the best of the best", *Prism*, (Fourth Quarter), pp.25-39.

Siguaw, J. A., Penny, M. S., and T. L. Baker. (1998). "Effects of supplier market orientation on distributor market orientation and the channel relationship: The distributor perspective", *Journal of Marketing*, 62 (July), pp. 99-111.

Slater, S. F., and J. C. Narver. (1994). "Market orientation, customers value, and superior performance", *Business Horizons*, 37 (March-April), pp. 22-28.

Trim, P.R.J., and Lee, Y-I. (2004). "Enhancing customer service and organizational learning through qualitative research", *Qualitative Market Research: An International Journal*, 7(4), pp.284-292.

Trim, P.R.J., and Lee, Y-I. (2007). "Chapter Four: A strategic marketing intelligence framework reinforced by corporate intelligence", pp.55-68. In: *Managing Strategic Intelligence: Techniques and Technologies*. Xu, M. (Ed). Hersey, PA: Information Science Research.

Vera, D., and Crossan, M. (2004). "Strategic leadership and organizational learning", *Academy of Management Review*, 29(2), pp.222-240.

Walters, D. (1979). "Manufacturer/retailer relationships", *European Journal of Marketing*, 13 (7), pp. 179-222.

Webster, F. E. Jr. (1997). The future role of marketing, pp 39-66. In: *Reflections on the Future of Marketing,* Lehman, D. R., and K. E. Jocz (Eds), Cambridge, MA: Marketing Science Institute.

Young, E. (1989). "On the naming of the rose: Interests and multiple meanings as elements of organisational culture", *Organisation Studies*, 10 (2), pp. 187-206.

In: Strategizing Resilience and Reducing Vulnerability
Editors: Peter R.J. Trim and Jack Caravelli

ISBN 978-1-60741-693-7
© 2009 Nova Science Publishers, Inc.

Chapter 13

SOME SUGGESTIONS FOR MAKING EMERGENCY RESPONSE EXERCISES MORE CONSISTENT AND MORE SUCCESSFUL

David Upton

ABSTRACT

Emergency response exercises or crisis management simulations are essential tools for testing and validating response plans and building organizational resilience. However surveys of exercises, and real-life examples, show that exercises vary greatly in quality. Sometimes this is due to faulty exercise design or conduct, sometimes to underlying social or 'political' agendas, sometimes to a culture of 'semi-confidentiality' which prevents lessons being learned and discourages scrutiny. This paper suggests some criteria for successful exercises, including consistency of design and of documentation, and building ability to learn from experience. It outlines several attempts to achieve these goals, including a software framework for exercise design and assessment.

INTRODUCTION

Hundreds, probably thousands, of emergency response exercises are held every year in the US and UK. They have become a part of many people's lives. Not just refineries and chemical plants, but schools, hospitals, transport infrastructure, sports arenas and other public bodies now take the time to simulate or imagine some disaster, and to work through the consequences.

As an example, reports available on the internet, by Emergency Planning Officers to their local authority masters, in Norfolk[1], Wakefield[2] and Lothian[3], list 50 exercises in which they

---

[1] Report by Head of Emergency Planning to Fire and Community Protection Review Panel, covering Norfolk Emergency Planning Performance Review for 2005/2006, available at: http://www. norfolk.gov.uk/consumption/groups/public/documents/committee_report/firecom120906item10pdf.pdf

participated during a one-year period. (Of these, 35 were 'table top' exercises.)[4] This pattern is replicated throughout the UK: some counties would have appreciably more exercises.

Exercises fall into two broad categories: table top; or walk-through exercises, in which participants discuss a scenario whilst sitting around a table, and more complex exercises in which the scenario is simulated by role-players, or sometimes even by physical representations of an actual incident – eg a vehicle crash may be simulated using actual vehicles, an oil spill by spilling a harmless dye, and so on. Most exercises are designed to test or train on a particular response plan, or set of plans. They usually have explicit formal objectives, and an underlying scenario or story which is passed to players by means of injects from a facilitator or from role-players. Exercises can range in size from a handful of participants to several hundreds, and exceptionally thousands, of people. Once completed, there is usually a formal analysis process, starting with a 'hot-wash' debrief as soon as the exercise ends, and sometimes including other discussion sessions later. Usually a post-exercise report is produced, and this is then fed back into the preparedness cycle (assess risk - plan – validate plan – and so on).

The recent growth in exercises has largely been driven by the counter-terrorism 'industry' which has grown up since 9/11, but also by increased concerns for safety of those living near industrial facilities (Buncefield) and by response to environmental incidents (flooding) and epidemics (avian flu).

This paper examines whether current exercises are successful, and how they can be improved. It looks at the exercises themselves, and at the contexts in which they take place and the way that they are perceived and used.

Terminology varies. What some people call an 'emergency response exercise', others call a 'crisis simulation' or 'major incident drill'. This paper will use the term 'exercise' throughout. It is not intended to develop a taxonomy of exercises. To a large extent the differences in descriptive language do not represent real differences in practice: they are simply inconsistent use of language between different organisations.[5]

A CULTURE OF SEMI-CONFIDENTIALITY

It is difficult to study exercises, because they are often semi-confidential. The author has been involved with many which were not announced to the public, and as far as is known never became public knowledge. When they are announced beforehand, this is usually in general terms, often because the scenario is not yet known to most of the participants.[6] It is

---

[2] Wakefield Council, Emergency Planning Annual Report 2005-2006, available at: http://www.wakefield.gov.uk/Environment/EmergencyPlanning/AnnualReports/2005-2006.htm

[3] City of Edinburgh Council, Second Annual Report on the work of the Lothian and Borders Area Emergency Planning Steering Committee, 2004-2005: available at: http://download.edinburgh.gov.uk/emergency_report_final.pdf

[4] This is not necessarily a representative survey. The reports are for different years, and the councils are selected purely because they publish reports on the internet.

[5] Upton, D (2007). "Official crisis simulations in the UK and elsewhere", p 70, in International Simulation and Gaming Research Yearbook Vol 15, Trim P R J and Lee, Y-I (Eds), SAGSET, Edinburgh.

[6] Eg Transport for London, press release, June 2005, at: http://www.tfl.gov.uk/corporate/media/newscentre/4027.aspx

rare for outsiders or the media to be invited to observe: this is usually done only where the exercise will be highly visible to the public.[7]

Organisations often cite security and commercial confidentiality as reasons for not publishing details of exercises, or their results. Sometimes these concerns are genuine, but more often the motives for reticence include the following.

1. Fear of causing local alarm. Some emergency scenarios may postulate deaths outside the perimeter of a site – eg a toxic gas escape from a chemical plant. Under UK COMAH legislation, local residents must be officially notified in general terms by the site of what risks exist and what to do about them. However, many locals appear to live next door to major hazard sites with little consideration of the risk to themselves.[8] This is not illogical: the risk is usually very small, that is, it is highly unlikely to occur, on a statistical basis. However, if it was regularly drawn to local residents' attention that their lives and properties might be devastated by a possible but unlikely major incident, plant operators and local authorities would face demands for expensive or difficult action. In addition, property prices would fall, insurance might be harder to obtain and local employment would suffer. There is thus a de facto 'conspiracy of silence', from the householders upwards. When exercises are announced, the announcement often seeks to reassure the public[9] or to emphasise the 'routine' nature of the event.[10]

---

[7] Eg ChannelOnLine TV, 26 April 2006: available on http://www5.channelonline.tv/news /templates/guernsey news2.aspx?articleid=3409&zoneid=1

[8] See for example comments on an internet 'chat room' hosted by Hampshire News about a minor but highly visible incident at Fawley refinery in September 2007, available at http://www.thisishampshire.net/news /hampshire news/display.var.1684904.0.power_fault_blamed_for_fawley_flares.php
Comments include:
"... I haven't got a problem living anywhere near Fawley but I have got a problem with a rather large explosion taking out my home and family. These oil refineries are supposed to be safe otherwise they wouldn't put homes, schools and shops so close by..."
" Trouble was the school at Hardley was there before the refinery. When they started extending the school, the refinery was still relatively in its early stages (60's/70's). I have lived here all my life, and can't complain about it one bit, its provided life long work for members of my family, and if Esso hadn't had built there, then the other plants on Charlton Industrial Estate probably wouldn't have done either....We do have a right to know the truth though, and as per usual its always dumbed down. That noise last night was not normal!! Nearly made me spill my G&T!"
" To all the people who have nothing better to do than moan about something they have no idea about, You choose to live in Fawley, Holbury and the surrounding areas, I myself live in Holbury and I can confirm that the flames were not white but infact orange and were coming from the flares, there is no damage to any of the flares either! My husband works for Esso and was on shift last night when the incident happened everything that is being said by people who have no idea about the matter is total rubbish. Esso have, and did deal with the problem quickly and safely. So just remember, Esso and the other supporting companies provide jobs for a lot of people so please get your facts right before you judge!"

[9] South Somerset District Council, press release, 10 October 2006, available at: http://www.southsomerset.gov.uk/index.jsp?articleid=5374 is headed: "Emergency exercise, don't panic".

[10] British Airports Authority press release, 13 February 2008, available at: http://www.baa.com/portal/page/Corporate%5EMedia%20Centre%5ENews%20releases%5EResults/623316a8eaf08110VgnVCM200000 39821c0a____/a22889d8759a0010VgnVCM200000357e120a____/which says: " Travellers using Glasgow Airport are reminded that this is simply a routine exercise, designed to ensure passenger safety in the event of a real incident. Passengers should not be alarmed at the presence of emergency services. "

2   Societal changes. Industrial sites which were once in remote areas now have residential and office buildings immediately outside their perimeter fences.[11] For all of us, new threats, or new awareness of risks, mean that things we used to do without a second thought are now potentially more hazardous (eg riding on London buses or the London Underground, which were targeted by terrorists in 2005, or H5N1 avian flu, which emerged as a threat in 1997. In fact, two terrorist bombs exploded simultaneously on the London Underground in October 1883[12], and epidemics have been with us since Mediaeval times, but both are perceived as 'new' threats.). We cannot change our lives completely – eg stop using public transport and avoid all birds – therefore we do not want to be reminded in too much detail of the risks we face, nor is it judged to be in society's best interest that we should be.[13] There would be adverse effects on psychological health, national morale, national efficiency, and the popularity of our governments.

In addition, the sheer volume and frequency of exercises means that they are not 'news'. The exercise documents and reports are often quite long, and only of local interest. Even if they were available, few would read them.

Some organisations do publish reports on exercises. These vary in helpfulness. One criterion is the extent to which recommendations are made, recommendations which are specific enough for anyone auditing them after a period of time to say confidently whether the recommendation had been achieved. Another is the extent to which specific issues are linked to organisations, and 'ownership' of improvement is made clear.

As an example of the bland and uncommunicative, one UK report[14] says; " Both exercises successfully met their aim which was to validate management and safety procedures for the visit of the Tall Ships to Newcastle/Gateshead. The majority of participants supported the conduct, location, facilitation and pace of the exercises. The main outcomes of the exercises were the clarification of issues relating to command and control of various scenarios, along with a greater understanding of the roles and responsibilities of partner organisations." It is not at all clear from this public document if any recommendations were made, what they were, or who was responsible for carrying them out.

By contrast, some exercise reports on the UK Marine and Coastguard Agency web site provide good examples of clarity and helpfulness.[15] These give specific recommendations, and responsibility for implementation is also clear: for example "Not enough information regarding the progress of the incident was posted on information boards in response centres such as the Salvage Control Unit and Marine Response Centre. Digital projectors are advised for this purpose (and have been procured by MCA)."

---

[11] For example, the Buncefield site: see Buncefield Major Incident Investigation Board, 29 March 2007, Planning History: available at http://www.buncefieldinvestigation.gov.uk/history/index.htm .

[12] Short, K R M. (1979). The Dynamite War, p.160. Gill and MacMillan, Dublin.

[13] See Hazel Blears MP (Home Secretary), speech to RUSI, February 2005, available at: http://press.homeoffice. gov.uk/Speeches/02-05-sp-tools-combat-terrorism : "We must be mindful of the need for a measured, proportionate response, which does not generate unnecessary alarm. Our aim is to keep the public 'alert but not alarmed'. A difficult balance."

[14] UK Resilience website, 'Case Studies: Recent Local Exercises: Exercise Collingwood/Exercise Bon Voyage: May/June 2005" : available at http://www.co-ordination.gov.uk/preparedness/exercises /regionalcasestudies /collingwood.aspx

[15] See for example: "Exercise Hadrian", MCA 2006: available at http://www. mcga.gov.uk/c4mca/mcga07-home

ACADEMIC AND GOVERNMENT STUDIES OF EXERCISES

Two recent studies have been published in the UK and USA, both assessing health agency exercises in the context of overall emergency preparedness. One is a report by the RAND Corporation [16] in 2005. The other is a report by the UK National Audit Office [17] in 2003.

Both documents examine the whole range of emergency preparedness activity of a number of health agencies in the US and UK respectively, mostly by means of a self-completed questionnaire. The main conclusion of both, at least as far as is relevant to this chapter, is that exercise performance varies greatly. The RAND study analysed 37 exercises. Each exercise was scored on a range of factors. The scores were aggregated to give an 'overall performance' rating for each exercise between 1 (meets all criteria) and 0 (meets none), The exercises they assessed had 'overall performance' scores ranging from 0.97 to 0.33 [18]. This wide range suggests that exercises at the lower end must have been sadly inadequate.

(A) Level of Documentation

The RAND study actually attempted to analyse 100 exercises, but in only 37 of those 100 was there enough documentation for them to study the exercise properly. (Even though RAND defined 'minimum documentation' only as "an after-action report or an exercise plan, plus at least one other document".) The NAO also found inadequate documentation. Exercise lessons were not published or shared: "Debriefing reports were prepared ...by health authorities after most multiagency live exercises and most major incidents, and after two-thirds of tabletop exercises. Our review of those produced showed that quality was generally poor, with few bringing out the key messages. Few were circulated outside the health authority, including less than 30 per cent to the Emergency Planning Co-ordination Unit. "[19]

Some exercise reports did not include any exercise lessons, and were not objective: " [they]...concentrated on the performance of the trust without any direct consideration of whether plans were activated effectively or if they performed in a way that enabled the plan's objectives to be met. They also tended to lack objectivity in identifying areas that posed difficulties." [20] (Refer back to the Tall Ships' exercise quoted above for another example!)

(B) Frequency of Exercise and Fitness for Purpose

NAO found that exercises were not frequent enough: "Acute trusts are required to test their communications every six months, and participate in a live multiagency exercise at least

---

[16] Shugaran, L.R., Eiserman, E., Jain, A., Nicosia, N., Stern S., and Wasserman, J. "Enhancing Public Health preparedness: Exercises, exemplary practices, and lessons learned", RAND Corporation 2005: available at http://www.rand.org/pubs/technical_reports/2005/RAND_TR249.pdf
[17] Report by the Comptroller and Auditor-General, "Facing the challenge: NHS Emergency Planning in England", HC 36 Session 2002-2003: 15 November 2002, London , UK, HMSO, available at http://www.nao.org.uk/publications/nao_reports/02-03/020336.pdf:
[18] RAND study, page 34
[19] 'Facing the challenge', para 3.10
[20] 'Facing the Challenge', para 4.

every three years. We found that 17 per cent of acute trusts did not test their communication systems (including one third of acute trusts in Eastern region), and that around half did not participate in any multi-agency live testing. Around half of acute trusts considered that they do not test their major incident plans frequently enough to ensure that they remain effective and up-to-date, and a quarter said their testing was not very effective, in both cases mainly because of time pressures and lack of resources." [21] (Note: UK National Health Service (NHS) services are provided by Trusts. 'Acute Trusts' manage hospitals; 'Primary Care Trusts' manage general practice doctors, dentists, and other care providers with whom the public make initial contacts.)

The NAO added that: "visits to a small number of trusts to validate completed questionnaires showed they had all overstated, in key areas, their degree of preparedness to tackle major incidents, or could not provide evidence of claimed improvements since our survey in February 2002, and were basing their assessment, in part, on anticipated future developments." [22]

It was also clear that UK agencies opted for cheaper 'table top' exercises: for instance the NAO found that, during their review period, 15% of authorities had tested their plans with a live exercise, and 49% with 'table top' exercises. (Similar figures were found for other types of scenario.) [23]

RAND's methodology did not allow it to judge exercise frequency. However, on the face of it, a recent report by the 'Trust for America's Health' [24] appears to suggest that exercise frequency is adequate. Authorities in every US state were invited to fill in a questionnaire. The one question to which every US state was able to answer 'yes' was: did it hold "an emergency preparedness drill or exercise in 2007 with health department officials and the state National Guard?"

However, this result was no doubt partly because states are legally obliged to hold exercises. The December 2006 Pandemic and All-Hazards Preparedness Act (PAHPA) requires tabletop exercises including outcomes measures, lessons learned, and future planning. Quite large amounts of money have been put into emergency response preparations.

Secondly, the Trust found that the exercises held were not adequate. "Often, emergency plans are evaluated using written assessments that include surveys, checklists, and written reports. .... Written assessments are favored by many preparedness officials because they tend to be inexpensive, especially when compared to the cost of holding live exercises or drills. A growing number of experts, however, both within and outside of government, are urging federal, state, and local emergency planners to incorporate drills and real-time exercises into their preparedness training and evaluation..... The PAHPA legislation ties state and local preparedness funding to states' incorporation of drills and exercises to test emergency preparedness. While many public health experts applaud this, they caution that simply holding an exercise or drill does not mean the state or local government would be able to respond adequately in a real emergency situation. One major flaw with the current drilling system is a lack of clear criteria for evaluating the quality of performance. At present, there

---

[21] 'Facing the Challenge', para 4.11
[22] 'Facing the Challenge', para 16.
[23] 'Facing the Challenge', figure 10.
[24] "Ready or Not? Protecting the Public's Health from Disease, Disasters, and Bioterrorism", Trust for America's Health, 2007, available at: http://healthyamericans.org/reports/bioterror07/BioTerrorReport2007.pdf

are no evidence-based guidelines from the federal government regarding conduct of an emergency preparedness exercise in terms of what outcomes are expected from each drill."[25]

(C) Follow-up

There is repeated evidence from all three reports that exercises are not held often enough or done well enough, and that reasons for this include cost, and lack of time and resources. It is also suggested that government criteria or legislation are not specific enough and do not set success criteria, encouraging the 'tick in the box' mentality. It is suggested that some exercise reports are written to reassure, rather than to appraise the exercise honestly and objectively. As a result, the NAO report found little evidence that aspects of the debriefing reports had been followed up. [26]

The NAO recommended that the UK Department of Health should: "Underline, in the revised national guidance the Department intends to issue following the current review, the need for full testing of major incident plans, to a timetable and with subsequent evaluation"[27] and that Primary Care Trusts should:

"(r) Draw up a formal structured programme for the regular testing of their plans;

(s) Identify those staff likely to be involved in dealing with a major incident and devise and implement appropriate training programmes; and

(t) Produce debriefing reports after each significant test and each major incident."[28]

The Trust For America's Health says: "There remains limited, non-systematic testing and exercising of emergency health plans, and inconsistent mechanisms for incorporating lessons learned into future planning."[29]

By the way, nothing in this section should be taken to imply that health agencies are any worse than other agencies, or the UK or US worse than other countries.

THE SOCIAL CONTEXT OF EXERCISES

Most exercises are conducted because of an external requirement to do so. This may be enshrined in legislation (such as the US PAHPA referred to above, or UK COMAH [30] legislation, which requires major industrial hazard sites to hold an off-site exercise at least once every three years).

It may be an internal requirement. ExxonMobil, for example, has an internal Operations Integrity Management System (OIMS) against which all parts of the business are regularly and thoroughly audited[31]. Whilst OIMS does not include observing actual exercises, it does

---

[25] "Ready or Not?', page 24
[26] 'Facing the Challenge', para 4.14.
[27] 'Facing the Challenge', recommendation 'h'
[28] 'Facing the challenge', recommendations 'r', 's' and 't'.
[29] 'Ready or Not?', page 6.
[30] UK Statutory Instrument 2005 No. 1088, "The Control of Major Accident Hazards (Amendment) Regulations 2005", see http://www.legislation.gov.uk/si/si2005/20051088.htm
[31] "Operations Integrity Management System (OIMS)", ExxonMobil UK, see http://www.exxonmobil.co.uk/UK-English/Responsibility/UK_CR_HS_OIMS.asp

examine the frequency with which they are held, the perceived results, and the extent to which recommendations are subsequently implemented. This is an example of industrial 'best practice' and is driven by concepts of corporate responsibility: sadly, not all companies are as conscientious.

In at least two cases the author has recently come across, but cannot identify for reasons of commercial confidentiality, exercises were held in response to a direct threat from a regulator to close down part of an operation if the regulator's specific and serious concerns for public or workforce safety in a major incident were not addressed. The exercises were seen as 'proof' that the issues were being addressed.

Once again, the risk is a 'tick in the box' mentality. In the best exercises, however, participants are there to learn: they are prepared to find faults with their own performance, and see the exercise as part of a process of improvement.

Given this background, most participants approach exercises with mixed feelings.

a) Institutional participants tend to feel that their reputation is at stake. No system is perfect. Every good exercise unearths several problems with emergency preparedness. So the result of the exercise may be seen as a comment on someone's plans, institution, processes, or readiness. This feeling is particularly common in 'multi-agency' exercises, where (say) a large company, the fire service, police, regulators, ambulance services, and others are all exercising together. In the current climate, they are understandably concerned that reported problems may be picked up by pressure groups[32] or the media[33] and used against them in future. Under these circumstances, most participants have an 'unofficial' objective, of ensuring that their organisation comes out well of the exercise in comparison to its rivals. Fear of being seen to fail is a real factor, but not usually admitted.[34]

b) Individuals may also be apprehensive. If they are partly responsible for the emergency preparedness of a site or an organisation, they feel that their work and abilities are being put on trial. Even if not directly involved, the exercise puts them into unfamiliar situations, under a certain amount of pressure. Very often exercises involve a 'vertical slice' of staff from an organisation, so junior staff are working immediately alongside their own senior management, people who can have a direct influence on their careers, and with whom they do not normally spend much time. Under these circumstances, most individual participants have an 'unofficial' agenda, namely avoiding damage to their own careers.

Examples of these two 'unofficial agendas' can clearly be seen.

---

[32] BBC News Report, "Terror test criticised", October 2003, available at: http://news.bbc.co.uk/1/hi/england/london/3167030.stm. We make no judgement about this exercise or this reported criticism, but the critique was by a Fire Brigades' Union official, who clearly had an interest in securing better conditions for Fire Service officers.

[33] Eg Edwards, R, Environment Editor, Sunday Herald, February 2008, "Response to nuclear accident exercise like 'Keystone Kops'" available at: http://www.sundayherald.com/news/heraldnews/display.var.1315298.0.response_to_nuclear_accident_exercise_like_keystone_kops.php

[34] See Staten, C L, "ERRI General Analysis of Disaster Drills ", EmergencyNet News, November 2006, available at: http://www.emergency.com/2006/critique_disaster_drills.htm

1. 'Common Ground'

Exercise "Common Ground" was held by the EU Commission on 23rd and 24th November, 2005, in response to growing media concern about threats from avian flu. There were 1,075 national participants, involving most or all EU countries. The exercise was announced on 4 October 2005; a coordinator was chosen on 19 October; the exercise was held on 23-24 November; the "Evaluation Meeting" was held on 1/2 February 2006; and the Final Evaluation Report" was issued on 30 March 2006. In other words, it took three months to hold the evaluation and a further two to prepare the report. Five weeks to write the exercise, five months to write the report: this suggests where the political priorities lay.

The report[35], when it emerged, was a miracle of diplomatic language clearly designed not to damage the institutional reputation of any member state. It made only 12 recommendations, of which these are typical:

- "a system to improve the collection of information and situational awareness should be developed";
- "teleconferencing facilities in some Member States should be improved";
- "Some national pandemic influenza plans did not sufficiently consider international aspects".

As with examples quoted earlier, these recommendations are not specific enough for anyone later to audit whether they have been met, and deliberately do not allocate responsibility to any nation or body. This may have been a political necessity, but in exercise terms this result has to be seen as a failure.

2. 'Hurricane Pam'

'Hurricane Pam' was an exercise held in New Orleans, one year before Hurricane Katrina. Its scenario was eerily similar to what actually happened a year later. Participants' statements after 'Pam' (but before Katrina) were blandly reassuring:

"We made great progress this week in our preparedness efforts," said Ron Castleman, FEMA Regional Director. "Disaster response teams developed action plans in critical areas such as search and rescue, medical care, sheltering, temporary housing, school restoration and debris management. These plans are essential for quick response to a hurricane but will also help in other emergencies.... "Hurricane planning in Louisiana will continue," said Colonel Michael L. Brown, Deputy Director for Emergency Preparedness, Louisiana Office of Homeland Security and Emergency Preparedness. "Over the next 60 days, we will polish the action plans developed during the Hurricane Pam exercise. We have also determined where to focus our efforts in the future." [36]

---

[35] EU Commission: "EXERCISE COMMON GROUND Serial 5.0 Final Report 27 March 2006", published by the EU Commission, 2006. Full text is at: http://ec.europa.eu/health/ph_t hreats/com/common.pdf#search =%22exercise%20%22common%20ground%22%20report%22 See also summary at http://europa.eu/rapid/pressReleases Action.do?reference=IP/06/406&format=HTML&aged=0&language=EN

[36] Federal Emergency Management Agency (FEMA) "Hurricane Pam Exercise Concludes", Press Release Number: R6-04-093, July 23, 2004, available at: http://www.fema.gov/news/newsrelease.fema?id=13051

Clearly some participants were largely concerned to demonstrate that they had taken, or were taking, action. There was no identification of shortcomings or issues.

In the event, preparations and the subsequent response to Katrina were widely felt within the USA to be inadequate, and a Congressional enquiry was held. This found that: " Some state and parish officials said they saw Pam as a "contract" of what the various parties were going to do, and the federal government did not do the things it had committed to doing... Beriwal [....the contractor who coordinated Exercise Pam...] said, however, the plan derived from the Pam exercise was intended as a "bridging document" designed to serve as a guide and roadmap to be used by emergency operational officials at the state and local level. In other words, it was up to state and local officials to take the Plan and turn it into more detailed individual operational plans.. Yet, according to Scott Wells, Deputy Federal Coordinating Officer from FEMA, there were several Hurricane Pam Exercise "to do" items state or local governments did not complete... " [37]

It is clear that major issues were obfuscated – ie, who was responsible for what? Although the 'Pam' reports suggested that all was well, the results were not fed back into the planning process and the result, a year later, was a disaster.

That such failures can have a real impact on individual careers, and a reason why individuals may be apprehensive during exercises, is shown by the removal of the director of FEMA[38] from command of the response in New Orleans, and his resignation[39] three days later. Exercises, and even more so the real events they imagine, are surprisingly high-profile.

3. French Avian Flu Exercise

A blatant example of a 'showcase' exercise was held by the French government in Lyons in 2006 at the height of the avian flu scare. The scenario was the arrival of an airliner from a 'South-East Asian country' with two suspected flu sufferers on board, who were taken off by doctors and given suitable treatment. However, a number of key points can be noted.

- a) The exercise was watched on closed circuit TV by the French Prime Minister and 135 journalists specially invited for the occasion.. ("Devant des journalistes venus en masse -135 au total dont des Anglo-saxons et des Japonais" – 'in front of massed journalists – 135 in total, including US, UK and Japanese')[40].. This suggests that it was intended to reassure the public that the government was taking action, and that no part of the 'exercise' would be allowed to go wrong. Sure enough, it did not. No-one will want to fail in front of the Prime Minister, several other ministers, and the world's press.

---

[37] Final Report of the Select Bipartisan Committee to Investigate the Preparation for and Response to Hurricane Katrina: "A failure of initiative" (2006), available at http://www.gpoaccess.gov/katrinareport/mainreport.pdf
[38] BBC News report (September 2005) " US emergency aid chief sidelined ": available from: http://news.bbc.co.uk/1/hi/world/americas/4231170.stm
[39] CNN News report, September 2005, "FEMA director Brown resigns" available at: http://www.cnn.com/2005/POLITICS/09/12/brown.resigns/
[40] Nouvel Observateur for 23 February 2006 , "Exercice de simulation réussi à Lyon", available on http://archquo.nouvelobs.com/cgi/articles?ad=societe/20060224.OBS8208.html&host=http://permanent.nouvelobs.com/

b) At the time the exercise took place, over 11,000 turkeys were being slaughtered at a farm in the Bresse region of France. The turkeys were suspected of having the flu virus, and came from near where two wild ducks died of it recently. So the exercise scenario, whilst not implausible, was at best only partly relevant: Nouvel Observateur also said, "Le scénario était purement virtuel puisque, aujourd'hui, aucun cas de transmission de l'animal à l'homme, ni d'homme à homme, n'a été détecté dans l'Union européenne".('The scenario was hypothetical, as so far no case of flu being transmitted from animal to human, or human to human, has been seen in the EU'.)

c) This appears to have been purely a propaganda exercise, designed to demonstrate government activity on a sensitive and topical issue. "Cet exercice, qui s'est déroulé sur toute la matinée, a été une "réussite" selon le Premier ministre. "Nous avons vérifié le bon fonctionnement de la chaîne d'alerte, nous nous sommes assurés de la qualité de la réponse médicale. Les agents du Samu, les personnels hospitaliers, les experts en virologie sont préparés à une telle situation", a-t-il déclaré à la presse". ('This exercise, which lasted all morning, was a "success" according to the Prime Minister. "We verified the proper working of the alert chain, we feel reassured about the quality of the medical response. SAMU [*Service d'Aide Médicale d'Urgence*, Emergency Medical Assistance Service], hospital personnel and medical experts are prepared for a situation like this.." ') It is clear from the tone of the 'Nouvel Observateur' report that the press were suitably sceptical.

It does not appear that any problems were identified or any recommendations for improvement made. The comment attributed to the French Prime Minister suggests that the value of the exercise was to demonstrate 'success' and to provide reassurance. Whilst good exercises often do provide reassurance, the evidential value of such a tightly-scripted demonstration is another matter.

However, many exercise participants do have 'hidden agendas' to show off how well they are doing. For example, in a statement after Osiris 2, held in 2003 to test response to a terrorist incident on the London Underground railway system, a UK Government Minister said "Our early view at the end of the exercise, is that the elements that we have planned to test, have worked well. There will of course be lessons to learn for all those involved.... Once the emergency services and exercise planners have looked in detail at their responses to the incident and how it went, we would hope where appropriate to publish the major findings..... I hope the public will be reassured that today's exercise, part of an extensive programme, demonstrates our commitment to ensuring that London is as prepared as possible to cope with all eventualities. "[41]

The major findings', published shortly afterwards, began its list of lessons with: "The exercise found that a great deal of work has already been done by Government, Emergency Services and the Mayor of London to improve London's capability to respond to emergencies through improved equipment and planning".[42]

---

[41] Raynsford, N, Minister for Civil Resilience: press statement. Available on: http://www.ukresilience.info/preparedness/exercises/londoncasestudies/osiris3.aspx

[42] London Resilience Website: "Case Studies, London Region Exercises: Osiris Two" available at http://www.ukresilience.info/preparedness/exercises/londoncasestudies/osiris4.aspx

It does not need an exercise to show what is (presumably) a historical fact: a more relevant question, as we have seen, is whether that work was relevant or adequate. There were only five other 'major lessons', which were bland but curiously disturbing, eg "we must not underestimate the number of people and specialist equipment required to respond to such emergencies." (Does this mean: despite the 'great deal of work' already done, and despite being 'as prepared as possible', we still do not have enough people and equipment? Once again, the lesson is not specific enough for anyone to audit later on whether the problem had been tackled, and responsibility to improve the situation is not allotted to anyone.)

WHERE DO WE GO FROM HERE?

Exercises, then, mean many things to different people. They are sometimes forced upon organisations and people who would rather spend the money and time on other things, and who feel threatened by the exercise. However, in the author's experience, most participants accept the need for exercises and take part cheerfully and conscientiously. Much depends on the corporate culture of the organisation to which they belong. If this is a 'learning organisation', which accepts occasional mistakes and shortcomings and focuses on improvement rather than blame, exercise participation is more honest and productive, at both the institutional and personal levels. In such circumstances, exercises do produce genuine benefits.

However, the findings of the studies quoted in this chapter suggest that the process can be greatly improved in three ways.

a) By making the exercise writing process more consistent. It should be easier to compare, say, a COMAH exercise by Category 1 responders in one UK county to a 'similar' exercise written in another. But usually there is no common process involved: objectives, participation, choice of scenario, and many other factors vary. They are only comparable in that each is a 'tick in a box'.

b) By making exercise documentation more consistent. Reports should be more structured, and more open. The public, a critical stakeholder, should have enough information to be able to judge what happened, rather than being forced to 'read between the lines' as it often is now. If there are good reasons why parts of the report have to be confidential, then the rest should still be made available.

c) By formal mechanisms to collect and then follow up exercise results and recommendations.

Attempts have been made to realise these criteria by legislation or 'top down' action. One step towards a consistent process is the US Government list of 'National Planning Scenarios'.[43] This is a detailed piece of work that identifies 16 scenarios designed "to be the

---

[43] "NATIONAL PLANNING SCENARIOS: Created for Use in National, Federal, State, and Local Homeland Security Preparedness Activities", dated April 2005. This is available on the internet via the Washington Post website at http://media.washingtonpost.com/wp-srv/nation/nationalsecurity/earlywarning/Nationa lPl anning ScenariosApril2005.pdf . The copy is marked 'for official use only'. No indication is given as to who wrote it, although the introduction ascribes it to "The Federal interagency – coordinated by the Homeland Security Council (HSC) and in partnership with the Department of Homeland Security (DHS)".

foundational structure for the development of national preparedness standards from which homeland security capabilities can be measured because they represent threats or hazards of national significance with high consequence....The scenarios are broadly applicable and focus on a range of capabilities.... the scenarios can provide the design basis for exercises throughout the Nation. They have been developed in a way that allows them to be adapted to local conditions. Although certain areas have special concerns ... every part of the United States is vulnerable to one or more major hazards."

The report has been criticised[44] but the scenarios are detailed and well worked out, and seem to be a laudable attempt to create a standard against which to measure. (There is an extensive literature about the use of scenarios for forward planning,[45] but the term has a slightly different use in emergency response exercises. Schwartz[46] defines the scenario in a planning context as 'a tool for ordering one's perceptions about alternative future environments in which one's decisions might be played out. Alternatively, a set of organised ways for us to dream effectively about our own future.' However, the 'National Planning Scenarios' report uses the term to mean: "... the foundational structure for the development of national preparedness standards from which homeland security capabilities can be measured because they represent threats or hazards of national significance with high consequence."[47] They are perhaps intended more as an auditing tool: this is a set of possible events against which to test your preparedness, rather than a means of thinking about the future. It is not intended that users should question why the scenario took place, but that they should take it as a given and react to it.)

A related example might be the attempts of the UK government to create standard assessments of major risks. UK 'Category 1 responders' (eg fire services and police forces) are required by the Civil Contingencies Act 2004 to carry out risk assessments. The guidance document, "Emergency Preparedness", devotes a chapter and several annexes to how this should be done.[48] The intention of this process is to compare different risks – which needs comparable assessments of the various impacts on society if a given event takes place. To help with this process, specimen 'impact descriptors' are given, as a means of ranking risks.

However, a recent study[49] by John Wilson of the Northern Ireland Fire and Rescue Service found that Category 1 response personnel rated these very differently. He invited responders to rate 50 impact descriptors. Some descriptors were from 'Emergency Preparedness', some he wrote himself. The descriptors were detailed and often quantified, eg '250+ family units requiring alternative accommodation for in excess of 2 years'.

Each responder was asked to rate each impact description as 'insignificant', 'minor', 'moderate', 'significant' or 'catastrophic'. The result: "Although it was anticipated that there would be different views of the impacts, the sheer scale was quite amazing. Four impact

---

[44] "Emergency preparedness against the universal adversary" by Michael Chossudovsky, Centre for Research on Globalisation, June 2005, available at http://globalresearch.ca/articles/CHO506A.html
[45] For instance, Schwartz, P. (1991). The Art of the Long View, Century, London and Upton, D. R. (1996). Waves of Fortune, John Wiley and Sons, Chichester.
[46] Schwartz, ibid, page 4.
[47] National Planning Scenarios, page 4
[48] HM Government, "Emergency Preparedness", 2004. Available on the internet at http://www.ukresilience.info/preparedness/ccact/eppdfs.aspx See Chapter 4 and annxes 4a to 4f.
[49] Wilson, J. 'Community Risk Registers: a firm foundation?", blueprint, Issue 52 Spring 2008. This article is based on his unpublished MSc thesis submitted to the University of Leicester.

descriptions were put into three different categories, thirty four into four different categories, and twelve into all five." (That is, some practising UK emergency response professionals rated each of these twelve incident descriptions as 'insignificant', whilst others rated the same descriptions as 'catastrophic', and others assigned them to intermediate levels.)

This example is quoted not to denigrate the UK attempt, but to emphasise the subjectivity of the whole process. If professional responders differ so completely over the description of an incident, how can they standardize, create and systematically assess simulations?

A third example relates to documentation and follow-up. The UK Government guidance 'Emergency Preparedness'[50] tackles this, requiring that, as well as a post-exercise report, "Within 12 months of the exercise, an implementation report should be produced, indicating which of the exercise report's recommendations have been carried out in the form of revisions to procedures in the plans... Lessons learned from multi-agency exercises should be publicised through the Local Resilience Forum". Very few 'Implementation Reports' seem to be prepared or published: in fact this author has never seen one. (See the earlier reference to the number of exercises conducted by, amongst others, Norfolk County Council in the UK. Neither an internal 2006 report to Norfolk Council's own 'Fire and Community Protection Review Panel'[51] nor the Norfolk Local Resilience website[52] appear to refer to any formal 'implementation reports' on any exercises, although they do cover, in passing, some of the lessons learned. In the author's experience this is typical: it is not intended to single the county out.)

It seems clear that the 'top down' approach is not always successful. Within the UK alone there are several different 'guidances' on how to design and organise exercises.[53] They are inconsistent, and in the author's experience few exercise planners appear to use them, or indeed to be aware of all those that are relevant. Added regulations and recommendations and central government standards can too easily become just another bureaucratic requirement on over-worked emergency response professionals.

An alternative 'bottom up' approach is to use a software system to design and to collate reports on exercises, thus silently internalizing a regular procedure, and moving away from subjectivity and its temptations. The author and colleagues have now developed and use in professional practice a software package, which starts from a series of factual inputs (descriptive lists of stakeholders, locations involved, and possible incident and response scenarios) and then uses artificial intelligence to create individual scenarios, down to and including detailed injects for roleplayers. This seems to offer several advantages.

Firstly, most of the work of constructing an exercise is shifted towards providing the initial descriptive lists, which only has to be done once per industrial site or set of issues. Exercise documentation can then be automatically (and almost instantly) prepared, in standard formats. The preparation time and cost of exercises is radically reduced, but a consistent process is followed and the same basic data are used each time, subject of course to

---

[50] HM Government, "Emergency Preparedness", 2004. Available on the internet at http://www.ukresilience.info/preparedness/ccact/eppdfs.aspx See sections 5.167 and 5.168.
[51] Report by Head of Emergency Planning to Fire and Community Protection Review Panel, covering Norfolk Emergency Planning Performance Review for 2005/2006, available at: http://www.norfolk.gov.uk/consumption/groups/public/documents/committee_report/firecom120906item10pdf.pdf
[52] 'Norfolk prepared – Norfolk Resilience Forum' website: http://www.norfolkprepared.gov.uk/
[53] There is a summary of them in Upton, D. (2007). "Official crisis simulations in the UK and elsewhere", pp. 73-75, in International Simulation and Gaming Research Yearbook Vol 15, Trim P R J and Lee, Y-I. (Eds). SAGSET, Edinburgh.

data updates over time. This means that smaller exercises (such as 'table tops') can be prepared at a few minutes' notice, and tailored to small groups, allowing more frequent use for training.

Arrangements for providing feedback can be standardized, and once again feedback can be prepared in standard formats and stored in a database. Feedback can be compared over time. Individual comments will always contain a subjective element, but overall subjective bias is minimised if the report is prepared by a system rather than a human. It is also felt that, whilst individual assessments of any one exercise may be subjective, over a group of similar exercises (say within a large multinational company), and over time, patterns will emerge which will help managers to assess resilience priorities and to plan future training and improvement work.

It is hoped that the result will be a gradually accumulating body of data, which will allow genuine objective comparison between exercises held at different times and places. Statistical reports can be produced quickly. (At the moment, it is the author's experience that even well organised responders find it difficult rapidly to answer questions like: 'How often have you exercised this scenario?' Or 'How often have your exercises included that stakeholder?' As a result, the exercise planning cycle is often driven by imperfect recollections.)

Many organisations also find perennial difficulty in following up exercise recommendations. Sometimes this is because recommendations are vague (as described above), but sometimes it is because they are scattered over different documents and not easily available to the person designing the next exercise. Putting them automatically into a database eases this problem.

A software approach has also been taken by other groups, though this is not the place to compare the different offerings. The UK Emergency Planning College has launched its 'Gold Standard[54]' package. 'Emergency Command System[55]' also has a training and exercise package. There are other packages which simulate exercises or incidents largely on computer screens, concentrating perhaps less on flexibility of design and objective data acquisition, and more on the graphical or haptic presentation of a pre-determined generic set of scenarios, often with amazing realism. Some of these are extremely expensive to set up and run, and focus on particular technical issues, eg how to put out a fire.

CONCLUSION

Benefits from exercises are many. Even relatively poor exercises can have many advantages, for instance.

a) They alert participants to the need to study response plans.
b) They bring responders together and help them to understand each others' problems.

---

[54] Strickland, K. "Going for Gold – Project Gold Standard The next step forward for UK Resilience" : available on-line at http://www.epcollege.gov.uk/upload/assets/www.epcollege.gov.uk/gold_standard_article.pdf

[55] See internet site at http://www.emergencycommandsystem. com/index.php?option=com_content&task =view& id=16&Itemid=31

Many exercises achieve considerable success in doing this, and in addition they provide a reasonable means of validating response plans, training responders, and drawing attention to issues and difficulties which need to be resolved.

However, studies and anecdotal experience both suggest that exercises vary greatly in the quality of their design, documentation and reporting, and in the way in which they are followed up. The three examples of 'bad' exercises quoted above all failed largely because no-one seemed prepared to listen seriously to the lessons they taught. However, even 'good' exercises can be improved, and it is quite clear that standards vary greatly between organisations and countries. If not done well, exercises can become opportunities for governmental or corporate self-deception, and in a climate of 'semi-confidentiality' this self-deception can easily go unchallenged.

To work well, exercises need authority and high quality. They also need integrity on the part of the organisations that commission and prepare them, as well as the participants.

In the author's view the key is a clear and consistent process, as much transparency as is commensurate with security and commercial constraints, and the gradual and automatic growth of a body of comparable data on exercise results. This is most likely to come about in the longer term through the use of specialised software.

Using software rather than humans to design exercises has many advantages, eg cheapness and convenience. The most relevant one for the purposes of this chapter is that good software enforces a consistent process, lessens the requirement for highly-experienced exercise writers, and yet produces a more objective and systematic result, which can be meaningfully compared with other examples of exercises.

Improved objectivity may not be easy to accept in cultures where 'semi-confidentiality' has become a habit. However, it seems likely that the benefits of a more structured approach to the whole resilience cycle will gradually become clearer. They are likely to include a more consistent follow-up process. Those who follow up exercises are often not limited to those who design and take part in them: they include the senior managers and politicians who have a top-down view of organizational needs and resources. More objective reporting will give them better tools to work with. It will also give them fewer opportunities for avoiding difficult issues. Otherwise, these issues may never come to light until a real disaster follows the simulation, and the lives of real people are affected.

In: Strategizing Resilience and Reducing Vulnerability
Editors: Peter R.J. Trim and Jack Caravelli

ISBN 978-1-60741-693-7
© 2009 Nova Science Publishers, Inc.

Chapter 14

PLACING DISASTER MANAGEMENT POLICIES AND PRACTICES WITHIN A STAKEHOLDER SECURITY ARCHITECTURE

Peter R.J. Trim

ABSTRACT

Developing a security architecture that embraces disaster and emergency management policies and practices can be considered complex and highly political. Furthermore, a robust stakeholder security architecture requires that attention is given to intra-government and inter-government working arrangements based on information sharing. It also requires that trust-based relationships between companies that provide disaster relief services and institutions that coordinate disaster relief operations are solidified through time. Hence integrating more fully international disaster relief management operations and holding individual government ministers accountable for their actions, should see a more robust global disaster and emergency management policy and strategy emerge and be implemented. The points put forward in this chapter reinforce the fact that a more pro-active approach is needed with respect to dealing with disaster and emergency situations and that the international community need to view disaster and emergency management from the perspective of stakeholder security.

INTRODUCTION

In order that government ministers and their policy advisors think in terms of planning adequately for disaster management situations, it is necessary that a distinction is made between a single event/incident and a series of events/incidents. As regards the latter, it is important that attention is paid to what is known as the cumulative effect that a series of events/incidents have on both intra-government and inter-government relations, and how government representatives interpret various man-made and naturally occurring disasters, which appear to be increasing in number and intensity. The ramifications associated with both man-made and naturally occurring disasters go beyond placing organizations in simply defined states of vulnerability, indeed, crisis and disaster management theory needs to be placed in the context of a stakeholder security architecture, if that is a long-term solution is to be found to managing disaster relief situations on an international scale.

It is important that disaster relief specialists and government policy advisors think in terms of the nature and scope of events/incidents, and find a way to quantify the economic, social and political consequences as well as the psychological aspects and technological dimensions. Indeed, disaster relief management needs to be viewed from a collaborative and community oriented security perspective, if that is, past mistakes made with respect to security in the context of a failing state are not to be repeated. During a crisis or emergency, a government is required to implement immediate and effective action, in order that it is judged by the general public to possess the ability to put workable and timely emergency solutions in place. A capable and credible government is important as it reassures members of the general public, pacifies the media, and appears to have integrity vis-à-vis dealing with inter-government relief relations. Maintaining confidence is necessary with respect to ensuring that financial markets remain stable and that a period of destabilization does not result in prolonged periods of uncertainty. A calming and reassuring approach to disaster management relief also makes it easier for government officials to influence positively top managers based in key financial and non-financial institutions, hence, a pro-active approach to formulating and implementing disaster management policies and practices is necessary in order to reduce the potential number of shocks to the world economic system. This means that a stakeholder security architecture needs to be devised that ensures that certain threats and potential disasters are identified in advance and action is taken to ensure that should they occur, an effective damage limitation policy and workable relief management process is in place, which can also deal effectively with secondary issues as and when they arise.

The chapter is divided into a number of sections starting with information relating to developing a disaster management architecture. This is followed by two sections, the first relates to mainstreaming disaster risk management and the second focuses on the role of the international community and key considerations. Next, attention is given to putting partnership development in context, and this is followed by a section entitled the collectivist security approach. The work ends with a conclusion.

DEVELOPING A DISASTER MANAGEMENT ARCHITECTURE

Issues relating to the human rights of both the victims and their families of a disaster/incident and the protagonists responsible (in the case of a man-made incident), can result in much debate and sometimes a conflict of interest between governments. As well as government, stakeholders include international institutions, independent bodies and agencies, the military, law enforcement agencies, the intelligence and security services, charitable organizations and foundations, various activist groups and the media for example. It is for this reason that those involved in planning, organizing and managing disaster relief operations, need to be able to negotiate with various stakeholder representatives and at the same time embrace the security issues that arise and which need to be placed within a politico-economic context that embraces the broad-based body of knowledge referred to as global governance.

Conflicts of interest that arise vis-à-vis disaster relief management operations are often due to a fundamental change in a government's economic policy which restates what the economic priorities are. The need for both direct and indirect government funding is a crucial point and what needs to be remembered is that both donor countries and non-donor countries may view a disaster differently, and act accordingly. Events such as war and famine have profound effects upon those immediately affected and can bring about emotional reactions from people in non-affected countries that are sympathetic to those that have/are suffering hardship. However, governments are becoming more accountable for their actions (via national auditing procedures, the direct political lobbying of activist groups and the influence of media organizations), and a government may find itself in a situation where money is provided for relief assistance and then later, when the situation deteriorates further, faces hostile lobbying from those against the provision of military support. As regards military support, there is an increasing need for military personnel and equipment to be supplied for peacekeeping duties, however, this is sometimes viewed from a less than friendly and somewhat critical perspective. Indeed, military personnel seconded to a country/region in order to carry-out peacekeeping duties, are wary of the fact that they may be judged to be acting in a provocative manner in the sense that the domestic government in the country in which the disaster has occurred, may hold the view that their arrival is underpinned by a hidden agenda. In which case, cooperation from domestic government representatives may not be forthcoming and a conflict of interest may arise involving all the stakeholders as political objectives override economic and social objectives. As a result, a long, drawn-out bitter struggle may arise which results in groups/factions disrupting the actions of those governments that are genuinely concerned with providing relief management assistance.

It can be suggested that disaster/emergency relief operations are multi-faceted and that some government officials may appear welcoming but are in fact inwardly resentful of outside assistance, because they consider that they have lost control of the situation. As regards placing emergency relief in a security context (Trim, 2003 and 2004), it can be pointed out that those government representatives charged with providing security solutions may be required to undertake an adequate long-term risk assessment of the situation in order that the new problems that emerge through time have been anticipated and that the unique solutions put forward are perceived as fit-for-purpose, and are not misinterpreted as being associated with a hidden agenda. Indeed, in the case of a failed or failing state, disaster relief management can be placed more firmly in the context of political and economic support programmes that are spread over many years and are most likely to cost billions of dollars.

A disaster management architecture can be thought of from the perspective of a collectivist responsibility as it embraces the "community". In such a case, it is necessary to think in terms of what organizations are in existence and how a disaster relief operation is managed by a range of skilled individuals from both the public and private sectors. Hence it is important to suggest that all those involved in a disaster relief operation need to be able to identify who does what at which stage of the disaster relief management process, and also, who is charged with providing the necessary leadership on both an intra-organizational and inter-organizational basis. As well as coordination, communication is key and it is important that first responders liaise effectively, and are perceived as being sensitive to events. An open, transparent and sensitive style of decision-making should manifest in information sharing and this should ensure that the disaster management relief process works as well as expected. Harnish (2002, p.124) has acknowledged this and suggests that attention needs to be given to how information is stored because this may determine the way in which the information is drawn on and how it "flows through the system".

MAINSTREAMING DISASTER RISK MANAGEMENT

Referring again to the issue of a failed or failing state, it is useful to note that Hilary Benn (2005), in his capacity as British Secretary of State for International Development, provided a comprehensive explanation of why it is essential for nations, to achieve the Millennium Development Goals set. If the international community is to achieve the goals set, a workable partnership needs to be created that is sustainable. This means that political leaders will have to think through the ramifications of not providing financial support to nations in difficulty and the immediate and long-term consequences of their actions. Adequate and immediate disaster relief management requires that staff from the various economic development and disaster management organizations work closely with people from a variety of international organizations, and need to have workable, disaster management programmes in place. La Trobe and Davis (2005) have outlined a number of factors that need to be taken into account when managers employed by non-government organizations (NGOs) and staff within development agencies, identify and prioritise methods encompassing mainstreaming risk reduction. It is clear that leadership is a key concern and La Trobe and Davis (2005, p.8) suggest that an organization needs to appoint somebody who is able to promote, from an internal perspective, the disaster risk reduction concept, if that is, the overall strategy is to be successful. It is at this point necessary to reflect upon what is meant by the term mainstreaming. La Trobe and Davis (2005, p.16) state: "This word obviously derives from the metaphor of a small, isolated flow of water being drawn into the mainstream of a river where it will expand to flow smoothly without loss or diversion. Therefore 'mainstreaming risk reduction' describes a process to fully incorporate disaster risk reduction into relief and development policy and practice. It means radically expanding and enhancing disaster risk reduction so that it becomes normal practice, fully institutionalised with an agency's relief and development agenda. Mainstreaming has three purposes:

- To make certain that all the development programmes and projects that originate from or are funded by an agency are designed with evident consideration for potential disaster risks and to resist hazard impact.
- To make certain that all the development programmes and projects that originate from or are funded by an agency do not inadvertently increase vulnerability to disaster in all sectors: social, physical, economic and environment.
- To make certain that all the disaster relief and rehabilitation programmes and projects that originate from or are funded by an agency are designed to contribute to developmental aims and to reduce future disaster risk".

With respect to the above, Sharma (2005) has provided a number of useful observations when outlining the disaster risk management programme initiated by the Indian government in 2002. It is clear that mainstreaming is about risk reduction, however, stakeholders are not always clear about what should be mainstreamed, how something should be mainstreamed, and who should do the mainstreaming (Sharma, 2005). What is clear however, is that academics, researchers and practitioners do need to adopt a robust methodological approach to studying disaster management (Mitchell, 2005). This is a useful point to note because policy advisers need to be aware of the role that the international community is expected to play during a disaster (either man-made or occurring naturally). For example, research undertaken into disaster risk reduction, has established that communication is a problem (between sectors and departments), and that the expertise and knowledge of risk reduction specialists was "confined to their immediate sphere of influence and was not shared with development departments as a matter of course" (La Trobe and Venton, 2003, p.14).

As regards knowledge sharing, La Trobe and Venton (2003, p.17 and p.29) have highlighted the approach adopted by staff at the Canadian International Development Agency (CIDA): "CIDA's International Humanitarian Assistance (IHA) division has adopted a focused approach and 'started small' with the task of knowledge sharing. It has begun working with CIDA's Climate Change Working Group and the geographical programmes that are already interested in, or working on, disaster prevention. From this starting point it will then try to broaden awareness more generally by taking advantage of other networks within the organization...........CIDA is working to integrate disaster risk management at the policy and programme levels. Its climate Change Working Group (CCWG) is comprised of representatives from each branch, who provide guidance to programme managers and share lessons learned about issues including disaster risk reduction. The CCWG also plans to adapt or design relevant tools to help CIDA officers integrate disaster risk management into development programming".

The UKs Department for International Development (DFID, 2005, p.1) has indicated that both the number of disasters is increasing and so too is the level of seriousness of these disasters, hence it is not surprising to learn that over fifty per cent of disaster related deaths "occur in low human development countries, even though only 11% of people exposed to hazards live there". It is important to remember that a pro-active approach to disaster management and in particular disaster risk reduction, can prove useful. Indeed, DFID (2005, p.2) make a crucial point: "*Disaster risk reduction* entails measures to curb disaster losses by addressing hazards and people's vulnerability to them. Good disaster risk reduction happens well before disasters strike, but also continues after a disaster, building resilience to future hazards".

What is clear is that the international community cannot detach itself from the effects of a disaster. There are several reasons why a disaster may occur, and DFID (2005, p.3) has suggested the following: "Disasters do not just happen – to a large extent, they result from failures of development which increase vulnerability to hazard events. Failure of institutions governing development can be found at all levels, from local and national institutions weakened by skills shortages or corruption, to institutions of global governance influenced by powerful countries and powerful interests within them".

Twigg (2005, pp.1-2), reporting on the outcome of the Fourth Integrated Planning Against Risk seminar, held at University College London on 21st April, 2005, indicated that "development programming should adopt a disaster risk management (DRM) approach – a systematic approach to identifying, assessing and reducing risks of all kinds associated with hazards and human activities.....The modern DRM approach recognises that a wide range of environmental, technological and socio-political hazards threaten society – individually and in complex interaction. Risks are located at the point where hazards, communities and environments interact, and so effective risk management must address all of these aspects.......This means that risk reduction initiatives must be multidisciplinary partnerships, both vertical and horizontal, involving a range of stakeholders".

One cannot rule out the influence of civil war or war with a neighbouring state, and also, climate change. Amanor and Brown (2003, p.3) have made several valid points when addressing the issue of improving natural resource management decision-making and have suggested that it should be possible to establish local platforms vis-à-vis the users of the key resources; promote feedback from locations relating to the environment and production systems; and create information systems to be used by members of the public and policy makers so that particular groups can make known the conditions that effect their daily lives. Initiatives in these areas should increase awareness and result in robust communication systems, which are then used to prompt positive government action (local, domestic and/or overseas).

Pelling and High (2005, p.15) have questioned the role played by formal management education and professional training, and suggest that practitioners need to engage in social interaction and develop productive networks of exchange. In other words, attention needs to be paid to the contribution that social relationships make and how these relationships are underpinned by learning. These points are critical with respect to assessing how international economic development organizations, donors (including governments and institutions), and disaster management specialists, tackle recurring problems and devise contingency plans that can be implemented when necessary.

THE ROLE OF THE INTERNATIONAL COMMUNITY AND KEY CONSIDERATIONS

It is useful at this juncture to reflect on the work of the United Nations. The Hyogo Framework for Action 2005-2015, has been well thought through and should do much to focus the attention of various actors in the international community (Valdes, 2005). The summary of The Hyogo Framework for Action 2005-2015: Building the Resilience of Nations and Communities to Disasters (HFA) (Expected outcome, strategic goals and priorities for action 2005-2015; and Implementation and follow-up) (UN/ISDR, 2005) are worth further analysis. It is clear that when scrutinizing the information, a number of points are raised, which require further clarity. For example, a disaster and emergency management framework needs to be underpinned by a security architecture that is considered robust. A well thought through disaster and emergency management policy and strategy will have integrated activities, workable support programmes, and draw on research output from university research centres as well as privately funded research institutes, and will be integrated in the work of various government agencies, relevant NGOs, and other interested parties. Indeed, should this be the case, it is likely that an operational security network alliance will emerge. The operational security network alliance will facilitate communication and provide leadership initiatives. If this is the case, it can be suggested that the resulting architecture will take into account what various governments are required to do; at what specific points in time they are required to do them (from the forecasting of a disaster; to the co-ordination of support and relief work and afterwards in the post event phase); and who is to be held responsible and accountable for the project management activities.

In order to be effective, the various relief and emergency services and organizations (as well as relevant NGOs) need to be identified and integrated into what can be called an event-action plan database. The database will detail what various governments are expected to do in the way of co-operation, and how they are expected to communicate. The main advantage of this is that the specialist disaster and emergency management organizations and support activities would be linked; the knowledge they hold would be stored for immediate access; and the various local government support units and teams would be linked with the law enforcement agencies, the intelligence and security services, and the armed forces.

It is not possible to suggest if the various public-private partnerships in existence have received enough attention vis-à-vis funding, intra- and inter-organizational co-operation, and the necessary management and leadership. For example, how do public-private partnerships underpin the concept of sustainability in the post disaster management period? And, how can government representatives ensure that the reports that appear in the media are accurate and timely? Further identifiable questions that need an answer are: What constitutes disaster management knowledge? Where is the knowledge stored? In what form is it stored? By whom is it to be stored? Can one assume that a number of inter-linked databases will be developed/are in existence that facilitate knowledge and information sharing? And also, are these databases accessible to all relevant parties that have received security clearance?

Some critics might suggest that it is not useful to think in terms of the international community taking responsibility for disaster/emergency management situations in individual countries and that it is not possible to develop a community oriented disaster/emergency relief management model. This argument can be counteracted as it should be possible to produce country/regional specific models that are generic in form. Furthermore, it is possible to develop a typology of disaster/emergency relief oriented community management models that allow those involved in disaster risk reduction to select an appropriate management model for implementation. If a limited number of generic but country/region specific disaster/ emergency management models are developed (and they may already exist and be available from the various emergency planning research centres), emergency and disaster management planners will be able to harness relevant knowledge and engage in information sharing.

With respect to building multi-stakeholder partnerships to facilitate disaster and emergency management knowledge and working practices, it can be noted that the issue of trust and continuity need to be firmly addressed. The key point must be the development of regional organizations and institutions that are sustainable and it may be useful to establish how facilitating technology such as the Internet (connectivity and interactivity) can be used to achieve community involvement. Again, the issue of sharing information (and research data) is a key consideration. Planners and policy makers will need to pay increased attention to issues such as inter-cultural disaster and emergency management cooperation and to cross-cultural communication that facilitates the implementation of crisis management programmes, and which ultimately results in the development of realistic risk assessment methods and models. As regards producing a generic model of disaster and emergency management, two points surface: (i) the model(s) need to be adapted to a specific type of threat and (ii) the model(s) need to be adapted to the required level of response that the affected community finds acceptable.

PUTTING PARTNERSHIP DEVELOPMENT IN CONTEXT

As regards partnership development within the context of disaster and emergency management vis-à-vis security implications, a number of issues need to be addressed. For example, international economic development organizations and overseas governments need to establish which companies and individual investors own parts of the critical national infrastructure. This is so that organizations from both the private and public sectors can work together in times of need, but also, Hyslop (2007, p.5) is right to point out that: "To protect the Critical Infrastructures of the future will require a new approach to defining threats. Such an approach has to both acknowledge and manage risk". By establishing a critical national infrastructure knowledge ownership bank, it should be possible for the international community to focus on restoring facilities quickly (when they have been damaged by natural means or indeed acts of war/sabotage). The concept of business continuity is important and this should be a priority (reconnecting the water supply or repairing broken drains and sewers for example). If essential services are not restored quickly, the effected community may be at further risk from disease and any delay in restoring essential services may result in political unrest. Bearing this in mind, it can be suggested that disaster management relief, business continuity and information sharing need to viewed as essential activities, if that is, those involved in partnership development are to be convinced that their actions are worthwhile.

There are a number of implications that need to be borne in mind, if that is, partnership development is to occur in the way that it should. Clarkson and Banda (2004, p.315) suggest that those that establish a policy area are required to fight in order to take control of the content, and also, there is competition vis-à-vis alternative policy fields. Clarkson and Banda (2004, p.315) also make it known that both popular political discourse and the necessity for budgetary allocations determine which policies are more acceptable than others, and it can be concluded that political choice and societal values play a major part. It is at this point that one can reflect on some of the points covered in the above and reflect on the issue of what is meant by the term "community". It is important to pay attention to what the word community represents and to think in terms of an "extended community", often referred to as a stakeholder group. Hodgett and Royle (2003, p.310) have indicated that the term community is about people with common ideas forming a grouping and that "community allows people to become acculturated, so it seems that community and culture cannot easily be pulled apart".

If the various organizations and institutions that deal with international economic development are to reform, it may be necessary for senior management to embrace the organizational learning concept and to implement an organizational cultural change process. However, McMahon (2004, p.326) asks if it is possible for staff to create a sense of mission bearing in mind the cultural groupings that exist, and whether a reformed organization can emerge. This focuses attention on a new set of questions: Is organizational reform too closely linked with political processes? Is organizational reform only possible if governments commit themselves to higher levels of funding? And ultimately, who in society shapes the governance mechanism parameters?

Peters (2004, p.6) has viewed governance from the perspective of society being more involved in the public sector decision-making process. But this raises several questions relating to the quality of information made available to the public; the timing of the released information; and how the public are expected to respond to the information provided. Bearing the fact in mind that security is essentially about national considerations, it would be foolish to suggest that the public sector decision-making process should be entirely transparent and that all information should be released into the public domain when it is available.

Table 1 below outlines the type of professional expertise that is needed during a disaster/emergency and the various stakeholders are made reference to. Figure 1 below represents an extended multi-cultural communication model for disaster and emergency management simulation exercises, and it can be noted that the various stakeholders identified, form long-term relationships. The importance of local disaster and emergency management expertise is made clear and it is important to note that research findings underpin skill development.

It is a well known fact that disaster and emergency simulation exercises have many uses (Trim, 2006; Trim and Lee, 2006). They allow those trained to undertake emergency management routines to become more expert in their duties and also, during a man-made or naturally occurring event, equip first responders to co-ordinate and communicate matters effectively. This is all essential with respect to maintaining public confidence. It can be argued, therefore, that in order to be effective, simulation exercises need to be based on fact; have specific and measurable objectives; and be linked with various aspects of management knowledge such as leadership theory for example. By viewing the work of the first responder from the perspective of providing management solutions in the case of adversity, through leadership and motivation, it is possible to place the body of knowledge in the context of theory building. This should also allow staff based in voluntary organizations to relate to each other better than is the case at present and to identify areas of activity, which require joint action. Again, this underpins the concept of sustainability through community action.

Another point that needs to be considered is, if a crisis, disaster or emergency situation results in a major dislocation, then how can a government deflect unnecessary pressure and thus avoid a backlash from various pressure groups that seize on issues that can be manipulated via the media? This requires that there is adequate co-operation between private sector organizations and public sector organizations, and that increased flexibility provides a platform upon which a sustainable security agenda that embraces reasonably full disclosure can be made. This raises the issue of how a central intelligence-security agency (Trim and Caravelli, 2007, pp.141-142) can assume responsibility for co-ordinating recovery work in times of crisis/disaster/emergency, as well as intelligence gathering that is related to peacekeeping activities. Policy advisors need to be realistic about the usefulness of a single central intelligence-security agency and in particular, be clear about the role that it would play. Even if it were possible, how would such an organization function? How would it be funded? Who would it be accountable to? How would it be constrained vis-à-vis the law and the current legal system? If such an organization was considered necessary and assumed the role of a think tank only, then what value would it have?

Trim and Caravelli (2007, p.142) state: "Such an organization would be charged with identifying future/potential threats and quantifying them; and would link these threats (in the case of pandemics) to health care provision and initiatives in bio-security, the location of health providers (hospitals) and improvements in hygiene and the mobility of people (travelling from one country to another in order to take up employment and in extreme cases, the evacuation of towns and cities during a disaster for example)". The term sustainable security is being used therefore to convey the point that a collectivist approach to security requires that a partnership approach be adopted to what can be called security for the community.

Table 1. Type, level and degree of interaction during a disaster/emergency

Professional Expertise			Media Personnel	Politicians	People
Scientific and Technical Personnel	Geologists Seismologists Civil Engineers Others	Geographers Geophysicists Economists Others	Report the facts and the situation to the general public; disseminate information vis-à-vis government policy; investigate the situation (interview experts and government representatives); provide various analyses and interpretations; act as a monitoring force and stimulate interest among politicians and interested parties; and ensure that once a story enters the public domain that it is kept alive and that a 'solution' is achieved. Staff are persistent, inquisitive, pro-active in their search for information and answers, and have an investigative disposition.	Provide advice and guidelines for the general public and make decisions relating to how the disaster/emergency is to be handled; introduce new policies; act as network facilitators vis-à-vis the accident and emergency services; liaise with various professional representatives, local government officers and members of the community; and undertake trips to view domestic scenes and disaster areas abroad. Politicians are informative, provide answers to questions posed, are keen to influence policy, and appear calming in times of uncertainty.	The general public obey the rules and regulations; remain calm and help in the rescue process; offer personal views when interviewed by staff from the media; join voluntary groups; lobby politicians; provide a voice for the community; and engage in fund raising activities. The members of the public want to be assured that they are safe, that their loved ones are protected, are keen to ask questions, and are keen to offer criticism.
Disaster and Emergency Personnel	Police Service Ambulance Service Fire Service Medical Staff Others	Army Navy Air Force Reservists Others			
Exchange information, knowledge and expertise; are aware of each other's working practices and views; communicate and co-ordinate rescue activities, clean-up activities and offer ongoing support and advice; and inform government representatives as to what the situation entails and how policy changes should be incorporated in order to improve the situation (eg viewed from a number of perspectives including less fatalities and greater value for money). Individuals: possess expertise, experience, tact, motivational and leadership qualities, a sensitive disposition and are prepared to take risks. Groups: are well co-ordinated, have clearly defined operational procedures to follow and all communications are through established communication networks and channels.					

Source: (Trim and Lee, 2007, p.113).

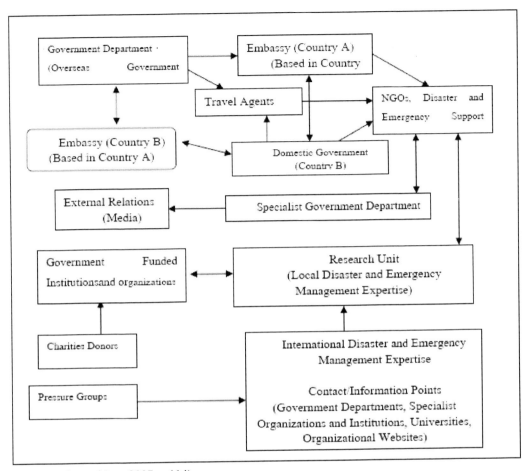

Source: (Trim and Lee, 2007, p.114)

Figure 1. An extended multi-cultural communication model for disaster and emergency management simulation exercises

THE COLLECTIVIST SECURITY APPROACH

Alexander (2002, p.63) has highlighted the fact that people are inclined to let qualified experts establish risk-reduction measures. This may militate against the formation of adequate disaster management implementation programmes by the community as it means that policies are imposed upon a community as opposed to being tailor made to meet what can be described as expected or unexpected needs. Government representatives will need to pay increased attention to how development funds are utilized and financial management procedures need to be put in place to ensure that the funds made available are deployed in an appropriate manner (Rienstra, 1999, pp.23-25). If this is not the case, donors may withhold funds or may not be prepared to inject funds into the disaster and emergency management process. By abstaining in this way, the logic behind collective security will be called into question and additional questions will be raised relating to governance leadership.

The English School approach to international politics, according to Bellamy and McDonald (2004, pp.307-308 and p.309), "focuses on the idea of an international society of states bound together by shared rules and norms". Hence the term security can be interpreted as people being free from danger and harm. The role played by the state is key because it is the state that provides society with security (Bellamy and McDonald, 2004, p.314). It is also important to note that displaced people have the right to protection and to be placed in a safe environment (Chalinder, 1998, p.36). So the terms stakeholder and governance are interlinked, and feature prominently in the relationship building process.

A number of geopolitical issues need to be placed in an historical context if that is a deeper understanding relating to current development problems is to be forthcoming (Middleton and O'Keefe, 1998). Development and disaster management experts need to be more in tune with the problems/potential problems of people living in an area that is under threat, if that is, the needs, hopes and frustrations of local people are to be fully appreciated (Salmen, 1989, p.6). It is clear that the term sustainability encompasses such issues as the quality of life; protection of the environment; and the maintenance of economic growth and employment (Meale, 1999, p.4). Walker (1989, p.7) has added to the body of knowledge by stating: "Sustainable development is about people's capacity to manage their natural environment, and the systems they use to exploit it in a manner which safeguards their and their children's future".

A collectivist approach to security requires that a country "might be capable of, and willing to, subordinate their own sovereign rights, and their own particular interests and needs, to a common interest in peaceful and stable international relations, and to take part in the creation of a global system capable of restraining its members from the threat or use of force" (Gareis and Varwick, 2005, p.59). The key point to note, is that a government that adheres to a collectivist approach to security is held accountable for its actions by the other participating/donor governments, and that any agreement is underpinned by a set of obligations that are reinforced through the threat of sanctions (Gareis and Varwick, 2005, p.59). The threat of sanctions can be viewed as logical in the sense that those participating in a collectivist security approach are bound by a set of rules and expectations. This does bring to mind the issue of participating/donor nations having an ethical foreign policy in place that can be classified as sustainable. However, if nations are going to devise and implement an ethical foreign policy and incorporate it within a collectivist security approach, then the governments of these countries may want a more pronounced voice in world affairs. This will always be an issue of concern and one that will intensify as governments lobby for increased international recognition. Indeed, Masci (2005, pp.93-114) has made it clear that questions have been raised regarding the composition and enlargement of the Security Council of the United Nations, and also, whether the United Nations should participate more directly in a country's affairs. This will no doubt fuel further debate in the field of international relations, and will one might suspect lead to discussions about past associations as well as present and future relationships.

CONCLUSION

During a crisis/disaster/emergency, a government is required to take action that not only puts in place a recovery operation but also, a communication strategy that ensures that the general public do not generate and suffer from what is known as psychological fear. In order not to generate fear that results in panic and looting for example, government representatives need to be visible and provide adequate leadership, and ensure that the various agencies and experts involved in the clean-up phase are visible. It is important to note that during periods of disaster and emergency, it is essential that government draw on the expertise available in organizations in both the private and public sectors, and that additional disruptive acts/events, should they materialize, are dealt with in a timely and decisive manner.

As well as establishing what the role of government is during a crisis, disaster or emergency, it is necessary for policy advisors to think in terms of what expertise is available at the regional, national and international level; and how this expertise can be integrated into a sustainable recovery programme that is being assembled to alleviate suffering and psychological trauma. Essential services need to be restored as soon as possible and key infrastructure needs to be repaired/rebuilt as quickly as possible if that is disease and unrest are to be contained, and economic and industrial development is to continue. The contingency plans drawn up need to ensure that the potential threats identified do not materialize or if they do, are containable. This means that various areas of vulnerability are identified and the various threats/weaknesses are made secure. A key point to note is that if a threat is not dealt with satisfactorily, the level of vulnerability will increase and further system failures will result.

Bearing these points in mind, it can be suggested that national security budgets may need to be reconfigured in order to take into account additional disaster implications. This means that the term security needs to be interpreted more widely than is the case at present. As regards the training of first responders, there is no doubt that simulation exercises prove useful with respect to preparing disaster and emergency personnel for a range of situations, and they can be used to develop an individual's/group's knowledge and expertise to carry out their duties adequately. Furthermore, by involving the general public in emergency simulation exercises, it is hoped that people can be hardened to such events and can adopt a sensible approach to handling uncertainty, which makes them feel confident that in situations of vulnerability they are indeed 'as safe as possible'.

ACKNOWLEDGMENTS

Dr. Peter Trim was a Visiting Fellow, from October 2000 to December, 2000, at the Benfield Greig Hazard Research Centre, University College London, University of London, and is grateful for the assistance provided by staff based in the centre.

Dr. Peter Trim was a Visiting Fellow, from October 2004 to December, 2004, at the Institute of Commonwealth Studies, University of London, and is grateful for the assistance provided by staff based at the institute.

REFERENCES

Alexander, D. (2002). *Principles of Emergency Planning and Management*. Harpenden, Herts: Terra Publishing.

Amanor, K., and Brown, D. (2003). "Making environmental management more responsive to local needs: Decentralisation and evidence-based policy in Ghana". *Forestry Briefing Number 3* (April). London: Overseas Development Institute.

Bellamy, A.J., and McDonald, M. (2004). "Securing international society: Towards an English school discourse of security". *Australian Journal of Political Science*, 39 (2), pp.307-330.

Benn, H. (2005). "The millennium development goals: The 2005 agenda". *Committee Room 14, House of Commons*, London (17th March), from 12.30pm to 1.45pm.

Chalinder, A. (1998). *Temporary Human Settlement Planning for Displaced Populations in Emergencies*. London: Overseas Development Institute.

Clarkson, S., and Banda, M. (2004). "Congruence, conflict and continental governance: Canada's and Mexico's responses to paradigm shift in the United States". *The American Review of Canadian Studies*, 34 (2), pp.313-347.

DFID. (2005). *Disaster Risk Reduction: A Development Concern*. London: Department for International Development.

Gareis, S.B., and Varwick, J. (2005). *The United Nations: An Introduction*. Basingstoke, Hampshire: Palgrave Macmillan.

Harnish, R.M. (2002). *Minds, Brains, Computers: An Historical Introduction to the Foundations of Cognitive Science*. Oxford: Blackwell Publishers Limited.

Hodgett, S., and Royle, S.A. (2003). "Conceptualising community: Policing implications for Atlantic Canada". *British Journal of Canadian Studies*, 16 (2), pp.309-318.

Hyslop, M. (2007). *Critical Information Infrastructures: Resilience and Protection*. New York: Springer.

La Trobe, S., and Davis, I. (2005). *Mainstreaming Disaster Risk Reduction: A Tool for Development Organisations*. Teddington, Middlesex: TEARFUND.

La Trobe, S., and Venton, P. (2003). *Natural Disaster Risk Reduction: The Policy and Practice of Selected Institutional Donors*. Teddington, Middlesex: TEARFUND.

Masci, D. (2005). "The United Nations and global security", pp.93-114. In: *Global Issues: Selections from the CQ Researcher*. Washington, D.C.: CQ Press.

McMahon, R.K. (2004). "Changing the organisation but maintaining the culture: The centrality of organisational mission to the reform process. An overview of the United States Environmental Protection Agency and the Environment Agency for England and Wales". *Strategic Change*, 13 (6), pp.323-332.

Meale, A. (1999). "Sustainable development: The view from government". *Earthwise*, Issue 13 (January), pp.4-5.

Middleton, N., and O'Keefe, P. (1998). *Disaster and Development: The Politics of Humanitarian Aid*. London: Pluto Press.

Mitchell, T. (2005). "Participatory disaster risk reduction: A trial of "Future Search" in St. Kitts and Montserrat". *Mainstreaming Disaster Risk Management: Organisational Learning and Change, Integrated Planning Against Risk Seminar 4*. London: University College London (21st April).

Pelling, M., and High, C. (2005). "Social learning and adaptation to climate change". *Benfield Hazard Research Centre Disaster Studies Working Paper Number 11*. London: University College London.

Peters, B.G. (2004). "Governance and public bureaucracy: New forms of democracy or new forms of control". *The Asia Pacific Journal*, 26 (1), pp.3-15.

Rienstra, D. (1999). "The cost of humanitarian aid – Are tax payers getting value for money? *Humanitarian Affairs Review*, 4 (Winter), pp.20-29.

Salmen, L.F. (1989). *Listen to the People: Participant – Observer Evaluation of Development Projects*. Oxford: Oxford University Press.

Sharma, A. (2005). "Risk, culture and government orders". *Mainstreaming Disaster Risk Management: Organisational Learning and Change, Integrated Planning Against Risk Seminar 4*. London: University College London (21st April).

Trim, P.R.J. (2003). "Disaster management and the role of the intelligence and security services". *Disaster Prevention and Management*, 12 (1), pp.6-15.

Trim, P.R.J. (2004). "An integrative approach to disaster management and planning". *Disaster Prevention and Management*, 13 (3), pp.218-225.

Trim, P.R.J. (2006). "Disaster and emergency scenarios: Pointers for educationalists, trainers and practitioners", pp.111-119. In: *The International Simulation and Gaming Yearbook Volume 14: Simulations and Games for Risk, Crisis and Security Management*. Borodzicz, E. (Ed). Edinburgh: SAGSET.

Trim, P.R.J., and Caravelli, J. (2007). "Counteracting and preventing terrorist actions: A generic model to facilitate inter-government cooperation", pp.135-152. In: *Terrorism Issues: Threat Assessment, Consequences and Prevention*. Merkidze, A.W. (Ed). New York: Nova Science Publishers, Inc.

Trim, P.R.J., and Y-I, Lee. (2006). "A multi-cultural communication model to be used in disaster and emergency management simulation exercises", pp.120-130. In: *The International Simulation and Gaming Yearbook Volume 14: Simulations and Games for Risk, Crisis and Security Management*. Borodzicz, E. (Ed). Edinburgh: SAGSET.

Trim, P.R.J., and Lee, Y-I. (2007). "An extended multi-cultural communication model for use in disaster and emergency simulation exercises", pp.108-118. In: *The International Simulation and Gaming Research Yearbook. Volume 15: Effective Learning from Games & Simulations*. Trim, P.R.J., and Lee, Y-I. (Eds). Edinburgh: SAGSET.

Twigg, J. (2005). "Mainstreaming disaster risk management: Organizational learning and change". *IPAR Integrated Planning Against Risk Briefing Paper 4*. London: Benfield Hazard Research Centre, University College London.

UN/ISDR. (2005). *Reducing Disaster Risk: A Challenge for Development*. United Nations/International Strategy for Disaster Reduction.

http://www.unisdr.org/eng/mdgs-drr/undp.htm (Accessed on 18th June, 2005).

www.unisdr.org/wcdr (Accessed on 19th April, 2005).

Valdes, H.M. (2005). "Mainstreaming disaster risk reduction within the UN: The Hyogo Framework for 2005-2015". *Mainstreaming Disaster Risk Management: Organisational Learning and Change, Integrated Planning Against Risk Seminar 4*. London: University College London (21st April).

Walker, P. (1989). *Famine Early Warning Systems*. London: Earthscan Publications Limited.

In: Strategizing Resilience and Reducing Vulnerability
Editors: Peter R.J. Trim and Jack Caravelli

ISBN 978-1-60741-693-7
© 2009 Nova Science Publishers, Inc.

Chapter 15

A CONCEPTUAL ENVIRONMENTAL AND INFRASTRUCTURAL RISK ASSESSMENT MODEL TO FACILITATE SECURITY MANAGEMENT AT MAJOR SPORTING EVENTS

Peter R.J. Trim and Jack Caravelli

ABSTRACT

Major sporting events have become increasingly important show cases as they provide an opportunity for a country to raise its profile. Owing to the fact that a major sporting event has a great deal of international appeal, it is not surprising to learn that law enforcement officers, and security and intelligence officers, are becoming increasingly concerned that activists, criminals and terrorists, will use major sporting events for their own means. Security and intelligence officers in particular are hard at work counteracting potential disruptions and are working with a range of other experts on developing a collectivist security partnership approach that can produce workable strategic security management policies. In order for this approach to be sustainable at an international level, those involved in the planning, organization and management of a major sporting event need to share and exchange information on a regular basis and give advice to and take advice from government representatives when necessary. It is important to note that managers employed by private sector companies need to work more closely with staff from the public sector, in order to ensure that the strategic security management policy that emerges is in fact sustainable. In particular, Internet service providers need to be more directly involved in providing online security and the general public need to be more adequately informed about the potential risks that are associated with the Internet. In order to safeguard those competing in or those attending a major sporting event, it is necessary for those involved in the organization of the event and the various sponsors, to introduce a number of security management initiatives that reduce the possibility of a man-made attack at the event. A conceptual environmental and infrastructural risk assessment model can be deployed to ensure that possible threats are identified and neutralized before they manifest. By putting in place robust counterterrorist measures, the authorities can ensure that a major sporting event is the cultural, social and economic success that it is supposed to be.

INTRODUCTION

Organizers and sponsors of major sporting events need to be aware of the risk associated with a man made attack on the venue itself. This requires that all those involved in the sporting event have a sound appreciation of what risk is and how an individual, group or community can be considered to be at risk. Issues such as who is responsible for establishing that a community is safe and what emergency plans and contingencies need to be put in place are the responsibility of a group of people ranging from local and national government officers, security and intelligence officers, corporate security staff, law enforcement officers to international security experts. Contingency planners need to place locational risk in context and also, ensure that the media provides both timely and accurate reports as an incident unfolds. This is to ensure that members of the general public are provided with as much help and assistance as is indeed possible, and that a panic situation is averted.

The arguments put forward in this chapter will show that security management is not an isolated activity, but is in fact a core activity that needs to be underpinned by theoretical insights. The work can be considered an extension of that undertaken by Trim and Caravelli (2007a and 2007b), and will hopefully stimulate more discussion and research in the area of security management initiatives that reduce the possibility of man-made attacks at major sporting events. The structure of the chapter is as follows. First, risk and the community are addressed and this is followed by a section dealing with the media and sports events. Security management initiatives are covered and this section is followed by a section entitled government and interagency cooperation at sporting events. Terrorism and the disruption of public events appears next and this is followed by a collectivist approach to security. A conceptual environmental and infrastructural risk assessment model is presented and the chapter ends with a conclusion.

RISK AND THE COMMUNITY

Risk is a broad based term that is often applied in various contexts and settings. The term risk is often linked with probability theory and this means that risk can be interpreted in a quantifiable manner. Experts involved in security and intelligence work are aware of the different definitions of risk that exist and make objective risk assessments that support policy decisions. The study of risk, uncertainty and vulnerability is therefore complicated and not as clear cut as one would expect. Issues such as psychological risk are difficult to quantify and need possibly to be associated with inner feelings of confidence, emotion and the 'feel good factor'. Furthermore, one needs to distinguish clearly between natural disasters and man made disasters, if that is an objective analysis of risk is to be made. Risk also needs to be viewed from the perspective of an individual, a group and a community, if that is, the term is to have meaning.

Both man made and natural occurring incidents/disasters can have a debilitating affect on a community as well as on isolated groups of people that are to a certain extent self sufficient. As regards the purpose of this chapter, the term risk has been interpreted rather broadly, in the sense that the term risk is used in an umbrella form to cover threats that have the potential to manifest in harmful consequences. Acts of terrorism are therefore, the result of deliberately orchestrated acts of aggression that result in the loss of life, injuries, physical damage to property and resulting panic and fear amongst a wider population. Denney (2005, p.74) has stated that: "Professionals are required to make risk assessments in relation to dangers posed by individuals to the 'community' and can become caught in a complex web of blame. The complexities of these situations are often exacerbated when professionals and organisations attempt to prove that another is to blame and had created the risk in the first place."

What one has to understand, is that both the business environment and developments in technology as represented by the Internet, are increasing customer choice but at the same time placing the customer at increased risk. Often, security and safety are linked and it is government's responsibility to ensure that an individual or group of people or community are placed within a bounded environment and thus protected against acts of aggression, which can include a programme of repeat hostile actions. It is a natural process for mankind to embrace technology and to improve the quality of life. However, by embracing technology, other unforeseen threats suddenly materialize. For example, one can assume that Internet safety is the responsibility of the Internet service providers and thus the end user is provided automatically with anti-virus and anti-spam software protection. The logic is, that the Internet service provider will assume responsibly for protecting the end user against attacks by unscrupulous individuals and organized criminal gangs. However, some might argue that it is the end user that needs to assume responsibility for protecting their computer files and thus need to ensure that they have adequate security measures in place, even if it means that they have to encounter additional costs in the process.

An issue that arises is trust and how the word trust is interpreted. For example, open-source software is readily available on the world wide web and the end user assumes that it is safe to use because it is the genuine article. However, the source code is openly available and allows those so inclined to modify the software. Should an unscrupulous individual decide to tamper with the software in order that it causes damage, it has to be said that those that download it would not be aware of the potential problem(s) associated with its use unless they deployed sophisticated software in their computer system that was capable of recognizing potential computer related threats. The point being made is that with the rapid advancement of technology it is unrealistic to expect that the end user will take responsibility for ensuring that they are secure and safe, because they have a certain expectation, rightly or wrongly, that the branded computer software will perform to the required standard because it is considered to be reliable.

The same line of argument can be adopted when an individual consumer purchases a ticket to attend a major sporting event and is required either to organize their own security for the duration of the period or are expected to pay an additional (premium) price whereby a percentage of the ticket price includes a security levy. Other issues also surface, for example, the issue of identity management is a hot topic and what is concentrating the attention of security and intelligence officers is the illegal movement of people. Law enforcement officers are keen to ensure that, if a person's name is on a ticket, the person holding the ticket, is the person attending the major sporting event. Furthermore, monies being used to purchase tickets abroad may be recycled through money laundering bank operations and thus provide organized criminal gangs with new ways of legitimizing their activities, and this is also of concern to law enforcement officers.

A number of scams have become evident in recent years, for example companies run by unscrupulous individuals have promoted their services with the intention of defrauding the general public. Bank accounts have been opened at various high street banks and then closed after a relatively short of period of time. The monies paid into these accounts has been transferred to other bank accounts and then retransferred or cashed. The Internet has witnessed several illegal activities whereby companies have established rogue websites that have advertised tickets for sporting events. Unfortunately, members of the general public have been defrauded and then face a long and arduous battle to recover their funds. Organized criminal gangs realize very few people would pursue their embezzled funds owing to the fact that they will need to encounter more expense and are guaranteed very little for their efforts. It is also important to recognize that money laundering is also associated with counterfeiting and the provision of fake tickets. Again, there have been a number of occasions when individuals have paid money for what they think are legitimate sporting event tickets only to realize that the tickets are invalid. What needs to be noted is that as well as the price of the counterfeit ticket, in many instances, individuals have travelled long distances to attend a major sporting event, and as a consequence have had to stay in overnight accommodation, and purchase food and beverages, only to find that they cannot be admitted to the event. The costs can amount to hundreds of pounds sterling and as well as the psychological hurt inflicted, one has to realize that there is an opportunity cost involved.

THE MEDIA AND SPORTS EVENTS

The media can play a central role in determining how a crisis/disaster is handled and can also be a major influencer vis-à-vis shaping and influencing future government policy relating to disaster management and planning. For example, any major crisis such as the 7/7 bombings in London receive instant and continuous news coverage, and tend to appeal to a worldwide audience as opposed to just a national audience. Although the aim of the news provider is to provide instant and accurate coverage as an event unfolds, it has to be remembered that experts are consulted, past decision makers are interviewed and comparisons are made as to how previous governments handled a similar but different crisis/disaster. This may in itself add to the confusion and resentment prevailing at the time. It also has to be remembered that the media operates 24/7 and some overseas media companies report events that may not be shown by domestic news providers, and this may act as a trigger for instigating or increasing news coverage. It also has to be stated that the government provides information to the general public via the media and rely on the media for impartiality and objectivity. During a period of crisis, key government figures need to demonstrate that they are in control and need to reassure people that they do not have anything to be afraid of. However, some interviews are ill timed and contain fragmented and disjointed information that adds to the confusion that prevails.

Bearing these points in mind, government representatives need to think through the issue of risk amplification. Denney (2005, p.84) has stated: "Risk amplification is used to explain why some events have both a primary, secondary and in some cases tertiary impact. The hazardous event moves through a series of stages of amplification. Although the media are regarded as the primary definers of risks in this model, other agents, including experts, government agencies and pressure groups, respond to the imagery and signs which have been communicated through various forms of media discourse. The initial signal can transform the risk message itself, while the amount of information made available for mass consumption can regulate the impact of these messages, though ripples can be felt through local communities and industry".

A major crisis/disaster once past, tends to live on in the sense that documentaries are made and new slants placed on the subject matter as new facts and evidence come to the fore. One also has to say that secondary events also trigger a new interest in the original crisis/disaster and new voices emerge that call on government to introduce additional laws or enforce existing government policy in a more direct manner. What is clear, is that the degree of government action, will to some degree, be determined by the resources available and how government allocates its priorities. It also has to be borne in mind that the general public's tolerance level, and the issue of value for money are key factors. If a general election is near, the issue of value for money is very important, but so too is the issue of making people feel good.

Another concern of law enforcement officers, is the deployment of fraudulent (phishing) websites by organized criminal gangs. For example, research undertaken by academics in the US suggests that a good phishing website can fool people and the percentage of people fooled can be as high as ninety per cent (Dhamija et al., 2006, p.1). What needs to be realized is that as the battlefield changes, so too does the expertise required, and a renewed emphasis needs to be placed on technology and infrastructural support. What becomes evident is that immediate and future investments are required in computer technology, to combat the actions of organized criminal syndicates.

A problem does emerge however. The term security can and does have multiple meanings and Denney (2005, p.121) is right to suggest that "'Security' is a problematic concept since it appears to have different meanings in different contexts". The word security can be placed in an individual context (someone attending a sporting event on their own); a group context (a group of supporters or a team travelling to a venue in a coach); or a community context (the spectators at the stadium, the local residents living and working in close proximity to the stadium, and those working on site or in the immediate neighbourhood). The degree of risk that each is subject to depends upon a number of risk factors and how likely a threat is to materialize. What can be noted is that the media, during a crisis or disaster, should focus on providing local people and organizations with as much information as is possible about the situation so that they can cope with the situation and feel reasonably confident to deal with the after affects. Fischer (2002, p.126) has recognized this and made a very useful point when suggesting that: "Accuracy was greater as long as the focus remained on live broadcasting of local responders and their needs".

The downside is that costs rocket during an incident (man made attack) and for sometime afterwards, because police and other law enforcement officers, as well as various government representatives, and the military for example, are deployed in a focused and concentrated manner to rectify the problem. As costs escalate, government needs a sympathetic public that is firstly willing and sympathetic to the government taking on terrorists and secondly, duty bound and prepared to pay higher taxes to fund counter-terrorist measures. Due to the fact that the nature of terrorist activities are highly unpredictable, it means that fighting terrorist aggression is both time consuming (preventive measures) and stressful (constant worry that the various systems in place will not be able to eradicate all the threats). Bearing these points in mind, various contingencies need to be put in place and also, additional funds need to be found during the long-term, because additional investment needs to be found for increasing law enforcement, security and intelligence personnel; upgrading equipment; and providing more office space for the extra staff.

SECURITY MANAGEMENT INITIATIVES

Those involved in disaster and emergency management and planning, can deploy scenario planning in order to establish how adequate the existing business continuity planning process is and can identify and develop more effective operational planning activities (Kennedy et al., 2003, p.4). Smart and Vertinsky (2006, p.336) state: "Techniques such as building scenarios of the worst possible outcome will aid in evaluating the seriousness of proposed actions realistically and reduce the propensity toward high-risk alternatives". It is useful to note that Smart and Vertinsky (2006, pp.330-334) have produced a number of design features for preventing crisis pathologies, indeed, their work is of interest because they not only state what major problem might materialize, they define the characteristics and symptoms, and then provide various prescriptions.

As regards the consumer, it is important to distinguish between uncertainty and risk (Littler and Melanthiou, 2006, p.432) if that is, security is to be adequately promoted in the minds of those buying tickets and attending major sporting events. Those that apply for tickets to attend an event need to be assured that the ticket that they purchase is genuine and they also need to feel safe in the sense that if they pay for the ticket using electronic means, that their personal details are encoded and held securely. So the issue of data transfer security is vital as it relates to an individual's confidence vis-à-vis using an online payment system for example. From a marketing point of view, it is also essential to note that if such technology is made available, that the general public have confidence in the security of the network itself. Deperimeterization is the term given to protecting data that needs to be encrypted and given authentication. The issue of identity management is important vis-à-vis the ticket operator, because the person receiving the sporting venue tickets needs to be known and needs to be traceable. Biometrics can be used to identify people as the technology locates and identifies "individuals who have already registered for a program or service" (Nanavati et al., 2002, p.6). Biometric systems are therefore focused on eliminating fraudulent behaviour and can be linked with various forms of population movement control. Identity cards can be used to monitor the movements of individuals across borders and can help to eliminate the use of double and treble identities. Government representatives, influenced by their policy advisors, staff employed by the security and intelligence agencies, law enforcement staff and independent international counter terrorist experts, have over the years been influential in introducing laws that make domestic security more effective. The key point to note however, is that a significant threat to national security does not have to materialize from ideology alone, it can be the result of any one of a number of factors including disease, politics, economics and demographics (Wirtz, 2007, p.353). What is of increasing concern to governments is the possibility of pandemics that are brought about by breakdowns in bio-security. If people do travel on mass to an infected area and then travel back to their homeland, the ramifications could be serious as some governments may need time to get the full medical provision in place. Hence a pandemic would require a collectivist security approach as it would need to be dealt with quickly and effectively.

GOVERNMENT AND INTERAGENCY COOPERATION AT SPORTING EVENTS

Trim and Caravelli (2007a, pp.13-15) have reported that a number of major sporting events have been affected by various direct and indirect man made actions. For example, on Saturday 7th October, 2000, after only one race, racing at Ascot was abandoned after police discovered an unidentified suspect package and ordered spectators to make their way to the centre of the track. The 2010 World Cup is due to be staged in South Africa and concerns have been raised about the safety of both the footballers themselves and the spectators. The South African government has indicated that it will spend 250 million pounds sterling to counteract crime during the tournament (there will be large additions of police and security personnel), however, the security measures will need to be approved by FIFA by June, 2009. There is a depth of security expertise available to visiting teams, for example, when the Australian national cricket team tour England, they not only receive advice from the Australian Cricketers' Association, they also receive advice from the Metropolitan Police.

Trim and Caravelli (2007a, p.14) have indicated that in the aftermath of the September 11, 2001 terrorist attacks against New York City and Washington, DC, the US government began developing a comprehensive list of domestic targets that would receive priority security upgrades. In 2003, a Congressional study placed the number of these high value targets at 300. The resulting political clamour since then has swelled the target list to over 10,000 targets. Some cynics might wonder if this number did not represent targets in search of terrorists.

While the importance of many of those locations or their potential as terrorist targets has been and remains subject to controversy and debate, the US government has taken the unambiguous and broadly supported policy decision to commit considerable resources to supporting in various ways the security measures of foreign governments hosting Olympic Games. Heavily attended, high profile events that stretch across two weeks at numerous venues provide an enticing set of opportunities for a terrorist group. From a US perspective, its large national contingent of athletes and the substantial number of Americans who travel to every Olympic Game regardless of location require offers of support to host organizers and officials. During the recent Olympic Games in Athens, Greece and Turin, Italy, US assistance was offered, and accepted, as an integral part of overall security measures set in place for the Games. While the primary motivation for such assistance was to contribute to the safety of US citizens, US officials also recognized that any successful attack on the Olympic Games could have a "chilling effect" and result in substantial financial losses, a long established and continuing goal of terrorist attacks.

The types of assistance provided have varied depending on the facility and the priorities of the host government. For example, radiation portal monitoring equipment, suitable for detecting attempts to smuggle radioactive material into Olympic venues, was installed for the Athens Games. The equipment worked as expected and did not detect any attempts at smuggling radioactive materials. There also were various types of information sharing among security officials from various nations.

US government support took on far broader dimensions at Turin. A US office was established there to serve as a coordinating hub for all US government assistance and the US ambassador to Italy took a direct interest in its operation. Concurrently, the State Department led interagency meetings in Washington, DC to ensure domestic coordination and cooperation prior to any US government entity providing assistance in Italy. Overall, the departments of State, Justice, Homeland Security, Defense and Energy provided various forms of assistance. Lessons learned from the Athens Games were incorporated into US planning for Turin. In addition, to a comprehensive approach to planning before the Turin Games, the US government also recognized the importance of coordination during the Games, establishing an operations centre at the Games that served as a useful clearinghouse for information.

The needs and interests of the host government in accepting assistance from other nations has not been a source of concern for the United States in the recent Olympics. Both Greece and Italy, US allies and NATO members, were excellent partners for the Americans.

The issue of intra-government and inter-government co-operation is highly important with respect to whether a man-made attack is launched at a major sporting event or whether an attack is launched prior to a major sporting event (possibly in a different country from the one hosting the event), the aim of which is to spread fear and create panic. What is clear, is that governments draw on various types of expertise from organizations in both the public sector and the private sector, and that in the event of an incident occurring, "genuine co-operation among emergency responders must not be taken for granted by planners and cannot be overemphasised" (Granot, 1999, p.21).

TERRORISM AND THE DISRUPTION OF PUBLIC EVENTS

It is important to realise that the word terrorism has different connotations to different people. For example, "Historically, members of militant groups who use violence have regarded themselves as freedom fighters, although they are often defined by governments as terrorists. Nelson Mandella, imprisoned as a terrorist, was elected head of the South African state which had imprisoned him soon after his release from prison" (Denney, 2005, p.135). It has to be remembered that as well as killing and maiming people, terrorist actions are aimed at causing as much disruption as possible and the resulting news coverage (world wide media coverage) is aimed at promoting the activities of terrorist groups and their causes. The propaganda generated by a terrorist incident allows terrorist groups to intensify their fund raising activities and develop additional links with organized criminal groups. It is fair to suggest, therefore that terrorist networks and organized criminal syndicates understand each other and embrace the concept of mutuality.

Bearing in mind that terrorism has been in existence for many centuries, it can be suggested that terrorist networks will continue to consume the attention of government and counter terrorist professionals for years to come. There is a genuine fear among law enforcement personnel and security and intelligence officers, that terrorist groups working in collaboration with organized criminal gangs will raise the stakes by focusing on chemical, biological and radiological weaponry. Should this be the case, terrorist activity will be elevated to a higher level of complexity than is the case at present. One can suggest therefore, that the general public will need to have a better understanding of the level of risk that they are potentially subject to and also, will need to understand that if a number of antecedent conditions are met, that a potential threat could turn into an actual incident. It is also important to point out that managers in the private sector need to review their corporate security and business continuity plans, if that is, they are to manage risk in a systematic and strategic manner (Slywotzky and Drzik, 2005).

It is useful to reflect on the point raised by Adams (2005, p.17): "The 191 people killed by the Madrid bombers on 11 March 2004 were equivalent to the number killed in road accidents in Spain every 12 or 13 days". The general public have been informed that it is not possible for the authorities to prevent every terrorist attack on their mainland, but what is of concern to people in position of authority is that if a chemical, biological or radiological attack occurs on a large and densely packed population, the consequences could be far reaching. For example, a radiological attack unleashed at a major sporting event would affect thousands of people in the immediate vicinity and in a certain radius, as wind carried the radioactive material over many miles. Contaminants would cover a very wide geographical area and possibly render wide tracks of land unusable and buildings uninhabitable for many, many years. So although it is useful to prioritize risk incidents, it is also essential for government representatives and their policy advisors to think in terms of what might happen and if it does, what resources need to be deployed to make the surrounding area safe.

Another important issue that has to be borne in mind is that if a major incident (a man made or naturally occurring disaster) does occur, a certain portion of the population may act in a selfish and reckless manner. For example, individuals may loot property and this may result in Martial law being implemented (Fischer, 2002, p. 124). Although, law enforcement officers, the military and disaster and emergency services personnel would be on the scene within a relatively short period of time, a chemical, bacterial or radiological attack could take a very long time to clear up, and such an attack would produce psychological trauma.

Reflecting on the above, it is useful to take into account the advice provided by Fuerth (2006, p.59) who states that: "In particular, the habit of heavily discounting the future in favor of the near-term must be abandoned, for the simple reason that the future – defined here as the rate of incidence of major social change – is accelerating. That acceleration represents, in turn, the dramatically quickened pace of science and technology, translated into ethical, political, economic and social consequences. If we are overtaken and swamped by the accelerating rate of change, then it is likely that our society will fail to grasp major opportunities for advancement and forfeit them to others who are more alert. We will also fail to take action in time to mitigate the societal impact of major, abrupt dislocations.

It is especially important to keep our eye on dislocations so extreme as to represent a permanent, new phase of existence for which previous experience offers little guidance...."

A COLLECTIVIST APPROACH TO SECURITY

As proven by recent past successful Olympic Games, a collectivist approach to security also will provide the organizers of the London Games with the best opportunity for a successful outcome. It should be possible to put in place adequate security measures that safeguard all those competing in or attending a major sporting event. Those living and working in close proximity to a major sporting venue will from time to time need to consider the threat level that they themselves face, however, sponsors of sporting events also need to consider the ramifications associated with sponsoring high profile sporting events that get worldwide coverage. As regards sponsorship, it is an established fact that the Olympic

Games, denoted by the five interlocking rings, is a powerful international brand in its own right. Companies sponsoring the Olympic Games understand well the importance of brand association and the national pride that goes along with hosting the games. Indeed, victory in the games means a great deal to the athletes competing and their respective coaches, and the final medal table gives some overall indication of the success of the athletes and the standard of sport in the competing countries.

With respect to the 2012 Olympic Games, London can draw much attention to itself and promote its role as a leading financial centre. Success in the games would no doubt reinforce London's standing as a vibrant city. No doubt the thousands of athletes, support staff, media personnel and tourists, will spend significant sums of money that will give the economy a boost. A successful games will also result in inward investment into the UK and this will be another measure of the Games' success. It should be remembered however, that sponsors of the 2012 Olympic Games consider their sponsorship activity to be somewhat all embracing. For example, Visa is one of the main sponsors of the games and has already mapped out a large and diversified sponsorship programme that is viewed as partnership oriented (Grannell, 2007). Visa aims to increase their brand association with both consumers and retailers, and this will be achieved by sponsoring the UK school games (an appreciation of culture and art as well as sport); the Paralympics world cup; providing hospitality services; promoting business activities to trade representatives; and gaining public recognition for 'access, convenience, and trust' at what is going to be a 'cashless games' (Grannell, 2007).

As regards the cost of security for the 2012 Olympics, it has been suggested that the original sum of 200 million pounds sterling is an underestimate and the actual figure could be as high as 850 million pounds sterling (Davey and Laurance, 2006, p.5). The figures put forward are for the provision of security guards and electronic surveillance during the games, but it also has to be borne in mind that security will have to be in place well before the buildings are ready for use (Davey and Laurance, 2006, p.5). What needs to be noted, is that some valuable lessons have been learned from the 9/11 attacks, and this has resulted in a number of security initiatives being put in place. A permanent unit, located within the Metropolitan Police, has been established to take control of security planning for the 2012 Olympic Games, and a number of additional security and intelligence initiatives have been taken that facilitate multi-agency planning and co-operation, prior to the Games and during the Games. Furthermore, those attending the games will need to travel to hotels and various other forms of accommodation, will need to have food and drink available, and will most likely want to travel to other parts of the UK and/or visit the main tourist attractions in London. As a result, there is expected to be additional pressure on both local and national government representatives to increase and improve transport facilities and the transportation infrastructure. It is not surprising to learn that in an unpredictable world, security is a key factor and much attention still needs to be put into assessing the UK's airport facilities, bus terminals, port facilities, train stations, and road networks for example. It is clear that security companies, the organizing companies associated with the major sporting event, the various company sponsors, local and government agencies, and various other participative bodies and organizations, need to adopt a partnership approach to managing the major sporting event. The British Security Industry Association is playing an influential role vis-à-vis the 2012 Olympic Games and this should raise the profile of security management.

In order that a major sporting event is successful, it needs to attract high quality athletes, imaginative sponsors, enthusiastic spectators and a pro-active media. Due to the fact that it is the current major sporting event that sets the standard for future sporting events, all those involved need to pay careful attention to meeting customer expectations. Indeed, managers of partner organizations can combine their expertise and engage in information sharing. A customer service policy can be devised that is underpinned by relationship management. It is important, however, to understand that sponsoring companies may well be competitors and because of this appear reluctant at times to cooperate and share information. Owing to the fact that the security issues are so very important one can argue that the sponsoring companies are morally obliged to cooperate and act in unison. It also has to be made clear that even if a security company or a sponsoring company has been involved in a major sporting event in the past that there will need to be a renewal of organizational learning because some key members of staff may have retired and may no longer be available for consultation. By advocating a collectivist approach to security, it is hoped that additional spin-offs will occur.

It is important to place the relationship marketing approach (Gronroos, 1997) within the context of customer relationship management (Baker, 2003). Should this be the case, the transformational leadership style (Hughes et al., 1999, p.291) can be harnessed by mangers throughout the partnership arrangement to inspire subordinates into embracing and managing change. For example, marketing and security are linked in the sense that a successful major sporting event will enhance the names of the organizers and the various sponsoring companies, and will impress government officials who realize that the knowledge and expertise developed can be made available to other sporting event organizers. One might suggest that marketing is by definition a competitive activity, however, a major sporting event can be considered within the public domain and also a truly international major sporting event, will invoke national pride and foster better working relationships between and among government representatives. It is clear therefore, that there is a link between organizational learning and knowledge management (Vince et al., 2002). Another important point to reflect upon is that the security dimension needs to be viewed from a skills based perspective and security officers in particular need to familiarize themselves with advances in biometrics. Identity management technology is developing rapidly and stand alone systems are now being superseded by Internet linked biometric systems. Brislin (2000, p.112) has highlighted the fact that different generations need different skill levels, and this is further evidence that the organizational learning concept needs to be embraced by all those participating in the organization and management of the major sporting event.

The organizers and sponsors of a major sporting event can ensure that there is no dilution of the brand by ensuring that a high quality after sales service is provided. Wright et al., (2007, p.141) state that "well-known brand names may suffer reverses as well as successes" and this is a useful point to note. Indeed, with respect to the London 2012 Olympic Games, it can be suggested that if the main aim of holding the games in London is to regenerate a large area of East London (Kornblatt, 2006, p.3), then attention needs to be given to how the investment in the games is going to produce sustainable results in the long-term. This suggests that marketing intelligence officers (based in the organizing company) need to work closely with customer service policy staff, and develop training programmes (Trim and Lee, 2006, pp.155-156) for small local companies. This should provide further business opportunities and result in employment security.

A Conceptual Environmental and Infrastructural Risk Assessment Model

Elliott (2006, p.403) has provided a useful explanation of what risk assessment is, by stating that it is a process that gauges "the most likely outcomes of a set of events and the consequences of those outcomes". Bearing this in mind, it can be argued that business continuity planning needs to be placed within both a strategic context and an operational context. The reader will note from Figure 1, that the main output from the conceptual environmental and infrastructural risk assessment model is a strategic security management policy that can be implemented in the context of a partnership arrangement. The term partnership arrangement is rather undefined but includes a formal association of all the organizations involved in the major sporting event.

The model's inputs are derived from a whole range of experts that have knowledge relating to past, present and possible future threats. They operate at the highest political level and deal with journalists on a need to know basis. The experts undertake various types of risk assessment: they produce reports outlining known factors and reports dealing with anticipated factors. The latter type of report incorporates scenario planning and other forms of forward thinking. As a result, the organizers of a major sporting event are able to produce a strategic management security policy that incorporates business continuity plans. It is also evident from Figure 1 that government representatives deal with the media, and that during times of crisis/disaster, media personnel are expected to report in an objective way, the main benefit of which is that it has a calming effect on the population. Should the military need to get involved, it can be said that their actions would be interventionist and problem resolution oriented. Military personnel can be deployed to invoke martial law and/or to stabilize a situation and to help with clearing up for example.

It is also clear from Figure 1 that overseas government representatives are involved in the collectivist security partnership approach and that law enforcement personnel, and security and intelligence officers in particular, are also involved in carrying out surveillance of known activists and suspected terrorists; monitoring the tourist population (and in particular front companies associated with the trafficking of people); and monitoring known money launderers and counterfeiters for example. They also work closely with independent security personnel that guard sports men and women, key guests and political dignitaries for example. The issue of drug abuse among sports men and women is a key concern and this is also under the auspices of law enforcement officers and the police, as well as the governing bodies responsible for the sporting event.

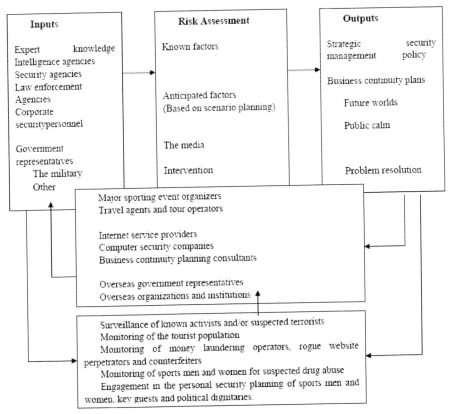

Source: (Trim and Caravelli, 2007a, p.24 and 2007b).

Figure 1. Conceptual environmental and infrastructural risk assessment model.

CONCLUSION

There is no doubt that major sporting events are of interest to activists, terrorists and criminals, as they provide an opportunity for causing disruption, propaganda to support a cause, and the means to earn a fast profit. A clearly focused strategic security management policy that is the result of a collectivist security partnership approach can do much to put in place realistic and workable business contingency plans that can be called upon if a potential threat manifests in an incident such as a terrorist attack.

What is clear, is that in the years ahead, there will need to be greater cooperation between the various government agencies, international organizations and international institutions charged with counteracting the work of terrorist networks and organized criminal syndicates, if that is, disruptions to major sporting events are to be avoided. This can only be achieved however, if the resources made available to the law enforcement agencies, and the security and intelligence agencies in particular, are increased so that they can become more pro-active in their duties. It can also be suggested that politicians worldwide will be required to introduce and/or amend existing laws so that the new type of threat envisaged is dealt with in a firm and timely manner.

REFERENCES

Adams, J. (2005). "Risk assessment: placing terror threats in context", *The Monitor*, 4 (8), pp.17-19.

Baker, S. (2003). *New Consumer Marketing: Managing a Living Demand System*. Chichester: John Wiley and Sons.

Brislin, R. (2000). *Understanding Culture's Influence on Behaviour*. Fort Worth, Texas: Harcourt College Publishers.

Davey, J., and Laurance, B. (2006). "Going for gold". *The Sunday Times Business Supplement Section 3* (26th November), p.5.

Denney, D. (2005). *Risk and Society*. London: Sage Publications.

Dhamija, R., Tygar, J.D., and Hearst, M. (2006). "Why phishing works". *Center for Research in Computation and Society Working Paper*. Boston, MA: Harvard University.

Elliott, D. (2006). "Chapter 24: Crisis management into practice", pp.393-412. In: *Key Readings in Crisis Management: Systems and Structures for Prevention and Recovery*. Smith, D., and Elliott, D. (Eds). London: Routledge.

Fischer, H.W. (2002). "Terrorism and 11 September 2001: does the "behavioral response to disaster" model fit?" *Disaster Prevention and Management*, 11 (2), pp.123-127.

Fuerth, L. (2006). "Strategic myopia: the case for forward engagement". *The National Interest*, 83 (Spring), pp.58-63.

Grannell, C. (2007). "Financing and sponsorship. London 2012 – What does it mean for UK PLC?" Portcullis House, London: Industry and Parliament Trust.

Granot, H. (1999). "Emergency inter-organizational relationships". *Disaster Prevention and Management*, 8 (1), pp.21-26.

Gronroos, C. (1997). "Value-driven relational marketing: from products to resources and competencies". *Journal of Marketing Management*, 13, pp.407-419.

Hughes, R.L., Ginnett, R.C., and Curphy, G.J. (1999). *Leadership: Enhancing the Lessons of Experience*. Boston, MA: Irwin/McGraw-Hill.

Kennedy, P., Perrottet, C., and Thomas, C. (2003). "Scenario planning after 9/11: managing the impact of a catastrophic event". *Strategy and Leadership*, 31 (1), pp.4-13.

Kornblatt, T. (2006). "Setting the bar: preparing for London's Olympic legacy". *Centre for Cities Discussion Paper No 8* (December). London: IPPC.

Littler, D., and Melanthiou, D. (2006). "Consumer perceptions of risk and uncertainty and the implications for behaviour towards innovative retail services: the case of Internet Banking". *Journal of Retailing and Consumer Services*, 13, pp.431-443.

Nanavati, S., Thieme, M., and Nanavati, R. (2002). *Biometrics: Identity Verification in a Networked World*. Chichester: John Wiley and Sons.

Slywotzky, A.J., and Drzik, J. (2005). "Countering the biggest risk of all". *Harvard Business Review*, 83 (4) (April), pp.78-88.

Smart, C., and Vertinsky, I. (2006). "Chapter 21: Designs for crisis decision units", pp.321-342. In: *Key Readings in Crisis Management: Systems and Structures for Prevention and Recovery*. Smith, D., and Elliott, D. (Eds). London: Routledge.

Trim, P.R.J., and Caravelli, J. (2007a). "A strategic approach to security management at major sporting events". *Sport Business Campus '07 Conference, Sport Business in the*

21ˢᵗ Century: Challenges and Opportunities. London: Birkbeck College, University of London (17th April), pp.1-31

Trim, P.R.J., and Caravelli, J. (2007b). "A conceptual environmental and infrastructural risk assessment model to facilitate security management at major sporting events". *The Third CAMIS Security Management Conference: Strategizing Resilience and Reducing Vulnerability.* London: Birkbeck College, University of London (5th to 7th September).

Trim, P.R.J., and Lee, Y-I. (2006). "Vertically integrated organisational marketing systems: a partnership approach for retailing organisations". *Journal of Business and Industrial Marketing*, 21 (3), pp.151-163.

Vince, R., Sutcliffe, K., and Olivera, F. (2002). "Organizational learning: new directions". *British Journal of Management*, 13 (Special Issue), pp.S1-S6.

Wirtz, J.J. (2007). "A new agenda for security and strategy?" pp.337-355. In *Strategy in the Contemporary World.* Baylis, J. Wirtz, J.., Gray, C.S., and Cohen, E. (Eds), Oxford: Oxford University Press.

Wright, L.T., Millman, C., and Martin, L.M. (2007). "Research issues in building brand equity and global brands in the pc market". *Journal of Marketing Management*, 23 (1-2), pp.137-155.

ABOUT THE CONTRIBUTORS

Kevin Brear is currently a Senior Manager with Deloitte LLP, responsible for the UK firm's internal business continuity programme. From 1986 to 2005, he served as a police officer in the City of London Police and for the last 5 years of that service, he was the Force Major Incident Officer. He is a member of the Business Continuity Institute, the Emergency Planning Society, the Institute of Civil Protection and Emergency Management and is currently the National Secretary of the Society of Industrial Emergency Services Officers (SIESO). Kevin represents the interests of the SIESO members on a number of British Standards Institute Committees. He holds an MSc in Risk, Crisis and Disaster Management from the University of Leicester.
Contact e-mail: kbrear@deloitte.co.uk

Jack Caravelli, PhD., is a Visiting Professor at the United Kingdom Defence Academy, Cranfield University, Shrivenham, England. Jack has over 25 years of experience in national security, including service at the highest levels of government. He served on the White House National Security Council staff as Director for Nonproliferation from 1996-1999. In this capacity he was the President's advisor on Russian and Middle East nonproliferation issues and was responsible for the formulation and day-to-day implementation of the US government's non-proliferation policies in those regions. From 1999-2002 Jack was Deputy Assistant Secretary for the Department of Energy and Director of the Office of International Material Protection and Cooperation. He most recently served as a senior advisor to the Department of Energy's Office of Plans and Policy. Jack's book entitled: *Nuclear Insecurity: Understanding the Threat from Rogue Nations and Terrorists*, was published by Praeger in 2007.
Contact e-mail: jcaravelli@earthlink.net

Nick Edwards has a strong interest in intelligence and security work, having spent a lifetime in this area including 28 years at GCHQ/CESG. On leaving CESG in 1996, he worked for Nortel, and this was followed by time spent at a start up company, and then a US technology company. Nick has spent time as a self employed consultant and in 2005/06 was Principal Security Consultant for Hyder Consulting (an international infrastructure design company). In May 2007, he undertook consultancy for Thames Water (via Hyder). He is a founder member of IAAC, a member of the IAAC Management Committee and a guest lecturer at various universities.

Contact e-mail: windsorlodge@btopenworld.com

Ann Fitz-Gerald, PhD., is the Director of the Centre for Security Sector Management (CSSM) at Cranfield University and the Associate Dean (Research). She holds degrees in Commerce, International Relations, War Studies and Security and Defence Management. Her PhD evaluated the impact of national disparities across multinational military forces on local development programmes and confidence-building measures in post-conflict states. Following an initial career in the financial sector, she worked for the Canadian Government which included posts at the Pearson International Peacekeeping Centre and NATO Headquarters. Before joining Cranfield, she worked at the Centre for Defence Studies, King's College, London University where she managed a number of large research programmes, including one on "Failed and Collapsed States". Ann has worked in both research and practitioner capacities in Africa, Asia, South-East Europe and the Caribbean. She led the Global Facilitation Network for Security Sector Reform (GFN-SSR) between 2002-2006. Ann currently leads CSSM's National Security Research Programme, chairs the International Working Group on National Security and manages a large UK Government-funded stabilisation and SSR research project.
Contact e-mail: afitzgerald.cu@defenceacademy.mod.uk

Marc Glasser's career in homeland security includes serving as a Special Agent with the U.S. Department of State and U.S. Department of Transportation (USDOT). He has directed risk management programs involving critical U.S. government facilities in multiple states and territories. He has conducted Federal criminal and civil investigations. He has been a FBI Joint Terrorism Task Force and FBI Organized Crime Task Force member. He has served as a USDOT Regional Emergency Transportation Representative Team Member in support of the National Response Framework (NRF) and Emergency Support Function #1. He is an adjunct professor at the University of Nevada, Las Vegas and Regis University. He holds a Masters of Science Degree in Crisis and Emergency Management from University of Nevada, Las Vegas and a Bachelor of Science Degree in Law Enforcement and Police Science from Sam Houston State University. Profession accreditations include CPP, CHS-V and MCAS.
Contact e-mail: marc@marcglasser.com.

Robert Hall has worked for both public- and private-sector companies in risk and security management. He currently works for an international organization in London. Until August 2006 he was the Group Strategic Assessments Manager for a large financial services company where he was responsible for analyzing the threats to the business worldwide from terrorism, crime, activism and natural disasters, as well as designing contingency measures that would minimise the risks. He dealt with the consequences of the terrorist attacks of 7 July 2005, as well as prepared plans to deal with pandemics, floods and protest. From 2000 to 2003 he worked as the Project Director for an international company, designing and managing all aspects of a global security forum. The forum brought together senior executives from governments and business to discuss strategic issues over the long term. The activity was a continuation of work he carried out as Head of Analysis at the National Criminal Intelligence Service in London (1997-2000). From 1991 to 1997 he was Managing Editor of a number of threat and security titles published by Jane's Information Group. He left the British Army in 1992 after 17 years. Much of his military career was devoted to intelligence matters; he served three years as a senior staff officer in the Defence Intelligence Staff (MoD). Robert has written extensively on strategic intelligence and security issues and authored a book on Russian military affairs.

Contact e-mail: robert.hall33@btopenworld.com

Maitland Hyslop was previously Director of the EC's acclaimed eJustice Project, named as an eEntrepreneur of the decade in 2004, member of one of the USA's most prestigious think tanks on 9/11 responses, member of the Science Committee of Brussels' Politech Institute, formerly an adviser to the European Network Information and Security Agency, and author of Springer's 'Resilience in Critical Infrastructures and Critical Information Infrastructures'. Maitland is also affiliated to the Disaster and Development Centre at the University of Northumbria and is at present a Director of Market Development and Management in the UK National Health Service.

Contact: e-mail: maitland.hyslop@btopenworld.com

Nigel A. Jones, QinetiQ, is Director of the Cyber Security Knowledge Transfer Network. Since joining QinetiQ in 2004, he has led a team delivering a consultancy and research business in the domains of security, resilience and intelligence. He has a special interest in understanding and analysing risk environments, the use of intelligence systems to aid decision-making and in the integration of human factors into security systems. Nigel's experience is derived from a military career in Information Operations and the design and delivery of education and training prior to joining QinetiQ.

Contact e-mail: Najones1@qinetiq.com

Yang-Im Lee, PhD., has studied and worked in South Korea, Japan and the UK. She is at present a Lecturer in Marketing in the School of Management at Royal Holloway, University of London. Yang-Im is a Strategic Marketing specialist who has provided a number of guest lectures and presented papers at various international conferences. She has undertaken research in the areas of international marketing, strategic marketing, and international management and culture. At present she is focusing her research effort in the areas of comparative management and international marketing. In 2008, Yang-Im had published a co-authored book entitled: *Strategic Marketing Decision-Making Within Japanese and South Korean Companies*, by Chandos Publishing.

Contact e-mail: yang-im.lee@rhul.ac.uk

Andrea C Simmons is an experienced information assurance evangelist with expertise in consulting, training and speaking, across several disciplines: information security management (ISO27001 – risks assessment, ISMS, strategy and planning, policies and procedures development and implementation etc.); Information Rights Legislation/Regulation and Standards (including Data Protection and Freedom of Information) and Information and Records Management. Andrea is currently running her own consultancy business (www.simmonspsrofessionalservices.co.uk) and works associatively with several organisations in both the Public and Private Sector. Simultaneously, Andrea writes a Security blog for the BCS (www.bcs.org/blogs/security) and is on the Management Committee of the Information Assurance Advisory Council (www.iaac.org.uk). Andrea's academic achievements support the above – holding the Certified Information Systems Security

Professional (CISSP) status and completing the Certified Information Security Manager (CISM) exam. Andrea has also successfully undertaken the British Computer Society/ISEB Certificate in Data Protection and is registered on the DP Experts Directory (http://www.sbu.ac.uk/dpaexp/dpa/index.php3). Andrea has also achieved the ISEB Certificate in Freedom of Information and the BSI BS7799 Lead Auditor course. She is also an active member of the BCS and its' relevant specialist groups – Security, Audit, Law – and is on the BCS Register of Security Experts.

Contact e-mail: andrea.simmons@bcs.org.uk

Peter R.J. Trim, PhD., is a Senior Lecturer in Management and Director of the Centre for Advanced Management and Interdisciplinary Studies (CAMIS) at Birkbeck College, University of London. During his academic career he has taught a range of Marketing and Management courses in France, The Netherlands and the UK. He has also taught in Hong Kong and has published widely in a number of areas including Strategic Marketing, Industrial Marketing, Management Education, Corporate Intelligence, Corporate Security and National Security. Peter has worked in several industries and has participated in a number of academic, government and industry workshops, both in the UK and abroad. He is a member of a number of professional institutions, is a member of several editorial boards and is the current Chairman of the Society for the Advancement of Games and Simulations in Education and Training (SAGSET).

Contact e-mail: p.trim@bbk.ac.uk

David Upton is a Director of Stirling Reid Ltd, a specialised consultancy company based in London UK, which has organised emergency response exercises in all continents and many industrial sectors. These have covered business continuity issues, industrial emergency response, and top-level crisis management. Clients include government organisations, agencies, utility companies, oil, gas, pharmaceutical, shipping and transportation companies. David is a member of the National Council of the Society of Industrial Emergency Services officers (SIESO), the Emergency Planning Society, and the Institute of Energy. A graduate of Cambridge University, he also studied at London Business School. He was formerly in the British Diplomatic Service, where he served in British Embassies in South Africa, Iran and Australia, and was also a Foreign Office Spokesman dealing with the world's media. He is fascinated by the whole question of simulation and the representation of reality, about which he maintains a weblog (www.simulation.cc).

Contact e-mail: david@stirlingreid.com

INDEX

9

9/11, 13, 32, 52, 61, 90, 104, 198, 238, 242, 247
9/11 Commission, 13, 52, 61

A

absorption, 104
academics, vii, 23, 33, 82, 83, 98, 109, 166, 175, 217, 233
accidental, 169
accidents, 106, 237
accommodation, 123, 126, 137, 161, 209, 232, 238
accountability, 18, 57, 144, 168, 170, 173
accounting, 124, 125, 129, 150, 163
accuracy, 32
achievement, 7, 78
ACM, 177
acquisition of knowledge, 81
activation, 130
activism, 75, 85, 90, 246
acts of aggression, 231
acute, 202
Adams, 177, 237, 242
adaptation, 30, 227
adjustment, 106
administration, vii, 1, 2, 3, 4, 5, 7, 8, 9, 11, 12, 13
adults, 75
adverse event, 130
advertising, 160
aetiology, 105
Afghanistan, 1, 2, 3, 5, 6, 7, 8, 11, 14, 17, 19, 22, 23, 43
Africa, 23, 40, 60, 235, 246, 248
age, 10, 84, 114, 143, 171, 194
agents, 49, 57, 71, 207, 232

aggression, 3, 233
aggressiveness, 8
agricultural, 41, 46
agriculture, 40, 43, 54
aid, 8, 16, 23, 116, 128, 206, 227, 234, 247
air, 46, 52
Air Force, 68, 222
airline companies, 106
Al Qaeda, 4, 5, 8, 43, 48
alienation, 12
allies, 5, 13, 236
alternative, 4, 5, 31, 68, 80, 108, 123, 125, 126, 129, 160, 209, 210, 220
alternative energy, 68
alternatives, 44, 124, 234
ambulance, 204
amendments, 35, 48
analysts, 17, 23, 70, 72, 84, 86, 157
anger, 47
animals, 40
annihilation, 4
antecedents, 194
anthrax, 30, 50
Anti-Terrorist Business-Politico (ATBP), 99
antiviral, 139
antiviral drugs, 139
anxiety, 187
apathy, 172
application, 72, 97, 109, 121, 175
aquifers, 42, 43, 44
Arab countries, 12
Arabia, 43
argument, viii, ix, 53, 93, 105, 166, 219, 231
arid, 44, 46, 52, 59
Arizona, 46, 55
armed conflict, 39, 40
armed forces, 2, 219
Army, 52, 53, 68, 222, 246
arrest, 92, 94

Index

articulation, viii, 4, 15, 24, 26, 28, 137
artificial intelligence, 210
ASD, 155
Asia, 40, 227, 246
Asian, 206
assassination, 9
assault, 32
assessment, x, 3, 5, 8, 11, 20, 21, 23, 24, 25, 27, 28, 31, 47, 59, 67, 70, 84, 105, 170, 176, 197, 202, 240, 242, 247
assets, 8, 9, 10, 23, 25, 26, 54, 81, 93, 130, 153, 166, 176, 211
assumptions, 82, 192
asymmetry, 70, 72, 150
ATBP, 99
Athens, 235, 236
athletes, 235, 238, 239
Atlantic, 19, 226
attachment, 190
attacks, vii, 1, 2, 3, 4, 5, 9, 13, 15, 27, 30, 48, 49, 50, 67, 72, 85, 104, 110, 114, 116, 138, 149, 150, 230, 231, 235, 238, 246
attitudes, 54, 57, 173
attractiveness, 48
auditing, 66, 174, 200, 209, 215
Australia, 150, 155, 248
Austria, 150
authentication, 32, 175, 234
authority, 31, 32, 34, 35, 41, 55, 125, 137, 197, 201, 212, 237
autonomy, 6
availability, 44, 47, 50, 59, 69, 75, 87, 133, 155, 169
avian flu, 198, 200, 205, 206
awareness, 49, 51, 53, 57, 58, 123, 125, 132, 169, 171, 173, 174, 200, 205, 217, 218

B

backlash, 221
bacterial, 237
Baghdad, 48
balance sheet, 160
Balanced Scorecard, 179
ballistic missiles, 10
bank account, 232
Bank of England, 113, 117, 122, 123
banking, 52, 168
banks, 78, 127, 151, 154, 155, 232
Barack Obama, 2, 6, 11
barrier, 119
barriers, ix, 22, 33, 45, 103, 107
Basel Committee, 117, 121
Basel II, viii, 67, 169

basic needs, 21
behavior, 156
behaviours, 170, 173
Beijing, 42
Belgium, 150
beliefs, 57, 105, 192
benchmark, 23, 48
benefits, vii, 17, 20, 29, 33, 66, 88, 91, 94, 138, 141, 145, 147, 158, 172, 186, 190, 193, 208, 212
Best Practice, 194
beverages, 232
bias, 211
binding, 81
biometrics, 239
bioterrorism, 63
Bioterrorism Act of 2002, 48, 53, 63
bipartisan, 41
birds, 200
black hole, 32
blackouts, 42
blame, 166, 172, 208, 231
blog, 142, 247
blood, 7
blurring, 82
bomb, 111, 116
border control, 94
Bose, 89
Bosnia, 17, 19
Boston, 121, 150, 155, 179, 195, 242
Botswana, 19, 22, 24
brain, 87
brainstorming, 27
breaches, 134
breaking set, 3
Britain, 13, 25
broadcaster, 32
Brussels, 247
buildings, 110, 126, 146, 171, 200, 237, 238
Bulgaria, 150
Bureau of Reclamation, 53
bureaucracy, 8, 227
buses, 124, 126, 200
Bush administration, 1, 2, 3, 4, 5, 6, 8, 9, 11, 13, 52
Bush Doctrine, 2
business, 157
business environment, 98, 182, 183, 185, 189, 193, 231
business model, 167
buyer, 70, 194, 195

C

call centers, 163

Index

campaigns, 6, 7, 85
Canada, 16, 23, 24, 150, 226
capitalist, 150
career development, x, 95
Caribbean, 246
case study, 148
cash flow, 153
cast, 35
catalyst, 2, 80
catastrophes, 29, 68
causation, 105
cell, 107
Census, 55, 62
Census Bureau, 55, 62
Central Intelligence Agency, 40, 60
CEO, 149, 163, 170
certification, 168
certifications, 169
chain of command, 138
channels, 31, 141, 174, 222
chaos, 6, 115, 118
charitable organizations, 214
charities, 153
chemicals, 49
children, 45, 46, 75, 138, 161, 224
China, 4, 40, 41, 42, 43, 47, 68, 92, 163
chlorination, 50
Christmas, 111
CHS, 246
CIA, 40, 43, 60, 63, 90
CISM, 248
citizens, 3, 12, 56, 57, 69, 79, 235
civil liberties, 3
civil servant, 118
civil society, 20, 22, 24
civil war, 218
classes, 41, 86
cleanup, 44
clients, 108
climate change, 16, 46, 58, 59, 60, 218, 227
Clinton administration, 8
clustering, 27
clusters, 126
CNN, 206
Co, 13, 17, 18, 36, 139, 182, 193, 194, 201, 205, 235, 245
coaches, 118, 238
coal, 68
codes, 105
coffee, 161
cognitive biases, 70
cognitive dissonance, 30
coherence, 16, 18, 28

cohesion, 79
Cold War, 5, 13, 93
collaboration, 39, 52, 57, 73, 83, 85, 89, 114, 142, 171, 178, 236
Collaboration, 83
colleges, 161
Colombia, 8
Colorado, 46, 51, 52, 54, 55, 59, 61, 62
Columbia, 50, 89
Columbia University, 89
comfort zone, 158
commerce, 66, 70, 71, 72, 80, 82, 86
commercialization, 56
commodity, 77
commons, 89
communication, 69, 88, 95, 98, 99, 106, 107, 109, 114, 115, 116, 123, 124, 125, 129, 130, 138, 139, 140, 141, 142, 143, 153, 170, 171, 174, 189, 191, 193, 202, 215, 217, 218, 219, 221, 222, 223, 225, 227
communication systems, 116, 130, 153, 202, 218
communication technologies, 170
communism, 5
communities, viii, 13, 26, 34, 51, 54, 55, 75, 76, 77, 79, 80, 81, 82, 85, 86, 89, 139, 217, 233
community, x, 2, 13, 18, 19, 20, 22, 23, 27, 28, 30, 33, 48, 55, 57, 60, 75, 77, 79, 80, 81, 82, 87, 89, 90, 104, 111, 128, 135, 139, 173, 213, 214, 215, 216, 217, 218, 219, 220, 221, 222, 223, 226, 230, 231, 233
community support, 135
competence, 139, 173, 185
competition, 39, 59, 78, 81, 220
competitive advantage, 79, 144, 154, 167, 182, 186, 194
competitiveness, 56, 71, 72
competitor, 79, 87, 182, 184
complex systems, 172
complexity, 13, 84, 141, 166, 170, 174, 175, 188, 195, 236
compliance, 35, 65, 66, 67, 112, 130, 132, 154, 155
components, 167, 169, 187
composition, 27, 224
computer, 157
computer software, 78, 79, 87, 231
computer systems, 49, 67, 94
computer technology, 233
computer virus, 80
computing, 31, 79, 150
concentrates, 114
concentration, 70
concrete, 42, 49, 129
conductor, 31

confidence, viii, 6, 31, 32, 33, 34, 68, 85, 96, 144, 169, 187, 214, 221, 230, 234, 246
confidentiality, 69, 112, 113, 169, 197, 199, 204, 212
configuration, 181, 183, 184, 187, 193
conflict, 5, 17, 18, 19, 20, 23, 39, 40, 44, 50, 58, 60, 89, 150, 166, 172, 214, 215, 226, 246
conflict of interest, 214, 215
conflict prevention, 17, 18
confrontation, 1, 7
confusion, 32, 232
Congress, 6, 10, 11, 45, 48, 53
congressional elections, 6
Connecticut, 14, 72, 100
connectivity, 75, 77, 219
consciousness, 11, 110
consensus, 7, 51, 126, 129, 172, 185
consent, 112
conservation, 41, 44, 55, 56, 57, 61
consolidation, 21
conspiracy, 199
Constitution, 52
constraints, x, 51, 86, 172, 212
construction, 51, 115
consultants, 113, 171
consulting, 247
consumer protection, 169
consumerism, 78
consumers, 45, 54, 160, 161, 169, 238
consumption, 40, 42, 43, 55, 57, 58, 70, 197, 210, 233
consumption patterns, 57
contaminants, 56
contamination, 46, 48, 49
contingency, 70, 114, 115, 126, 135, 137, 167, 172, 218, 225, 241, 246
continuity, viii, ix, 3, 30, 37, 65, 66, 68, 72, 76, 84, 96, 98, 103, 104, 107, 108, 109, 110, 111, 112, 113, 114, 115, 116, 117, 118, 119, 120, 121, 125, 131, 132, 133, 134, 135, 136, 137, 143, 144, 146, 148, 149, 151, 152, 154, 155, 156, 163, 167, 169, 192, 219, 220, 234, 237, 240, 245, 248
contractors, 69, 127, 146
control, 30, 31, 34, 35, 49, 53, 68, 92, 109, 123, 124, 156, 157, 158, 168, 172, 185, 190, 192, 200, 215, 220, 227, 232, 234, 238
convergence, 168
cooking, 58
cooling, 42, 138
corn, 42
corporate governance, 144, 155, 172
corporate life, 108, 170
corporate responsibility, 168, 173, 204
corporate sector, 91, 92, 93

corporate social responsibility, 137, 144
corporations, 78, 84, 155, 167
corruption, 9, 56, 57, 79, 217
cost effectiveness, 44
cost saving, 167
costs, 6, 30, 33, 44, 45, 50, 57, 68, 77, 113, 153, 154, 168, 172, 177, 231, 232, 233
counterfeit, 232
counterfeiting, 88, 92, 93, 94, 174, 232
counterintelligence, viii, 73, 75, 77, 78, 80, 88, 174, 178
countermeasures, 97, 99, 157
counter-terror, 18, 198, 233
counterterrorism, vii, 1, 2, 3, 4, 5, 8, 13
counterterrorism strategy, vii, 1, 2, 3, 4, 5, 8, 13
covering, 197, 210
CPA, 156
cracking, 80, 92
credentials, 134
credibility, 6, 12, 129, 137
credit, 33, 52, 77
creditors, 147
crime, 23, 33, 69, 73, 83, 90, 92, 100, 101, 169, 174, 178, 235, 246
crimes, 110
criminal activity, 91, 92, 94
criminal gangs, 93, 231, 232, 233, 236
criminality, 92
criminals, x, 25, 87, 91, 92, 94, 96, 109, 229, 241
crisis management, ix, 66, 109, 111, 117, 125, 127, 128, 136, 197, 219, 248
critical infrastructure, 49, 85, 99, 149, 155, 167
criticism, 22, 135, 204, 222
cross-cultural, 219
crude oil, 53
CSR, 134
cultural differences, 168, 191
cultural influence, 89
cultural perspective, 172
culture, ix, 24, 32, 51, 67, 69, 71, 77, 79, 83, 94, 106, 141, 144, 165, 166, 167, 168, 170, 171, 172, 176, 177, 182, 192, 193, 194, 195, 196, 197, 208, 220, 226, 227, 238, 247
customers, 48, 76, 77, 78, 86, 137, 154, 160, 161, 170, 182, 185, 186, 195
cyber crime, 174
cyber terrorism, 85
cybersecurity, 81
cyberspace, 81, 177, 178
cyberterrorism, 73, 90, 178
cyberwar, 137
cycles, 137
Czech Republic, 150

D

danger, 51, 69, 106, 224
data collection, 104
data mining, 85
data transfer, 234
database, 85, 110, 211, 219
dating, 1, 33
death, 48, 58, 124
deaths, 33, 45, 199, 217
debt, 22
debtors, 147
decision makers, 99, 232
decision making, 117, 183
decision-making process, 79, 83, 84, 95, 99, 172, 181, 183, 185, 189, 192, 220
decisions, 3, 7, 24, 25, 54, 57, 83, 95, 127, 128, 130, 138, 154, 156, 182, 183, 189, 209, 222, 230
defecation, 46
defense, 154
deficits, 56
definition, 44, 58, 97, 107, 108, 114, 135, 143, 151, 239
degradation, 45
dehydration, 58
delivery, 76, 107, 141, 143, 146, 163, 247
democracy, 5, 12, 24, 227
Democratic Party, 6
demographics, 234
denial, 32, 49, 51, 120, 124
Denmark, 23, 150
dentists, 202
Department of Agriculture, 41, 52, 53
Department of Commerce, 52
Department of Defense, 8
Department of Energy, 10, 54, 62, 245
Department of Health and Human Services, 53
Department of Homeland Security, 2, 49, 62, 97, 208
Department of Interior, 45
Department of Justice, 49, 62
Department of State, 246
Department of the Interior, 46, 51, 52, 53, 62
Department of Transportation, 246
derivatives, 24
desalination, 41, 44, 45, 54, 55, 57, 60, 62
desert, 55
designers, 77, 80, 174
destruction, 2, 8, 50, 132, 169
detection, 49
deterrence, 33
developed countries, 19, 41, 42, 47, 51, 56
developing countries, 21, 45, 57
Development Assistance, 18
development policy, 216
diarrhoea, 46
diets, 41
Director of National Intelligence, 2
disaster, vii, ix, x, 32, 33, 50, 51, 65, 66, 97, 105, 106, 107, 109, 110, 114, 115, 120, 126, 131, 133, 145, 149, 151, 156, 163, 167, 197, 204, 206, 212, 213, 214, 215, 216, 217, 218, 219, 220, 221, 222, 223, 224, 225, 226, 227, 232, 233, 234, 237, 240, 242
disaster relief, x, 213, 214, 215, 216
discharges, 49
discipline, 103, 120, 133, 137
disclosure, 48, 132, 169, 171, 221
discounting, 237
discourse, 57, 220, 226, 232
discretionary, 173
discriminatory, 86
discs, 69, 142
diseases, 16, 45
disenchantment, 9
dishonesty, 177
disinformation, 84, 85
dislocation, 221
dislocations, 237
dispersion, 10
disposition, 100, 222
disputes, 39
dissatisfaction, 129
disseminate, 120, 222
distribution, 40, 112, 140, 141, 147, 150, 194
divergence, 168
diversity, 91
dividends, 6, 12
division, 170, 217
DNA, 146
doctors, 202, 206
dominance, 144
donor, 16, 18, 19, 20, 21, 22, 28, 215, 224
donors, 218, 223
doors, 127
download, 83, 114, 198, 231
draft, 20
dream, 209
drinking, 41, 42, 44, 45, 48, 49, 58
drinking water, 40, 41, 42, 45, 48, 49, 58
drought, 41, 42, 46, 51, 52, 53, 55, 56, 59, 61, 62
Drought, 45, 52, 53, 61
droughts, 52, 53
drug abuse, 240
drug sales, 8
drugs, 5, 92, 93
drying, 41, 42

duplication, 78, 174
duration, 231
duties, 78, 97, 145, 190, 215, 221, 225, 241

E

early warning, 166
earth, 44, 49
earthquake, 50
East Asia, 206
Eastern Europe, 19
e-commerce, 68, 170, 174
economic, 156
economic activity, 161
economic development, 19, 83, 87, 93, 192, 216, 218, 220
economic growth, viii, 39, 224
economic policy, 215
economic theory, 87
economics, 58, 90, 178, 234
ecosystem, 45, 141
Education, 22, 162, 248
education/training, 66
educators, 169
Egypt, 12
elasticity, 145
election, 3, 6, 9
electricity, 140
electronic surveillance, 238
electronic systems, 84
email, 123, 129, 171
e-mail, 31, 85
e-mail, 123
e-mail, 123
e-mail, 245
e-mail, 245
e-mail, 246
e-mail, 246
e-mail, 246
e-mail, 247
e-mail, 247
e-mail, 247
e-mail, 247
e-mail, 248
e-mail, 248
e-mail, 248
embargo, 53
emergency management, vii, x, 61, 120, 213, 218, 219, 220, 221, 223, 227, 234
emergency planning, 34, 135, 136, 219
emergency preparedness, 201, 202, 204
emergency relief, 215, 219
emergency response, ix, 48, 49, 52, 124, 197, 198, 202, 209, 210, 248
emerging issues, 130
emotion, 230
emotional, 33, 143, 144, 190, 215
Emotional Intelligence (EI), 143, 144
emotional reactions, 215
emotions, 143
employees, 75, 76, 83, 115, 123, 144, 147, 166, 171, 172, 174, 182, 187, 189, 190, 191, 193
employment, 103, 111, 112, 120, 199, 221, 224, 239
empowered, 70, 117, 169
empowerment, 47, 58
encapsulated, 52, 107
encouragement, 52
energy, 4, 11, 27, 42, 44, 58, 62, 65, 68, 71, 114
energy supply, 68
engagement, 15, 18, 32, 125, 139, 146, 242
England, 201, 226, 235, 245
enlargement, 224
enterprise, 108, 144, 173
enthusiasm, 7
entrepreneurs, viii, 76, 77, 80, 87
environment, ix, 16, 19, 27, 31, 32, 47, 54, 58, 70, 79, 90, 95, 98, 114, 150, 157, 158, 163, 168, 172, 175, 181, 183, 187, 216, 218, 224, 231
Environmental and Infrastructural Risk Assessment, vi, 229, 240
environmental impact, 51
environmental issues, 44
Environmental Protection Agency (DPA), 45, 49, 53, 63, 226
environmental sustainability, 100
EPA, 63
epidemics, 198, 200
equilibrium, 39
equipment, 157
equity, 243
erosion, 170
espionage, 69, 73, 83, 85, 94, 97, 173, 178
Estonia, 150
ethical issues, 92, 111, 112
ethics, 123
ethnic groups, 85
ethnicity, 86
EU, 22, 23, 66, 71, 93, 94, 205, 207
Europe, 10, 92, 94, 96, 246
European integration, 93
European Union, 16, 23
Europeanisation, 94
evacuation, 140, 221
evening, 127
evidence-based policy, 226

Index

evolution, 105, 139, 177
Executive Order, 41
exercise, x, 15, 20, 26, 78, 120, 139, 141, 188, 197, 198, 199, 200, 201, 202, 203, 204, 205, 206, 207, 208, 210, 211, 212
exercise participation, 208
exercise performance, 201
expertise, 26, 81, 82, 92, 168, 217, 221, 222, 225, 233, 235, 236, 239, 247
explicit knowledge, 193
exploitation, 39
explosions, 31, 104, 106, 110
external environment, 70, 72, 78, 94, 171, 174, 175, 184, 185
external relations, 166
extraction, 43
extremism, 40, 58
eyelid, 30
eyes, 2, 3, 173

F

face-to-face interaction, 161
facilitators, 26, 80, 222
factor analysis, 163
failure, viii, 2, 11, 12, 42, 46, 60, 66, 69, 107, 123, 140, 141, 146, 205, 206
fairness, 190
family, 88, 126, 128, 199, 209
family units, 209
famine, 51, 215
farmers, 41, 43
farming, 41
farms, 41
fatalities, 222
fatigue, 6
faults, 204
FBI, 36, 90, 92, 94, 246
fear, viii, 2, 29, 30, 31, 32, 33, 50, 56, 225, 231, 236
fears, 9, 31, 32, 42, 59
February, 6, 7, 9, 13, 14, 26, 56, 59, 152, 156, 160, 195, 199, 200, 202, 204, 205, 206
Federal Deposit Insurance Corporation, 156
Federal Emergency Management Agency, 34, 53, 205
Federal Emergency Management Agency (FEMA), 53, 205
federal government, 13, 52, 203, 206
Federal Reserve, 156
Federal Reserve Board, 156
fee, 80
feedback, 114, 115, 139, 211, 218
feelings, 33, 58, 144, 204, 230

feet, 151
FEMA, 34, 52, 53, 205, 206
filters, 144
filtration, 50
finance, 163, 169, 172, 192
Finance, 162
financial instability, 93
financial institution, 117, 155, 168, 169, 214
financial loss, 235
financial markets, 117, 214
financial sector, 114, 117, 119, 120, 168, 246
Financial Services Authority, 112, 117, 122, 123, 169
financial support, 216
financial system, 169
Finland, 150
fire, 7, 31, 107, 108, 118, 129, 151, 157, 204, 209, 211
fires, 106, 110
firms, 72, 96, 112, 117, 119
first aid, 128
first principles, 25, 26, 28
first responders, 50, 215, 221, 225
First World, 49
fissile material, 10
flexibility, 24, 78, 99, 115, 137, 211, 221
flood, 108, 151
flooding, 46, 56, 198
flow, 43, 46, 59, 136, 143, 153, 170, 216
focus group, 21, 50
focus groups, 21
focusing, vii, 33, 57, 97, 106, 115, 236, 247
FOIA, 48, 62
food, viii, 27, 39, 40, 41, 43, 44, 45, 46, 47, 58, 59, 65, 68, 111, 127, 128, 232, 238
Food, 162
Food and Drug Administration, 45, 48, 53, 63
food production, viii, 39, 40, 46, 58, 59
Food Supply, 162
forced migration, viii, 42, 58
forecasting, 19, 218
foreign affairs, 24
Foreign Corrupt Practices Act, 156
foreign direct investment, 83
foreign language, 79
foreign nation, 2
foreign nationals, 2
foreign policy, 1, 3, 4, 6, 224
Forestry, 226
Fort Worth, 242
fossil, 43, 62
Fox, 59
fragility, 9, 11

France, 7, 54, 56, 150, 207, 248
fraud, 169, 174
free association, 33
freedom, 25, 236
freedom fighter, 236
Freedom of Information Act, (FOIA), 48, 61, 112, 122, 236
freedoms, 26
fresh water, 40, 44, 56
freshwater, 44, 60, 61
frustration, 69
FSA, 112, 117, 118, 119, 120, 122, 169
fuel, 40, 47, 66, 78, 111, 224
functional approach, 163
funding, 10, 11, 18, 20, 51, 57, 67, 202, 215, 219, 220
funds, 10, 155, 223, 232, 233
futures, 51

G

G8, 150
games, 238, 239
gas, 33, 68, 199, 248
gauge, 58
gender, 79
gene, 192
General Accounting Office, 89
general election, 23, 72, 233
generalizations, 192
generation, 59, 148
Georgia, 4, 41
Germany, 7, 14, 150
global climate change, 56
global economy, 169
global terrorism, 10
global trends, 25
globalised world, 94
goals, 5, 17, 22, 24, 26, 27, 28, 53, 57, 78, 94, 106, 186, 187, 189, 190, 197, 216, 218, 226
gold, 211, 242
goods and services, 58
Gordon Brown, 8, 13, 14, 16
governance, ix, 7, 18, 46, 65, 66, 67, 137, 149, 168, 170, 172, 214, 217, 220, 223, 224, 226
Government, 162
government policy, 24, 85, 96, 99, 214, 222, 232, 233
grain, 41, 42, 43, 44, 47, 60
grass, 55
Great Britain, 3, 13
Great Depression, 13
Greece, 5, 150, 235, 236

Gross Domestic Product, 41
grounding, 134
groundwater, 41, 42, 43, 54
grouping, 220
groups, viii, 6, 68, 70, 71, 75, 77, 79, 80, 81, 82, 83, 84, 85, 87, 91, 92, 94, 95, 98, 104, 135, 143, 144, 150, 160, 172, 178, 187, 191, 197, 204, 210, 211, 214, 215, 218, 221, 222, 230, 232, 236, 248
growth, viii, 15, 39, 40, 41, 54, 58, 61, 185, 187, 198, 212, 224
guardian, 160
guidance, x, 20, 27, 48, 66, 70, 92, 107, 109, 110, 112, 113, 123, 125, 169, 183, 187, 203, 209, 210, 217, 237
guidelines, 24, 52, 81, 156, 175, 203, 222
guiding principles, 21, 25
guns, 33

H

H5N1, 200
hackers, 71, 80, 84, 87
hacking, 49, 80, 92, 173
Haiti, 16, 19
handicapped, 5
handling, 106, 161, 225
hands, 10, 31, 66, 99, 167
haptic, 211
hardening process, 158, 163
hardware, 157
harm, 25, 48, 70, 76, 87, 144, 187, 190, 224
harmful effects, 174
harmony, 70, 144, 187, 190
Harvard, 72, 179, 195, 242
harvest, 41, 42, 43, 44, 156
hazards, 46, 50, 59, 60, 105, 106, 107, 162, 209, 217
health, 8, 12, 23, 46, 47, 49, 58, 63, 201, 202, 203, 205, 221
Health and Human Services, 53
health care, 8, 12, 49, 221
hearing, 25
heart, 42, 69, 108, 135, 161
heating, 23
height, 206
heroin, 8
Hezbollah, 5
Higgs, 155
higher education, 169
higher quality, 77
high-risk, 93, 234
highways, 32
HIPAA, 155
HIPC, 22

hiring, 84
HIV/AIDS, 16
HM Treasury, 113
holistic, 33, 35, 66, 71, 82, 96, 97, 108, 134, 144, 149, 163, 173, 176
holistic approach, 66, 71, 149, 176
Holland, 36, 48
homeland security, viii, 2, 13, 72, 86, 91, 96, 97, 100, 209, 246
Homeland Security, 2, 23, 49, 60, 62, 97, 205, 208, 236
honey, 99
Hong Kong, 248
horizon, 34
hospital, 207
hospitality, 238
hospitals, 197, 202, 221
host, 30, 116, 206, 235, 236
hostile environment, 150
hostilities, 5, 6
hostility, 9
hot spots, 97
hotels, 127, 238
House, 13, 25, 26, 90, 226, 242
household, 21, 46
housing, 205
HSC, 208
hub, 235
human, ix, 3, 6, 7, 12, 25, 29, 30, 40, 41, 45, 46, 58, 68, 69, 79, 82, 83, 85, 92, 94, 110, 114, 116, 117, 124, 141, 142, 147, 149, 157, 163, 165, 166, 167, 171, 176, 177, 185, 207, 211, 214, 217, 247
human development, 217
human dimensions, 166
human resource management, 185
human resources, ix, 114, 147, 149, 163
human rights, 3, 12, 25, 79, 83, 85, 92, 94, 214
humanitarian, 26, 227
humanitarian aid, 227
humans, 40, 58, 141, 212
humiliation, 47, 58
Hungary, 150
hurricane, 29, 60, 205
Hurricane Katrina, 34, 50, 68, 205, 206
hurricanes, 53, 110
husband, 199
hybrid, 190, 192
hydroelectric power, 49
hydrologic, 43
hydrological, 41
hygiene, 45, 221
hygienic, 58
hysteria, 33

I

ICM, 114, 115, 119, 122
Icons, 162
ICT, 170, 172
id, 23, 53, 62, 63, 122, 205, 206, 211
identification, 23, 26, 27, 108, 117, 206
identity, 80, 112, 117, 231, 234
ideology, 83, 234
imagery, 232
images, 29, 31, 33, 82
imagination, 48, 50, 144
IMF, 22
immigration, 23
impact assessment, 144
implementation, viii, 17, 44, 56, 57, 67, 71, 95, 115, 125, 135, 170, 175, 182, 184, 185, 190, 192, 200, 210, 219, 223, 245, 247
imports, 44
in situ, 83, 225
in transition, 19, 88, 89
incentives, 54, 55, 77
incidence, 19, 110, 237
Incidents, 103
inclusion, 143
income, 8, 47
incomes, 58
incubation, 105, 106
incubation period, 105, 106
indebtedness, 56
independence, 22, 34, 45, 48, 86
India, 9, 40, 41, 42, 43, 47, 48, 163
Indian, 216
Indians, 43
indication, 30, 174, 208, 238
indicators, 187
indices, 12
indigenous, 12, 68
individual characteristics, 191
Indonesia, 47
industrial, 56, 69, 73, 83, 85, 94, 97, 173, 178, 198, 203, 204, 210, 225, 248
industrial sectors, 248
industrialization, 40
industry, ix, 41, 48, 54, 55, 60, 66, 67, 70, 71, 72, 77, 78, 80, 81, 82, 83, 85, 86, 87, 89, 92, 97, 103, 107, 109, 114, 115, 118, 120, 121, 132, 134, 135, 136, 138, 140, 145, 151, 161, 167, 169, 171, 177, 185, 198, 233, 248
infection, 59
infectious, viii, 42, 58
infectious diseases, viii, 42, 58
influenza, 139, 205

Information Age, 90
information and communication technologies, 170
information exchange, 75, 96, 188
Information Operations, 247
information sharing, 65, 69, 81, 82, 87, 91, 95, 96, 213, 215, 219, 220, 235, 239
Information System, 45, 66, 88, 132, 145, 148, 156, 247
information systems, 132, 133, 142, 160, 218
Information Technology, 31, 90, 152, 159
infrastructure, 2, 8, 13, 41, 48, 49, 51, 57, 62, 67, 77, 85, 89, 99, 126, 138, 142, 147, 163, 167, 169, 170, 197, 220, 225, 238, 245
inherited, 2
injection, 23
injuries, 33, 103, 231
injustice, 12
innovation, 57, 79, 87, 88, 90, 194
Innovation, 88, 89
insecurity, viii, 30, 47, 58, 60
insight, 31, 93
inspiration, 189
instability, 40, 41, 58, 85
institutions, 19, 23, 79, 80, 81, 88, 98, 100, 121, 155, 169, 171, 195, 213, 214, 217, 218, 219, 220, 241, 248
instruments, 15, 17, 18, 19, 20, 22, 27
insurance, 155, 199
intangible, 176
integrated intelligence, 82
integration, 19, 93, 171, 187, 247
integrity, 69, 71, 169, 170, 212, 214
intellectual appreciation, 183
intellectual development, 77
intelligence, vii, viii, x, 2, 4, 20, 30, 34, 67, 70, 71, 72, 73, 75, 77, 78, 79, 80, 81, 82, 83, 84, 85, 86, 88, 89, 90, 91, 92, 93, 94, 96, 97, 98, 99, 100, 107, 143, 167, 173, 174, 176, 178, 179, 185, 186, 193, 195, 196, 214, 219, 221, 227, 229, 230, 231, 234, 236, 238, 239, 240, 241, 245, 247
intelligence gathering, 30, 174, 221
intentional attempts, 71
intentions, 67, 157
interaction, 117, 140, 177, 187, 188, 217, 218, 222
interaction process, 188
interactions, 55, 85, 161
interactivity, 75, 77, 219
interdisciplinary, 98
interest groups, 172
interface, 72, 178
interference, 34
internal controls, 155, 156, 169
internal environment, 174, 183, 184

internalizing, 210
international law, 63
International Monetary Fund, 22
international relations, 79, 97, 224
international terrorism, 73, 90, 100, 101, 178
International Trade, 16
internet, 111, 117, 121, 122, 129, 138, 197, 198, 199, 208, 209, 210, 211
Internet, 66, 69, 75, 76, 78, 80, 82, 84, 85, 89, 90, 92, 123, 174, 219, 229, 231, 232, 239, 242
interoperability, 92, 96, 100
interrelationships, 167
intervention, 12, 19, 20
interview, 16, 117, 118, 120, 222
interviews, 26, 50, 104, 106, 111, 112, 117, 120, 232
introspection, 30
investment, 11, 56, 83, 96, 185, 187, 233, 238, 239
investors, 220
IPPC, 242
Iran, 10, 12, 43, 68, 71, 248
Iraq, 1, 2, 3, 5, 6, 7, 11, 12, 14, 17, 19, 25, 34, 40
Ireland, 139, 150
irrigation, 42, 43, 44
Islam, 14
Islamic, 1, 3, 4, 6, 9, 11
Islamic law, 11
ISO, 73, 159, 169
isolation, 71, 79, 109, 134, 143, 147
isomorphism, 106, 107
Israel, 12, 39, 45
Italy, 150, 235, 236
IUCN, 57

J

Jamaica, 22, 23, 24
Japan, 27, 150, 195, 247
Japanese, 27, 195, 206, 247
jobs, 199
journalists, 81, 83, 206, 240
judge, 11, 199, 202, 208
Jung, 192, 195
justice, 19, 21, 24, 25, 26

K

Katrina, 34, 50, 60, 68, 205, 206
Kentucky, 26
killing, 4, 236
King, 48, 103, 122, 246
knowledge economy, 176
knowledge transfer, 77, 95

Korea, 150
Korean, 247
Kosovo, 17, 22, 23
Kurds, 6

L

lakes, 42, 44
land, 41, 44, 45, 48, 57, 61, 93, 237
lland-use, 44, 57
language, 19, 26, 79, 81, 131, 137, 198, 205
large-scale, 44, 50
Latvia, 150
laundering, 92, 93, 231, 232
law, vii, viii, x, 2, 4, 5, 6, 11, 19, 24, 25, 26, 30, 49, 53, 62, 63, 69, 70, 75, 80, 81, 83, 84, 85, 86, 87, 91, 92, 93, 94, 96, 97, 98, 99, 100, 167, 174, 214, 219, 221, 229, 230, 231, 233, 234, 236, 237, 240, 241
Law and order, 162
law enforcement, vii, viii, x, 2, 4, 5, 69, 70, 75, 80, 81, 83, 84, 85, 86, 87, 91, 92, 93, 94, 96, 97, 98, 99, 100, 167, 174, 214, 219, 229, 230, 231, 233, 234, 236, 237, 240, 241
laws, 53, 105, 233, 234, 241
leadership, viii, ix, 6, 9, 18, 29, 32, 34, 51, 57, 86, 94, 95, 98, 138, 146, 174, 175, 179, 181, 182, 183, 185, 188, 189, 190, 191, 192, 193, 194, 195, 196, 215, 216, 218, 219, 221, 222, 223, 225, 239
leadership style, ix, 94, 175, 181, 183, 185, 189, 190, 191, 192, 193, 195, 239
learning, ix, x, 51, 58, 79, 92, 94, 95, 105, 106, 107, 108, 109, 110, 111, 115, 127, 131, 132, 161, 175, 179, 181, 182, 183, 185, 186, 187, 188, 189, 191, 192, 193, 194, 195, 196, 208, 218, 220, 227, 239, 243
learning environment, x, 161, 187
learning outcomes, 131
learning process, 95, 181, 183, 186, 187, 189, 194
legislation, 6, 10, 35, 48, 65, 67, 79, 168, 169, 177, 199, 202, 203, 208
leisure, 88
lending, 22
lens, 12
LexisNexis, 122
licensing, 80
life cycle, 175
lifestyles, 41, 61
lifetime, 245
likelihood, 85, 141, 144
limitation, 214
limitations, 5, 13, 17, 43, 138
linguistic, 100

linkage, 18
links, 70, 84, 89, 91, 93, 100, 108, 109, 110, 117, 118, 121, 124, 136, 139, 143, 236
Lithuania, 150
litigation, 32, 52
lobby, 222, 224
lobbying, 215
local authorities, 116, 135, 199
local government, 66, 118, 202, 206, 219, 222
locus, 13
logistics, 117, 171
London, vii, viii, x, 3, 18, 30, 31, 34, 36, 63, 88, 89, 90, 93, 100, 101, 103, 104, 107, 111, 112, 114, 115, 116, 118, 120, 121, 122, 123, 124, 125, 148, 152, 155, 158, 177, 178, 194, 195, 198, 200, 201, 207, 209, 217, 225, 226, 227, 232, 237, 238, 239, 242, 243, 245, 246, 247, 248
long distance, 48, 127, 232
long period, 192
long work, 199
longevity, 24, 147
longitudinal studies, 82
Los Angeles, 3
loss of control, 30
losses, 6, 11, 31, 71, 217
Louisiana, 205
loyalty, 182, 185, 186, 190
Luxembourg, 150

M

machinery, 147, 192
machines, 41, 106
maiming, 236
mainstream, 98, 216
maintenance, 27, 144, 171, 224
management technology, 239
mandates, 17
man-made, 29, 55, 106, 213, 214, 217, 221, 229, 230, 236
manufactured goods, 41
manufacturer, 150
manufacturing, 31, 161, 162, 163
market, 31, 33, 43, 55, 76, 78, 149, 153, 155, 156, 160, 169, 175, 185, 186, 194, 195, 243
market position, 155
market research, 156
market segment, 153, 160
market share, 186
marketing, ix, 72, 78, 79, 86, 88, 149, 154, 160, 161, 163, 173, 174, 178, 179, 181, 185, 193, 196, 234, 239, 242, 243, 247
marketing mix, 160, 161

marketing strategy, 72, 79
markets, 77, 87, 93, 117, 140
martial law, 240
mass media, 4
Massachusetts, 72, 90, 179
matrix, 162, 163, 172
maturation, 132, 133, 146
MCA, 200
meanings, 196, 233
measures, x, 30, 35, 41, 48, 49, 50, 57, 66, 69, 85, 86, 104, 121, 137, 138, 139, 157, 169, 170, 173, 202, 217, 223, 229, 231, 233, 235, 237, 246
meat, 41
media, 4, 25, 29, 31, 32, 33, 35, 94, 104, 108, 112, 124, 129, 131, 198, 199, 204, 205, 208, 214, 215, 219, 221, 222, 230, 232, 233, 236, 238, 239, 240, 248
medical care, 205
membership, 7, 114, 119, 144, 169
memory, 69, 171
memory lapses, 171
men, 8, 240
mentoring, 183
mergers, 195
messages, 107, 118, 124, 129, 131, 139, 141, 201, 233
metaphor, 216
metric, 10, 43
metropolitan area, 55
Mexico, 39, 46, 52, 55, 56, 150, 226
middle class, 40
Middle East, 1, 2, 4, 11, 39, 48, 60, 71, 245
migration, viii, 39, 42, 58
militant, 236
military, 2, 3, 4, 5, 6, 7, 8, 9, 17, 19, 20, 27, 29, 34, 39, 66, 68, 71, 81, 97, 99, 100, 141, 150, 214, 215, 233, 237, 240, 246, 247
milk, 111
Millennium Development Goals, 45, 195, 216
mining, 41, 42, 43, 86, 90
mirror, 143, 169
MIT, 72, 90, 177, 179
mobile phone, 31, 104, 123, 124, 126
mobility, 221
MOD, 20
model, 157
modeling, 156, 157
models, 13, 56, 66, 95, 100, 167, 172, 174, 181, 183, 219
modernization, 12
momentum, 23, 186, 189
money, 10, 56, 92, 93, 157, 160, 202, 208, 215, 222, 227, 231, 232, 233, 238, 240

money laundering, 92, 93, 231, 232
morale, 200
morning, 207
motion, 9
motivation, 51, 52, 56, 182, 185, 221, 235
motives, 199
mouth, 66, 68
movement, 4, 41, 146, 163, 182, 231, 234
multidimensional, 17, 186
multidisciplinary, 218
multi-ethnic, 26
multilateral, viii, 15, 16, 19, 21, 28, 83
multinational companies, 93
Muslim, 2, 9, 11, 12, 43
Muslim League, 9
Muslims, 43
mutuality, 87, 185, 236
myopia, 242

N

naming, 196
narratives, 33
nation, 2, 7, 8, 9, 25, 26, 43, 49, 71, 81, 83, 85, 97, 99, 137, 150, 205, 208
nation building, 8
nation states, 150
National Academy of Sciences, 60
National Commission on Terrorist Attacks, 13, 52, 61
national culture, 192
national emergency, 52, 53
National Guard, 202
National Health Service (NHS), 132, 139, 202, 247
national interests, viii, 15, 18, 24, 25, 27, 28
national policy, 52, 53
National Response Framework, 246
national security, vii, viii, 1, 2, 4, 13, 15, 16, 17, 19, 20, 21, 22, 23, 24, 25, 26, 27, 28, 35, 40, 52, 65, 70, 72, 77, 87, 89, 97, 98, 112, 173, 178, 225, 234, 245
National Security Council, 245
National Security Strategy, 15, 17, 20, 23, 25, 37
National Strategy, 13
National Weather Service, 53, 55, 61
NATO, 5, 7, 14, 19, 22, 66, 150, 236, 246
natural, 29, 33, 39, 40, 41, 44, 46, 65, 76, 134, 218, 220, 224, 230, 231, 246
natural disasters, 33, 65, 230, 246
natural environment, 224
natural hazards, 46
natural resource management, 218
natural resources, 40

Navy, 68, 222
NEC, 96
negative consequences, 51, 56
negotiating, 67
negotiation, 52
neighbourhoods, 55
Netherlands, 150, 248
network, 77, 78, 79, 80, 83, 88, 97, 98, 123, 124, 129, 144, 148, 165, 170, 218, 222, 234
networking, 79, 82
Nevada, 46, 52, 54, 55, 56, 61, 246
New England, 59
New Jersey, 3, 195
New Mexico, 46, 52
New Orleans, 29, 205, 206
New York, 1, 3, 13, 14, 17, 29, 32, 36, 59, 60, 61, 62, 72, 89, 90, 100, 101, 104, 142, 155, 168, 194, 195, 226, 227, 235
New York Stock Exchange, 155
New York Times, 3, 14, 59, 60, 61
New Zealand, 150
news coverage, 232, 236
newsletters, 82
newspapers, 78
next generation, 78, 132
NGOs, 216, 218, 219
NHS, 132, 201, 202
niche market, 76
niche marketing, 76
Nigeria, 84, 89
noise, 199
nongovernmental, 53
nonproliferation, 10, 245
Norfolk, 197, 210
normal, 41, 55, 83, 105, 117, 118, 125, 133, 143, 199, 216
norms, 78, 79, 105, 145, 187, 224
North Africa, 40
North America, 55, 114, 121
North Carolina, 13
North Korea, 10
Northern Ireland, 20, 32, 139, 209
Norway, 150
NRC, 42
nuclear, 9, 10, 12, 34, 42, 43, 59, 68, 71, 93, 150, 204
nuclear energy, 68
nuclear material, 10
nuclear power, 42, 68
nuclear reactor, 42
Nuclear Regulatory Commission, 42
nuclear weapons, 9, 10, 12, 43
NYSE, 155

O

OAS, 19
objectivity, 201, 212, 232
obligations, 224
observations, 114, 115, 119, 216
Obstructive Marketing, 157
oceans, 44
OECD, 17, 18, 19, 21, 23, 150
oil, 11, 29, 43, 53, 57, 68, 151, 160, 168, 198, 199, 248
oil refineries, 199
oil spill, 198
Oklahoma, 41, 50
Olympic Games, 235, 237, 238, 239
omission, 59, 109
online, 89, 90, 121, 145, 229, 234
on-line, 75, 76, 79, 80, 82, 84, 85, 211
on-line news, 82
open source information, 75, 76, 86, 87
openness, 77, 82
operating system, 94, 106
operator, 234
opinion polls, 6
opium, 23
opportunity costs, 77
opposition, 5, 56
organic, 137
organization, 156, 157
organizational culture, ix, 91, 92, 94, 95, 181, 182, 183, 185, 189, 190, 192, 195
organizational development, 100, 183, 189
organized crime, 73, 90, 100, 101, 178
orientation, 32, 84, 166, 179, 194, 195
osmosis, 45
outrage, 30
outsourcing, 131, 147
overload, 30
overseas aid, 23
oversight, 20, 34, 55, 118
ownership, 21, 130, 170, 200, 220
ozonation, 50

P

Pacific, 45, 227
pain, 30, 31, 33
Pakistan, 3, 6, 7, 8, 9, 13, 14, 23, 43, 48, 60
Pakistani, 8, 9
pandemic, 32, 33, 34, 60, 125, 139, 205, 234
paradigm shift, 70, 107, 226
paradox, 30, 172

parasites, 45
Paris, 18
Parliament, 20, 22, 24, 242
partnership, ix, x, 56, 57, 67, 80, 81, 91, 94, 97, 98, 99, 122, 135, 165, 167, 170, 173, 181, 183, 185, 186, 193, 208, 214, 216, 220, 222, 229, 238, 239, 240, 241, 243
partnerships, ix, 57, 82, 89, 94, 181, 193, 194, 218, 219
passenger, 199
passive, 25
password, 112, 114, 120, 171
pathogens, 49
Patriot Act, 86
PCs, 147
peacekeeping, 215, 221
peer, 185, 193
peer group, 185, 193
peers, 166, 171
penalties, 155, 156
Pentagon, 15, 50
People, 162
perception, vii, viii, 1, 5, 7, 12, 29, 32, 35, 144, 192
perceptions, 4, 6, 8, 13, 21, 30, 32, 72, 166, 182, 209, 242
permit, 150
Persian Gulf, 45, 48
persuasion, 88
Petroleum, 53, 54, 62
pharmaceutical, 248
philosophical, 163
philosophy, 134
Phoenix, 46
phone, 31, 118, 125, 128
pipelines, 48, 49
planning, vii, 5, 15, 16, 17, 18, 20, 21, 24, 26, 27, 28, 30, 35, 51, 57, 72, 86, 96, 108, 127, 133, 135, 136, 137, 138, 139, 142, 145, 147, 154, 158, 163, 167, 170, 186, 202, 203, 205, 206, 207, 209, 211, 213, 214, 219, 227, 229, 232, 234, 236, 238, 240, 242, 247
plants, 41, 42, 44, 45, 48, 49, 54, 59, 197, 199
platforms, 29, 132, 218
play, 7, 20, 77, 79, 81, 95, 97, 98, 166, 217, 220, 221, 232
PLC, 242
pleasure, 31, 33, 76
plug-in, 166
poisoning, 48
Poland, 150
police, 7, 20, 34, 67, 91, 92, 93, 94, 97, 118, 125, 204, 209, 233, 235, 240, 245
policy, 157

policy choice, 6
policy initiative, 83
policy instruments, 15, 19, 24, 26, 27, 28
policy makers, vii, viii, 45, 51, 65, 67, 70, 71, 81, 87, 96, 98, 218, 219
policy making, 58
policymakers, 8, 16, 21, 25, 26, 27, 50, 57
political instability, 39, 41
political leaders, 70, 216
political opposition, 5
political parties, 3, 6, 9, 10
politicians, 34, 35, 57, 66, 97, 99, 212, 222, 241
politics, 9, 39, 57, 58, 63, 172, 224, 234
pollution, 47, 49, 58
polyurethane foam, 106
poor, 10, 11, 43, 47, 58, 152, 201, 211
poor health, 47, 58
poor performance, 11
population, viii, 25, 27, 30, 33, 40, 43, 44, 55, 56, 58, 61, 62, 63, 98, 231, 234, 237, 240
population growth, 40
portfolio, 23, 126
Portugal, 41, 150
post-Cold War, 93
posture, 5
poverty, 12, 19, 22, 39, 41, 47, 50, 56, 58
poverty reduction, 22
power, 4, 8, 31, 39, 42, 49, 57, 68, 72, 87, 110, 129, 135, 150, 188, 189, 199
power plant, 42
powers, 6, 13, 19
PPP, 9
pragmatism, 33
precedents, 2
precipitation, 46, 61
prediction, 129
preference, 110
premium, 231
premiums, 159
preparedness, 37, 198, 200, 201, 202, 205, 207, 209, 210
presidency, 2, 9
president, 2, 6, 9, 11, 13
President Bush, 5, 7, 48
President Vladimir Putin, 11
pressure, viii, 9, 79, 93, 99, 128, 140, 204, 221, 232, 238
pressure groups, 204, 221, 232
prevention, 17, 18, 50, 86, 92, 133, 217
preventive, 2, 3, 233
prices, 43, 71, 160, 199
prisoners, 6
privacy, 86, 155, 175, 178

private, viii, x, 13, 35, 53, 54, 56, 65, 66, 73, 75, 80, 82, 85, 87, 90, 97, 98, 100, 117, 138, 146, 150, 154, 155, 167, 178, 215, 219, 220, 221, 225, 229, 236, 246
private investment, 56
private ownership, 54
private sector, viii, x, 35, 54, 56, 65, 66, 73, 75, 82, 85, 87, 90, 97, 98, 100, 138, 146, 167, 178, 215, 221, 229, 236
privatization, 56
proactive, 30, 96, 98, 144, 189, 191
probability, 30, 142, 156, 230
probability theory, 230
problem solving, 95, 166, 187
producers, 42
production, 25, 41, 43, 44, 81, 140, 159, 161, 218
productivity, 41, 49, 58, 110, 191
professional development, 169
professionalism, 144, 169
profit, 35, 81, 93, 115, 241
profitability, 154
profits, 56, 153
program, 10, 54, 63, 234
programming, 217
proliferation, 17, 245
propaganda, 207, 236, 241
property, 55, 88, 125, 199, 231, 237
property owner, 55
property rights, 88
propriety, 168
prosperity, 58, 59
protection, 7, 9, 13, 49, 51, 53, 54, 67, 94, 108, 140, 149, 163, 169, 175, 224, 231
protocol, 66
protocols, 49, 94
psyche, 69, 71, 75
psychological health, 200
psychologist, 166
psychology, 70
public awareness, 53, 169
public domain, 65, 83, 111, 112, 221, 222, 239
public health, 49, 202
public interest, 92
public opinion, 55
public relations, 80, 174
public sector, 87, 115, 117, 135, 145, 155, 158, 189, 220, 221, 225, 229, 236
public-private partnerships, 82, 219
pumping, viii, 42, 43, 49, 140
pumps, 43, 49, 140
punishment, 76
purification, 41, 56

Q

qualifications, 121, 122
qualitative research, 196
quality control, 81
quality of life, 58, 94, 224, 231
query, 60, 161
questioning, 11
questionnaire, 117, 119, 201, 202

R

race, 29, 31, 32, 86, 235
radar, 32
radiation, 50, 235
radiological, 10, 236, 237
radiological dispersion device, 10
radius, 237
rail, 30
rain, 59
rainfall, 41, 46, 55
RandD, 152
range, vii, viii, x, 10, 16, 17, 18, 19, 20, 21, 22, 35, 44, 65, 76, 80, 81, 83, 84, 87, 95, 99, 108, 110, 132, 144, 154, 155, 160, 161, 167, 170, 198, 201, 209, 215, 217, 225, 229, 240, 248
raw material, 27, 68
raw materials, 27, 68
reading, 56, 135, 161, 168
real estate, 155
real time, 29
realism, 33, 211
reality, 4, 7, 11, 12, 30, 43, 56, 138, 144, 186, 248
recall, 69, 125
reception, 118
recession, 87
recognition, 7, 11, 19, 76, 106, 137, 224, 238
reconcile, 137
recovery, ix, 30, 65, 66, 105, 108, 110, 114, 120, 131, 133, 138, 141, 149, 151, 154, 163, 167, 221, 225
recreational, 48
recruiting, 40, 47, 58, 84
recycling, 44, 57
Red Cross, 153
refineries, 197
refining, 27
reflection, 7, 94, 118, 176
reforms, 20, 57
refugees, 43
regenerate, 239
regular, 51, 124, 203, 210, 229

regulation, 55, 154, 168, 169
regulations, 106, 156, 168, 210, 222
regulators, 145, 204
regulatory bodies, 81
regulatory requirements, 169
rehabilitation, 216
rehabilitation program, 216
relationship, 8, 13, 32, 66, 72, 78, 82, 86, 113, 117, 167, 179, 182, 186, 189, 190, 191, 193, 194, 195, 224, 239
relationship management, 78, 86, 186, 239
relationship marketing, 72, 179, 193, 239
Relationship Marketing, 174
relationships, viii, 71, 72, 76, 81, 82, 83, 96, 131, 144, 157, 166, 172, 176, 182, 190, 195, 196, 213, 218, 221, 224, 239, 242
relatives, 123
relevance, 34, 66, 84, 105, 129, 160
reliability, 45, 82
religion, 79, 83
Republican Party, 6
reputation, 108, 137, 144, 168, 204, 205
Research and Development, 159
resentment, 232
reserves, 62, 160
reservoir, 48, 55, 56
residential, 54, 55, 200
resilience, viii, ix, 1, 24, 29, 30, 31, 33, 46, 65, 66, 67, 71, 88, 108, 115, 121, 123, 129, 130, 131, 132, 133, 134, 135, 136, 137, 138, 139, 141, 142, 143, 144, 145, 146, 147, 148, 149, 150, 154, 163, 167, 168, 169, 170, 173, 176, 177, 185, 193, 197, 211, 212, 217, 247
resilient, 157
resistance, 166
resolution, 111, 240
resource management, 55, 185
resources, ix, 2, 4, 5, 7, 8, 13, 30, 34, 39, 40, 41, 47, 48, 56, 57, 60, 61, 62, 77, 79, 86, 87, 91, 97, 99, 105, 114, 117, 123, 135, 138, 142, 144, 147, 149, 163, 166, 173, 189, 202, 203, 212, 218, 233, 235, 237, 241, 242
responsiveness, 71
restructuring, 86
retail, 114, 115, 120, 126, 140, 155, 161, 242
retaliation, 2
returns, 186, 189
revenue, 6, 31
revolt, 33
Reynolds, 104, 105, 106, 108, 109, 123
rhetoric, 2
rhythm, 158
rings, 238

risk assessment, x, 65, 68, 86, 108, 143, 147, 158, 169, 171, 174, 176, 182, 209, 215, 219, 229, 230, 231, 240, 241, 243
risk aversion, 31
risk factors, 233
risk management, viii, ix, 65, 67, 68, 109, 132, 133, 135, 137, 144, 155, 169, 171, 173, 214, 216, 217, 227, 246
Rita, 60
river basins, 42
rivers, 41, 42, 44
roadmap, 206
Roads, 22
Robert Gates, 3, 7
robustness, 84
Romania, 150
routines, 30, 33, 34, 75, 95, 166, 221
routing, 66
Royal Society, 122
rule of law, 19, 24, 25, 26
runoff, 41, 46, 47, 55
rural, 19, 48, 54, 138
rural areas, 48
rural communities, 54
Russia, 4, 10, 11, 23, 47, 59, 68, 71, 92, 93, 150
Russian, 10, 11, 93, 94, 245, 247
rust, 242

S

sabotage, 166, 173, 174, 220
safe drinking water, 40, 58
safeguard, 87, 187, 229, 237
safeguards, 50, 108, 177, 224
safety, 69, 71, 127, 141, 152, 198, 199, 200, 204, 231, 235
salary, 190
sales, 8, 108, 239
salts, 44, 60
sample, 106, 115
sanctions, 224
sanitation, 39, 45, 46, 47, 58, 59, 63
Sarbanes-Oxley Act, 155
sarin, 33
SARS, 33, 36
satisfaction, 186
Saturday, 235
Saudi Arabia, 43, 48
scams, 231
scarcity, 39, 40, 43, 44, 45
scepticism, 30
school, 26, 75, 108, 197, 199, 205, 226, 238
scores, 42, 201

scripts, 129
search, 82, 88, 205, 222, 235
search engine, 82
searches, 1
searching, 77, 84
Seattle, 13
seawater, 60
Second World War, 32, 33
secret, 79
Secretary of Defense, 3
Secretary of State, 9, 216
secrets, 88, 99
secular, 11
Security Council, 208, 224, 245
security services, 9, 77, 80, 174, 214, 219, 227
segmentation, 194
selecting, 76
self-image, 12
self-interest, 81
semantics, 4
senators, 10
sensitive data, 69, 80, 97
sensitivity, 157
sensors, 10
separation, 25, 137
September 11, 1, 2, 3, 13, 48, 49, 50, 235
sequencing, 20
Serbia, 20, 21
service provider, 80, 82, 116, 150, 161, 229, 231
services, 9, 31, 49, 58, 72, 75, 76, 77, 80, 81, 84, 89, 94, 111, 114, 115, 116, 124, 138, 145, 151, 155, 156, 172, 174, 178, 199, 202, 204, 207, 209, 213, 214, 219, 220, 222, 225, 227, 231, 237, 238, 242, 246
seven Ps, 160
severity, 46
sewage, 46
shape, 31, 183
shaping, 1, 12, 33, 169, 232
shareholder value, 85, 160
shareholders, 163, 186, 187
shares, 54, 85
sharing, 39, 65, 69, 77, 81, 82, 83, 86, 87, 90, 91, 93, 95, 96, 135, 138, 142, 183, 213, 215, 217, 219, 220, 235, 239
Shell, 160
shelter, 47, 128
Shiite, 7
Shiites, 6
shipping, 248
shock, 165, 167
shocks, ix, 141, 214
short period, 237

shortage, 44, 58
short-term, 11, 57
siblings, 146
Sierra Leone, 19, 20, 21, 22
sign, 7, 30, 61, 128, 145
signals, 183
signs, 62, 232
silver, 54
simulation, x, 198, 206, 212, 221, 223, 225, 227, 248
simulations, ix, 197, 198, 210
Singapore, 45, 194
singular, 106
sites, 67, 78, 85, 124, 125, 126, 128, 146, 159, 199, 200, 203
skills, 65, 66, 76, 95, 143, 166, 167, 169, 170, 176, 177, 181, 182, 186, 187, 191, 217, 239
skills base, 239
Slovenia, 150
slums, 47
Small Business Administration, 52
SME, 160
smuggling, 10, 88, 235
social activities, 75
social capital, 23
social change, 237
social consequences, 237
social costs, 172
social development, 12
social group, 75
social justice, 24, 26
social network, 83
social relations, 218
social relationships, 218
social responsibility, 33, 137, 144
social sciences, 165
social skills, 143
social systems, 141
software, viii, x, 75, 76, 77, 78, 79, 80, 81, 83, 84, 85, 86, 87, 88, 89, 90, 171, 175, 197, 210, 211, 212, 231
soil, vii, 1, 3, 46
soil erosion, 46
sole trader, 151
South Africa, 235, 236, 248
South Korea, 247
Southeast Asia, 40
sovereignty, 53
Soviet Union, 2, 8, 10, 13
space shuttle, 50
Spain, 13, 41, 59, 150, 237
spam, 231
spectrum, 94, 111, 133
speculation, 115, 129

speech, 23, 200
speed, 79, 82, 125, 143
spin, 17, 239
sports, 197, 230, 240
stability, 4, 5, 7, 8, 40
stabilize, 240
staff development, 95, 184, 185, 189
staffing, 67
stages, 5, 21, 32, 105, 199, 232
stakeholder, x, 20, 26, 146, 168, 174, 208, 211, 213, 214, 219, 220, 224
stakeholders, 26, 39, 79, 96, 107, 108, 111, 115, 135, 137, 146, 163, 167, 170, 171, 173, 174, 176, 210, 214, 215, 216, 218, 221
standards, viii, 2, 12, 35, 81, 96, 97, 168, 169, 170, 175, 176, 209, 210, 212
Standards, 37, 108, 121, 148, 245, 247
State Department, 235
statistics, 156
statutory, 169, 177
steel, 150
stimulus, 76
stock, 168
stock exchange, 168
stockpile, 53, 127
stockpiling, 127
storage, 82, 140, 159
storms, 46, 110
stovepipes, ix, 103
strain, 111
strategic management, 26, 173, 174, 182, 183, 189, 240
Strategic Petroleum Reserve, 53, 62
strategic planning, vii, 15, 16, 20, 21, 26, 163, 186
strategies, 2, 3, 5, 17, 58, 62, 63, 70, 76, 83, 98, 106, 108, 134, 135, 150, 151, 165, 184, 185
strength, vii, viii, 24, 31, 107, 144, 187
stress, 40, 41, 55, 128, 187
stress reactions, 128
strictures, 69
strikes, 157
structural changes, 35
structuring, 160
students, vii, 75, 122
subjective, 130, 143, 211
subjectivity, 210
subsidies, 43, 44
substances, 106
suburban, 13
Sudan, 19
suffering, 33, 59, 215, 225
suicide, 9, 33, 96, 151
suicide bombers, 33

summer, 3, 4, 41, 134
Sun, 61, 62
Sunday, 204, 242
Sunni, 6
Sunnis, 6
superpower, 2, 26, 29
suppliers, 56, 78, 80, 82, 111, 114, 137, 154, 155, 167, 173
supply, viii, 39, 40, 41, 42, 43, 44, 45, 46, 49, 50, 51, 52, 53, 54, 55, 56, 58, 59, 63, 65, 66, 68, 76, 80, 106, 116, 140, 154, 159, 167, 171, 187, 220
supply chain, 66, 154, 159, 167, 171
support staff, 143, 145, 238
Supreme Court, 52
surplus, 31
surprise, 4, 27, 40, 47, 76, 153, 188
surveillance, 1, 2, 13, 85, 90, 171, 238, 240
survival, 27, 43, 152, 185, 187
surviving, 153
sustainability, viii, 21, 76, 79, 88, 98, 100, 167, 219, 221, 224
Sweden, 150
Switzerland, 150
symbiotic, 113
sympathetic, 9, 166, 215, 233
symptom, 30
symptoms, 50, 143, 234
synergistic, 185
Syria, 40

T

tactics, 150, 151
Taliban, 7, 8, 9
tangible, 145, 176
tanks, 16, 81, 100, 247
targets, 48, 235
task conditions, 195
taxes, 233
taxonomy, 3, 198
teaching, 51, 83
technical assistance, 10
technological advancement, 57
technology transfer, 83
teeth, 35
telecommunication, 155
Telecommunications Act, 156
teleconferencing, 171, 205
telephone, 104, 116, 124, 129, 161, 171
television, 31
temperature, 46, 61
tenants, 118
terminals, 238

Index

territory, 5
terrorism, 3, 4, 5, 9, 10, 11, 12, 13, 14, 16, 18, 33, 35, 39, 40, 43, 47, 48, 49, 50, 58, 60, 72, 73, 85, 90, 92, 93, 99, 100, 101, 178, 198, 200, 230, 236, 246
terrorist, vii, viii, 1, 2, 3, 4, 5, 10, 13, 15, 27, 29, 30, 32, 33, 40, 47, 48, 49, 50, 58, 65, 70, 71, 72, 79, 81, 83, 87, 91, 92, 93, 94, 98, 99, 101, 108, 110, 111, 114, 200, 207, 227, 233, 234, 235, 236, 237, 241, 246
terrorist acts, 32
terrorist attack, vii, 1, 3, 13, 15, 27, 29, 32, 48, 49, 50, 72, 108, 110, 114, 235, 237, 241, 246
terrorist groups, viii, 79, 81, 83, 87, 91, 92, 98, 236
terrorist organization, 5, 10
terrorists, x, 3, 4, 5, 25, 32, 33, 47, 48, 60, 85, 86, 87, 92, 94, 97, 200, 229, 233, 235, 236, 240, 241
Terrorists, 13, 14, 72, 100, 245
Texas, 41, 242
theft, 92, 166, 173
thinking, 11, 15, 19, 21, 44, 78, 147, 167, 209, 240
third order, 24
third party, 54
threatened, 208
threatening, 108, 192
ticks, 69
time consuming, 233
time factors, 113
time frame, 192
time pressure, 202
timetable, 7, 203
timing, 13, 220
title, 166
Tokyo, 33, 193
tolerance, 24, 25, 26, 27, 233
Tony Blair, 20
top management, ix, 95, 176, 181, 182, 188
top-down, 34, 212
tourism, 10, 120
tourist, 48, 55, 238, 240
toxic, 49, 199
tracking, 3, 4, 53, 125, 127, 179
trade, 18, 78, 81, 83, 84, 86, 87, 99, 134, 145, 150, 167, 173, 238
trade union, 145
trade-off, 84
trading, 83, 87, 96, 117, 166
traffic, 118, 138, 150
training, 19, 34, 49, 66, 69, 89, 96, 108, 123, 128, 143, 147, 157, 168, 169, 173, 174, 186, 187, 189, 202, 203, 211, 212, 218, 225, 239, 247
traits, 183, 192
trans, 71

transcript, 23
transfer, 41, 83, 88, 142, 188, 234
transformation, 186
transitions, 19
translation, 79, 80
transmission, 104, 107, 207
transparency, 57, 77, 174, 185, 212
transparent, 91, 94, 95, 181, 183, 215, 221
transport, 3, 104, 118, 120, 123, 125, 126, 127, 128, 197, 200, 238
Transport, 162
transportation, 124, 238, 248
transportation infrastructure, 238
traps, 70
trauma, 2, 103, 143, 225, 237
travel, 32, 81, 123, 125, 127, 146, 147, 234, 235, 238
Treasury, 113, 117, 122, 123
treatment methods, 50
trial, 204, 226
tribal, 7, 8, 9, 53
tribes, 8, 80
trucks, 47
trust, viii, 29, 32, 33, 34, 67, 72, 77, 80, 81, 82, 83, 111, 120, 143, 144, 171, 172, 176, 179, 190, 201, 213, 219, 231, 238
trusts, 201, 202
tsunamis, 53
turbulent, 26, 36
Turkey, 39, 150
turkeys, 207
typology, 219

U

U.S. Department of Agriculture, 41, 52, 53
U.S. economy, 53
Uganda, 20, 21, 22
Ukraine, 22
ultraviolet, 50
UN, 19, 23, 45, 47, 62, 218, 227
uncertainty, 19, 30, 70, 71, 72, 98, 137, 144, 156, 167, 172, 214, 222, 225, 230, 234, 242
undergraduate, 121, 122
UNESCO, 45, 47, 58, 62
unforeseen circumstances, 115
UNICEF, 45, 46, 58, 63
uniform, 40, 92
United Kingdom, 3, 19, 25, 108, 113, 114, 115, 121, 150, 245
United Nations, 19, 40, 45, 46, 218, 224, 226, 227
United Nations Development Program, 40, 46

Index

United States, 1, 2, 3, 4, 5, 12, 13, 14, 42, 45, 46, 47, 48, 50, 51, 52, 53, 54, 55, 56, 60, 61, 150, 209, 226, 236
universe, 86
universities, 83, 121, 161, 245
university students, vii, 75
unpredictability, 156
unstructured interviews, 104, 117
updating, 123, 125, 129
upholstery, 106
upload, 211
uranium, 10
urbanization, 40
USA Patriot Act, 86
Utah, 46

V

vacuum, 4
validity, 80
values, viii, 15, 24, 25, 26, 27, 28, 77, 95, 166, 174, 181, 182, 190, 192, 220
vehicles, 140, 198
vein, 31
venue, 39, 230, 233, 234, 237
victims, 108, 214
Victoria, 90
video clips, 31
Vietnam, 19
violence, 6, 9, 56, 236
violent, 40
virus, 80, 108, 207, 231
viruses, 80
Visa, 238
visible, 91, 134, 199, 225
vision, 9, 11, 79, 95, 134, 174, 181, 182, 189, 192
voice, 12, 32, 34, 47, 58, 66, 94, 129, 222, 224
volatility, 32
voluntary organizations, 221
vulnerability, viii, 32, 47, 48, 49, 58, 59, 65, 66, 67, 69, 70, 84, 96, 98, 135, 167, 170, 176, 182, 214, 216, 217, 225, 230
vulnerable people, 139

W

wages, 49
Wales, 139, 226
walking, 124
Wall Street Journal, 60
war, 2, 3, 4, 5, 6, 7, 9, 13, 33, 34, 39, 48, 60, 90, 148, 150, 215, 218, 220
war on terror, 4, 9, 90
warfare, 2, 150
warrants, 16
Washington Post, 13, 14, 36, 63, 208
wastewater, 44, 46, 48, 49, 57
wastewater treatment, 48, 57
water, viii, 35, 39, 40, 41, 42, 43, 44, 45, 46, 47, 48, 49, 50, 51, 52, 53, 54, 55, 56, 57, 58, 59, 60, 61, 62, 63, 65, 68, 138, 216, 220
Water, 162
water policy, 51, 52, 54
water recycling, 57
water resources, 39, 40, 41, 47, 48, 57
water supplies, 43, 48, 56, 57, 59
water table, 41, 42, 43, 47
waterways, 56
weakness, 107, 128, 170, 175
wealth, 50
weapons, 2, 9, 10
weapons of mass destruction, 2
web, 67, 73, 76, 77, 78, 79, 80, 84, 85, 88, 114, 129, 200, 231
web sites, 67, 78, 85
weblog, 248
websites, 111, 112, 119, 161, 232, 233
Weinberg, 182, 185, 195
welfare, 12, 116, 140
wellbeing, 26, 127, 137
wells, 41, 42, 43
Western Europe, 97
wheat, 42, 43
White House, 13, 245
WHO, 36, 45, 46, 58, 63
wholesalers, 167, 173
wild ducks, 207
wind, 237
wine, 127
winning, 4, 7, 8
winter, 41
wireless, 79
wireless technology, 79
wiretaps, 86
withdrawal, 6
witnesses, 84
women, 240
work activity, 171
work environment, 173
workers, 23
workflow, 171
workforce, 69, 134, 170, 204
workplace, 76, 170
World Bank, 21, 22, 42, 43, 44, 90
World Health Organisation, 139

World Trade Center, 50
World War I, 7, 13
World War II, 7, 13
World Wide Web, 88
worldview, 2
worry, 30, 233
writing, 19, 24, 208
writing process, 208
Wyoming, 46

Y

yang, 247
Yemen, 43
yield, 12, 42, 43, 189
young adults, 75

Z

zero-risk, 32
Zimbabwe, 19